The Author

Photo courtesy of Rob Gray

Joey Berlin is a veteran entertainment journalist who has conducted more than 4,000 celebrity interviews over the past two decades. As a reporter his outlets have stretched across the media, from newspapers to the Internet. He is the president and co-owner of Audio Magazines Inc. (AMI), a repository of audio interviews. He is also executive director of the Broadcast Film Critics Association.

The newspapers Berlin has written for include the *Los Angeles Times*, *Newsday*, and the *New York Post*, where he wrote the weekly column "Reel Life." For the past 10 years, he has written the "Film Close-Up" column syndicated by the Copley News Service. He has contributed to a large number of magazines on a regular basis, including more than a dozen entertainment and general interest publications in countries ranging from the United Kingdom to Japan. On radio, Berlin is the head writer and producer for four daily programs syndicated on approximately 700 stations across America: "Sixty Second Preview," "Video Viewer," "Sixty Second CD (pop/rock)," and "Sixty Second CD (country)." On television, he has been a correspondent on "Tomorrow's Television Tonight" and for the World Entertainment News Network. Berlin is also one of the most visible entertainment reporters online. He is the official host of Hollywood Online, which provides content to the leading consumer online services, including America Online and the Microsoft Network.

The bicoastal Berlin divides his time between Los Angeles and New York City.

TOXIC FAME

TOXIC FAME

CELEBRITIES SPEAK ON STARDOM

Joey Berlin

DETROIT NEW YORK TORONTO LONDON

CELEBRITIES SPEAK ON STARDOM

Published by Visible Ink Press™, a division of Gale Research
835 Penobscot Bldg.
Detroit, MI 48226-4094

Visible Ink Press is a trademark of Gale Research

Most Visible Ink products are available at special quantity discounts when purchased in bulk by corporations, organizations, or groups. Customized printings, special imprints, messages, and excerpts can be produced to meet your needs. For more information, contact Special Markets Manager, Gale Research, 835 Penobscot Bldg., Detroit, MI 48226-4094

Art Director: Mary Krzewinski

Cover Photographs courtesy of The Kobal Collection

ISBN 0-7876-0874-2

Printed in the United States of America

10 9 8 7 6 5 4 3 2 1

A Cunning Canine Production™

If you wish to live long, don't become famous.
—Israel Ba'al Shem Tov (1700-1760)

I'm going to stay in show business until I'm the only one left.
—George Burns (1896-1996)

Contents

Preface

Mel Gibson once told me that being a movie star is like walking through life with a skunk on your head. The adoration of strangers is generally thought of as a wonderful thing, to be sought after, fought for, sacrificed for. Fame is believed to be a sure-fire path to wealth, power, and happiness. But while it generally brings wealth and power, happiness is another story. In fact, fame guarantees immense pressure, alienation, and temptation while often destroying the joy that went with the achievement of fame in the first place.

Simply put, fame is toxic. It's a disease that makes being comfortable in public impossible. Extreme cases are often fatal. We would love to play basketball like Michael Jordan, sing and dance like Michael Jackson, and act and look like Julia Roberts, but would we really want to live their lives? Bill Murray suggests that those striving to gain fame and fortune should start off with the fortune and see if that doesn't do the trick.

Imagine wearing Mel Gibson's skunk around. Everywhere you go, people stare at you, whisper about you, shove pieces of paper at you to sign, snap flashbulbs in your face—or worse. No meal can be taken in public without interruptions. The guy running toward you probably just wants to shake your hand, but he could be Mark Chapman. What if your children are with you? What about your children when you are not with them? And the rest of your family?

Suffering from a bad case of fame, seclusion is the obvious prescription. But inside the fortress you are surrounded by a tight-knit circle of "friends." Of course, how can you be sure? They are all on your payroll. Even assuming you are lucky enough to have good people around, you are still removed from the daily give and take of the world outside. This might not hamper the performance of athletes, but for "artists" in film or television or music, the distance from the audience makes honest and meaningful communication harder and harder to achieve. Fame can commission an artistically rewarding project that otherwise would never be funded. If it bombs, the accumulated rewards of earlier successes come in mighty handy. However, as those who achieve great wealth usually realize, money doesn't buy happiness. And when you are living in the self-imposed quarantine that fame demands, it is all too easy to blot out the unpleasant realities of loneliness, fear, and self-doubt with corpulence, alcoholism, and drug addiction. The list of casualties of fame is a long one.

I have spent my career talking to the stars of film, television, and music, the touchstones of our popular culture who have replaced political, military, and religious leaders as our heroes and role models. What do those "lucky" few who really know say about living with celebrity? From Mel Gibson's skunk quote to Madonna's desperate plea for a man able to share the glare of her ceaseless spotlight, my library of interviews is filled with victims of toxic fame syndrome. ***Toxic Fame*** gathers their thoughts on this subject as a collection of concise and pithy quotes illuminating this modern predicament as only they can.

Joey Berlin
March, 1996
Los Angeles, California

Acknowledgements

The interviews that form the basis of ***Toxic Fame*** were done in a variety of settings for a range of media outlets. Some were conducted by my staff and I would like to thank all of them over the past decade, beginning with Don McLaughlin and including Jenny Peters, Robin Milling, Greg Srisavasdi, Dera Revel, and Jeff Shore. For their cooperation, patience and camaraderie, I want to thank "the radio gang," Shep Morgan, Mike Reynolds, Bob Healy, Barry Krutchik, Gayl Murphy, Ron Brewington, Mari Cartel, Cathy Cogan, Alan Silverman, Cameron Turner, Laura Gross, Howard Benjamin, Randy Bush, Bonnie Churchill, Bill Diehl, Joanna Langfield, Robin Sagon, Lisa Carlin, Matt Levitz, Ann Lieber, Mary Lyon, Suzanne Whatley, Dave Weber, Leo Quinones, and Susan Granger. Publicists too numerous to mention individually but too important not to acknowledge made and continue to make my work possible. I could not have assembled my library of interviews without the support of Jeff Craig, Steve Katinsky, Sue Byrom and Vincent Musetto, Nanette Wiser and Alison Ashton, Jonathan Ashby and Lloyd Beiny, Charles Morrissey and Neil Williams, and Terry Winsor, who understood the value of my approach to celebrity journalism.

At Visible Ink Press, Martin Connors and Julia Furtaw have been invaluable allies. Kelly Cross and Michelle Banks were a great aid in choosing photos.

Personally, my father, Frank Berlin, remains my moral compass. My mother, Thelma Frankel, provides an unconditional rooting section. My brother and sister are part of my own soul. Their families are mine. No one means more. Along with the Laurens, Byes, Stuchiners, and the rest of the Berlins, they are the foundation for everything I do.

I also treasure the good counsel and friendship of Peter Hartz, Kathy Hartz, Randy Cohen, Jennifer Edson, Jim Schwebel, Karen Sherman, Rod Lurie, Steve Sobel, Susan Goran, John DeSimio, Paul Taublieb, Jaime Taicher, Charlie Paikert, and Rob Gray, more than I can say.

Finally, my wife and best friend, Ivy, has inspired me by her example to reach for everything I can imagine.

Photos were supplied by The Kobal Collection and Shooting Star.

Introduction

The price of fame includes being forced to grant a lot of interviews, often dozens in a single day. Stars hear the same questions over and over again, often going on automatic pilot until those rare occasions when a subject truly interests them. Literally hundreds of times in the past several years, I have seen stars perk up when I told them I was working on a book about the toxicity of fame. In spite of all the glamorous rewards, they know best of all that life in a fishbowl is no walk on the beach. In fact, a recent study reports that celebrities are almost four times more likely to kill themselves than the average American. The average life span of a celebrity is only 58 years, while the average for everyone else is well into the 70s.

Meg Ryan—Fame as a toxin? Boy, that's a really interesting question.

Sally Field—This is a study. You're talking about what is it like to be a celebrity, basically. Boy, there's a long answer to that. I wish I had the answer. I don't know. I know it's very, very difficult.

Emma Thompson—I think it is poisonous. I really do. You have to be very careful. It is toxic. I think that's a very good word for it.

Jason Alexander—I don't know if it's a toxin as much as a drug—and if you get hooked on it it's a bad monkey.

Kim Basinger—You feel like there's an earthquake every day of your life. It disrupts your brain waves from being able to comprehend or respond.

John Malkovich—I don't have any desire to be popular. It's humiliating, I think. And deadly. And confusing.

Harry Belafonte—It's a pollutant. It has a terrible downside to it. Those of us who have experienced it have a huge struggle with dealing with it. I think, in the final analysis, it's personal values that shape how you take and deal with power, visibility and perceived omnipotence. All the VIP treatment, sometimes it's nice to have. It gets you, on a hot muggy day, up front into an air-conditioned room. But other than that it's about how we perceive power and what it is there for. What do you do with it?

Kurt Russell—We live in a time when we have not yet fully understood the abilities of mass communication. When we as a society gain knowledge all at one time, it creates this toxicity of celebrity. I don't if we'll ever evolve as a society to where we just accept mass knowledge all at one time and it doesn't create celebrityism. Maybe that's just the nature of the beast. It's certainly worth writing a book about.

Keanu Reeves—It's going to be a thick book.

Bill Murray—When people say they want to be rich and famous, just try rich and see if that doesn't get most of it for you.

Author's Note

T*oxic Fame* not only spotlights the wide range of problems associated with celebrity, it also illuminates the individual celebrities themselves. The ways that people react to the stresses and strains of fame are as varied as the number of people grappling with them. As revealing as what they say is the way that they say it. Who is wise enough to understand the forces rocking their world? Who is resigned? Who is angry? Who is hurt? Which demure actress on screen swears like a teamster in real life? Which macho action hero is as sensitive as a small child?

Quotes have been cleaned up in some cases because literal word for word (and "um" for "um") transcriptions of interviews do not do justice to oral comments translated onto the printed page, but care has been taken to retain the speaker's original tone and flavor. It is also important to note that fame is a double-edged sword and this book focuses on the side celebrities try to hide from public view. Many prefaced their remarks by noting that they did not want to be perceived as whiners and acknowledged the advantages they enjoy as stars. (In fact, stars never use the word "star" to describe themselves, preferring "public personality" or "celebrity.") The above not withstanding, everything that follows is true. And I have the tapes to prove it.

The Nature of Celebrity

The explosion of celebrity journalism has had a profound effect on its subjects in recent years. Once, even the biggest stars could put on a hat and dark glasses and give newshounds the slip, but today there are armies of reporters out there relentlessly stalking their prey. They have spies not just in restaurants, but in rest rooms. They use helicopters to stake out territory. Michelle Pfeiffer says she acts for free—and charges for being a celebrity. Being a celebrity means never letting your guard down for a minute. Once there were powerful publicity machines that could protect a star, but one slip today and you're tomorrow's Hugh Grant.

Denzel Washington

You pray for rain, you gotta deal with the mud, too.

Tom Hanks

It's like I've got a special pin that I wear and everybody recognizes on my lapel. "Oh, you're that guy."

Emma Thompson

All that attention, it can really knock you for six. It doesn't make you feel very well, too much attention. It's actually like having too much to eat.

> *Everybody dreams of being rich and famous. Once you get rich and famous you think, "This isn't it."*
>
> *—George Harrison*

Kim Basinger

It all becomes such a mad dog frenzy. Who's stabbing you in the back—or doing it in front of your face.

Johnny Depp

It's getting odder. I'm starting to feel like a Hunter S. Thompson book.

Demi Moore

When you really look at these few people, just regular people who don't choose a public life for their career, yet get picked on by the press, you really see how frightening and scary it is.

Bo Derek

Can you survive with your sanity? The record shows you end up a drug addict, an idiot, or whatever it is. I don't think you can see the forest for the trees. You can start out the most sound, well-adjusted person, but if you're alone in life you won't come through it.

Michael Maloney

Anybody who craves fame is not aware of the consequences. Sure, you can have fame. You also get your laundry inspected. When you go home at night, don't think that you can put your feet up because we've got spectravision coming in through the air grate to have a look at you. There is no stop button.

Anthony Kiedis

(Member of the Red Hot Chili Peppers)

If you reach a certain point where you can't go out in public or you can't go to your favorite restaurant or your favorite club because you're afraid of people hassling you, that's when it becomes less fun.

Jason Patric

People recognizing me in public? That's something you know going in and that's part of it. But the intrusion into your life that is not only willful but accepted—not only by the perpetrators but by the public in general—is something that is not only unfair to people who have chosen this direction in their life, it's really unfair to everybody. To have such a lack of value for human life in all regards. People seem to revel in a celebrity's pain, or catching them in moments. I don't think that the average Jones family in Cleveland would be very happy if even their block knew about their daughter's bulimia or abortion or broken marriage. However, they're very happy to hear about it, about their favorite star who they go to see twice a year in a movie. I find that very strange and unfortunate. People aren't public figures. They're public beings. Even that term, "figures," sort of gives people the license to throw darts at will.

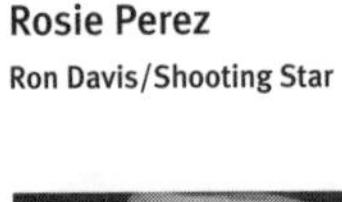

Rosie Perez
Ron Davis/Shooting Star

Rosie Perez

You never understand how dear your privacy is until you lose it.

Uma Thurman

It's indescribable. I can't imagine people who relish it. It's just not easy to be separated out like that.

The Nature of Celebrity

Liam Neeson

I have had a couple of telephoto lens shots, most notably at my son's christening recently. At least I wasn't cavorting naked on a beach, but it's a bit of an invasion.

Priscilla Presley

It's very difficult to raise children and be in the public eye without them looking at you through the microscope. Everything is exposed. If you have a spat or some kind of an argument it's in the news. It makes you reclusive.

The right to be left alone is the most comprehensive of rights and the right most valued by civilized man.

—Supreme Court Justice Louis Brandeis

Shelley Long

The only place that I can go to be in a bad mood or to be quiet or nonsociable, all those things I can't do out in public, is my own home. It's why you read about celebrities feeling that their homes are prisons.

Leslie Nielsen

I think O.J. [Simpson]'s probably in a different kind of prison now.

Clint Eastwood

I've been around for forty years, and for maybe thirty of it I've been a well-known figure. You give up your privacy. That's the one thing I have the greatest regret about, giving up your privacy.

Martha Plimpton

Fame is a price to pay. Some days it's a larger price than other days. Absolutely. Losing my anonymity, my position as a neighborhood girl, was difficult. Having to take my name off the front door buzzer hurt.

James Garner

When I leave the gate at the house I'm a public figure. I get back home as soon as I can. I really value my private time.

Steve Walsh

(Member of Kansas)

I'm really afraid of the public interfering with my private life. I'll let a lot be known about me, privately, but that belongs to me. I want to keep it that way.

Laurence Fishburne

I've given up a great deal of my privacy. Certainly not all of it. I've had to be a public person. That's the price you pay. We all have to give something up.

John Malkovich

When you become a public figure everything you do becomes suspect on some level.

Earvin "Magic" Johnson

It was a shame that Arthur Ashe was forced into revealing that he had HIV. Just because he's a national figure, he's still entitled to his privacy. I don't think it was right. It definitely wasn't right.

Rob Lowe

There's a certain line. I don't have as much right to privacy as the average person, but you can't tell me that absolutely everything that I do in my life in private or behind closed doors is public domain. I don't buy it. I refuse to buy it—and the Constitution wouldn't buy it, either.

Carrie Fisher

I've never felt that I had a really private life anyway.

Michelle Pfeiffer

I've moved into a much more private homestead, with a taller wall. That's a bit saddening, but what are you going to do?

Richard Dreyfuss

It sucks. It's awful. If I had to do it again I may very well have made another choice. If I had known about the invasion of privacy, the permanent lack of privacy and people's feeling that they have a right to

Jennifer Capriati, the precocious tennis prodigy who earned her first million on the pro circuit by the age of fifteen, dropped out of pro competition late in 1993, pleading for anonymity and privacy. Several months later, the once effervescent Capriati, bleary-eyed and overweight, was arrested on suspicion of possession of marijuana in a dingy Florida motel room. She did not return to the tour until February, 1996.

some part of me that they have absolutely no right to under any civilized code of ethics or behavior, I might very well have said, "Pass."

Jack McDowell

(Baseball player and recording artist)

It's strange. And it's hard to explain to people. People don't get it unless you're there. It's a strange thing to go to any city and have at least somebody come up to you and know who you are—and know something about you. I can't go to any shows any more and just watch the show. It's like, "What are you doing here?"

"I'm watching a rock show."

Dennis Hopper

Sometimes when I'm in a store buying a pair of socks and I look up and I see people watching me, I think, "Do they think I'm a pickpocket?" Then I realize, "They must be looking at Dennis Hopper. Oh yeah."

Tommy Lee Jones

I'm a little bit more famous than I used to be, but I haven't been comfortable in public places in a long time.

Andrew McCarthy

I don't find it very relaxing to go to some party where there are going to be TV cameras. You go when it's part of your job, but I don't really want to live in a fish bowl.

Jodie Foster

I've never, certainly not in recent years, had any kind of Hollywood social life. First of all, I don't care about it. You know, "Oh damn, I don't want to go to that meeting because I've got to go to Planet Hollywood tomorrow." I will always pick the job first—and my home life first. I'll always pick going home and watching TV after a day of working. What am I going to do? Go to an opening after a day of working? I lead an entirely public life. I'm always talking to people. It's seven o'clock, I'm going to go home. I don't want to go out and be with five hundred people and get photographed. I focus on the parts of the process that I love the most and the parts of the process that I hate, I don't do.

Madonna

Most stars are misconceived by the public. People make up their mind. They give you one attribute and that's all you're allowed to have. You're not allowed to have a full life. Everybody does, but not everybody sees it. I'm a human being like everybody else.

Sean Connery

I like Sidney Lumet's comment: "I know he's not a legend because I go to the toilet with him."

Michael J. Fox

I'm not saying, "Woe for pitiful me, you don't understand what it's like to be in the limelight." Life is what life is. But you do want to sometimes take somebody by the arm and go, "You know, I'm a guy. We're just people, living our lives like anybody else."

Winona Ryder

I spent a couple of years just at this war with myself, with my popularity, and people looking at me. I felt really vulnerable. I could never understand why. I felt like if I complained about it then I was being a brat, like I should never complain because I'm so lucky and I have money and other people don't, all this stuff. But if I tried to enjoy it, then I was conceited. There was no way to win.

Helena Bonham Carter

It does inhibit your freedom. I think that's rather an ironic thing—the more successful you get the more your freedom seems to be circumscribed. When you're going down and shopping you have to be prepared that people are going to watch you or make comments, or then something that you say gets repeated around. So you have to be a nice person all the time. Otherwise you're known as a bitch if you're slightly in a bad humor and you're short with somebody. You can't care too much about what other people say. That's the key.

Sarah Jessica Parker

I think I've become more sensitive to it for some reason. I can't tell you why. I was always a late bloomer.

The Nature of Celebrity

Alfre Woodard

I'm not that famous. I'd say I'm known. I've got some famous friends. It's a real pain in the ass to be around them, too.

Leonardo DiCaprio

People who have been famous for twenty or thirty years are still trying to get accustomed to it. It's still hard for them. It's something that you can never quite get comfortable with. It's a weird thing to have people watch you. It hasn't been that bad for me. My movies have only made about $8 million apiece. I'm sure if I do something like a *Forrest Gump* it'll be a different story.

Al Pacino

You hate to say you get used to it, because you don't really get used to it, but it gets easier. You accept it more. And you finally have to become more comfortable with it. That's what's happened to me, I think.

James Caan

A lot of the actors are so full of crap. They don't want to be bothered with the autographs. They want to hide. I remember telling Al [Pacino], "What are you doing? God forbid somebody doesn't recognize you. You'd have a heart attack." It's such bullshit. You pray when you start to become recognizable. Sometimes it's not pleasant to sign autographs, but what if they stopped?

Patrick Swayze

I'm actually very excited about my life now. I've dealt with the celebrity and stardom stuff, where it's not blowing my mind and scaring me to death and making me fear that I'm going to go off the deep end in some way or get stupid. Of course, I'm stupid anyway. (Laughs)

Anouk Aimee

If you want to be a star, or if you are a star. There's a difference. Do you want to be somebody, or do you want to be you? It's like being young, rich, and beautiful, it's better.

Mary Elizabeth Mastrantonio

How does one become a star? I saw Sally Field on a chat show and she said, "It's not about talent." That's painful.

Shaquille O'Neal

Things are different now. I'm dealing with companies. My image is real simple. I'm just being myself. Most of my commercials, you see me tearing down backboards. That's what I do. You see me going to the park and playing with little kids. That's what I do. I'm just being myself. They're not going to make me something that I'm not.

Juliette Lewis

I don't want people to look at me as something extraordinary. A star. That's so weird. It's like not real. They should just be able to relate to me —and I to them—as a person. I don't have an urge to be hot or famous or cool or sexy or anything.

Clint Eastwood

I'm not a star. I'm just me. I'm just another guy trying to have a good time and trying to exist like everyone else.

Elijah Wood

You know what a star is? It's a big huge ball of gas. You want to be noted for a ball of gas. It makes no sense to me. And then they think you're special. If you're a star you're supposed to be special? You're like a god to most people—and that's so untrue. You're normal. People think they can just fly through life, but they can't. It's so ridiculous. Even the famous part of it, being a household name. I can't say that I like it. The more famous you become the harder it is to live a normal life. Why do you want to become Macaulay Culkin famous? People mobbing you and screaming your name at you. Ugh.

Annette Bening

When people ask me about being "the woman who got Warren Beatty to settle down," I never know what to say. I try to come up with something snappy, but it doesn't have anything to do with that in my own life. I'm learning that if there's any kind of life where you have to reaffirm that it doesn't matter what people think, it's a life when you're famous. I was raised in a world where you did mind what people thought and you made

Juliette Lewis Ron Davis/Shooting Star

a lot of choices based on what the neighbors think, so I've had to really address that issue personally.

Jodie Foster

I never needed to be famous. I still don't. It's annoying. It's the last thing that I looked for.

Jason Alexander

I love fantasy, but I don't like living in one. I think that fame is a fantasy.

Clint Eastwood

Burt Reynolds used to say, "The trouble with Clint is he doesn't realize he's a star." Who wants to be? There are a lot of nice things about it and I suppose a lot of people would like a certain recognition for what they do, but you want to get recognition for what you do without having it be your physical being. It's nice that people want to see a musician play his horn, but they don't want to pester him in a restaurant.

Shannen Doherty
Ron Davis/Shooting Star

Shannen Doherty

It's really a lot of pressure. Everybody is watching you. You're under a microscope 100% of the time.

Elliott Gould

People ask me about celebrity, having been on the cover of *Time* magazine. I say that some of us have to make a bigger fool of ourselves than others.

Christian Slater

I've always dealt with it brilliantly.

Jane Fonda

It's so much a part of my existence that I don't even notice. Hey, we get paid well, it's a great job, we travel to interesting places and meet interesting people. The least you can do is put up with the by-product.

Kyra Sedgwick

To have stardom on a Julia Roberts level, certainly the invasion, certainly the press interest, certainly the media, it would be so detrimental to my family and me. I don't know how she does it.

Campbell Scott

I was hugely impressed with Julia Roberts and her ability to deal with her fame, because at the time I worked with her [on *Dying Young*] she was about as big as she was ever. She dealt with it with aplomb. To be twenty-one and deal with that is something that I'll never understand. Horrifying.

Alannah Myles

I hope that people like Madonna enjoy it. I'm sure she does. Otherwise she wouldn't be so successful at it.

Sandra Bernhard

I like the balance I have. If I go into certain situations, I know I'm going to get recognized and acknowledged and validated. If I want to be away from it, I can be away from it. I don't think I'd want Madonna's fame. You have no time, you have no opportunity to be yourself. It's next to impossible—and I think it really limits your ability to be creative. I think it's dangerous.

D.B. Sweeney

I never got into this to be a celebrity. I have friends who—I think they're great guys—but they really get off on it. For me, I'm a little wary of it. I feel like the next person that comes down the line is gonna hit me with a stick.

Belinda Carlisle

If you have too much fame, you become a prisoner of your own success. What fun is that? I can't imagine being Michael Jackson or Madonna. To me, that would be the biggest curse in the world. I would never want to live my life like that.

Mary Stuart Masterson

Some people have that meteoric kind of thing, with huge amounts of money and huge fame and huge pressure. I don't have that. That would terrify me. How do you have your privacy at all? Mine is challenged, but I deal with it. But how do you do that and maybe have kids, or your own parents, or family? It's very hard on all your relationships, on everything. It's weird that my job is dependent on that. I love what I do, but a big part of what I do is that I don't do it in a vacuum. It's about reaching—at some point—somebody's heart somewhere. But, darn it, I want my privacy.

Liam Neeson

I'm glad I'm not Tom Cruise. And I think Tom's a magnificent screen actor and very, very underrated. It's nothing to do with his craft. It's he's a major young star. It's important for me to be able to walk down to the deli and get a bottle of milk and a pound of butter and not think twice about it. In Tom's case he can't do that. When it starts to interfere with who you are as a human being, which includes things like being able to go to the grocery store or go for a walk and not feel like you've got to put on a hat and shades and scurry through the streets.

Treat Williams

Any all-American red-blooded kid that gains stardom at an early age has a hard time with it. I don't know many that handle it very well. Tom Cruise seems to have handled it very well and gotten through all that without going ballistic. But I can name you so many names, so many of us who just were too young to handle that kind of energy.

Sam Neill

I just spent some time in Italy with Tom Cruise and Nicole Kidman. Their lives are very, very constrained. I would find that intolerable.

Nicole Kidman

At first I was quite naive. I didn't realize how much attention he did get and suddenly I would be thrown into all that. It did affect me in the sense that I was not Nicole Kidman, I was now Mrs. Tom Cruise.

Mary Elizabeth Mastrantonio

I see people whose careers I envy. I wouldn't change lives with them, not for one second.

Patricia Arquette

Nobody is getting a right to be alive, if you have this celebrity. That's the price you pay, but it doesn't make it right.

Rob Schneider

Billy Crystal hates me because I did him on *Saturday Night Live.* Al Franken wrote it and I did it. Billy called up, "Why are you attacking me?" We did Woody Allen on the show. That was kind of tough. I had to play Soon-Yi [Previn], of course.

The most surprising thing to me about fame is that people think it's important, that it necessarily makes you happy.

—Linda Fiorentino

Arnold Schwarzenegger

I loved Hans and Franz on *Saturday Night Live.* "Get rid of those love handles or pull them over your head and use them as a shopping bag."

Liam Neeson

I was at the Evander Holyfield/George Foreman fight in Atlantic City. I bought this ringside ticket for myself and flew down to Atlantic City just to see this fight. Bobby Duvall and Kevin Costner and these fellas are all riding in. I'm sitting in my little seat. I've got my tuxedo on.

During the preliminary fights the "Let's get ready to rumble!" guy comes over and says, "I'm going to mention your name in the introductions."

I'm thinking, "Now I've made it! I'm going to get announced from the ring!"

He says, "I just want to get the pronunciation of your first name."

I tell him, "It's pronounced LEE um."

So he goes up and says, "And we have the Darkman himself here, Liam Nissin."

I thought, "Damn, 50% there."

Mia Farrow

I don't even know what to do about being famous. This has been my life. I don't have the objectivity to say whether it would have been better another way, whether your life has been easier than mine or mine maybe was easier because of this. Who knows? I've had a good life. My children have given me immeasurable satisfaction. I'd be a fool to complain.

Alan Bates

I don't think you can go into this kind of work without knowing that you will become recognizable in public. You don't actually want that, but there's no point in doing the work if it's not recognized. Therefore, it's a natural part of it. I think as long as you don't live off that, you can live with it, even to a point of often not noticing it. It's slightly easier in Europe than it is here. People tend to make slightly more of the fact that they've recognized you or like you. The complete openness of the American reaction is sometimes a very attractive thing. It's nice to have people recognize you for what you've done, because that's why you do it.

Nicolas Cage

I've found a way to enjoy it. You have to, otherwise you're in hell. If you don't like it, you're in trouble because you can't escape it.

Matt Dillon

After a while it just becomes a part of your life. That's all there is to it. There's nothing you can do about it, even if you try to pull your hair out and scream, "Why don't these people leave me alone?" It's never going to happen. Then there's that old cliché, when it does, that's when you're in trouble.

Gary Sinise

If you resist it your life will be more difficult, in a way. If that's happening to you and you fight it, you're just going to end up slugging people, getting mad, and having the press go after you and paint a bad picture of you.

John Goodman

Fame? It sucks. I'd rather not be famous. I'm sorry if it sounds weird, but it's the truth.

Ellen DeGeneres

There's a scene in *Mr. Wrong* where ants are crawling all over me while I'm tied down. It really is a good metaphor for stardom. It appears to be really nice, but if you look closely there are gnats all over me.

Pat Benatar

I'm always trying to explain to people that it's not always what it seems. Don't think that your life is so bad and mine is so good. Because it's not. Everybody's got their problems, just different ones.

John Hall

People see rock stars when they're on stage or on TV or on album jackets and it looks glamorous. They don't see the Holiday Inns and Howard Johnsons and the plane rides and the six hours to get to a gig in West Virginia or the twenty hours in a bus to drive from Austin to Iowa City. They don't see the eight months a year away from home. There are times when I don't know what town I'm in. There are times when it's fun, but there are other times when I've got a two-year-old at home saying, "Papa, Papa, don't go."

Elliott Gould

I believe there's nothing of value other than what we have to share. It's one thing to share goodness and wealth. It's another thing to share problems. Once we can open up and share our problem, I think we discover that we all have the same problems. Nobody has a problem that somebody didn't have before.

Alec Baldwin

Public performers are always presented to be childish, drug-taking, money-splurging, fornicating, hedonistic people. Actors are all having sex with each other all the time, and they're all spending all their money, and they're all oversleeping, and they're all pretty indulgent. Beautiful pigs. Write that down. That could be the name of your book. "Beautiful Pigs." That would be the name of my book about the current crop of motion picture actors. "Exquisite Pigs."

Alec Baldwin
Ron Davis/Shooting Star

Nicole Kidman

There have been a lot of attacks on him [husband Tom Cruise]. It goes in different cycles. Different people get it at different times. He was supported for so long. We call it in Australia "the tall puppy syndrome." You build somebody up and you have to cut him down. It hurts him.

Elle MacPherson

Australia does have a tall puppy syndrome, where they build you up and then they want to cut you down.

Michael Douglas

In direct proportion to how successful one is, that's how much the need is to chop him or her down.

Samuel L. Jackson

Bruce Willis told me that the bigger that you get, the more things people try to find wrong with you. I believe that, in certain kinds of ways. But there are certain kinds of ways that you can act that cause people to do those things to you.

Jason Patric

People create types or heroes because they want the possessive identity that goes along with that. They project themselves onto people. Once that person grows and becomes larger than the people, they no longer identify with them or project to them. The shadow that looms over them makes them appear small. That's when they need to cut down the archetypes they created for their own needs anyway. Unfortunately, it's reached savage proportions of late. The people involved can deal with it, but the ethical question behind it is a much, much larger issue. There seems to be an idea that the fact that you have fame or make money means that you forfeit your right to privacy. If you were to go to the other end of the spectrum and say that someone who makes under $20,000 a year has no protection or privacy, you'd have your head handed to you.

Nathan Lane

Mickey Rooney once said to me, "They build you up to knock you down." Everyone has been very nice to me. I'm due for a beating very soon.

Whitney Houston

"She has no problems whatsoever, she's famous." That's bull. Everyone knows that's bull. Money doesn't solve your problems. It creates problems. Fame doesn't solve anything. It just makes people more dangerous. You've got people who love you so much they hate you. Hate to love you. What kind of shit is that? All I want to do is sing.

Jack McDowell

The money brings way more problems than it takes care of. I found that out. One of the problems it does get rid of is that it enables me to live at a certain level to avoid all the other shit that would go with celebrity. If you have celebrity without having the money you're in deep shit. You really are. You're in trouble.

Kevin Costner

I think fame is a useless thing. It's never helped me pick a script. It's never helped me go to work in the morning. It's not helping me right now. The things that I like about movies have nothing to do with fame. I like story. I like being in an editing room. I like that stuff. Maybe I'm living my life wrong.

Howie Long

The NFL is so overrated. So are movies. John Travolta pretends to be other people. I hit people for thirteen years. What is the big deal? What is the fascination?

Steve Walsh

Forget it. It's too much work. It'll make you gray-headed before your time. One of the hardest ways to live—and maintain your sanity—is in show business. I'm insane myself.

Steve Martin

The easiest part about being Steve Martin is you can get restaurant reservations almost any time you want. And the hardest is everything else.

Christian Slater

I went out last night and instead of having to wait outside in the cold they said, "What party are you here with?" I said, "I'm here with the Slater party. Let me in you bastard." Because these guys can be tough at the door. And then when you go in to a place you get harassed a little bit. It's not like you can just go in and relax in a corner and hide out.

Madonna

The best thing is that I never have to wait for a table at a restaurant. The worst thing is that I can't put my trash out in front of my house because people always go through it. That's the spectrum.

James Earl Jones

The orbit of so-called stardom and the sparks and lights that shine from that orbit can attract unusual things. It can attract insanity, whether it's stalkers or people who have these projects that they want you to do and you're the only one that's going to save their script.

Sylvester Stallone

It's like having neuroses as a household pet. It really is. It's just something that I have to say, "Okay, I'm living a very unbalanced, very confrontational life. A very stressful life." The way I hold a fork, if your shirt is messed up. Everything I do is held up under a microscope.

Screen superstar Sylvester Stallone is primarily known as a two-fisted action hero in the Rocky and Rambo series. Not as well-known is his love for art. He has used some of his riches to acquire a valuable fine art collection that includes works by Claude Monet, Auguste Rodin, and Andy Warhol [a silk screen of Stallone himself]. He also likes to paint. Stallone says the subject of many of his own canvases is how fame destroys celebrities.

Hugh Grant

I still in the back of my mind genuinely think that it'll be my brief flash in the pan and then it'll all be over. It would be an alarming thought if someone told me that it definitely would go on forever.

You become this thing. You feel that you're riding in this huge hot air balloon and not sitting on top of something made of rock. I think that's my worst metaphor ever.

Denzel Washington

It has nothing to do with what I do, other than that it's a result of what I do. I didn't go into the business to become a movie star. I was an actor in New York hoping to make three hundred bucks a week one year. And when I did, I thought I was on top of the world. Then all of a sudden California started calling. I came out, green and naive. I'm not green or naive anymore.

Mimi Rogers

I have a private mailbox. I don't have mail delivered to my house because fan magazines and services always find your address and sell it.

Sean Connery

Some arse put my address out in some magazine somewhere and the mail coming to my house in Spain got so bad the postman stopped delivering the mail.

Bruce Willis

I don't know, at the end of the day, what is the real appeal of celebrities and movies and everything that surrounds Hollywood? Why are there a hundred TV shows that deal with Hollywood and what gossip is the current thing? I truly don't understand it. I don't know why that stuff is more important than politics or why people know more about film actors than the guys who are spending their tax dollars. But that's the way it is right now and I think Planet Hollywood [the chain of theme restaurants he owns a piece of] is just an extension of that. It's a little module of Hollywood that comes to these twenty-five cities that it's in.

> *The things that are very precious to you, that mean a lot to you, that are very private, are interesting to people. I know. I'm curious about celebrities' lives myself.*
>
> *—Annette Bening*

Ellen DeGeneres

It really doesn't take much to be a celebrity now, so to me it's not much of a flattering thing. If you look at the people who are supposedly celebrities. Joey Buttafuoco is a celebrity.

James Cameron

(Director of True Lies *and* The Terminator*)*

If you were living in a small town in the Midwest a hundred years ago, it would take the form of gossip. Now it's broadened to the point where that gossip is not just about the people that you know but the extended global community and it's much more interesting. Video makes that seem much more immediate. You can look at how other people are living. You can see them baring their souls on midday television.

Paul Reiser

Mad About You *is not really autobiographical.* Very few of the stories have ever happened to me, but a lot of the little sidebar conversations are real. Biographically, it's lagging two years behind. I was married three years when we started the show about a couple that just got married. If we have a kid this year in life, I imagine next year I may go, "You know what? I said we don't want to have kids on the show, but I just thought of twenty episodes."

Paul Reiser

Once in a while my wife will see my eyes glaze over in the middle of a conversation and she'll go, "Go ahead, type it up and we'll finish the conversation later."

It's sad. My wife was sleeping outside, taking a nap in the afternoon, and I was just watching her sleep. And instead of thinking, "Oh wow, there's my wife," I went, "This could be something." As Billy Joel said, it's hard to leave a tender moment alone.

With the success of his first book, Couplehood, Paul Reiser is putting together a sequel, tentatively titled Parenthood, to expand his commentary into the world of being a parent. This is a relatively new world for Paul who, in 1995 welcomed a son into the life he shares with his wife. Not surprisingly, his experiences are coloring his TV show Mad About You—the 1995-96 season revolved around the attempts of the Buckmans, portrayed by Reiser and Helen Hunt, to have a baby.

Oliver Stone

There are no private vices any more. The concept of having private vices is fine with me. I like it. I don't think they should be shared. It's your business. This public morality is very difficult. Gary Hart was a brilliant man, but he was publicly condemned for his morality.

Val Kilmer

The Doors *is a film about fame.* I think Oliver Stone was confronting what's happening to him and using the character of Jim Morrison to do that.

Robin Williams

The one awards show that isn't televised is the Nobel Prizes. That would be wonderful. "Mother Theresa—and her host, Pia Zadora."

Geena Davis

"Renny [Harlin, her husband] is the absolute most famous person in Finland. He is a super-superstar in Finland. It's like going around with the Beatles. He is so famous and so recognized there—every single person

Geena Davis and Renny Harlin Ron Davis/Shooting Star

can't believe it when they see Renny Harlin. The front page of the newspaper at least once a week will be "Renny Does Something," whatever it is. "RENNY GIVES A PARTY!" It's like "O.J. NOT GUILTY!" The whole country goes crazy.

And now they've adopted me as their imported celebrity. *Angie* did genius over there. It was just a huge hit. [*Angie,* starring Geena Davis, was a box office flop everywhere else.]

Sean Penn

Fame on any level is something to be very wary of. You know the Phil Ochs song? "Found him on the stage last night, he was breathing his last breath. Gin and a cigarette was all that he had left. Make some music and carry a guitar, but God help the troubadour who tries to be a star. So play the chords of love my friend, play the chords of pain, but if you want to keep your song, don't, don't, don't play the chords of fame." There's a lot in that.

Emma Thompson

I regard it with a certain degree of jaundiced skepticism at the moment. And certainly if it were to snowball into something worse I'd stop. I'd stop acting. Why would you do it? Why would you put yourself through it? Pointless. If being famous takes your life away, then stop being famous. Say no. Walk away. Simple.

> *I would give all of my fame for a pot of ale, and safety.*
>
> *—King Henry V, in William Shakespeare's Henry V*

Debra Winger

I always pray that I'll wake up one morning and say, "Well, that's that. I've finished that. I'm going to do something else now." That's a big dream of mine.

Al Pacino

You simply have to adjust to it. It's part of the deal. I knew someone who had difficulty with it and I've known of people who have left because they had difficulty with it. You have a choice. They left. I stayed, but I like it when it's difficult.

Robert Redford

I quit all the time. I get fed up and say, "This isn't worth it. I'd rather be with my horses or studying something of another culture or painting." I do that for a while—and then I come back. It does get frustrating and it's getting worse and worse.

George Harrison

The Beatles? Are we still talking about them?

Tony Curtis

Some people suffer dreadfully from fame. They become so intimidated, so neurotic about it. And it kills a lot of people. It did away with Marilyn [Monroe]. She was fulfilling her personal life in the press—and that's what did her in.

Jason Patric

You couldn't be more famous than Elvis [Presley]. You couldn't have more money than Elvis. You couldn't be more influential than Elvis. And look at Elvis.

First Finding

The bright lights, the glamour, the big bucks. Who wouldn't want to be famous if that were all there was to it? That's what a lot of people believe when they start up the ladder, but once they reach the top they quickly discover it's a very precarious position. Suddenly you're playing a whole new game—and they don't hand out a rulebook.

George Harrison

Every day was like living ten years in concentrated experiences. We [The Beatles] met everybody in the world and we didn't have a moment's peace. You have to grow up quick.

Jack Casady

(Member of Jefferson Airplane/Starship)

There wasn't a Rolling Stone *volume* on "How to Be a Rock Star."

Ariana Richards

Going around the world three times for all the promotions and premieres was a very big change for me after making *Jurassic Park.*

Kate Jackson

All of a sudden there was all this incredible attention when *Charlie's Angels* hit. There was this big media thing that happened. Being in the middle of it was a strange place to be, looking out and seeing all this. It was like being in the middle of a hurricane. There was all this STUFF flying around. You really had to duck and look out—and if you forgot to duck something would hit you. It didn't completely die down for a long time. It was surreal, that's what it was.

Would I do it again? At what age? At the age that I was then, yes. At the age that I am now, I wouldn't. At this stage of my life, having learned what I've learned, I wouldn't put myself into a goldfish bowl or in the middle of a hurricane like that. But if I were twenty-seven, yeah, I'd jump right back in.

Roman literature portrays Fame as a monster. According to the poet Virgil, "Fame is an evil and no plague is swifter than she. She grows by moving, gains strength by going. Small and timid at first, she suddenly rises up to the air and yet simultaneously walks on the ground."

Kiefer Sutherland

Even being a second generation actor, [his dad is actor Donald Sutherland] I don't think there's anything that helps you prepare or understand any of it. I remember there were times when people would say amazing things about me when I first started out. That made me feel uncomfortable, too, because I knew I wasn't that. I felt a horrible pressure about trying to fulfill that.

Garth Brooks has sold more albums than any other recording entity, except for the Beatles. He told The Los Angeles Times: "Going from nowhere to platinum with the first album was like being hit with a tidal wave. And I used to try to calm myself by saying things will eventually get easier. But it doesn't."

Charlie Sheen

I was twenty-one years old and *Platoon* had just won Best Picture and grossed $100 million. Suddenly you're not paying for meals or drinks. You don't drive anymore. You get successful. The more money you make the less people want you to spend. It's very bizarre.

Elliott Gould

I couldn't fully accept nor appreciate all the privileges that were given to me because I was so successful so soon. No matter what privilege, working with the outstanding people in any area—director, writer, conductor, composer—I believe the great privilege is to be conceived, born and know yourself. Everything else will follow. It's true. But we're told that we have to make something of ourselves. It's dangerous, if we make something of ourselves before we know what we are, before we can accept what we are.

George Michael

I understand the whole star system. There's one level on which I'm probably the same as every big star that's ever been. I wanted to be a star because I wanted to make up for whatever weaknesses I felt I had as a person. There is that element of people that I've met, though, who generally want to become someone else the moment the public takes them into their arms and says, "We accept that you're something special." They want to become something else because they weren't at all happy with the person they were in the first place.

Richard Dreyfuss

My dream was to become a movie star. Because it was a dream and it was unknown territory to me, the reality is far more complex and has more dark sides to it than up sides, compared to what I'd anticipated. It still has more up sides, obviously, but when I was nine and ten and fifteen years old, I only thought about being able to choose what I did. I never anticipated how horrible fame was. I thought fame would be great. I didn't know about the invasion of privacy.

Jason Priestley

You never think about the price of fame when you start out. You're far too busy trying to work. All of a sudden you find yourself a working actor and six months later you've got *Hard Copy* camped out on your doorstep.

Keanu Reeves

In the early days I wasn't used to being asked personal questions and most of the questions don't pertain to work. To a certain degree, I was not leading an examined existence, even internally, so I was unable to speak about what I was thinking or feeling. I was just being. So I think that inability to express my thoughts about feelings and being unable to categorize and put things in context was amusing, especially for journalists. So they made fun of the monkey.

Keanu Reeves
Ron Davis/Shooting Star

Robin Givens

The fact that people see you and think they know you, that "fame," whatever that is, it's difficult to prepare somebody for.

Natasha Henstridge

Especially female models, who leave at a very early age, it can be difficult on them.

To be away from home and living on your own at such a young age when you don't really have your roots established yet, then all of a sudden you're in this whole different lifestyle and whole different world that's kind of like a fantasy world. You're making more money than your family half the time. There's drugs and people telling you how great you are. Then if something changes, you can be on top and then hit bottom. When those things happen it can be very hard on people.

As an attractive, moderately successful model trying to make it big in New York, there was nothing extraordinary about Marla Hanson. Then an ex-boyfriend had a couple of thugs slash her face with razor blades and she became a media sensation. Her hospital room filled up with thousands of letters. One wealthy man sent her a $20,000 check, with a promise to send another each year for the rest of her life. After her release from the hospital, Hanson reported that when some people saw her on the street they would burst into tears—and run over to get her autograph. In 1989, a TV movie was made about Hanson's ordeal—starring Marla Hanson.

Goldie Hawn

The toughest time for me in my whole life was when I became known. I was very afraid of falling into a category of what I considered fairly neurotic and self-centered people who led unhappy lives. All that I'd read, and how Hollywood was perceived by me as a small girl growing up in Washington D.C., I didn't want to be that way. Suddenly I was challenged as to who I really was when people started to think they knew who I was. I individualized myself at a very young age from the masses, masses meaning people who focus on you and perceive you to be a certain way. It isn't the way I am. I learned that through some very difficult times. That was pre-*Laugh In*, when I did a show called *Good Morning, World*.

Mick Jones
(Member of Foreigner)

You have to be ready to sacrifice most everything in life, just about, to be successful in the first stage. And then you have to be strong enough to keep it together after that. It's a very demanding life. People think it's glamorous, but it's a high-pressure job.

Belinda Carlisle

When The Go-Go's went number one and we were, like, "IT," for the moment, it was one of the worst memories I have. It was horrible. I hated it. People tend to focus on the lead singer and I was a complete prisoner of our success. I could not go out of the house. I would get bugged all the time. No one wanted to go out with me because it was such a pain in the ass to go out. I hated it.

Then you go through the whole thing, "Do I deserve all this fame? Do I deserve all this success?" And you sabotage it. From that moment on—and for the next five years of my life after that—it was a downhill spiral. It was horrible.

Peter Tork

I don't really have a lot to compare it with, since I didn't have a normal life going on at the time to which I could refer, but at the time when the Monkees hit, the fame thing was very difficult for me. I thought that kids liked our records and that they came to the shows to hear us play the music. That's why I go to shows. I couldn't believe it.

Ozzy Osbourne

The initial success of Black Sabbath, to go to America all those years ago, it was like going to the moon. I expected to see Superman flying around New York when I first got here. Then I got spoiled with the way of life and started taking it for granted and started to abuse everything.

Judge Reinhold

A lot of young actors are thrown into fame knowing that they don't know what they're doing, not having trained or not being prepared, and they behave badly because they're scared.

I went through that. I went through a period where I wished I hadn't worked so much. I went through a crisis point in my life where I had to face fifty people every day. I'm not trying to paint myself into this tragic figure, but imagine you going through the roughest times in your life in front of fifty people every day—and having people write about it. It's not pretty.

John Turturro

You see a lot of these young people who get out there and they don't have the skill to do different things. They don't even know how. You've got to build a foundation.

Cyd Charisse

I think the old studio system was very fortunate for us all. If you signed a contract at MGM or Warners or Columbia or Universal, no matter where it was, you were trained. I came out from a ballet company knowing absolutely nothing about films, except watching them. So when they signed me at Metro, it was like going to school. I had to learn to act, to lose my Texas accent, and to show up for publicity. It was an education for me and I absolutely felt very fortunate. They would look for things to use you in so the public would get to know you. That is completely gone today. It does not exist. Without the studio system young actors today don't have that wonderful security.

Dennis Hopper

I was raised in Kansas on a wheat farm. I didn't see a way out of where I was except for sports or acting. I guess if I'd been in Spain I'd have probably tried to become a matador, in Italy I'd have probably tried to become a race car driver. I just happened to be in America and sports and acting seemed to be the only ways out of where I was. I love football, but I was a little too small to play professional football. When I moved from Kansas to San Diego when I was thirteen, I started working at the Old Globe Theatre. I wanted to be an actor really young. By the time I was eighteen I won a contract at Warner Brothers. I was good.

Kevin Pollak

My thirteen-year-old cousin took me to see the Dave Clark Five when I was six. Sonny and Cher were the opening act, in fur vests. When the show was over, my cousin and fifty other thirteen-year-old girls and I were waiting at the side stage door to get autographs. We waited like forty-five minutes. They never came out, or probably left through another exit. There were stairs leading up to a little platform and my cousin said, "Why don't you go up there and sing some of the Dave Clark Five songs." I was a natural ham, so I jumped up there. I guess the girls came to get somebody's autograph, so a couple of them asked for mine. I didn't know how to write yet. I had to print my name, literally. That was the beginning of the bug. By the time I was ten I actually had an act.

Alannah Myles

I was the most unhappy I've ever been in my entire life when "Black Velvet" hit the top of the charts. I pushed and struggled and with tremendous tenacity I managed to rise above the crowd and be heard. And then when I got there at the top of the heap all my dysfunction was reflective. All the things that I was trying to escape or hide from by becoming successful were the very things that I had to go and repair in order to be happy with myself inside.

How could people understand that? They've never become famous and won Grammys, sold five and a half million records and suddenly became—for fifteen minutes—the favorite of everyone. It doesn't happen to everybody. It's a very unusual thing.

Alannah Myles

I spent so much energy on trying to get there that by the time I got there I didn't want to be there. There was a lot of healing necessary before I was to escape the darkness that enveloped me.

Pat Benatar

I was desperate to be famous. It was making me crazy when I was twenty-two. I couldn't wait. Then something happened. By the time I was twenty-six, I wasn't so desperate any more. Then when I was twenty-eight I hated it, so it took me a long time to come to grips with "now look what you've done."

Sammy Davis, Jr.

First making it big, it's like being twenty-one. You're on top of the hill. "This is what I've fought for all my life. I've got the success and I've licked the critics in New York. Now why the fuck ain't I happy? Oh well, the hell with it. On to the next gig, on to the next challenge."

> *The stupidest thing in your life is to work for so many years to achieve something that you want—and then get there and be so unhappy. That makes no sense. I couldn't understand it. You sit there and say, "Why am I not enjoying this? Something's wrong!" It just came down to the fact that first of all you have to try and understand who you are. What is it about this that enticed you?*
>
> *I wasn't happy because the priority wasn't on music any more. The priority became interviews, television, album covers, and merchandising. You feel like an object instead of a person.*
>
> *—Pat Benatar*

James Garner

That was the thing that made me famous, so I have a fond memory of *Maverick*. I was just learning my trade then. I was busy working every day, ten or twelve hours a day, and I didn't know what I was doing. I didn't know the effect that it had. They sent me somewhere every weekend. I'd work up until Saturday at noon and Saturday afternoon they had me on a plane somewhere so I could promote on Sunday and back to work on Monday. I was so dumb, I did it.

Julia Ormond

When it all first started to happen I kind of froze. I was, "I don't know how to play this. I'll just take each moment, moment by moment." Woodenly, very rigidly. What I feared the most was that I would lose a sense of reality. If you've lost that sense of reality and you can't do things for yourself, then you can't be an actor. You cannot if you lose touch with people on the street. You have to have some sort of reminder of what people get put through, because you get put into such an extraordinary position.

John Leguizamo

At first there was a huge amount of pressure. That was the hardest time for me. I was used to being a lot more obscure and unknown. It was fun for a while, but then all of a sudden there was all this attention on me constantly. People were recognizing me and I felt like I had to be funny all the time. So I stopped leaving my house, just so I wouldn't disappoint anybody. And my management was telling me, "John, your next choice is really important. A wrong decision and your career will fail." Obviously, I made the wrong decisions, but I'm still here.

Jason Alexander

I would go home from a great performance on the stage, where the audience just was adoring. You'd go to the stage door and there were autograph people. You could really see that light in their eye. They thought that you were something special. And you'd go home.

And that's what happens. You go home. That is a fleeting moment. It is an illusion. It is a gift that you gave to a group of people. They appreciate the gift and they're very touched by the gift, but you don't own it. It's not something you can give each and every time. It's not yours. It's actually something they give you.

Richard Dreyfuss

I had always assumed that my stardom would happen in my early thirties and that I would spend my twenties doing regional theater and hustling more. Studying in London. Then I did this little, inconsequential movie, which turned out to be a movie of great consequence, called *American Graffiti*, which I had not a clue would be important. And then I went to Canada to do a film that I didn't think would get sold in the United States, *The Apprenticeship of Duddy Kravitz*. Then I did *Jaws*, and that was the end of that.

Lynn Redgrave

It was terribly exciting and quite frightening when *Georgy Girl* hit. It was very scary. I came to New York in a play with "The Phantom" himself, Michael Crawford, and Geraldine Page, as *Georgy Girl* had just opened. So I arrived not only going into what turned out to be quite a hit as a show, but also with this movie and all these nominations and awards and things. I really couldn't believe it. I was just in this sort of daze and people were being terribly nice, the way they are when you're the new flavor. I was the new flavor.

There's nothing that prepares you for that. I had done well up until that time. I was with the National Theatre in London and had made a couple of films. I was a working actress, but I wasn't recognized in the street and didn't have people writing things about me in the papers. I found it very unnerving and exciting. I started not sleeping very well, loving it and being scared of it at the same time, as I think most people are when it happens. I was young. It was my first time in America.

I was much helped by the fact that I met and married my husband [John Clark] at that time. My husband had been a child star and he knew what it was like, the fright when you're not used to people shouting at you, clamoring, wanting to touch you. It's very flattering, but it's very frightening.

Julie Walters

Educating Rita *was my first film* and it was such a massive shock that it was such a success. It's still with me now. I remember coming to America, the huge culture shock when I arrived in Los Angeles. I was put in a limousine that was bigger than the flat that I lived in. At the Beverly Hills Hotel there was enough gold by the swimming pool to revive the British economy.

Richard Dreyfuss

Imagine that attaining success is wearing a suit. Years ago I was handed a suit—and it was a good-looking suit, no question about it. But it was a suit I had never worn before and it didn't fit. And no one said to me, "Well, the sleeves have got to fit and it's got to be pulled in here." I walked around and it felt awkward and it looked awkward and I didn't quite understand why everyone respected and admired this suit of clothes so much.

Now I wear a suit of clothes better than I did before. Now I know, first of all, that it's only a suit of clothes. That's number one. You get it fitted and it looks right and it feels good. You feel like you're walking around in something that fits you. And you're walking around on a planet that has the right amount of gravity.

Sophia Loren

I was very young and for me everything was a joke. It was like playing. It was something fun, but I didn't take it too seriously. I always liked to be with my feet on the ground and I always liked to know where I was and where I stood. Always.

It was fun in the beginning, when the fame of Mork & Mindy happened. And then after a while it was like, "Okay. I've done this now." There's a fine line. You just have to temper yourself and not become a jerk.

—Pam Dawber

Henry Winkler

I didn't get too caught up in my fame, thank God no. The honest truth is I had very low self-esteem. I'm dyslexic. My parents were very, very strict and never allowed me to express myself, so I never had a point of view when I was younger. They did the best they could. They came from Europe, that's all right, whatever. The effect on me was that I didn't think that I was that special to begin with, so when people started to say that I was special I couldn't see it. So I didn't buy into it.

Lauren Holly and Jim Carrey Ron Davis/Shooting Star

Dennis Miller

I was a bit of an asshole for a while when I first got famous, but I think most people are a bit of an asshole with it for a while. I probably acted a little bit cooler than I should have acted when I was a little younger, but all you can ask anybody is that they get a stranglehold on that fakery in a quick manner—which I did. I didn't wear it well for a little bit. Then I thought, "You're being such a cretin, man." The reason you act like that is you can't believe you got it. You're firmly convinced they're going to knock on the door in the next second and tell you it's gone. And that shouldn't be that bad a thing, and you're kind of embarrassed that you've made more of it than it is. Or at least that's the way I felt.

Wesley Snipes

No one can train you for fame. Unless you've grown up in it, how do you learn how to deal with the loss of anonymity, the loss of privacy, managers and bodyguards and motorcycles? You just pray. Study and pray. Be disciplined. Go back to what works. You have to be sensitive to your own journey and your own destiny.

Lauren Holly

There's no doubt that I'm probably more well-known to people because of Jim. It's always, "Jim Carrey and galpal Lauren Holly." I have met more people because of Jim. But I don't think that's made studios want to hire me.

Keenen Ivory Wayans

I had the fortunate experience of having all my friends get famous before I did. So through their experiences I was able to learn a lot just being there and having a more objective point of view of things. I learned early on that anybody can be a bad person, but everybody is not a bad person. You learn to be a better judge of character when you have that point of view and give people the benefit of the doubt and not be paranoid.

Marlon Wayans

Hey, I just learned from Keenen [his brother]'s mistakes.

David Birney

You'll see the same thing, whether it's somebody in a high political office or an entertainer or anyone who's suddenly prominent. Mark Fuhrman. There is a sense, always, of shock. Your life is exposed to the news media. There's a sense of outrage. "Hey, that's not who I am. That's not the way I live my life. That's not what I said. That isn't what I did."

Laurence Fishburne

This is weird, man. This is the weirdest thing I've ever experienced. I'm an actor first. That's what I love to do. I wasn't anticipating any of this. So it's very flattering and it's very exciting, in more ways than one, but it is new. I'm doing the best I can to negotiate it and appreciate it and be as graceful as I can with it.

Al Pacino

The person who helped me the most, Marlon Brando, couldn't have been nicer to me on the first picture, *The Godfather.* I needed it on that picture because I wasn't wanted there the first six weeks.

Justine Frischman

It came pretty quickly, probably too quickly, and we [the members of Elastica] tried to run away from it. We've always been a bit worried about the hype that you can get involved in, but if you want people to hear your music and come and see you then they've got to have heard of you. So it's a very fine line really.

Robin Givens

After my first three days in L.A. I had a job with Faye Dunaway and I had two different people wanting me to do a TV series. In three days. Everything was so smooth. So for me, when I got married [to boxer Mike Tyson] it was like, "Okay, now we're going to teach you about life."

Quentin Tarantino

It's always a misconception that it happens—BOOM!—in a minute. When it's your life it's not happening overnight. It's a day-by-day process. When it's your life you're not in the abstract. Hopefully, you're living it, experiencing it.

Does that make any sense?

Liam Neeson

I'm glad [the success of Schindler's List*] came now* when I'm forty-two instead of when I was eighteen. I have a sense of who I am.

Rene Russo

As a teenage model I had very low self-esteem. I did not think I was pretty at all. It was the hardest time of my life. I think that the modeling career and going to New York, being put in front of a mirror, was unbelievably painful. Oh my God, I grew up fast. It's a tough business. Modeling was particularly difficult because it was all about how you look and I didn't like the way I looked. I don't care if you're on the cover of *Vogue* magazine, we all have our own insecurity in that area.

Eddie Murphy

I got Saturday Night Live *when I was nineteen years old.* That's a kid. I did *Beverly Hills Cop* when I was twenty-three. My kids are the first kids on both sides that weren't born to the projects. It's a lot to have the background that I have, the background that a lot of people have in this business, to go from nothing to everything. All of a sudden you've got power and money and fame and girls and drugs and the whole thing is laid out. Then it's on the artist to see what road they want to walk down. In the meantime, you're trying from every table and stuff. Your whole life used to be doing what you do and then it turns into celebrating what you did and being half-assed about your work. It becomes a party.

Keenen Ivory Wayans

Again, I had been there, so I knew what the trappings were. I knew how superficial most of those people are. A lot of them didn't even remember me. That's how funny it is. When it was my turn, the whole party came my way and it was like, "Hello. I know you. I was there." I know that you can't rest on your laurels. I've seen other people fall.

LL Cool J

When you start, you're not really aware of the power that the record sales and the celebrity status gives you. If you start believing your own hype you can't see what's really coming at you.

Michael Jackson

We auditioned for Motown at Berry Gordy's mansion in Detroit. It was this big, big, big estate with an indoor pool. Here we are singing next to the pool among all the Motown stars, the Temptations, Diana Ross, the Marvelettes. They were all there and we were singing and we did our show and they loved it. They gave a standing ovation. Berry Gordy came over and Diana Ross came over to us, too, at the end of the show. She kissed each one of us and said she loved what she saw and she wanted to pay a special tribute to the group and she wanted to be a part of what we do. So we moved to California and half of the group stayed with Diana Ross. I lived with Diana almost a year and a half and the other half lived with Berry Gordy. It was like paradise. We went to Disneyland. We had fun every day. We just screamed. I mean, this was a whole 'nother thing from Gary, Indiana. Hollywood. We went into the studio and we came up with "I Want You Back," "ABC," "The Love You Save," and "I'll Be There," four number one records in a row. And we never stopped going.

Marilu Henner

Usually when you first get out here the first six months you're going, "You're kidding! People do that?" Then after six months it's, "What's the phone number?" I've done it all. I've had the L.A. experience.

Martin Sheen

I don't think Charlie [Sheen, his son] had matured enough to handle what happened to him at such a young age. All his life he wanted to be a pitcher, a professional baseball player. When that faded he thought

After nearly eighteen months of marriage, Lisa Marie Presley, the daughter of Priscilla Presley and the late "King of Rock 'n' Roll" Elvis Presley, filed for divorce from the self-proclaimed "King of Pop," Michael Jackson, on December 10, 1995. She cited irreconcilable differences. She was said to be resentful that Michael was closer to his work and his younger, child friends than to her.

According to reports, Presley, as stipulated in a prenuptial agreement, will get $15 million, plus 50% of all property acquired during their marriage. When the New York Post learned of the news, on January 19, 1996, it ran a full page headline declaring, "Jacko Gets the Sacko!"

offhandedly that he would try acting. That's hardly a way to go into a career, but BOOM! He had an instinct for it. He had a love for it. He was good. Then he had this instant success. My God! How could he be expected to react normally to all that attention? His ego was constantly being stroked. A lot of very unscrupulous people came around him and created this entourage. He was isolated and protected and his ego was nurtured. He was bound to hurt himself. He's still dealing with a lot of demons that come from that.

Woody Allen

Fame has certainly not helped me these last couple of years. When you're an adolescent you think, "Gee, I'll do movies or plays and I'll be famous and it'll be so glamorous." Then, you quickly see that's an adolescent's dream and it doesn't mean anything.

Berry Gordy

All of a sudden I was this different person. I would find out then how other people started treating me. I was this big star. But I had no money and I thought I was going to have all the money. I thought I was going to be rich and, more importantly, have all the girls I ever wanted. I was wrong on all counts.

David Ogden Stiers

It was actually rather daunting [when joining the cast of *M*A*S*H* made him famous] and a bit uncomfortable. That's nothing I ever sought. I was never particularly gracious about it, either. I didn't evolve a way of dealing with it.

Richard Gere

I tried not doing anything—no interviews—because I was very shy. I didn't want to talk about myself. I just wanted to do the work. Part of doing the work, I thought, was being anonymous, putting the mask on. But once you start making movies you're co-opted in many ways. You become an icon. It goes with the territory. So you start to play with that energy, the original energy, the impulse to create, along with the new energy that comes from the icon, and hopefully use the new energy to do even better work.

Sharon Stone

When I first got famous, the image of the movie [*Basic Instinct*] really protected me. Everyone thought I had so much bravado and was so wild. So I could continue to be that. It was a blast. As the time has gone by and I had to continue to cope with it, things start to integrate with your own personality. I could bring it down and bring more of myself to the party. It's a learned thing.

I thought when I first made my first big mistakes in public that that was really going to be the end of me. My parents cried. My friends were desperate. I was just kind of dumbfounded, because everything was going great and then—Ba-Boom! It was just awful. It was very confusing and very overwhelming. I started thinking about my life in terms of just one day at a time, because it was just too much.

Ethan Hawke

The first time you're in a tabloid, there's a certain intrigue to the whole idea that people care about who you're sleeping with or what you're doing. You're kind of like, "Gosh I must be really neat." And then all of sudden you're like, "Wow, this is really sick." There's something intrinsically sick about the whole thing—and destructive.

Charlie Sheen

At first it was about really living that lifestyle that I had envisioned, that I had really hoped for. I'd hoped to be a very recognizable celebrity. I thought that's what it was all about: the women, the money, the fame, all the bullshit. When you get in it, when you're suddenly in the eye of the storm, it's not as good as it looks like from the outside. It's not as appealing as it looked when I would hang out with Emilio [Estevez, his brother] or Tom Cruise or Judd Nelson, the guys who were going through it when I was still on my way up.

Whitney Houston

Three women in my life who I grew up around and highly respected, Dionne Warwick, Aretha Franklin, and Cissy Houston [her mother], they used to talk to me all the time. When I first hit, Dionne said to me, but it's like a diva thing, "So, you wanted to be a star." Right, okay. I said, "Jesus, no, I didn't." My mother says it to me constantly. Aretha, in that very

Whitney and Cissy Houston Ron Davis/Shooting Star

Detroit drawl, says, "So, you wanted to be a star." That was the thing that they were saying to me. All of this stuff is cool, it's wonderful when you do something and people accept it and embrace it. But that fame is some crazy mess.

Lauren Holly

Jim [Carrey] and I are kind of new at it and we meet other people who are more ensconced in it and really handle it well and you pick up from them. Tom Hanks and Rita Wilson, we're friendly with them. I really like the way they lead their lives. Steven Spielberg and Kate Capshaw. You can set certain examples. Who has a nice home life and family life?

Luke Perry

I ask a lot of questions. I have people I go to for advice. When it starts to get a little crazy, I'm not too proud to ask. You don't let your ego get in the way. When you don't know, you don't know. So ask someone who does.

Laurence Fishburne

My hope is that I will contact other famous people who have had to deal with this and who have dealt with it successfully—because there are those who have—and get some good advice. I've talked to a few people. The advice I got was "go away four times a year to someplace very remote and quiet."

Shirley MacLaine

I would tell anyone who was going into this business to learn every technique they possibly could to go within themselves, because they're going to need that balance. When you lead a public life there are so many winds that come buffeting around your head and your feet that can knock you over. It's not only survival, it's evolution. It's too hard not to have that center because people are telling you what you're doing wrong all day long. They have to, to get the project right. So that's all you're trying to do, is please people all the time. You have to please yourself also.

Jack Lemmon

I'm very cautious about giving advice, even though I know everything.

Kimberly Williams

When I did the first Father of the Bride, *I just went back to school* [Northwestern]. I didn't know about unlisting my phone number. I hadn't thought about all these things that happen when you become a celebrity. You're completely exposed. I would get calls from people all the time. My dad would get calls at home. People would show up at my dorm. I remember this guy showed up once with flowers. He just didn't know that I didn't know him. I'm still not used to that.

Jennifer Beals

I was at school [Yale] a lot of the time when *Flashdance* hit, so I didn't experience it fully. Thankfully. I don't think I would've remained sane if I had. Somebody called me and said, "Isn't it so wonderful that your film made more money the third weekend than it did in the first two weekends?"

I said, "How do you know that?"

He said, "I saw it in *Variety*."

I said, "Are you one of the producers of the film?"

"No."

"Then what do you care?"

Jennifer Beals

The thing that was daunting was that people knew more about me. People suddenly knew my name. They knew my brother's name. They knew where I grew up—and I didn't know anything about them. I was really shy at that time, it felt kind of strange. But I was thankful for the film because it helped me pay for school.

Bruce Willis

When I was first pronounced a box office star I thought it was all bullshit. I didn't believe it. I just thought it was a hook-y thing to write to get people to buy stuff. Almost immediately it became a lot more interesting to write something negative about me than to write something nice about me, because it sells more newspapers or magazines. I just don't care anymore.

Marlon Wayans

I didn't understand any of the political aspect of this industry. I tend not to pay attention to it, because it can really get on your nerves, but sometime or another you're going to have to grab it by its throat and handle it. You have to get in your fighting stance and understand what goes on.

Mel Gibson

You learn how to live with celebrity. It used to really bother the hell out of me and I'd get quite upset about it. But the best thing to do is let it slide. I don't give a damn anymore. Fuck 'em.

Ricki Lake

At first I was like, "Me? You want my autograph?" That to me was exciting. I would write books. "To so-and-so. It was great meeting you. Hope you like the movie. See you soon...." Now it's just, "Ricki." Now it's like work.

Hugh Grant

Just turning left as you get on the airplane is a big thrill. Pathetic, isn't it? Of course, it's nice to have the opportunity to earn money, but the

Mel Gibson Ron Davis/Shooting Star

downside is the pressure. It's like being given a whole new set of ski equipment without actually knowing how to ski. You look a bit of the fool trying to come down the mountain.

Brendan Fraser

It's like being given something really intricate that doesn't have an owner's manual. I really wish I could read it sometimes, but then again it's kind of fun to figure out how it works.

Cathy Lee Crosby

I was begged by ABC to do *That's Incredible!* I turned down the pilot. I said it was the stupidest idea for a show I had ever heard in my entire life. That's what I said to them. They kept calling. Finally they said they'd do twelve shows in twelve days. Now I figured, twelve days of my life—and I was making an unbelievable amount of money for those twelve days. I hadn't made big money yet. I had done all these great feature films with Walter Matthau, Bruce Dern, Lou Gosset, all these great people, but I had never hit yet. So I thought, "I'll do this, get some quick money, and then I'll go back to doing films." Right? Wrong. It shot up into the top ten and stayed there for five years and that was it.

George Burns

I started at eight with the Peewee Quartet. We used to work for a candy store in the basement. We made syrup, chocolate and strawberry and

George Burns: 1896-1996

George Burns died peacefully at his home in Beverly Hills on Saturday, March 9, 1996. He was 100 years old. Burns had a long-enduring relationship with fame—the result of a nearly century-long career.

Burns was born on January 20, 1896 to a large family in New York City. He began his career with the Peewee Quartet in 1903 and then moved to the vaudeville stage, where he met Gracie Allen. Burns and Allen formed a comedy team and were very successful, both personally and professionally. They moved their act to radio, then to the big screen in feature films, and finally, to the new medium of TV. After his beloved Gracie's death in 1964, Burns launched a successful solo career, even playing God in the Oh God! series of movies. He wrote several books about his life in entertainment, including his final book: A Hundred Years, A Hundred Stories, published in 1996. He was active until his death.

George Burns's death turns off the spotlight he was under for most of his life and closes the door on an era. His career in "the business" lasted longer than anyone else's.

vanilla. There was a letter carrier on the Lower East Side, name of Lew Farley. He wanted the whole world to sing harmony. He saw four kids and he started to teach us how to sing harmony. We were pretty good. One day we were singing and I looked upstairs. At the top of the steps there were about seven or eight people listening to us. They threw a couple of pennies at us. I said, "Fellas, let's give up the syrup business and go into show business." We started to sing on ferry boats and on street cars and on corners. I fell in love with show business—and I love it as much today as I did when I was eight. But I'm doing better today than I did then.

Chazz Palminteri

I always used to say when I was broke, "Why is it that people with money say, 'Money doesn't make you happy'?" I've never heard a poor person say that. But then when I started to make money I realized they were absolutely right. The things that are inside you as a human being that bother you will always bother you, even when you become rich, even when you become famous. In fact, it will bother you even more, because now that you have all this money, you have nothing to worry about. You got the money for the rent. You got the money for the car. You got the money if your car breaks down. So all that you can think about now are the things that really bother you. It actually makes life worse.

Nathan Lane

You try to take it in stride. This is something to discuss with my therapist. You want to allow yourself to enjoy it, but sometimes it's hard. It's a little scary. Everyone is saying to me, "This is going to change your life." If you sit around waiting for your life to change you may be in for a big disappointment.

Sinbad

If you're not happy before you're successful, you're going to be miserable when you do become successful because all your problems just get magnified.

Roseanne

When I first got famous, everybody was saying, "She stands for this and for that, for the working woman, for the mother, for the fat woman." I was like, "God, I stood for so much, I've really gotta sit down."

Close Encounters with Fans

Fans present stars with their most vexing dilemma. Everyone knows that in theory fans are the lifeblood of their careers, but in practice they can be nuisances—or much worse. Remember Rebecca Schaeffer, Selena, and John Lennon? They were murdered by deranged fans. These are extreme cases, but there isn't a celebrity in the world who doesn't entertain that fear at some point. Some are haunted by it every day. Coupled with the resentment common to those who are dependent on others for their livelihood and the breakdown in common courtesy, it's no wonder that celebrities have such mixed emotions about their fans.

Bruce Willis

I can't go anywhere. I've accepted it. That's what my life is now. I wish that I could throw a switch and sometimes go out and be anonymous again. Six days out of seven I'm okay with it. I'll sign their autograph or acknowledge them. But I'm a human being, too. There are days when I'm just irritable or cranky or tired and I don't want to be somebody's movie star. I don't want to be somebody's hero. But you gotta do it, people expect you to do it, because that's the way it's been set up. When someone sees someone famous the first thing they want is that autograph. "Give me something, you gotta give me something!" There are days when I just don't feel like doing it, when I just don't care at all about being famous.

Tom Hanks

I've been a public figure since I was on *Bosom Buddies* in 1980. Some version of getting recognized in airports. Does it get worse? Yes. But I've learned how to not let that bother me. The problem is autograph hounds, people who want to make money off you. They're very rude people.

Kirstie Alley

I'm not good about people who point and tell their whole family to stare at me. That's where I draw the line—and that happens a lot. "LOOK AT HER! EVERYBODY LOOK!"

James Woods

I was at the Foxwoods casino in Connecticut with my family. I was playing the slot machine and I actually had, like that scene in *Annie Hall*, where a guy grabbed my arm and held me and said, "Hey look! I got James Woods here! Hey look!"

Martha Plimpton

One time I was on the subway and I was walking to get on a train and a woman getting out of the train grabbed my arm and said, "I knew it was you!"—and made me miss my train. Other times people make bets on your identity. "I got five dollars riding on you're the girl from *Goonies*."

Sigourney Weaver

I have stopped taking the subway. There is nothing more horrifying than being in a crowded subway and being recognized by the wrong person. But the bus is different. My daughter just loves to take the bus.

Alfre Woodard

You're walking along—you as yourself—and somebody just grabs you. It's like, "Whoa!" It's like being awakened out of your sleep, constantly, by somebody screaming at you. It's jarring, it's upsetting, and people don't understand that they've crossed the line. They think they absolutely have the right to do it. All your thoughts are constantly interrupted and people tell you their opinions of things. Everybody has an opinion about something; they need to let you know to make your life better.

> ***They yell at you. They point at you. I've had people talk about me five feet away in an elevator, like I don't exist. Either I'm too stupid to understand them or I'm still behind a glass and I'm not going to hear them. Like I'm this two-dimensional object.***
>
> *—Larry Drake*

Winona Ryder

When you're famous sometimes you have problems with weird people. I'm small. Sometimes you do feel scared. Sometimes people come up and they think that it's okay to touch you. That's always really terrifying to me.

Howie Long

Everyone whispers. One time I don't think they were whispering—and I thought they were whispering—but I was paranoid. But now I know they're whispering.

Alfre Woodard

People treat you like an object. They think you can't hear. They'll stand this close and go, "There's that woman."

"What woman?"

"You know. That woman. That's that actress."

"No, it's not."

I remember being on this train in New York and there were like five teenage girls and one of them said, "Ooo, there's a movie star." I'm sitting this close and they started laughing. "If that's a movie star, I'm a movie star." They just laughed and slapped each other five. Sometimes it's kind of wild.

Amy Brenneman

That's where the resentment starts. Then you hate the public who loves you.

Tia Carrere

I don't feel so bad for myself. I feel bad for my family or my friends that are with me. They have to sit there and deal with this whole thing. "Okay, now can we go and have lunch?" Or, "I'd like to go and try on swimsuits now, if you're done." It's harder on the people around you.

Jack McDowell

(Baseball player and recording artist)

My wife Meredith does a lot of the shielding for me. She tries to protect me from things that make me uncomfortable and a lot of that is the celebrity. People asking for autographs is an uncomfortable feeling. It's not that I don't want to do it or don't appreciate it—it's just strange.

But then, on the other hand, now I do music and expose even more of myself and what I'm thinking. So maybe that's it. Having people think that they know me because I come into their house for three hours every five days and they see this person who's in this baseball world. Maybe in my own mind I have a lot more to offer—and that's where the music comes in.

Steven Tyler

(Member of Aerosmith)

It depends on what mood you're in. If you walk down the street and people bother you, you either pass it off or go with it. If you don't walk around outside a show, the nuttiness we find of people pestering and coming on to us usually happens outside a show. If you're walking down the street they'll come on to you, but you try to avoid that.

Debbie Gibson

People say, "You have a dachshund? I have a dachshund, too." There are some kids, they know every fact about you, but they don't really know me as a person.

Iman

I never understood from the first day when I came to the United States and they asked me for my autograph. I didn't understand. What do they do with it? And I still don't. It depends on my mood now. I'll sign and or I won't. I'll just say I don't sign autographs.

Kirsten Dunst

Why do you want a human being's name on a piece of paper? It's kind of stupid. I saw in this magazine that it was $56 for Tom Cruise's autograph. It was really stupid.

Jason Priestley

You're standing at a urinal and people just follow you into the bathroom and start asking for your autograph. What do you say at that point? "Look, my hands are kind of full right now."

Tisha Campbell

I get followed into the bathroom. They knock on the stall, put the note under there, ask for the autograph. Those kind of things drive me nuts.

James Woods

Carol Burnett told a story once, where she was literally in the ladies room, riding the porcelain bus, and this lady put her head under the door and said, "I'm sorry to bother you but could you just sign this?"

Howie Long

After I finished my first movie [*Broken Arrow*], they gave me a football. The crew signed it and gave it to me at the end of the production, which was pretty fun. You're so used to signing things that when they handed it to me I said, "Does anybody have a pen?" I thought they wanted me to sign it, because you get on auto-sign. You're at a store, you're at a restaurant, you just sign.

Laura San Giacomo

Sometimes I feel like I must be wearing a sign or something. I'll be looking not at all like any of the characters I've ever played, no makeup, glasses, baseball cap, not because I'm trying to hide but because it's 7:30 and I'm running out for milk and coffee. People will just come up to me continuously. I have to say, that's really nice. I feel like it's a blessing that people like my work and they want to share that with me.

Adam Sandler

When you're eating in a restaurant, you chew your food and you look up. You see someone just staring at you and you feel self-conscious about the way you're chewing.

Winona Ryder

I don't like to be stared at. On the screen that's different, but I don't like to be stared at when I'm in a restaurant. I had this battle going on. Is that okay to feel like that, please don't stare at me? If I complain about it people would say, "What do you expect? You're an actress. Don't make movies if you don't want to be stared at." But it finally occurred to me that it's just common courtesy not to stare at someone. When I see someone famous, and it doesn't matter if I'm famous or not, you just don't stare at someone and make them uncomfortable. It has nothing to do with fame to me.

Nicolas Cage

No one can really prepare you for how people want to recognize you. Sometimes it's amazing how abrasive people can be—and how insensitive. Like I won't take pictures when I'm with my kid, because I don't want people knowing what he looks like and I'm afraid of kidnapping and all that.

Nicole Kidman

I go out in a baseball cap, sweat pants, and pull my hair all back. Then I tend not to get noticed, but my height, I'm six feet tall, tends to give me away. He [husband Tom Cruise] gets it no matter what you do. I say, "Why don't you wear a wig?" He says, "Then it'll be 'Tom Cruise Caught in a Wig!'" You pull that baseball cap down, avert your eyes, and hope for the best.

Julia Roberts

I don't like to be mean to fans, but I have to have cops around me now. The worst is when people come up and just grab you.

Ed O'Neill

I can't go anywhere. I wear hats and glasses and stuff—even that doesn't help much. They'll chase after you a lot times. "Sign this t-shirt." "Put your hands down your pants, let me get a picture." All that stuff.

Lauren Holly

Going any place crowded with Jim [Carrey] is really difficult. Disguises don't work. We tried that once. We were immediately seen through and then people were saying things like, "Nice black hair, Lauren." "Nice moustache, Jim." We felt like two idiots.

Paul Newman

When people spot me they say, "Take off your dark glasses so we can see your beautiful blue eyes," at which time I could puke. I hope that there's something working that's less accidental than that. I usually say, "I'm terribly sorry, ma'am. If I take off my glasses my pants fall down."

I have a reputation that I don't sign autographs. I stopped signing them after I was standing at the urinal at Sardi's and some guy came in and said, "Can I have your autograph?" I didn't know what to do with my hands, left-handed, right-handed? And then I thought about all the times that I was having dinner with the kids or walking down the street with the kids. When did somebody put down in *The Congressional Record* that if you were in films and somebody stopped you doing whatever it was that you were doing that you had to put your name on a piece of paper? I figured I wasn't around to vote on it.

Nicole Kidman and Tom Cruise Ron Davis/Shooting Star

James Woods

I can't understand actors who don't want to sign autographs. You're in a public service industry. If you don't want to sign autographs then become a computer programmer. What is your problem?

Henry Winkler

I don't get a kick out of people asking me for autographs. It's part of my life. You incorporate that in your life.

I don't say that you owe anything to the public except for the best performance you can get out of your body, but it's a lie if you say, "I want you to give me a half hour or an hour or two hours of your life. I want you to give me your money. I want you to watch me and listen to what I have to say."

And then when I say, "I really like what you do," and you say, "Get out of here!" that's not completing the circle. That's a lie. There's something very wrong with that.

Scott Bakula

There are times when there are just things you can't do anymore, but that comes with the territory.

Tom Selleck

I know a lot of people in this business—and I'm not criticizing them—who have a real appetite for public attention. They kind of feed off it. I don't mean this in a negative way. I wish I could do that. It energizes them. You see them almost buoyed by it and revitalized. Me, if I do a day in a public appearance or a charity event, I really do believe the Eastern cultural concept that photographs take a part of your soul. Believe me, at the end of a day where no matter what movement you make somebody's snapping a picture, I feel really drained. After a day like that you don't really know how you're going to get to the next day.

David Ogden Stiers

People interrupted some deeply emotional concentration at the Sistine Chapel by wanting to talk about *M*A*S*H*. Things like that have really put me off talking about it. It's so frequent a topic. I have nothing new to say about it. It's film. It doesn't alter. There you are. They're only reruns. Life is forward, not back.

Bronson Pinchot

You know, every once in a while, you try and get someone to date you and it takes like six months and finally you sit down to dinner. Well, I'm sitting with this woman and this guy comes up to the table—first he was outside the window for a long time—then he came up to the table and said, "My friends always said I looked like you." What do I do with that piece of information? And, of course, he was a complete dog.

Sam Neill

I'm often stopped by people who tell me, "I hated you in *The Piano.*" I walk as fast as I can around New York to keep this kind of thing to a minimum.

Sally Field

There was one person who kept calling with death threats [after she made *Not Without My Daughter*], but we didn't know whether to take it seriously or not. The President had just alerted the country about terrorist threats. The FBI was all over us because of it. I kept thinking "They're not going to come after me as their terrorist activity for the country. That's going to be it?" But we didn't know what was going to happen.

Arthur Richard Jackson, a drifter with a history of mental illness, left his home in Aberdeen, Scotland in 1982 to find Theresa Saldana, a young actress best known for her appearance in Raging Bull. When he found his "divine angel," he viciously attacked her, repeatedly plunging his hunting knife into her so fiercely that the blade bent. Saldana survived and Jackson was jailed. While in jail, Jackson continued to threaten Saldana's life in messages to several people, including a producer for television personality Geraldo Rivera. Saldana later starred as herself in a made-for-TV movie about the attack and her difficult recovery.

Pam Dawber

How can anyone have perspective on what happened to Rebecca [Schaeffer, her co-star on *My Sister Sam,* who was murdered by a psychotic fan]? I can get on my bandwagon again about television taking responsibility for itself. That was a sick boy who was obsessed with television, who actually said he wanted to become a famous celebrity slayer on *Hard Copy,* which gave him that opportunity. Two years after she was killed, they're still interviewing that guy? That guy should've been locked up and never heard from again. Why are they making him a celebrity? For any other sick, demented, obsessed person watching TV saying, "I can do that, too." You have no idea how many celebrities have death threats. It is so prevalent. You just don't hear about it because it does no good. It just inspires more.

Rob Reiner

It's a very tricky thing. First you create something for yourself. Then hopefully you want people to like it. You want people to love it. But then you also don't want them to confuse their love for your work with some kind of fantasy love that they might have for you. You hope that they are able to make the separation and keep on the right side of that line. Unfortunately, people can have trouble with that and cross over.

John Lennon was the worst tragedy of all in that area. If you saw the documentary, *Imagine*, there's that guy in Lennon's garden who says, "I feel like I am you. I know you. You wrote these things for me." I think any artist, whether they be a writer or musician or painter or director or whatever, you do things for people in hopes that they will identify so closely that they will have this kind of emotional experience when they see your work. But at the same time, you don't want them to confuse that with some crazy notion that you are somehow inside their mind or you

Robert Bardo, nineteen, went into the bathroom of a Los Angeles coffee shop and took a .357 Magnum pistol out of his plastic grocery bag. He slipped a final bullet into the gun, fully loading it with extremely deadly hollow-point cartridges, then walked the few blocks towards the modest house of a young actress, Rebecca Schaeffer. Bardo got the address of the beautiful star of the hit TV series My Sister Sam from the California Department of Motor Vehicles.

About an hour earlier, they had had a one-minute conversation on her doorstep, before Schaeffer politely but hurriedly closed the door, telling him, "Take care, take care." This time, when Schaeffer opened the door, Bardo shot her in the chest and killed her. Then he ran, taking his bag, which also contained a copy of Catcher in the Rye, with him. Bardo was captured and ultimately sentenced to life without parole in 1989. The case was tried by prosecutor Marcia Clark, who later became much more famous as the prosecutor who failed to get a conviction against O.J. Simpson, acquitted of two grisly murders in 1995.

Laws were changed after Schaeffer's death to prevent people from obtaining addresses through the DMV.

are them or they are you. Sometimes you run into mentally unbalanced people and then tragedy can result.

Yoko Ono

John [Lennon]'s death was so mind-boggling. I wasn't prepared for this. Every day seems like a new learning experience. I'm learning a lot, let's put it that way. Maybe it's a learning process that I have to go through. This is the reality. I have to learn it. I never thought that a title or label like "widow" would ever be mine.

Blair Underwood

I got letters from someone who had a "fatal attraction" thing for me. She felt as though she should be Mrs. Underwood. It was eerie.

Malcolm McDowell

I did get a couple of death threats. That's all part of the job. For killing Captain Kirk, the Trekkies [fans of *Star Trek*] all went nuts.

Leonard Nimoy

A lady recognized me in an airport and brought her child to me. She said, "Johnny, look who's here. Your favorite person." The kid is looking at me, dumbfounded. Really bewildered. Doesn't know what his mother is talking about. "This is your favorite person. You watch him on television every week [in *Star Trek*]." The kid is looking at me and still doesn't get it. She says, "That's Mr. Spock!" And she was wrong. And the kid knew she

Mark David Chapman was obsessed with the novel, Catcher in the Rye. In that famous book, the hero Holden Caulfield, reserves his most vitreous hate for phonies. When Chapman read the November 1980 issue of Esquire, which contained an article on his one-time hero John Lennon describing the ex-Beatle as a forty-year-old businessman with lawyers to squeeze him through tax loopholes, he was furious. Lennon, as far as Chapman was concerned, was now a phony. And so he purchased a gun and started hanging around Lennon's apartment at the Dakota in New York City. After a brief trip to Florida, Chapman was back, staying only a half a block away from Lennon's apartment building. On December 8, 1980, Chapman shot and killed his former idol as he was returning from a recording session with his wife, Yoko Ono.

was wrong.

Brent Spiner

Fan mail is a really interesting subculture of show business. It really gives you a clear indication of the phenomenal diversity of America. That to me is the most perplexing, the people who use someone they see on television almost as a confessor.

It's sad that they would spend their time writing to me, but it also reflects something that's missing for them, an emptiness, that they need to connect with somebody. So they connect with who they see on television.

I don't write letters back, but I send a picture to people when they ask for it.

Kim Hunter

I think people still remember me mostly as a chimpanzee [in *Planet of the Apes*]. God knows a great portion of my fan mail still comes for ape photographs, or sending me ape photographs to sign.

Harvey Korman

They say, "Hello Hedley," or "Hello Heddy," and I say, "It's Hedley!" and they just love that. I don't get so many people talking to me about *Blazing Saddles* as I get people around forty who come up to me and say,

Lieutenant John Lane is in charge of the Threat Management Unit of the Los Angeles Police Department. The seven members of the unit investigate about two hundred stalking cases each year, with about a third involving celebrities. Lane says obsessions with celebrities often last a decade or more. A 1990 California law allows the police to make arrests for exhibitions of bizarre behavior that people find threatening. Lane reports that one stalker, Joni Leigh Penn, barricaded herself into the home of actress Sharon Gless, at the time a star of Cagney & Lacey, with a rifle and hundreds of rounds of ammunition. Penn had previously sent Gless more than one hundred photos, including one picturing Penn holding a gun to her own head.

"I grew up with you. My family and I used to watch you on Saturday nights." I was to them what Cary Grant was on the big screen. This guy! It was so precious to them, this family thing. I get more mail today than when I was doing the Carol Burnett show. I don't know how they get the address, but they do.

John Ratzenberger

When you're strolling through Disneyland or some amusement park with your kids and every other step someone is saying, "Hey Cliff [his character on *Cheers*], where's Norm?" "Hey Cliff, where's Norm?," that gets real old. I just get annoyed because there's no dignity in it.

Shelley Long

I cannot walk out of my house without expecting someone to call me Diane [her character on *Cheers*]. That's still going on. Everybody has rude things said to them and that never feels good.

Rob Schneider

I haven't gone through a day yet without someone doing the "meister" thing to me. And you know what? It's not funny anymore. Believe it or not. It was funny the first three thousand times it happened, but then, "Hey, hey. Rob. The Rob-man." "Yeah. No one's ever done that to me before."

Janine Turner

I felt there was more of a buffer when people came up to me and said, "You're Maggie O'Connell [her character on *Northern Exposure*]." Now they come up to me and say, "You're Janine Turner." If there's anything that hits me as being a bit strange, it's that.

Kirsten Dunst

Everyone asks about Brad Pitt. "What was it like to kiss Brad Pitt?"

Walter Matthau

I find fans fascinating most of the time, except if I'm in the middle of some hot soup. Then I don't appreciate the intrusion.

Close Encounters with Fans

Adam Sandler

I was in New Hampshire with my family at a pizza place. The kid working there goes, "Hey, you look like Adam Sandler."

I said, "Yeah, yeah, I know."

He goes, "What's your name?"

I go, "Adam Sandler."

And he goes, "Whoa, that's a coincidence."

David Keith

Charles Barkley told me that Michael Jordan told him that he says, "How about I don't bother you during your dinner and you don't bother me during my dinner?"

People think they're the only person that's ever gone up and done that. They don't realize that twenty people did it right before 'em, twenty are gonna do it right after 'em, and the person that's signing that autograph can't pick that person out as an individual.

Luke Perry

I've learned to love delivery food.

Halle Berry

If there's ever a day when maybe I'm having a bad day and I don't want to be bothered or I can't be nice, then I just don't come out. I just stay home by myself, because fans and the public really don't understand that. In their minds, this is the first time they've ever approached you. They don't realize that it's happened a hundred times already today.

Shelley Long

When I walk outside of my house suddenly life becomes totally unpredictable. It's pretty unpredictable inside the house, too, but I have to be prepared to meet the public, whether I want to or not. I have to be nice because I think that's important, too. I think that's part of my job, even if I don't feel particularly sociable or chatty, I owe the public courtesy and respect. I wish that the public felt that they owed me that, too.

Will Smith

There's something about the television medium that makes people feel like they know you. When people see Madonna, they expect to get shoved away. When you see Bruce Willis or Arnold Schwarzenegger, you expect to not be able to get near them. But with television stars, because you let them into your house every day, it's like you know them. It's not like a celebrity, it's like a friend of yours. So you're insulted if you can't get near a television star. You start to get more negative backlash than actors or musicians.

Jean-Claude Van Damme

People watch you and they don't see you for twenty years and if one day you have a bad temper and you go out—because some days we all have bad tempers—you're very tired and you're traveling a lot, lots of stress, stay home. Because you may see a fan and maybe you don't want to sign an autograph and they go, "Oh, he's a bad guy." For the rest of his life Van Damme is a bad guy.

Chuck Norris

I know a lot of acting friends of mine just hate it. But I think they'd hate it more if no one noticed them. I don't let it bother me. If someone comes up and asks for an autograph, it's faster to sign the doggone thing than it is to say, "Get out of my face."

Walt Parazaider

(Member of Chicago)

A kid asks for an autograph or some advice about the business. How could I turn that down? People who don't sign autographs are so full of themselves. "Later. Wait in the traffic kid." No way. Those are the people that made us.

Chris Farley

It's really nice when people recognize me. I like that. That's probably really sad that I have to have that, but it feels really good when people say, "Hey, fatso! Get away from my car!" No, they don't say that. When they say, "Hey Chris, we like you on the show. You make us laugh." That makes me feel really good.

Robin Williams

A skinhead came up to me once. He said, "Sign my fuckin' head—and dot my eye. Aye! You literal bastard. You dotted my real eye!"

Macaulay Culkin

Michael [Jackson] asked for my autograph and I asked for his. We trade them, like baseball cards.

Sam Neill

I did one of the Omen *pictures*—it's well behind me now. I did get a lot of very strange fan mail from that. That was creepy. That was a work of fiction, but there were people who were slightly confused as to what was fact and what was fiction.

D.B. Sweeney

In England, they have the Royal Family, an object of mythic attention that's abstracted from ordinary life. In America, in this pseudo-democracy, our need for everyday myths is filled more by Arnold Schwarzenegger or Roseanne. It does serve some psychological need. Some people watch soap operas and have these figures that they invest with larger meaning than they actually have. Some people go to the movies. Some people use sports. But I think there's some kind of universal need that people get from it. I think when people start to really believe it and think it actually has the meaning that it seems to have, that's when it gets to be troublesome.

Peter Tork

When I became famous and the Monkees were up on stage, I didn't get what it was all about, so I was disappointed. Now I get it. Those little girls would come running in from school. They'd be full of piss and vinegar, rocketing into the house, and Mother says, "Shut up. Behave yourself." Goink! It's like hitting a brick wall. "You've got to behave yourself. You've got to be quiet. Got to be demure." And the only place they could let it out, the only place where it was all right to put it all on the line, was at a rock/pop concert. They would scream their little butts off. Years of frustration just poured forth into the air when they got the word that said, "It's okay to do that here." That's what it was all about.

I get it now and it's okay. I wish I'd gotten it then and I wish that I had known what it was all about. I don't think I would've done anything differently except felt better about it, but that would've been enough.

Marlon Wayans

Girls are strong. I used to have dreams about girls ripping my clothes off, but in reality them girls are too damn strong. They start ripping skin off. One time four thousand girls chased us in a mall, me and Shawn [his brother, Shawn Wayans]. It was scary. Big girls. Big chops.

David Keith

There's the famous story about Elvis [Presley] when he tried to go out the front gate once. He said, "I'm tired of sneaking out the back door in disguise. I'm going out the front gate. I'm going to be me." And they tore his clothes off, they pulled his hair out. They scratched hunks of skin off to say they had Elvis's skin under their fingernails.

Patrick Stewart
Ron Davis/Shooting Star

Patrick Stewart

There is always the possibility of something wild or dangerous happening. I did something very stupid in L.A. about eighteen months ago. I used one of those cash machines very, very late at night. Why should I need money so late at night? Well, for some reason I did. I realized when I parked my car that I was doing something that was foolish. It was a deserted car park and it was off a main street. However, I was standing there, waiting for this thing to spit out my cash, and a car turned the corner and cruised very slowly into the car park, went past me, and then stopped. I got nervous. I began to sweat. I really thought that something ugly was going to happen. And, just at the moment that my money came out, the car door was thrown open and this HUGE guy got out of the car. He stood looking at me very threateningly, and he said, "Patrick Stewart, right?!"

And I said, "Yeah."

"Captain Picard?!"

And I said, "Right."

He lifted his arms up and he said, "I LOVE THIS TOWN!" And he got back in his car and he drove away.

Olympia Dukakis

I've gotten to know Whoopi Goldberg—and the world loves this woman. They yell at her on the street. They hurl themselves at her. That's difficult to have a life.

The most people do with me is want autographs. The best thing that I love when they do, is they walk by and yell lines at me, lines that I've said, as if I've made these lines up.

Michael Palin

You have to make some sacrifices. You have to be prepared to accept that you can't live quite the life you think you can live. I like to think I haven't changed, but I can't go into a pub late at night, sit by myself and have a drink. People recognize me and one or two who've had a few drinks will want to come over and try the jokes on me.

Dana Carvey

It can be a little bit like a western movie."Looky what we got here!" Like you're their plaything. "We got one of them thar celebrities. You gonna dance for us? Come on, do the celebrity dance!" Some people get really aggressive, loud and hostile. I've had people go (breathlessly), "See that girl way across there? Walk over there. Go over there now. She wants to say hello to you. Then come back here, I want you to sign this."

You go, "I'll be right back. I've just got to go to the bathroom." Then you run for your car.

Pauly Shore

People are always wanting me to smoke bud with them, or drink beers with them, or hook me up with chicks. It's like I'm the Spuds MacKenzie of humans.

Matt Dillon

After a while, it's so predictable, being famous. That's the truth of it. It's so predictable, the things that people are going to come up to you and say. Just the fact that people come up to you constantly becomes a thing. It just becomes a part of your life and you can't change that.

Shelley Long

When they comment on the work—even if it's positive—it puts my head into a work mode. I may be very much into a personal mode. I may be with my child or with my husband, or even on my own thinking.

Connie Selleca

If celebrities are going to put themselves in a situation where they know that there are going to be fans, you have to accept that. But if it's something where you're in a place where you're obviously spending time with your family, I think there's a certain respect that a fan should have. Places like Disneyland, someone like me is either asking for problems or you can deal with it in a way where you can have your privacy too. You don't go to Disneyland in full makeup and full hair and stand around. You put on sunglasses and don't look around. Go and do what you've got to do.

Jack Nicholson

You've made yourself a public person. They're going to recognize you wherever you go. Would anybody choose it? No. Anonymity, if you're cool within your own ego and sense of self-worth, is a tremendous asset for living a life. My life is truncated. I can't sign for the three-year-old girl who asks me for an autograph at a baseball game because then everybody else in that row is not going to see that baseball game. It's a tough moment for any human being. There's nobody who wants to reject a three-year-old girl. But you have to do it.

Halle Berry

Sometimes giving autographs is harder for him [her ex-husband, baseball star David Justice] than it is for me because in baseball if someone is asking for his autograph it's not necessarily because they're fans. His autograph is worth money. That bothers him. I don't have Halle Berry cards that they trade, so if someone is asking me for my autograph it's because they're a fan and they enjoy what I do. And so I deal with it better. I feel good about it. When people come up to him he's not sure. Are they fans? Do they enjoy what he does? Or do they just see him as a big walking dollar sign and how they can make money off of him?

Kurt Russell

Goldie [Hawn] and I went to a Red Sox game and it was kinda freaky. By the fourth inning people were just standing up looking at us. We couldn't see the game anymore, physically couldn't see it, because people were standing up looking at us, like there was a fight in the stands.

Kevin Pollak

I think when there's sex involved, people can get a little nutty with their fanship. That I've seen firsthand in friends. It's a difficult lifestyle.

Kirk Cameron

I had a lot of problems with people following me home, literally people trying to run me off the freeway, getting into accidents. It was nuts. I sold the Honda Prelude and got another car with tinted windows, because the Prelude was on a Dick Clark bloopers show, so everybody knew what kind of car I drove. So now I don't say what kind of car I have.

Mary Stuart Masterson

I think men tend to have it worse than women usually, because their fans are more obsessive. The men that I've worked with who have that kind of stardom tend to have more of the rock star thing going for them.

Marlon Wayans

I had some girls chase me in my car. I felt like I was in some action movie and there was this chase scene. I was on my way to Shawn [his brother Shawn Wayans]'s house and they were chasing me and chasing me. I had no place else to go, so I took them to Shawn's house. I lured them into his house—then I backed up and left. I honked my horn, Shawn came out, and they went running to his house. I just pulled off and ran.

Shawn Wayans

I used to have this real, real, real big girl follow me to my comedy spots. She would show up to every spot I did. I had to give up doing stand-up for a while. I was really nice to her at first. That's what's really scary about these people. You start off being nice and then they think that they have this relationship with you. She was questioning me about how come I didn't come and do my spot. "Uh, 'cause you were here." It can be pretty scary. Look at Madonna.

David Keith

Some drunk guy will come over and tell me to go kiss his wife, she's in love with me. It's kind of a no-win situation. You say "No," he says "Why, she's not good enough for you?" Or if you say yes then you have to go kiss this woman. Then he gets mad, they get into a fight, he gets mad at you. That's happened a few times.

Robin Williams

People want me to be funny and I tell them, "I'm off today." Most people understand that, except for the guy who put me in a headlock to kiss his wife. And she wasn't that pretty either.

Robert Conrad

I had a good time doing that battery commercial and was never seriously challenged. On the other hand, I'm pretty much who I pretend to be. I can handle myself very well. I've had a lot of occasions to prove that. No one's going to jump in my face. Plus, I'm polite. I'm a nice man. I'm a grandfather. If a guy really needs his ass kicked I'll accommodate him, but I'd rather say, "I'm a senior."

Stephen Baldwin

It's really amazing the lengths some people will go to to be around famous people. I've had some offers in recent weeks that are inconceivable. Weird stuff, guys in relations to their wives.

"My wife loves you."

"Oh, really."

"Yeah, in fact, if you come over at ten tonight...."

"Go rent a video of mine, pal, 'cause I'll be home with my wife."

People are strange.

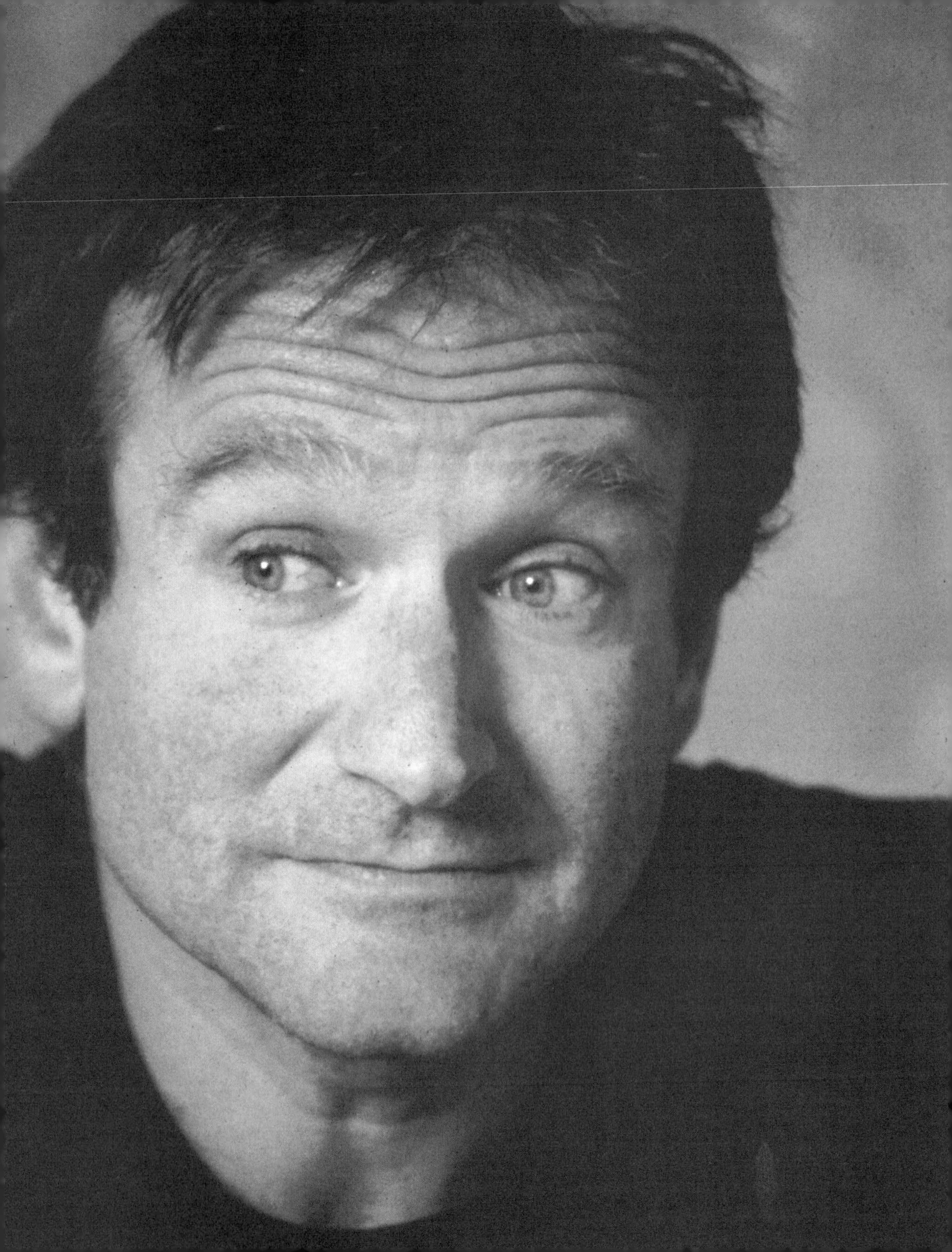

Dennis Miller

I had a guy ask me to autograph his wife's breast one night. I said, "I'm going to need something bigger to write on," and he hit me.

I said, "Listen, you fucking idiot. Don't come up to me with the most important person in your life and ask me to put my hand on her tit—and then when I point out how ludicrous that is—act like I'm the bad guy. That's your wife. Keep her breast in her bra."

What kind of goofball does that? Would you ever debase your wife like that?

Christian Slater

I had to initial a guy's penis once, because I couldn't fit my whole name on it. It was a sad thing for the guy.

Vincent Perez

I always get asked, "May I see you in your room?" or "Could you kiss me?," which is quite strange. Sometimes in letters people ask me to give them money. I'm always amazed by that.

Rosie Perez

There was this guy on the train and he recognized me and announced my name to everyone in that whole car. He wanted a kiss. I told him, "I'll shake your hand, but I won't kiss you."

Then he said, "No, I want a kiss." He was really adamant about it. I tried to get away from him and he wouldn't stop. Then he went into a brisk walk, then he was walking quicker, saying, "I want that kiss."

I started to break into a run and he started running after me, too. I was on the A train at night and since it's New York, no one wants to be involved. So I jumped over the turnstile, ran up the stairs and was running in the street. He was still running and yelling, "Just give me a kiss!"

I ran into one of those Euro cafe coffee shops where they had designer napkins and coffee costs three dollars a cup, you know? I go in there and say, "There's somebody after me!"

Robin Williams Yoram Kahana/Shooting Star

And somebody goes, "Celebrity attack! Celebrity attack! Someone call 9-1-1, damn it!"

I started screaming, "Help!" And another guy comes in and he's like this queen of queens, this thin waif of a man. He probably wanted to be Sandy Duncan in life. Well, he comes in and he has a nine millimeter gun and he's pointing it at the guy, who says, "Okay, sorry, I just wanted a kiss." And then he leaves. That was it.

I thought it was in my best interest not to take the train after what happened.

Scott Bakula

I had a wild experience in England a couple of years ago. I was in a castle walking around and about halfway through it we realized we were being followed by this family with a video camera. They finally got us in this corner of the castle where we couldn't get out and the woman says, "Would you stop right there?"

(Sheepishly) "Yes."

"Oh, God, I love you." And she turns to her husband and says, "See that? That's what a real man looks like."

I felt so terrible. Every week, this poor guy is at home and *Quantum Leap* comes on and she's going, "That's what a real man looks like."

Bob Barker

My wife and I were in Costa Rica. There's a huge volcano out there. When you go out to this volcano you think you're on the moon. A driver had taken us out there and left and we were walking. It was almost an eerie feeling. There was not another human being around—and then around a huge boulder came this man. He looked over at me—we were still maybe twenty-five or fifty yards apart—and he screams, "Hey, Bob Barker! COME ON DOWN!" It can happen anywhere.

Charlene Tilton

I was in Israel with my husband, as tourists. My hair is up under a hat, no makeup, sunglasses on, and there's a Bedouin woman with a couple of camels and a couple of kids. Her face is covered, but all of a sudden I hear, "There's Lucy!" They live in tents, they don't have bathrooms, but boy, they have TV antennas and they watch *Dallas*. That's the power of television.

Jim Varney

A guy called my hotel room about seven o'clock at night. Said his name was Jeff and asked if I wanted to come out and meet his girlfriend. The guy lived like thirty miles out of town.

I said, "I don't know you. I don't know your girlfriend. Why would I want to do this?"

"We just always wanted to meet you."

"Well Jeff, I have a date tonight."

So he calls me at midnight and says, "How you doing?"

I said, "Jeff, remember that date I had at seven o'clock? GUESS WHO'S HERE NOW?!"

He calls me at seven the next morning. I could not shake him. It's kind of creepy, with stalking and all that stuff. You never know when somebody's just trying to be friendly. Maybe that'll be our next film, "Ernest Gets Stalked."

Brent Spiner

I've had people who have written me every day for five years. I know so much more about them than they know about me. They know nothing about me. They know the character, Data [from *Star Trek: The Next Generation*].

There are a few people actually, who have written every day, but I don't think it's particular to me. You can ask anybody who's been on a television show for a long time. I'm sure Tom Selleck got mail every day

The nearly five thousand letters Michael J. Fox received from a deranged female fan threatening to kill him, his wife, and his unborn child were "perfectly normal" abnormal behavior, according to Gavin de Becker. De Becker, a leading celebrity security expert, has become quite wealthy by providing peace of mind for his clients. Among his methods for accomplishing this are around the clock protection from armed guards, armored cars, and sophisticated threat analysis of every letter and message.

from lots of people who wrote him and thought he was a friend, because he was in their house every day.

Mary Stuart Masterson

I had one crazed fan. Everyday I was getting huge bouquets of flowers—from a woman.

Eve Plumb

It was out of control when we were doing the *Brady Bunch.* We did a song and dance act that was probably hideous, but was very popular. There were people mobbing us. We had to sneak out of the theaters after the show.

About five years ago I was playing Nellie—of all things—in a production of *South Pacific.* It was in Bucks County, Pennsylvania, and I looked down in the front row of the theater. Someone was sitting there in a t-shirt with my picture on it. I could tell it was my picture, but I couldn't tell if they had hand painted it or what. It was very odd. I didn't stick around to meet the person after the show. I snuck out of the theater.

Anthony Hopkins
Yoram Kahana/Shooting Star

Anthony Hopkins

I wrote a fan letter to Charlie Chaplin when I was fourteen or fifteen years of age. He wrote me a letter back, you know, "Thank you for your kind and sympathetic letter." So obviously I tried to express something to him. Forty years later I played the editor in *Chaplin* and I went through his files trying to find the letter, but I didn't find anything.

Alfred Molina

I was filming in London. I was just parking my car when this Iranian gentleman came up to me and asked, "Are you the man from *Not Without My Daughter*?" Actors being the egotistical beasts that they are, I went, "Why, yes." And he just called me a very nasty name and punched me in the jaw, which left me in the very humiliating position of being sprawled across the bonnet of my car going, "But I'm only an actor!"

Eddie Murphy

The chink in our armor as black people is that when you embrace somebody, you need to hold onto that embrace. I guess we've been screwed over as a people so much, when we see another brother or sister get their stuff together, it's hard to hold that embrace.

I remember being at the Soul Train Awards and they were booing Whitney Houston. I was like, "Why are they booing this sister?" And then they thought she pisses ginger ale because she had a hit movie and got married to Bobby Brown. And Whitney hadn't changed. Only your perception of her has changed. She's always been cool, and any rumor that you've been hearing is just a rumor. It should only matter what you feel when you hear her sing. We're so judgmental.

Jada Pinkett

Black audiences are extremely finicky. We haven't even learned what we like.

Fred Williamson

My respect in the white neighborhood is different than in the black neighborhood. I'm not known as a butt kisser. I do what I think is right. So I can walk in any neighborhood, on any side of Harlem or Chicago or Watts, and get maximum respect. It's up to me to show that I am that guy that they know. When they see me in the ghetto, it's, "Hey brother! What's happenin'?"

It's up to me to say (in a deep growl), "Yeah, it's cool."

As I walk by they go, "Wow, that's a bad dude!"

But if I said, "Yeah! How you doin'?!"

"That's the Hammer? No, that's not the Hammer. Hammer's cooler than that."

So it's up to me to blow my own image. I'm not concerned about it. As long as I've got my cigar, I'm cool.

Ozzy Osbourne

I like to sit in a bar and talk to local people. I don't like to talk about my job all the time when I'm not working. I forget who Ozzy Osbourne is. When I'm John Osbourne I totally blank him out. Then you get somebody who goes, "It's him!" It comes rushing back to me and then I have to be him for ten minutes and it gets tiring.

I couldn't live where I want to live because it was just too much of a hassle. I couldn't deal with me being out of town and fans coming by my house and coming right up to the door. Your home is supposed to be where you can shut down from all this. I had to move away.

—Ice Cube

Sharon Stone

It was too much, to have people beating on my car windows. It was too much to have people in this obsessive behavior. I learned where it's appropriate to say, "I'm not working now, I'm having lunch. Nice to meet you, go sit down."

Deidre Hall

The Emmy [awards] people sell tickets to the fans, open the doors, and you're it. Literally. They can run at you, pin you down, go through your purse, grab your hair, snatch your dress. There is almost no security for it.

Luke Perry

Rudeness is unacceptable—on my part as well as theirs. I don't think I have any more right to be rude to them than they have to be rude to me. However, when you've been on a plane for ten hours and you're walking with your luggage through the terminal and some guy comes in front of you and just fires with his camera—this close to your face—you feel like you're going to fall down. You want to take a swing at people once in a while.

Bruce Willis

I'm always surprised at how famous I am. I really am. There are times when I can get away from Los Angeles or New York and not have to be confronted by how famous I am. Then we went down South Carolina to shoot *Die Hard 3* and people just lose their composure. They don't know how to behave when they see someone they might have just seen in a film last night. But it's still a surprise to me.

Al Pacino

I'm always a little surprised that people recognize me, a little bit. I hope I don't lose it for some reason. But I was out of the loop for about four years and I think that was a very important time for me, when I didn't work. When I came back to working again, to public life, those four years away had a positive effect.

Martin Lawrence

I try to keep it real. If I have a problem with somebody I'll tell him, "Man, get the fuck on outta here."

John Hall

For the fan who wants to have contact with a celebrity, the best thing to remember is the gentle approach is the only one. When people come up and get too effusive with someone they admire, they scare them off. It's the same thing if you're in love with somebody. You have to let things develop as they will and not force them to develop.

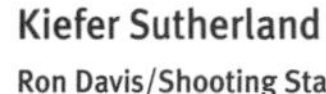

Kiefer Sutherland
Ron Davis/Shooting Star

Bruce Willis

I like to go up to them and say, "Hi, how are you? What's your name? Thanks for saying hi," and act like a normal human being. Freaks 'em out.

Kiefer Sutherland

I've driven back and forth across America probably twice a year. There's something that I find incredibly relaxing about staying a couple of days in a small town somewhere and feeling no worries about getting in the car and going to another one. Find out who the good pool player is and move out.

People come up to me and say, "I can't believe you're here. What are you doing here?"

I say, "I just came here to hang out and play pool for a couple of days and relax and get away from it." Boom. The second you talk to someone on an equal level they go, "Oh, that's cool. Well, see you around." And that's it.

The only times that I have ever gotten into trouble and ever really been embarrassed about being successful was when I acted like an idiot and tried to pretend like it was more than it is. That's the time when people react oddly to you or treat you on a very different scale.

Scott Bakula

It's a little shocking to go out of L.A. or go home or go into an area where people aren't used to seeing people in the business. It gets a little bit crazy sometimes. They're just kind of in shock about it—and then they want to argue about it with you, is it really you.

I was in a restaurant the other night and a girl said, "Well, prove it!" She bet her boyfriend ten bucks that it wasn't me. I don't think she actually really believed me until somebody else came up and asked for my autograph. Then she came back and said, "All right, I believe it's you. Can I have your autograph?"

Martha Plimpton

Sometimes they're very cordial, friendly, and polite and remember where they know you from. Other times they are convinced that they went to high school with you and you have to really argue. "Absolutely not! I did not go to Torrance High School!" And other times they're just outright rude. You try not to get too angry, because you don't want people to really hate you. No one wants to really be hated, but sometimes a firm response is necessary.

Pam Dawber

Only one time did I snap at someone who came up to me, but he was rude. He wrote me this nasty note and gave me back my autograph. I felt very bad, but he didn't realize what an idiot he came across as. People have no perception of what it is you do. They don't understand what it's like to be invaded.

Larry Drake

I was driving in L.A. and there were three young rather attractive women in the back of a cab. The one on the far side was looking out through the rear window at me and it seemed to be the look of recognition as I've come to know it over the years. We pulled up to the next stoplight and they were all looking at me. I usually just ignore it and let it go, but this one I gave them the roll down the window sign. They did and I said, "What's the question?" I don't want to assume too much.

The girl on the far side said, "Are you the guy from *L.A. Law*?"

I said, "Yes, I am."

She pointed to the girl next to her. "My friend didn't believe me."

So I turned to her friend and said, "Do you want to come up to my house and see my Emmys?" I knew she'd either laugh or panic—and she panicked.

Eve Plumb

I don't get recognized a lot [as Jan from *The Brady Bunch*] since I changed my hair color, which is actually a lot better. I'm a much nicer, friendlier person when I can just have a regular transaction or a regular conversation with a stranger, rather than always being about, "Hey, you're famous."

Julie Delpy

People recognize me, but they're not really sure. I have a lot of situations where people are totally convinced that they know me—or they even had an affair with me. I have guys come up to me. They're very cute, they're very sweet, but I don't know them. When people recognize me it's another problem, but sometimes people are just looking at me and thinking they know me or maybe they met me in another life. No, they just saw me in a film.

James Woods

I had somebody come up to me once and say, "What was it I saw you in?" Instead of the usual "I can't go through my whole resume," I thought, "I'm going to go through my resume and see how long she'll stay here." I did it. I went through twenty-seven movies. And she kept saying, "No, it wasn't that."

"Could it be *Salvador*?"

"No, it wasn't that."

"How about *Against All Odds*?"

"Which one was that? No, it wasn't that."

I thought, "This woman will stand here until next Groundhog Day." Finally, I said the one that always works, *RoboCop*, which, of course, I never did.

She goes, "Yeah."

Tea Leoni

I remember at the grocery store in New Jersey this woman said, "You know what. You sound like that girl on that show, that crazy beautiful girl."

And I said, milking it you know, "Oh yeah? What show?"

She said, "It's on Fox, *Flying Blind*. But no way."

"No way what?"

"No, I thought you were her for a second, but no way."

I was like, "Hey, wait a minute. I'm going to go put on my bustier. I'll be right back."

Dana Carvey

When twelve-year-olds meet me they usually get teary-eyed. "You don't look like Garth [from *Wayne's World*]. You look old and stupid and your hair is too short."

Robin Givens

I always hear, "You're much smaller in person." Everybody thinks I'm 5' 10". Fulfilling fantasies about looking great all the time, it's impossible.

Jean-Claude Van Damme

I'm very accessible and I talk to people all the time. I look very tough in movies, but in real life I'm more charming than in movies. They have a big surprise. They think I'm bigger, I'm stronger, but I'm just 5' 10", I'm not that big.

Yoko Ono

Most people, when they meet me, they say, "Oh, you're small." You know there's that classic thing about most people in the public eye, they look larger than life size. It's a comfort that in private life with your friends and relatives that you have this small, sort of secret side of you, which is the vulnerable side. Those people who love you will know that, and not know the other side of you. It doesn't matter. Maybe they don't have to know.

Patrick Stewart

I attended one of those glossy awards events in Los Angeles about a year ago. As I arrived, a very distinguished American film star looked in my direction and said, "My God! I love this actor! This man is my favorite! Sir, would you come over here. I want to have a photo taken."

I looked around to see who he was talking to. But he put his arms around me and he called his wife over. "Honey, this guy is so great! Where are the photographers?" And they took some pictures and he turned to me and he said, "Mr. Kingsley, I am your biggest fan."

Robin Givens
Stephen Harvey/Shooting Star

The problem was I was to give a speech that night and I had no way to possibly disabuse this man of his mistake, somebody whom I admired enormously.

So I told this story on one of the chat shows and a couple of weeks later Ben was on. He told how he had been on the street in Los Angeles and a woman had approached him and said, "Mr. Stewart, I love your work. I think you're so great on *Star Trek*."

Ben said, "I'm very sorry, but actually I'm not Patrick Stewart. My name is Ben Kingsley."

And she said, "Oh."

"But let me assure you, I'm a very good friend of Patrick Stewart's."

And she said, "Well, congratulations on being such a good friend of his."

In fact, I've invited Ben to my next premiere, because I thought it would be very good for the world to see us together.

Stephen Baldwin

Living with fame is far weirder than I had realized. Somebody can walk by me and smile, then ten minutes later come up to me in a Gap and say, "How's your daughter?" There's someone who has read an article on me. I don't know who they are but they know my whole life.

A lot of the time people come up to me and say, "Look, I just wanted to say that I like your work." They have this feeling that they can't talk to me because I'm not some normal person because of how I have affected them. Which is fine because I can relate to that. When I see Meryl Streep I can't talk because of how she has affected me.

Joe Mantegna

One time when I was living in New York in the mid-seventies, I remember seeing John Lennon walking with his kid in Central Park. I looked at him and I caught my breath, "Oh my God! It's John Lennon!" Then I realized, it's John Lennon—he's walking with his kid and he's just being like anybody else. People were mostly ignoring him, but ten years earlier they would've eaten him. They would've just grabbed him and eaten him alive.

Linda Fiorentino

When I met Kareem Abdul-Jabbar and Wilt Chamberlain they were patting me on the head, because they're so big! It was like, "Okay, little girl." Of course, I completely insulted Kareem. I called him Mr. Alcindor, because when I was a little kid that's who he was. And then I realized he hates that! He's suing General Motors for that.

I behaved exactly like people who come up to me. I knew how it felt, for once in my life, I knew exactly how a person felt. They come up to me and say, "Look, I never do this." I said the exact same words, exact same intonation, as a fan who would come up to me. And I was so embarrassed. I just walked away with my tail between my legs.

I made such a fool out of myself. I'm looking up at him saying, "You made me want to play basketball when I was a kid."

He was like, "Yeah, okay, fine little girl. Move on."

Kiefer Sutherland

I've been fascinated by actors and actresses. I can't count the number of times I've wished I was Harrison Ford. He's a guy's guy and he's sensitive. I get caught up in that fantasy all the time. Movies are a very enticing dream of a reflection of not only what we would like to be, but hopefully what we will attain. I understand that full well.

Glenn Close

I was intimidated by Michael Douglas. I thought he was this Hollywood prince. Not only an actor having this incredible background in Hollywood, but also a very, very successful producer. He told these jokes that I didn't always get. I knew he was telling them to try to make me laugh, so I think that both of us were kind of intimidated by the other one.

John Hall

I played with Bob Dylan briefly, back in my sideman days. I spent a couple of weeks rehearsing with Dylan in his loft and I saw how he reacts to people, the look he gets in his eyes when somebody comes up to him on the street. I made a fool of myself once that way with Joni Mitchell backstage at a Jackson Browne concert when my old group Orleans opened for him at the Shrine Auditorium in L.A. We had a couple of hit singles, "Still the One" was on the charts, and we thought we were doing pretty well. But Joni had been an idol of mine—and I was a little sloshed. I went up to her in dim light while Jackson was on and slobbered, "I love everything you've ever done." I saw her eyes glaze over and I knew she thought I was another stupid nitwit. It's hard to know, when you reach that level of success, how to react to people, or why they're talking to you.

Connie Selleca

I have been in some troublesome situations with fans. I think to talk about them makes it worse. Some have been frightening. The funny thing is when I'm out in public and someone says hello to me I always think, "Where do I know them?" I always think that everybody who says hello is somebody I worked with or broke bread with.

David Alan Grier

The thing that's really disconcerting is when you're out and you hear a voice and someone is calling you in an intimate way. "David." You turn around. I was in a grocery store and I go, "Hey, how are you doing?" I'm bluffing, you know. Then he goes, "You don't even know who I am."

"No, I don't, but you acted like you knew me so I'm trying to be nice." And he got angry because I'm trying to be nice. That's weird.

Robin Williams

Some guy, I didn't wave to him in a car, and he went, "No wonder you didn't win the Oscar, you prick!" That peels away any pretension.

Susan Sarandon

I was in a family situation with my baby, completely unprotected in a resort area. Someone came up to me, spat at me and called me a Commie cunt. I was very, very frightened and completely upset by it. I was very happy that my baby was so small that he didn't understand what was going on. To have that much animosity come from somebody, and you don't even know why, I then followed him into the bar and asked him why. He explained that he was a Marine, as if that explained it all. I can't believe every Marine is that stupid and that cowardly. He didn't even confront me.

Tab Hunter

Someone stopped me and grabbed hold of my arm in the middle of the street and said, "Oh! Tab Hunter! Blah, blah, blah," and screamed and yelled for me to sign an autograph.

I was late for an appointment and I said, "I'm terribly sorry, but I'm late."

She said, "Well, you owe it to us."

I remember saying to her, "I don't really owe you anything other than a good performance." A lot of people feel that because they know you they feel that they are entitled to become a part of your life. I don't think that's right.

Thomas Ian Nicholas

You go to get a bite to eat and all a sudden someone stops you and goes, "You were in *Rookie of the Year,* right?" And I go, "Yeah." "Oh my God!"

Even telling you, it's unexplainable. I know that I owe them, but it's so different than you can possibly imagine. It's something that I'll never get used to.

Ellen DeGeneres

I went to New York for Christmas. We went to Rockefeller Center to ice skate, but it was a big mistake. I don't know what I was thinking. It's the biggest tourist area and it was packed with people. But I thought, "Well, nobody's going to recognize you."

It was freezing cold and I had on a knit hat, a scarf, and sunglasses, so basically my nose was showing. People are going "Ellen!" and taking pictures of my nose.

Lauren Holly

When I was doing my holiday shopping, whatever store I went to, people would say to me, "Hi Lauren. Who are you buying for?" Every single time, until about the two hundredth time, I thought, "I'm supposed to know that person. Where have I met them?" I went through this panic of being rude—and then realizing that they just knew my name and I had never met them before.

> *James Taylor said it best: "Fame and fortune, a curious game. Perfect strangers call you by name." That line does it for me.*
>
> *—Whitney Houston*

David Morse

When I was doing St. Elsewhere *and I was on every week* in people's living rooms, people felt very comfortable about coming and sitting down at a table with me when I'm trying to be private with my dinner. They just sit down and think they're entitled, that we have a kind of relationship, because I've been in their living room. I try to be respectful of that, but, unfortunately, people are not always respectful of us as well.

Tom Arnold

I can do anything I want anytime I want, but you have to know that people are going to talk to you or people are always going to look at you.

If you're okay with that then you're fine. When you're on TV people feel you're even more accessible, that they really know you, especially when you do a lot of talk shows and do those afternoon talk shows. Once they've heard your life story they really bond with you.

Mary Steenburgen

[Her husband Ted Danson] can order pizza and not use his name and the guy over the phone will say, "You sound like Sam Malone [his character on *Cheers*]." He's been in your home for so many years that there is a sense of ownership of him.

Jason Alexander

I live with the awareness that when I walk into places there's a buzz. But that has become such a fact of life that unless it actually gets into my face I don't even notice it any more. Friends of mine will say, "Do you hear that?" I say, "No, I don't." But compared to other people on my show, Michael [Richards] has people knocking on his door at four o'clock in the morning going, "Is Kramer here?"

Tab Hunter

I remember an opening of a film in Chicago with Natalie Wood. We had police barricades and escorts and what have you. We had to take refuge in a warehouse because of all the screaming fans. I look back at it now and laugh, but it was frightening.

George "The Animal" Steele

The first ten years that I wrestled you very often had to defend yourself going to and from the ring. The security wasn't very good and the people were very violent. As it progressed and it's gone to where it is now, people seek autographs.

There was a time when I couldn't even walk the streets of New York. I was a wild, wild bad guy. I didn't change anything, but then my manager became a good guy, Lou Albano. He brought me under his wing and people changed their view of me. But I liked being a bad guy. I was a school teacher, so it was a release for me. Nine months I was coaching

Kurt Russell and Goldie Hawn Ron Davis/Shooting Star

football and wrestling and playing it straight down the middle. Then all of a sudden I could let all that go in the ring.

Steve Martin

As you get older, you get a little more respect, so it's not the sort of annoying intrusion. You're now "a man." When I saw *Father of the Bride* I said to myself, "I'm no longer an old young man, I'm a young old man." So you don't rush up to young old men and bowl them over and ring their doorbells.

Kurt Russell

I've lived with it for so long that I don't even see when people are looking. I basically live behind closed gates. When I go out, it's in a car. When I walk somewhere, I don't see people. I don't look. If I look at 'em then bang, they've got it, and you've got to move on or you just can't do the things you've got to do in a day.

Hugh Grant

I drive incredibly badly, especially in Los Angeles. I just about crashed into some car one day—I knew there was going to be a shouting match—and as I drove by the guy yelled, "Learn to drive, Hugh!" It was kind of embarrassing that he knew who I was.

Jason Priestley

Cary Grant was driving his car home at night and he was drunk. A cop pulled him over and said, "Cary, get in the car," and he'd drive him home and put him to bed. Now you've got Wesley Snipes getting knocked over on his bike, and he's carrying a gun because he's got a million death threats, and they throw him in jail. Hollywood has changed a lot. I go out and get in my car and people are honking and waving and wanting me to sign autographs at stoplights. I can't go to Disneyland.

Pierce Brosnan

There are some days when you don't want to be looked at. There's an energy which comes from adulation that is so powerful and so strong that it takes part of you. Some days you just don't have the strength, but being a public figure you have to walk down the street and meet it head on.

I wish that I could do what I do and still have another face to wear on the street, because that's where I like to be, out among people. I don't like to be out among people if I'm the object of their attention, when things are aberrated by my appearance. I like to go to a museum and look at the pictures, not go to the museum and sign autographs.

—Harrison Ford

Tom Selleck

If you're in public and you don't want to be bothered, you don't make a lot of eye contact. You don't say hello to too many people because it's kind of inviting them over. Some people get a lot of privacy sitting on a beach reading a book. You don't want to have to lock yourself away in a closet to get privacy or you'll go nuts.

Sigourney Weaver

I know I am going to be knocked down by a taxi, because I walk with my head down as a I walk. I do not like to be recognized. It can be a very scary thing. But I have an ability to fade away. There are some celebrities that just cannot do that. Madonna used to live in my neighborhood. She could not disguise herself at all.

Daryl Hannah

If I go out and people are staring at me I just get uncomfortable because I don't picture myself that way. I'm not naturally an extrovert. I don't know what to do with myself. I tend to get so scared that I just go inside or I fly right out of my body and disappear. It's not natural.

I was an unpopular kid. I was an outsider as a child, awkward and uncomfortable, and I've never really grown out of that. It's always kind of nerve-wracking for me, so I try to avoid it. It's not because I'm a snob or because I'm extremely private. It's just uncomfortable, period. I just don't know how to deal with it. I'm better off in the background, with my hair in front of my eyes, watching other people. That's where I feel more appropriate.

Quentin Tarantino

It's hard to go to a lot of the places that I love to go, that I used to love to go to, because a lot of the people who love my movies the most go to those places. The days of me going to a used record store and zoning out

On a sunny day in May, 1995, one of Madonna's bodyguards, Basil Stephens, spotted Robert Hoskins climbing the wall of the pop star's Hollywood Hills home after tossing two bags over it. "It looked like he was bringing his bags and moving in," testified Stephens at a later trial. Hoskins shouted that he lived on the estate and would fire any security guard who disturbed him. Moments later Hoskins was drying himself off after a dip in the pool not far from Madonna's bedroom. Stephens and another security guard drew their weapons and ordered Hoskins to lie on the ground, but instead he began pulling clothes out of his bags and getting dressed. Frustrated by Hoskins's refusal to respond, Stephens holstered his gun—and Hoskins jumped him. After a brief struggle Stephens shot Hoskins twice and believed he had killed the intruder. But ten minutes later Stephens found Hoskins sitting up near the pool with wounds in his arm and stomach.

"An ambulance is coming. I'm sorry I shot you," said Stephens.

"No problem," replied Hoskins calmly.

Not wanting to give Hoskins the satisfaction of seeing her in person, Madonna refused to testify, but was eventually compelled to give her testimony under the threat of being jailed on $5 million bail. He was convicted on stalking charges. She put the house up for sale.

for three hours while I look at every album that they have in the store might be gone. I can still do that, but I'm also going to be dealing with talking with people and everything. Going to a video store and checking things out—since I'm the patron saint of video clerks—and going to comic book conventions and horror film conventions and everything like that, those are the people who love my stuff. So that stuff is a little different.

George Harrison

I'd step on stage and you're playing to like twenty thousand people. Well, maybe ten thousand came because they wanted to see you. The other ten thousand came because they were with the people who went to see you, or half of them were there because it's what's happening in town that night. They're all smoking reefers and getting loaded. I ended up thinking, "I don't know if I even like these people." I'd rather play to twenty people who appreciate it than just to play to seventy thousand yabbos.

Sinbad

I think if we shot more fans, the word would get out there. Shoot people. You've gotta wound people, don't kill 'em. Wound 'em. That way they'll go home with a limp saying, "Man, I'll never do that again."

Jackals of the Press

If celebrities are ambivalent about their fans, they view the members of the press with crystalline clarity. They hate 'em. From Hollywood to Fleet Street, the mass media is the enemy. Professionally, with the cold precision of charts, ratings, and box office tabulations, every day is Judgment Day in show business. Personally, celebrities are the characters in our ongoing national soap opera, like it or not. Critics and reporters seem to take great pleasure in cutting celebrities down to size, mocking their carefully groomed images, and doing whatever they can to tarnish the stars's reputation. Nonetheless, the demands of marketing force actors and musicians to plug their products on release, which means venturing again and again into the lion's den.

Keanu Reeves

Critically, I'm the whipping boy, man. I'm like Saint Augustine. I'm like aaaggghhh, you know? I didn't take "Press" in acting school. They didn't have that course.

> *This has become a minefield. "No comment" doesn't save you from disgrace in American public life anymore. I specifically negotiate that I don't HAVE TO do any press. I only do it when I think it's going to make me extra money.*
>
> *—Jack Nicholson*

Mary Elizabeth Mastrantonio

I am ambitious in terms of getting better, not in terms of getting seen. But you have to be seen. Is it a matter of hiring a publicist to put your face on magazine covers that stay in people's bathrooms for a year? Am I supposed to hire a publicist at $3,000 a month minimum and retain this person to plant me places?

George Michael

It's a necessity in this business to do interviews, because if you don't do them everyone gets fucked off with you. So you have to do them. But to be really honest with you, if I could be a star just by making records and I didn't have to make videos and didn't have to do interviews, I would be in heaven.

I don't think anything that I can say can possibly enrich people's appreciation of what I do.

William Reid

(Member of The Jesus and Mary Chain)

Interviews to me are so hard to do. I don't have much to say about the music I make. If we sold four million records I wouldn't do interviews again. I wish I had the strength to just not do photo sessions and interviews. It does kind of interfere with your psyche. And it's unpleasant.

Barbra Streisand

It's hard to be articulate. I just do the thing. I don't talk about it or intellectualize emotional gut feelings.

Roger Daltrey

(Member of The Who)

I must admit, doing interviews takes an awful lot out of you. I like meeting people. I like talking with people. You'd be surprised, although the answers are very similar, it's the bits in between the main questions which are always different because it's always a one-to-one relationship with a different person. You survive through it because of that. But basically it's the same thing, you must sell the records, otherwise there's no point in making them. It's not easy.

Tom Arnold

It's a drag for people to know so much about my private life. But it's part of the game. I should have known. You marry a big star [he was married to Roseanne] who's in the public eye a lot, controversial, and then you contribute to that, people are going to be talking about you.

Sean Connery

I was in Japan to do You Only Live Twice *and I couldn't go* to the toilet. They were in the toilet. Seriously, they were under the door with the cameras.

Woody Harrelson

I find it just the oddest thing for people to actually be listening to me and at least pretending to be interested in what I have to say. It'll never make sense.

Bruce Willis

I wish people would ask me interesting questions. I wish people would get beyond the same ten things I get asked all the time.

Kirsten Dunst

I was scared about doing interviews and Tom Cruise told me, "Oh yeah, it's a pain. Everyone's going to ask the same questions, so just relax." You know what? You do ask the same questions.

Sean Connery Ron Davis/Shooting Star

Bruce Willis

There are other corporations in the United States that make the kind of dough that Hollywood does, but nobody gives a shit about the CEO of the space industry and what he does, and where he was last night, and who he was sleeping with.

Treat Williams

If you're not on People *magazine covers* and the audience isn't aware of you, they think that you've disappeared. There are hundreds and hundreds of actors in America who are doing wonderful work that just don't have that kind of presence in the press.

D.B. Sweeney

I don't know whether there's any more fascination with celebrity now than there has been through the history of human events. I just think that we have so many more ways of observing celebrities, so many more outlets to peek in on these people.

Lauren Holly

I went home to see my family for the holidays and Jim [Carrey] came with me. It was front page news every day in the paper, who sighted us where, what we were wearing. It was just a bizarre thing.

Madeleine Stowe

Even on the news shows, there's all this focus on celebrities. All these gossip shows. What is going on here? Why is that?

John Landis

The New York Times *is* Hard Copy *now.* Everything is "He's Over!" "He's Finished!" "He's Dead!" "He's Divorced!" I'm horrified that entertainment grosses are reported. Entertainment has become Entertainment News. Entertainment News? It's gossip—and you have to take gossip for what it is. Which is entertaining.

Steven Seagal

Most of the people in town know that some of the magazines with the shinier covers now are acting worse than the tabloids. It's a shame, because that stuff is even too shiny to work for toilet paper, so they're totally useless.

Johnny Depp

This tabloid ambulance chaser mentality, bloodsucker society, is nothing but a bunch of mosquitos flying around. Eventually a mosquito will land and try and suck your blood and you smash it. Kill it. Ha, ha.

Charlie Sheen

I'm personally trying to change my image and change things about myself, but they don't want to let it die. I guess there are more sales in controversy. They should change the title of *Hard Copy* to "Hard Charlie," or "Sheen Copy." Christ, I'm on there twice a week. I should get some royalties maybe. Are there so few things going on out there that my birthday party is news?

Melanie Griffith

I don't read the tabloids, only because they're not accurate. It's like a bad dream. People have no scruples anymore. It's really nobody's business. That's why I don't read the tabloids, because then it doesn't hurt.

Sally Field

There are these absolutely irresponsible people who sell addresses. You can buy a magazine today—I'd like to go and shoot these people myself—with celebrities' home addresses in it. I get a lot fan mail right to my house. Some are very, very nice people and I write back and say, "Could you just tell me how you got my address?" That's irresponsible. It's a scary world.

Lauren Holly

I get incensed sometimes because I don't understand how the law protects them and doesn't protect us, to a certain point. I'm allowed to be followed home. I'm allowed to have people hide in the garbage cans and even jump over the wall if they're not caught when they're in my yard. That's really bizarre. And there have been times when I've been being [sic] followed and Jim [Carrey] is out of town. I'm going home to an empty house and I'm scared the rest of the night. Maybe he's a tabloid person, but maybe he's a serial killer who's following me. That is really upsetting to me. I've been being followed and I've pulled into a police station and been told, "There's nothing we can do." They harass you in the car and drive recklessly and endanger people's lives on the road as you try to get away from them. It's craziness.

> *The invasion of privacy by the press is horrible—and morally indefensible, I think.*
>
> *—Emma Thompson*

Richard Dreyfuss

It's a sick absurdity. No one turns the focus of the media on the people who live in Wilmington, Delaware, and have shoe stores. "My God, another divorce in Wilmington!" But they do in Hollywood, which makes your attempt to live your life in some normal fashion more difficult. It's like living in Macy's window. It's an impossible thing to do. It's not impossible, but it's very tough.

Annette Bening

I usually don't put myself in a position where I'm going to get questions that I feel I can't answer. Quite frankly, when I get those kind of personal questions that I don't want to answer, part of it is that I want to be a good interview. That's my problem. I have to get over that. I have to say, "Look, you don't have to answer it if you don't want to. Just don't say anything." I'm learning to deal with it better. Of course, Warren [husband Warren Beatty]'s a big help because he's been doing it for so long.

Robin Givens

I have this mouth that speaks the truth, and that's not so good.

Sean Young

I look at my honesty as a virtue, but I really do have to pay a high price for it.

Jack McDowell
(Baseball player and recording artist)

I've never pushed myself to create some kind of cartoon character like a lot of athletes do. But then again, people don't deal with truth in sports, either. I've said a lot of things that are flat-out true and exactly the way I feel and that's just not the way things are done in the sports world. I've got myself in trouble because of that. That's been frustrating to me.

Jack McDowell

I can be truthful when I'm talking about music. In sports, you throw a bunch of clichés and lie a lot. That's what it comes down to. I'd love to get done with a game and just go, "We got screwed tonight," or "That guy really screwed that play up," or "I hate that guy on that other team," that kind of stuff. But you can't. You gotta go, "We did our best tonight." It's weird how that works because really it's a similar audience, people buying music are people watching sports. Yet they accept certain things from sports people and certain things from music people, but you can't cross them. Like talking about drug use.

Dennis Hopper

I doubt I'll write an autobiography. At this point in my life I don't think I'd be able to go public with a lot of stuff. I don't think I can be honest about my life. I think it would hurt too many other people. I was involved in things that weren't necessarily legal during my drug days. I don't want to do something until I can be really honest about it and really talk about it. I don't think I'm there yet.

Robert Downey, Jr.

Sometimes I think it takes more energy to doctor up a whole bunch of boundaries. There are certain boundaries, some stuff that I don't want to talk about and it's pretty obvious when it comes up. Or then I'll think—if there's someone that I don't like—"Oh, I shouldn't say anything." If you don't have anything nice to say, don't say anything, and usually I'll do that. But sometimes I'll just say, "Yeah, he was a prick."

(Is it true then, that he didn't get along with his Restoration *co-star, Hugh Grant?)*

I just thought he was a dick. That's all. And I still do. That could be something that has to do with me, or it could just be that not everyone in this industry is really someone that I'd care to hang out with.

Antonio Banderas

When they get into my personal life, of course, that is uncomfortable. I have to pay a price for being a public personality, or whatever you want to call it. And I do that with a sense of humor. I try to maintain some sort of dignity and integrity in front of the mass media. But I've always been very respectful with the lives of other people and I would like just to be treated in the same way. I'm not going to be angry or pissed all the time. I

think there are storms that cross your life and you have to confront certain situations. There is a time when everything calms down—and I am waiting for that.

Annette Bening

I don't feel completely invaded all the time in my life like I think a lot of celebrities do. I'm lucky. I don't have that situation a lot of the time. Sometimes I do. I've been in situations which were horrible and very uncomfortable with unwanted attention. But I think as movie actors you can really stay away from it if you don't like it. You don't go to movie openings. You don't go to restaurants where they photograph you. You can really avoid it a lot of the time. When you're doing interviews when you have a movie coming out, you can choose how much to reveal or not reveal. For a politician, I think they have so little say now. We've all decided that we can invade these people's lives to a degree that is so inhuman and unkind. I really feel great sympathy for our public servants. Whether or not we agree with their politics, they are trying to help us and make the world better. But in present-day politics they are really raked over the coals. We've become callous to that.

Blair Brown

It certainly happens to actors that certain incidents—true or untrue—may get blown out and people's careers are really changed. The slings and arrows that we get, they hurt you personally, but in some way I always figured that we were slightly fair game. In politics, it always seemed to me to be beside the point, all these ideas that people have that this really tells us about a person's character. You know, I've had people I work with, people I adore, business partners who are great to work with, I would never dream of wanting to be their wife or be their child. Actually, I've become a little more irate at even the way some actors and show folk are dealt with because it does seem fairly prurient. And I don't think it is always what the public is interested in.

Antonio Banderas Yoram Kahana/Shooting Star

Richard Dreyfuss

The press has done its own very good job over the past thirty years, without leadership, in cutting off at the knees the idea of integrity in leadership in government. Now, admittedly, integrity in leadership in government is rare, but what little there has been has not survived the scrutiny of the press.

Dustin Hoffman

Something is finally clicking I think with the American public for the first time since media became a part of the electoral process. Maybe we don't give a shit who's screwed who. That was kept under wraps. Then Gary Hart kind of broke the mold. Everyone's flawed. Maybe [Bill] Clinton tried to get out of the draft. So what? Who's perfect?

Comic books. We've never gotten away from that. Superman was all good. You could get him with kryptonite, but he didn't have a flaw in him. The President is this image—and it's not true.

Rob Lowe

There are so many more important people than myself who it really affects in a bigger way, political candidates and world leaders. Who cares about me? Forget that. Remember Gary Hart? We're talking about things that affect the world. It's very scary.

Something's got to give here. Somewhere the media has to reassess its role in creating the agenda. It can take an isolated issue and decide to make that the national debate. That shouldn't be chosen on the basis of "Is it a good headline?"

Emma Thompson

That's where it really gets scary. No wonder Colin Powell didn't want to run. Who would want to run? No wonder a decent man thought, "I'm going to have a vile time, I'm going to have a horrible time if I run for office. They will dredge through my dustbins." What will happen? That to me is really, really dangerous. I don't think that I matter, obviously I will protect my own life, but it doesn't really matter. But with politicians and our political systems to be so dangerously intermeshed with the media now, I'm very concerned about that.

I get concerned about it not just from a moral point of view, but also from the point of view of the bastardization of our language. The media requires politicians to be simplistic. We have all this information at our disposal, but it's all been simplified. I don't think that we write the same speeches anymore. Look at political speeches from fifty years ago even. These were brilliant, brilliant people who wrote complex ideas which were available to the public. Now it has to be a sound bite. And, of course, the more you go in that direction, the more simplistic your ideas become, that is absolutely the invitation to fascism. Those are the simplest ideas.

Look at National Socialism. If you read enough about the second world war and about Goebbels's propaganda techniques, then you know that the simple messages are the ones that get across. Actually, often, they are the extremes, either left wing or right wing, it doesn't matter, but they're the extremes. They're the messages that say, "There's us and there's them."

Our challenge, I think, as writers and communicators, is to examine the complexity of life and present it as it is.

From the beginning, Alma Powell was counseling her husband, Colin, not to run for President. As long ago as 1991, concerned about security risks and the intrusiveness of campaigning, Alma was clear on the subject. "I don't want any part of this. Public life is very difficult for people. You might start out as a saint, but I don't think you'd end up as one."

Oliver Stone

I set out to make Natural Born Killers *as an action picture* and it became something else. I see it as an exaggerated mirror to what I perceive as a culture in the nineties that has become more violent, and degenerated into a media-driven obsession with talk shows and fame. It disgusted me. Ice skaters and murderers getting headlines? There's a sickness about it that made me want to throw up and make that movie. And the movie is an act of throwing up.

Tina Turner

They used the idea of me and Ike [ex-husband Ike Turner]'s life to make a movie. How much of it is kept? It's twenty years all packed into two hours. I believe they did their best, but it's difficult to put my life into people's hands because a lot of people will believe what they see on the screen.

Lawrence Kasdan

I find the media repugnant in many ways. The way we treat celebrities in movies is nothing compared to the real issues of the day and how we treat those. I'm more alarmed by the way we treat politicians and the fact that the guy who gets to run the country has to go through this minefield of baloney. If you say the wrong thing the week before the election you're screwed. A lifetime of preparation doesn't matter because of one phrase that catches the media windstream.

Bill Cosby

The media is only interested in what's more fun and what's more entertaining. I don't think they're really interested in the intellect. It's more like, "That belongs to the *Wall Street Journal.* We just want to do excitement."

Oliver Stone

A woman cuts off her husband's penis and is celebrated for it—and acquitted. Two young men kill their parents in cold blood, bring up a child abuse thing, and again are acquitted. O.J. This stuff is going on. The burlesque of modern absurdity is upon us. The age of absurdity is here.

Rosie O'Donnell

(On Madonna cursing up a storm on Late Night*)*

I don't care who you are. To sit next to David Letterman, who is a trained prize fighter, and you are a ballet dancer, you're doomed. Even a trained prize fighter like myself works up a sweat sitting next to the Muhammad Ali of late night. She did her best. Unfortunately, when she's scared she goes to some sort of banal, fifteen-year-old response. Whatever. If David Letterman had to sing "Like a Virgin" before forty thousand people at Wembley Stadium I don't know whether he would hold his own either.

Oliver Stone Andy Schwartz/The Kobal Collection

Shirley MacLaine

Something about it must be working for David [Letterman]. Didn't work for me, but it must be working for him. It must be working for some of the people who go on and put themselves in that position. I knew that I would be in some position of metaphysical ridicule there, even though I knew—and it was agreed upon—that we would talk about my new film. I know better than that. I didn't just fall out of a tree. But I didn't think somebody would go on and on and on like he did. I understand he did that too with Donald Trump about his money. It is a bit of a waste of air time.

Brad Pitt

I asked for it, but what I didn't know was people's desire to turn things into negatives and constantly draw on negatives. I just wasn't prepared for that. No matter what you say, you can sit there for an hour and you can compliment this and feel that way about this positive thing, but if one thing has even borderline negative, that's what's there in the final print.

Juliette Lewis

The thing about the media is they don't get any consequences. No one punishes them for anything! I like people to be up front and a lot of time they aren't. They can be really nice to you and be thinking a whole other thing about you. I wish they would ask me about it.

Joan Armatrading

They'll come in to do an interview and they'll say, "I've heard you're this and I've heard that. You don't like interviews, you don't like to have a laugh and you never smile." But it's totally different, of course. We're having a great time, we're having a laugh, and then they go and write this same thing that they've read. I think, "What happened?"

Nathan Lane

The man who wrote the story seemed to have an agenda with me. I felt deceived by that. He was very complimentary and pleasant. He professed that he was a big fan. You'd be hard-pressed to believe that after reading the article.

Susan Sarandon

The most upsetting thing about taking the chance to be interviewed is that you can only be as smart and as clever as the person that's interviewing you. It worries me sometimes when I'm talking to someone and they only write down every fourth word. You say something that's a nice polished sound bite and then they ask you to explain it.

Martin Lawrence

One thing I learned is y'all gonna write what you want and you're gonna write what you feel from the way that you see it. You have one of two things to do. You can look in my eyes and say, "This person is positive, let me write positive things about him." Or you can say, "Let me write something negative about him and have people going crazy running around asking if this is true or if that's true." I believe it's in your hands.

Brad Pitt
Ron Davis/Shooting Star

Kiefer Sutherland

It's impossible to have a career as an actor and not have been helped by the press. And I have had a wonderful career, despite some people's dribblings. In the last few years I had a lot of things blown out of proportion, misunderstood, or flatly lied about. It's like a roller coaster. It goes up, it goes down. I do the best work I can do. I live my life how I see fit. I make mistakes. Other people make mistakes. I try to do my best to recover from those and I can go to sleep at night.

Janeane Garofalo

Journalists' agendas have hurt me very much and made life very difficult for me. Journalists have an agenda a lot of times and no matter what you say, if it doesn't fit into the sound bites they want or the way they want to go with it, they will print things—even though you've been as diplomatic as you could about a statement—they will choose the most caustic aspect of that statement and print it. Or even take liberties with the facts. They have painted such a harsh picture of me among my castmates and writers at *Saturday Night Live* that have made my friends think that I have betrayed them to the press. I have been in pain over certain things that journalists have printed.

Nick Nolte

I interviewed a lot of journalists before I played a journalist in *I Love Trouble*. I didn't find one journalist who said he'd allow another journalist to interview him. Ha ha ha.

Yoko Ono

Someone went to a friend of mine in 1981 and tried to sell his book. He was saying, "I want to spend the rest of my life trying to discredit John [Lennon] and Yoko." Now I don't know what that does to anybody. Maybe he's got some principle that there shouldn't be any legends, any myths, any statues, because that's wrong. I can understand that. People should trust in themselves, not in a legend, not in a statue. We believed that, too, but they don't have to defame our names to do that.

Geena Davis

I'm stunned. It's really amazing. I always used to think if I read something provocative about somebody, "Well, but it must be true, or there must be some part of it that's true. They did something that made this happen." Now I think, "They make everything up."

Gary Busey

The press has been after Steven Seagal. They came out with an article saying, "Steven Seagal has given an ultimatum—either Busey goes or I go." Two days later there was a story, "Steven Seagal says Gary Busey is a fine actor and a good friend, but it would be a cartoon if he brought him back for the *Under Siege* sequel." I agree with that.

John Landis

One of the things that's interesting about Hollywood to me is the vast majority of what is written and said about it is incorrect—but not wrong!

You read everything and it's so wrong. The numbers are wrong, things are wrong, but the attitude actually is probably right.

Johnny Depp

For a few years there I was ready to jump out of my skin—and that feeling comes back every now and again. The idea that your private life is displayed before the public and kind of dissected and a lot of fiction gets written about you is a drag—a real drag. But it's something you just have to deal with. How do I deal with it? I don't read anything. I haven't touched one of those magazines in probably eight years. Ever since they started writing fiction about me I just decided that it's not good to be a part of that.

Elton John

Most of the stuff I read about myself in the papers is absolute nonsense. That's why I don't do many interviews, because you spend so much time talking to the press and when you actually read it, why bother?

Madonna

I think it's impossible for anybody to say they know me or write as if they know me unless they actually know me. If you're going to judge my work, then judge my work. A lot of people do psychological profiles on me, as if they know who I am. I guess everybody believes them.

Madonna

I think a lot of what people write about me is uncalled for and unfair—and I can't stop it. I'm not going to try. It's just so ludicrous that anybody would think that it's their right to judge me in my personal life that I'm not going to bother addressing what they think.

Goldie Hawn

My life is a distortion. You start there. You don't know me, so you have a distorted idea of who I am. You have to. You can't look at me and know me, so that's a given. You put yourself in front of people and you do what you can. You stand on your head. You say a few things. You walk away. Then people write about you. They think they've met you, they know who you are. They don't.

Meg Ryan

(On her Vanity Fair *cover story)*

I like Kevin Sessums as a person, he seemed like a decent person, but I just feel like with the nature of that kind of article there's no hope to get it right. It's three thousand words. I spent two days with this person and he calls a few people. Definitely a particular portrait comes out. How could it represent all of me?

Demi Moore

You may not understand me, or at least share my perception. When do you do it for a national publication, you have to just do it and walk away. You can't take it too seriously.

Even with *Premiere,* which is supposedly a very serious, respectable publication, the nature of how most of the articles are written whether—it's me or anybody else—it's three compliments to two insults. That's just what it is.

Demi Moore

The danger of a profile piece is that you allow people to interpret you after spending a little while. You give of yourself and then they go and write it, and what they say becomes reality. I now have to defend or deny. It makes me vulnerable.

You talk to people for an hour and a half or two hours. They can say anything they want because you've given them so much. Things can get misconstrued. What are you going to do?

—Dana Carvey

Warren Beatty

I keep coming back to a metaphor that Robert Frost made about talking and writing. He said, "Talking is a hydrant in the front yard and writing is a faucet on the third floor."

Annette Bening

It's easy to get hostile and think,"Well they're not going to print the truth so why should I say anything anyway?" It's also tempting to get in there and try to set the record straight and say, "Now look, you're all printing wrong things, so we're gonna come in and tell you what." You can't do that.

Warren Beatty

For twelve or thirteen years I didn't do interviews. When you make movies you want the movies to be seen. You don't want the chatter about the movie or the publicity about the movie to override the movie. Along about the time I made *Reds*, I said, "This is ridiculous." There was such a high level of bullshit that was coming through all of our information sources that it was better to drop out. Now I think it was a mistake. I don't think, I know it was a mistake, because what happens when you are in a public business is the machine rolls on with you or without you. They're not that interested in you because someone will invent what they want to say about you, which in today's climate more often than not is negative.

Ally Sheedy

I've sat down with journalists on different movie projects and they'll come right out and say, "I hated it." Now I have fifteen minutes to talk to them. I'm really crushed. I don't know what's wrong with it. There's so much rejection in this business. You have to be a really strong person inside.

Isabella Rossellini

(On her work as a TV journalist before becoming a model and actress)

I had a hard time being a serious journalist. You meet people for twenty minutes and you have to write an in-depth profile that your editor forces you to do. That was a torment.

Jodie Foster

"A dramatic actor and not a comedic actor." "Short and not tall." All that stuff that we do where you feel objectified certainly, because what can you know about somebody unless you spend twenty years with them?

Esther Williams

One August in the fifties I was on twenty-eight magazine covers—and every one of those fan magazines had to have a story inside. Now Elizabeth Taylor sells magazines, she's on the cover, and there's not a word about her inside. You say, "Where's the story about Elizabeth?" It's just to sell the magazine. They don't give a shit about Elizabeth. But in those days they cared, my God, how they cared!

Madonna

(Asked for her response to a magazine story, "How to Protect Your Children From Madonna")

At this point I feel that people write articles about me with those kind of sensational headline catchphrases because it sells magazines. I've grown to expect it.

Richard Dreyfuss

At one time, the story of my life was my recovery. My arrest, my drug addiction, my recovery. It was played in every newspaper, in every weekly, in every this, in every that. Barbara Walters came up to me one day and asked to do an interview on television. And I said no, because there was only one story in my life then, and it had been done.

> *I love the power and the fascination of silence.*
>
> *—George Michael*

Sarah Jessica Parker

The hardest part of that curveball that fame throws at you is trying to not turn everything into an anecdote, trying really hard to be circumspect and to have some discretion. To keep things that are private, private and not feel forced into situations. I'm not really good at that. I tend to talk too much.

Robert De Niro

There are things that you have no control over. You can worry and angst over them and it just doesn't change anything. So I'd rather save that energy, conserve it, and use it where I know it's going to make a difference. Otherwise don't use it at all. Young actors always worry about this and that—and it doesn't mean anything.

Christopher Lambert

I'm never surprised. You just have to be strong. It doesn't affect me. I don't even read it. People write whatever they want to write. Most of the time they think they're going to hurt you and what they should realize is they don't. It slides on you, as if nothing happened. It's more of an ego trip than anything, regarding the people writing about you. "Look, I've the guts to say this or that," thinking they're going to hurt somebody. It doesn't. It doesn't even reach me.

Sarah Jessica Parker

It's hard to understand that when somebody writes something that's not true about my personal life that they're not trying to hurt my feelings, because it feels like it all the time. It feels like they know that I'm going to pick up the paper tomorrow morning at ten o'clock and they're going to hurt my feelings. I know that it's far more arbitrary and far less personal than that.

After Joan Rivers's husband, Edgar, killed himself, an anonymous article appeared in GQ about the family shivah, or mourning period. According to the article—written by Ben Stein—Rivers was her usual cut-up self during the shivah, telling off-color jokes and insulting her deceased husband. Rivers sued Stein for $50 million. The suit was settled out of court.

James Woods

You just ignore the mean-spiritedness of that kind of press and you let your work speak for itself. You live a good life and after a while people notice that you've never been in drug rehab, you don't have a gambling problem, you don't have a woman problem, and you don't have a professionalism problem. You always show up on the set. You always know your lines. You must be doing something right. After a while, they finally get it—and they stop.

Belinda Carlisle

I'm not that controversial, where you're always reading about me in the news. I've been there and I don't want that any more. I don't necessarily want to be the biggest star in America, or be Janet Jackson, or whatever. I've been there and done that. It's weird because you do hope to be successful, but I guess you don't hope to be recognized, is basically it. But you can't control it. I've thought about that. What if my next album is successful beyond my wildest expectations? What would my life be like? It's scary out there now.

Cybill Shepherd

I've finally got to the point where I feel like I can be myself in interviews. It took me a while to do that. I went through a period where I yattered on like an idiot. Then I went through a period where I didn't say anything because I was too dignified to speak. And then finally I became comfortable with being myself. So hopefully that will telegraph who I really am, whatever that is.

Lauren Holly

I have made a conscious decision to try to answer people's questions about my personal life as openly as I deem necessary—and maybe if I do that people won't try to find out more. Maybe they'll give me some respect. A year from now maybe I'll be sitting here at this same table telling you, "I am not going to say a word. I was taken total advantage of and I've been raped in that sense." I don't know. This is the tack I'm trying.

Rob Lowe

You've got to find a way to keep a certain amount left to yourself, otherwise you just feel like you've been invaded. I could walk away from all these interviews just feeling like I've been raped for hours. There are times when you feel like that.

Rob Lowe

(After a videotape of him having sex with a teenage girl was made public)

I've been beaten up pretty badly, so I have a lot of scars. But adversity is what gives people depth. I wouldn't say that it has been beneficial to me, but I would say that it's forced a lot of hard issues for me to deal with. It's made me grow up ten years worth in one summer.

Jennifer Jason Leigh

It's just hard for me because I'm self-conscious. I worry that I'm not going to sound smart. I get really nervous about it. It's not natural for me to talk so much. Also, it's hard for me to be myself with people I don't know.

That's why acting is the perfect profession for me. I don't have to be myself out there. I can be these characters. I can put myself into these characters. It chose me, in a certain way.

Steve Martin

If you're being asked personal questions and you don't want to talk about personal questions, you come off shy or aloof. If it's something people want to know and you don't want to tell them, you tend to close up. If you're around your closest personal friends, then you can be alive and funny. I don't jump around the room with strangers. I'm not a show-off.

Pauly Shore

You can't always believe what you read. That's the first thing. A lot of the stuff that I talk about is a joke. It's just for people to say, "Oh my God! He's a freak!" If I were to just do interviews about stuff that wasn't like "Oh my God," then how interesting would I be?

Daniel Day-Lewis

Most people get to read about a new film if you talk about it before they see the film. That's one of the problems. It's like seeing all the sketches before the painting. You might as well see the painting first. Sketches can be fascinating, but I've never been able to discuss the working process to my satisfaction. It seems to be like a recreation of the truth because it's a very subjective process and in this situation you are trying to talk about it objectively. So in most cases I don't even know what I'm talking about.

Jennifer Jason Leigh
Nancy Kaszerman/Shooting Star

Elliott Gould

I sometimes will get lost in the need to produce product to fill time and space without understanding any meaning. Sometimes the material, industrialized meaning for product, empties us out.

Sarah Jessica Parker

In a talk show environment, you think about everything. If you analyze guests on a talk show who have been through years and years of talk shows and have hurt people's feelings or said the wrong thing, you can see the moment of panic when they're asked something they don't know they're going to be asked. You can take a talk show I've been on and see the moment where I'm realizing, "How am I going to say this diplomatically, politely, correctly?" That's the sad part. I feel like I can't answer things honestly. That to me is sad.

Robin Williams

It's like one-way therapy. I tell you all these things and you go, "Okay." You don't

Julia Roberts The Kobal Collection

give me any feedback going, "I think you should...Maybe don't do that...Work out that stuff with your mom." It's not like that. I tell you about things and you just move on. You've got to get something to make the story interesting, but still find that human element. You want to find something new about myself that makes the story different than the other four hundred biographies you've read. "Jonathan Winters, John Belushi. Get on to something new." That's what interviews are about.

Andy Garcia

The journalists say, "We want to know more about you." They know more about me than I do already. I am up on the screen. How much more public do you want me to live my life? It's an interesting concept. They want to know something else. But what do they mean? That's me up there.

Ray Liotta

It's nobody's business. I don't think when the movies first started out that there was so much put on that. I chose this line of work because I like acting. When you start out you don't say, "I don't want to do this because I'm going to end up in the *National Enquirer.*" You don't even think of that. I don't think people have the right to go too far and cross those lines. I'm not free meat. That's why I'll just clam up and not talk about it. I don't think that me talking about my personal life is going to make somebody want to go and see a movie.

Maybe because I'm in the well and in the water here, I can't objectively look at this.

Julia Roberts

I'm tired of saying anything personal. It's never taken right or depicted properly. I just don't do it anymore.

Neil Simon

The news media has changed. They want more specific and grittier details of one's life.

Tim Robbins

I don't think I ever entered into a bargain where because I make films I have to tell you everything about the way I live personally. I just don't think that's part of the bargain.

It's the voyeur, the curiosity. I don't suppose there's anything wrong with it. I just don't feel like I should be offering my own personal life to the public. I want to keep that private. I'm happy in my life, but I don't feel like I should be offering advice, or should be saying because I do this that you should. I'd rather keep that sacred.

Jeff Goldblum

It sometimes is another little added irritant to complicated, sensitive, and private matters that I would rather keep private, but at the same time I understand that there's an industry that makes entertainment out of telling stories about people that we know. I wanted to do this and I knew that was out there, so it's entirely acceptable.

Laura Dern

I interviewed Robert Duvall for Interview *magazine* and it was such a funny experience. It showed me that, no matter what, you have to invade someone's privacy. It taught me two things. One, that I should be more conscious of the fact that people are going to have to try to get answers —and that it is my prerogative to answer them and protect my privacy or not.

I started doing interviews when I was twelve and I thought I was supposed to answer the questions. Now sometimes I'll look back on interviews and think, "I didn't really want to talk about that boyfriend so much." You don't have to talk about that relationship if you don't want to. Now I see there are choices.

Meg Ryan

You can always not answer a question. That's always within my realm of reality. It also feels like so much that's written is not true that you don't feel like you've lost any of your privacy at all. There's just this whole other myth that's getting spun out.

I feel more and more like there are less and less responsible people who are editing those things and letting them come out like they're actual news. It's insane. It helps mostly not to read them. You can do nothing about them. I have no control over what anyone thinks. I have no interest in making people like me, or not like me.

Nathan Lane

I've taken the radical—and unpopular—stance that my personal life is my own business. Yes, I realize that the questions are going to be asked and the more visible you are the more that comes up. I'd like to make it all about my work.

Ted Danson

(On his romance with Whoopi Goldberg)

I understand the curiosity, but I can't be part of the conversation. I need to have privacy in my life. This is a big conversation in my life. I need to have this conversation with those people in my life who are part of my personal private life, not with people I don't know. Truthfully, you and I want to sit and talk and share about our lives? I'd be happy to. I don't mean that as a push away. My life is incredible right now. Huge amount of stuff in life. I'd love to share it with you—on a personal level. But not to pick up and read in the paper. Not for people in my life to pick up and read in the paper. It's personal.

Whoopi Goldberg

(On her romance with Ted Danson)

Why would people want to answer questions about their personal lives? They're not questions that you would want to answer to people that you don't know, for the consumption of people you may never meet. As an interviewer, I stayed away from those kind of questions, because as an interviewee I know that it's nobody's business.

James Caan

I'll tell you who I'm fucking later.

Laura Dern

Doing movies I've come in contact with people who ask some pretty lewd questions. I had a very well respected reporter, he was talking to me about *Rambling Rose* and the scene with me and Lukas Haas, and said, "Do you come in real life like you did in the movie?" I was like, "Excuse me." It's so embarrassing.

Nick Nolte

I'm always a little shocked when the questions are more interested in my personal life. How many wives, all that kind of stuff. I get agitated with it and it's gotten more so. But I do understand. That sells. As I get older I just really don't want to pick up another magazine and see about testicle tucks. See, I always used to lie. It worked for a while, but it's not working much anymore.

Al Pacino

Sometimes I'm flattered if somebody wants to know about my personal life. That shows an interest. The only way I can think about it is when I identify with it, thinking about whose personal life do I want to know about and how does that manifest itself. Why are we interested in someone's personal life? It is interesting. I've just been reading books about Picasso, for instance. Not to compare myself with Picasso, but there are certain actors who I have been interested in the past whose biographies I've read.

Jean-Claude Van Damme

I don't know why they want to know stuff like that. The guy on the screen is not the same as the guy on the street. When women see a hero on screen, they fantasize without realizing that he's a normal person.

David Birney

I've been doing this for a while now and it's always been like there are two lives that you're involved with. One is the life that the media leads for you when you happen to be more visible. The other is your actual life—and the two rarely are coincident. They rarely have anything to do with each other.

Michael J. Fox

There's so much projection, so much bizarre Freudian weirdness. It's so laughable that you try to explain it to people.

Juliette Lewis

All my big affairs in the media have been completely fake. I really try not to be resentful. I don't want to be angry or cynical. I also don't want to ruin my natural thing, to be candid and to be honest. I don't want to become a restricted person who's like a robot. But it does upset me because I have good intentions. Like recently I did an interview and I think I could be a really great inspiration. Okay, maybe not really great, but a good inspiration for people in my generation. So I do an interview and then the interviewer will take that interview and make me out to be something so far removed from myself. I come across so dumb and arrogant and actressy, very shallow, and it's totally not what happened when we did the interview. She took out everything she contributed to the interview and made me into this bad person.

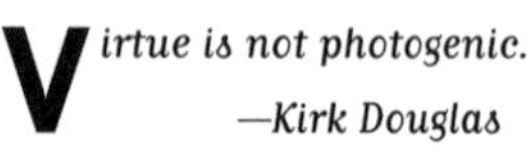

Virtue is not photogenic.
—Kirk Douglas

Mary Elizabeth Mastrantonio

You agree to do a magazine article and they use some horrible picture. Was I supposed to ask about that?

Emma Thompson

I think we have to start reeducating ourselves. You're asked by your editors to do what is required by the people who employ us, that we ask

Emma Thompson Ron Davis/Shooting Star

these questions or that we answer them. I've been thinking about this a lot lately, because it's no good just yelling at somebody or getting cross about it. You actually have to look at the practicalities of it and just think, "What purpose does this serve for any of us?"

It's inappropriate. The bottom line is: I wouldn't dream of asking you any questions about your personal life because I think that would be rude. I don't know you well enough. If you were my friend I would say, "I hear you're having a bit of a hard time. Are you okay?" But to be asked it in a public situation seems to me to be a kind of apoliteness, you know, it's like amorality. It's perfectly normal, suddenly, for well brought up people to behave as though they have never heard the words good manners or courtesy.

It's bizarre, actually, finally, because there is no place for it. I actually do not agree that because one's job involves publicity, because one has to go out and bang the drum for the work that you do, that you should be selling your life. I know that some people do. I understand that that is a syndrome. If you get that kind of attention it's very seductive and people think, "Well, I'll bare my soul." That happens particularly in America. I'm astonished what people will say on *Oprah* and things like that.

The young generation of actors coming up, when I read interviews with them, they seem to be much clearer about it and they just say, "I'm just not going to talk about that." There was a generation of movie stars, certainly in the forties, where the studio wanted that side of it as well. It was part of being a movie star, that personal side of it, the Elizabeth Taylor/Richard Burton angle on things. And if you make that a part of your life and that's how you want to present yourself and you're able to give that of yourself, then okay. But I think it's probably very difficult to live with, and very destructive.

Julia Roberts

I don't like having to explain myself. I resent having to make it comfortable for other people to understand.

My job is not being in the public eye. My job is acting, but it does have to be dealt with. I think anybody would want to be able to do their job and that's it, but it's silly to ponder it, because that's not the way it is.

Jason Patric

Being interviewed is not enlightening at all. The only thing you really have is your instinct. Instinct is something no one can seem to define and so you're very protective of it. No one knows why a salmon swims upstream or how a bird knows how to build its nest. They say instinct, but what is that? That very reason makes people, especially myself, extremely protective of what I don't necessarily know. So sometimes those boundaries become larger than they need to be.

Daniel Day-Lewis

Maybe I seem to be pathologically secretive, but if I am it's only because I'm aware that once you give something away you can't have it back again. Bearing in mind that the nature of the work is always drawing one into a public situation, you have to hold on that much more to your privacy.

Sandra Bullock

I'm as open as what I'm willing to lose. I'm very private when it comes to things that I really cherish and I'm not willing to lose. Like anybody who is a love interest in my life and is somebody that I care about, I'm going to protect. I'm going to protect a lot. My family, I'm going to protect a lot. I know it's an interesting subject, but I'm just very careful about it.

I'm sure everybody closes off. Once you get burned you don't go back there, but I don't learn from my mistakes and I keep going back out and getting burned again.

Tim Robbins

When Susan [Sarandon, his longtime companion and the mother of his three children] was pregnant, it went into the papers somehow. I was in Malta, in the middle of the Mediterranean, doing *Eric The Viking.* Before you knew it, everybody knew about it. We didn't have the chance to tell our friends yet. So I was robbed of the opportunity of going up to a friend of mine and saying, "Guess what? I'm going to have a baby!" and seeing the joy on his or her face and getting a hug. That's what I have a problem with.

Steve Martin

There's always a loss of privacy, but you've got to keep something for yourself. You don't want to have all your thoughts out there. I'm not qualified to talk about every subject. Sometimes entertainers are asked about every subject, as if their opinion actually means something. It's like on the news when there's a slaying and they ask the neighbor, "Did you hear any screams?" Does it matter?

Kelly Lynch

Watching a lot of daytime talk shows before I made *White Man's Burden,* I learned that America is a very scary place. Andy Warhol was so right about the fifteen minutes thing. There are people getting their fifteen minutes that we really don't want to know about. *Oprah* is a kinder, gentler show, I have to say. I'm talking about shows where I don't even know who the hosts were. There are hundreds of them. You can watch them all day long. It used to be soap operas, but now there are hundreds of these shows with "Aliens Ate My Husband's Car" or "Women Who Sleep With Men Who Sleep With Women Who Don't Have Children."

Geddy Lee

(Member of Rush)

I've been doing interviews six a day for the last couple of days and it's a little tiring, I must say. The shame of it is a lot of the people I've talked to I've really enjoyed talking to and I've had really good conversations, but talking about yourself so much over such a short period of time makes you insane. It really warps you. Last night when I went to bed I was twitching. I couldn't sleep, even though I was really tired. I kept flicking channels on the television, hoping I could just escape from it all.

Mimi Rogers

Talking about yourself gets really boring. I guess not everybody feels that way, but I do.

Kirk Douglas

I've been making movies for more than forty years, but what amazes me is that in this business you spend so much time talking about yourself. A lot of times I find myself in a group and I think, "You know, I'd like to know something about her." You're always talking about I, I, I. I once wrote an article called "I Bore Myself."

Robert Downey, Jr.

I'm either getting more in touch with myself lately or I'm just not good at this anymore. I just have a really hard time talking about all these "aspects of myself."

John Malkovich

I give an awful lot of myself to what I do, to my work, and I think I'm paid for my work. I can't imagine why my personal life would be of interest to anyone. I have absolutely nothing to teach them. I have absolutely nothing to give. There is nothing that I've learned. There's nothing that I can live by. It's completely beyond me.

James Garner

There aren't many people who enjoy doing what they do as much as I do. The down side is the press. I don't read it. I don't look at it. It's there, something you have to do, but I don't enjoy talking about myself much. I don't think I'm smarter than anybody else. Why are they asking me questions?

Arnold Schwarzenegger

We can't take ourselves too seriously. No matter what your job is there's a serious side to it and you want to do it as well as you can, but it's all a joke at the same time. You're sitting here with your recording equipment, going from one interview to another, thinking that you're re-creating the wheel or something like that, it's all funny.

Overheard from the next room, immediately after an interview:

Am I done? Please, God!

—Lori Petty

Yoko Ono

I remember John [Lennon]'s first gallery show. We go into this white show that we prepared and suddenly there's a lot of reporters and photographers. So I immediately thought, "Let's go in the back room." And John said, "No, no, no, we're gonna pose for them so they can take photos." I thought, "Why? We're artists, aren't we? We don't accommodate reporters." John was king of the world or something—and you mean the king does that, too? Why? Later he explained to me, "That's how we did it. We have to accommodate them." You know, in the art world that I come from, we were just snob artists. We never had to do that. Maybe even if you wanted to they wouldn't come around.

Harrison Ford

I've been characterized by the press from the very beginning as a person who didn't like to be interviewed and it's sort of become a part of my file. There's a constant reference to that. What I don't like is to be interviewed between times when I have a movie that's available, because I think people only have a certain amount of interest in you and you'll wear out your welcome. The press is voracious in its appetite. If you feed it all the time, it's not a good thing. The people are not as interested as the press.

Kevin Costner

We're told what's best dressed. We're told who's hot, who's not hot. It's not that we don't think for ourselves, but it's a noisy world that's constantly thinking for us. We're told if it's a good movie. We're told if it's a long movie. Fuck, why don't you just go see it yourself?

> *I don't ask everybody to write all these articles that they write. It's not really something that I'm in control of. I guess when everybody's sick of me they'll stop writing about me.*
>
> *—Madonna*

Madonna

I think that the people who are threatened by the idea of someone being forthcoming about their sexuality and sort of preaching sexual liberation will be swayed if they read articles written by writers who are threatened by it. They're going to form opinions of me. I do think it has an effect. It's unfortunate because I found that a lot of people were judging my book before they even read it, before they looked at it, before they got anywhere near it. It would be nice if everybody could listen to my music and watch my movies and read my books and whatever I do without anyone telling them how they should think or feel or accept it or not accept it, and then judge for themselves.

Kim Basinger

It's become a real tabloid world. Sometimes I'll have Alec [Baldwin, her husband] come to me and say, "Don't you get it? Are you still sitting here not accepting the fact that this is the way it is?" Because I still think there are good people out there to be entertained and see you be what they know you are capable of being. It's sad because one person can stand up and say, "This is what I saw. This is what it is. Go spread it around." And the herd are going to follow the leader. Some person with guts and integrity should stand up and say, "I'm not going on someone else's judgment. I'm going to talk to this person myself and see what I think."

Kevin Costner

There's a scene in Wyatt Earp *when he confronts the guy* with the pool ball. It's a very tense situation. But the moment after that is a very telling moment because he goes over and he picks up this gun and he goes, "This man was trying to shoot me down over nothing." And when the press wants to get at me in some way, I sometimes think it's over nothing. They would ruin my life, they would expose that I am a man, over nothing but a day's headline. And they can laugh and go on to their next story, but I live with the implications of what they've done. To me sometimes, it's over nothing. The weight of words sometimes has a lot of meaning to me.

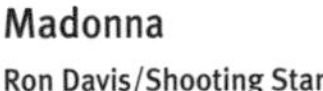

Madonna
Ron Davis/Shooting Star

Denzel Washington

Has the bottom line become such a factor that people will do anything, sell out anybody, talk about anybody, destroy anybody for the sake of a ratings point?

William Baldwin

The press has been frighteningly accurate some times and so absurdly inaccurate other times. I remember one time I went to an awards ceremony with a woman and—crossing the t and dotting the i—exact conversations that we had had during that evening were in print. I called her up thinking she must have told somebody. They paid off the limousine drivers! So the limousine drivers either recorded what we said or remembered specific quotes in the conversations. I remember, that day I had met her mother. I had never met her mother before and I was dating her. And all the conversation we had about her mother was in the article. Then the other half of the article about this woman and me was completely untrue.

Nastassia Kinski

It can be very distorted. Anybody who does this kind of job where they write about you, you can say, "Oh, it's nothing," but inside you know it's you. From a certain moment you drop it, but sometimes it just hurts you.

Michael J. Fox

(On the story he wrote for Esquire *about press coverage of his wedding)*

It was nice to be able to get it off my chest. It was, "You really want to know what this is like, to be getting married and have five helicopters buzzing overhead? Okay, I'll tell you." It was just too weird not to tell people about.

People magazine and the National Enquirer called Michael J. Fox bizarre and paranoid, leaving his heartbroken fans out in the cold, without even a picture of his wedding to look at. For his wedding to former Family Ties co-star Tracy Pollan, Fox spent top dollar hiring security expert Gavin de Becker and his team of guards and spies to prevent tabloid publications from getting a single picture. They went so far as to place moles within the very magazines trying to cover the wedding. Why? Because the same magazines who criticized them spent $250,000 attempting to get a picture of the wedding. They tempted Pollan's grandparents with a new car for information about their granddaughter's plans. They offered $10,000 to a hotel worker for a snapshot. They hired six helicopters to buzz the wedding [which was held in a tent]. They even contemplated dressing up as llamas to blend into the Vermont hillside and evade de Becker's guards. But the tabloids got nothing until a week later, when Pollan and Fox took their honeymoon on Martha's Vineyard and a scuba diving photographer popped up out of the water and took a picture. After that, Fox and Pollan changed their approach and began freely posing for pictures, even parading themselves in public. After a few weeks of that behavior the price on their heads—which tabloids had once valued at $50,000 or more—plummeted.

Lauren Holly

We're going to walk around with baseball hats with little mirrors taped on them, so every time they take a picture all they'll get is just a huge blinding white light. Ha, ha. Then I have this other idea. A bunch of us should band together and hire our own guerilla film crew that will shadow every move of every tabloid photographer. Follow their kids to school. Park in front of their house. Hide in their garbage and root through their stuff. Make a documentary on their lives. Create a lot of fake stories about them.

Sharon Stone

If you haven't made a mistake in your life, write an article and just fuck me, okay. If you have?

I live under a spotlight. If I break something at the supermarket by knocking it down with my cart, I'm going to read about that. I'm not just going to feel dumb. I'm going to feel dumb and then more dumb.

The concept of being exemplary means you also have to be exemplary in your failures. You have to be able to accept them with some dignity and learn something and go on. In the biggest crushes of the things that were hard for me, I learned a lot of lessons. Because of my fame I had to really look at myself. I had to really look at what I was doing. I didn't get to get away from it and forget it for a second. And I had to think about the part of me that was still naive, the part of me that was open. Maybe that's the hurtful part. Now I have to be careful in a way that you don't have to be as careful if you're not a target.

Disturbed by what he felt were untrue stories run about him in Time and Life magazines, Marlon Brando took revenge in 1957. The Academy Award winning actor hired a research organization to dig up every incontrovertible negative fact about Time Inc. Ammunition in hand—and thanks to Time/Life owner Henry Luce there was plenty—Brando went on TV and radio programs across the country to sling the mud himself. To this day, Brando feels that Time avoids mentioning his name.

Arnold Schwarzenegger

You have a lot of those journalists out there that for some reason or the other—although it's not their money, it's not their movie—they're very concerned that we bring the movie in on time and that we bring the movie in on budget. It's very clear that it's just for them, creating a story, filling some space in a newspaper, because they have nothing else to write about, or because we are riding on top of the wave. They say, "This guy is up there on top. His last five movies were a success. Every movie is making over a hundred million domestic, some even two hundred million. Let's take a shot at him."

Bruce Willis

The press has run out of things to say. So now the hook is: How much did this film cost? How much did this actor make? All these other things that really don't have anything to do with the actual filmmaking process. After *Hudson Hawk*, the gift that I got from that, after walking through that fire, is that I realized that I don't have to play that game anymore. I don't care what you say anymore.

Jason Priestley

I feel like with the success of *Beverly Hills 90210,* the first thing that goes is your privacy. If I go out to a bar and have too much to drink and fall down or get into a fight, I'm going to read about it the next day. That's just the reality of my situation. The positive side of things is that I get to buy a nice house to stay home in.

Tom Sizemore

I know what's out there. I did a little of that running around. It left me bereft and bored, running around with a bunch of B-level models and half-ass movie stars. There's nothing there really. The tabloids make it out like there's something going on. I'm here to tell you there's nothing going on.

Sharon Stone Yoram Kahana/Shooting Star

Gary Oldman

When people are writing gossip and following you in Central Park every time you go out the door, I can understand Sean Penn throwing rocks at people. You just want to go, "Fuck off. I'm buying a pack of cigarettes. I'm taking the dog for a walk." That can be tough.

Richard Dreyfuss

The public has no right to be gossiped to. There is no obligation to thrust gossip into people's faces. There is an obligation to make sure that the security of this country is taken care of. But to say that that allows the press any allowance of any gross behavior is despicable and thoughtless. Ultimately it belittles the press and clearly belittles the people that the press is dealing with.

Laura Dern

Since the beginning of celebritydom, people have wanted to know gossip. Gossip was around in the Roman era. Everybody wanted to know if Julius Caesar was gay. I know sometimes I thrive on it. You hear, "Oh, Princess Di...." You hear so-and-so left his wife. "Are you kidding me?!" It's so foul, but we all want to know certain things.

Ally Sheedy

There's not a single person I know who doesn't look at the *National Enquirer* headlines in the supermarket. It's natural. You're nosy. Everybody likes to gossip. But it can be a little scary to have people knowing secrets about me when I don't know anything about them. It's not exactly a two-way street there.

Lauren Holly

It's a very fine line because of what we do. We are public people. You have to give some back. People do have a right. I like hearing about other people and what they're doing and all that. To a certain point, you do have to give that. It's part of the trade-off. It's just that when people scream our address out and hide in garbage cans and climb over our walls into our backyard, things like that, that's where it gets incredibly intrusive and I think very low of those people.

We are public people and it's part of what propels us forward, but then there's a line. I don't want people to know what color underwear

I'm wearing that day. Is it really necessary to know if I put sugar on my cereal in the morning?

Whoopi Goldberg

People want to know what color drawers we wear to bed. I don't think that's anybody's business. I don't think anybody has the right to expect that they will be answered on those types of questions. It's fine to ask the question, but you were turning red because it wasn't a comfortable question for you. Let's help our audience expand beyond that, to get to another place.

Julia Ormond

The British are the worst. The British are appalling. I've been really shocked by the behavior of the British press. Richard Gere went out to dinner with Uma Thurman. They're old friends. Uma left the restaurant and she gets shoved up against a railing by journalists trying to get her photograph. She gets a cut above her eye that needs stitches. And his driver gets stabbed in the stomach trying to get them out. What's going on? For what?

Hugh Grant

We [Grant and supermodel Elizabeth Hurley] rented a house in the country in England, which we thought would be peaceful. We were wrong. The first day all the newspapers, and in fact the TV stations, gave out the address.

Kenneth Branagh

I try and stay away from the British press. The British press can certainly be very savage—or they can be very obsessed, as they were over that television interview with [Princess] Diana, which played, as you know, to an awestruck public. Two minutes after which, I saw on a news program reporting it a complete perversion of everything she had said, without blinking.

After fifty minutes we finally got into, "Other news today, in Bosnia, some trouble there, but anyway back to another reaction to Lady Di. Apparently someone saw an eyebrow flicker. It's a body language expert and that says she's guilty. So, Di guilty with the eyebrow there, and back to Philly Schmilly who's outside the gym where she may be in one hour coming out to walk to her car. Later in the week more on Bosnia, but right now this world-shattering stuff about the movement towards the BMW."

It was bizarre. It was like the whole nation was gripped. It was like we were all over the garden wall talking to our neighbors. And afterward, as you may well know, there was a power surge in Britain as the entire nation got on the telephone and put the kettle on.

Michael Maloney

I find the higher the profile the Royal Family gets the less credibility they are inevitably going to have as figureheads for English society. They're digging their own grave and I really wish they wouldn't do it. I support them, that's the problem. I just wish they wouldn't get hooked up in the PR system.

Hugh Grant

In England the police are totally in the pocket of the press, and vice versa. They should be called the "pless," or the "preice." I'm pretty bitter about that.

Thandie Newton

The British press? It's like animals in a zoo for celebrities in England.

Justine Frischman

(Member of Elastica)

The British press are a pretty evil bunch. When I'm traveling around and I'm in hotel rooms, I don't feel my privacy is being invaded in the same way that I would if I had it somewhere that was my home and there's people turning up on the doorstep. Generally when I'm on tour I don't feel the pressures the same way as I do when I'm at home.

Robert Downey, Jr.

The Hollywood Foreign Press, they come in, some of them don't even take notes [during the press conference], and then they want to take pictures with you at the end.

Irene Jacob

In Paris we are very careful about private lives. It's very difficult for journalists to be too aggressive about knowing where you are, with whom, and what are your pains. I think this is very healthy.

Richard Gere

I remember in Paris these guys followed us around for four hours. There was a caravan of them, motorcycles and everything. I was just jet-lagged and tired. I just wanted to ride around Paris. Finally, I said, I can't even repeat what I said. You can imagine. They wanted me to go with the girl I was with to the Eiffel Tower and pose for pictures there—at which point I totally blew up. If there hadn't been somebody there I probably would have ended up in jail. In fact, we went to a police office and said, "Get these guys off us. This can't be legal." The cops wouldn't do anything. They posed for pictures.

Gary Oldman

I was in the jury at Cannes. I was walking along the street and two guys were in the shrubbery. I heard this guy with a British accent say, "Gary." He was with a friend and his friend took a picture of me...So this guy said to me, "Got some great pictures of Uma [Thurman] by the swimming pool. She's your ex-wife, right? Just thought I'd keep you up to date and let you know what was going on." What he wanted me to do was hit him, probably. This was the gutter press. It was a set up, probably for me to hit the guy and his friend to take a picture of me. "Jury Member Hits Photographer!" "Wild Man Gary Oldman!" All I did was bite my lip and walk away. What gives them the right to walk up to me and say that?

Mary Steenburgen

Having President [Bill] Clinton [an old friend] at my wedding [to Ted Danson] made a lot of things easier. It meant that no nasty helicopters flew over and spoiled the whole thing because they couldn't invade his air space. I told him that was his big gift to me.

Lauren Holly

When the guy jumped out of our garbage can, Jim [Carrey] was out of town. I was pulling into the gate and the garbage cans were outside

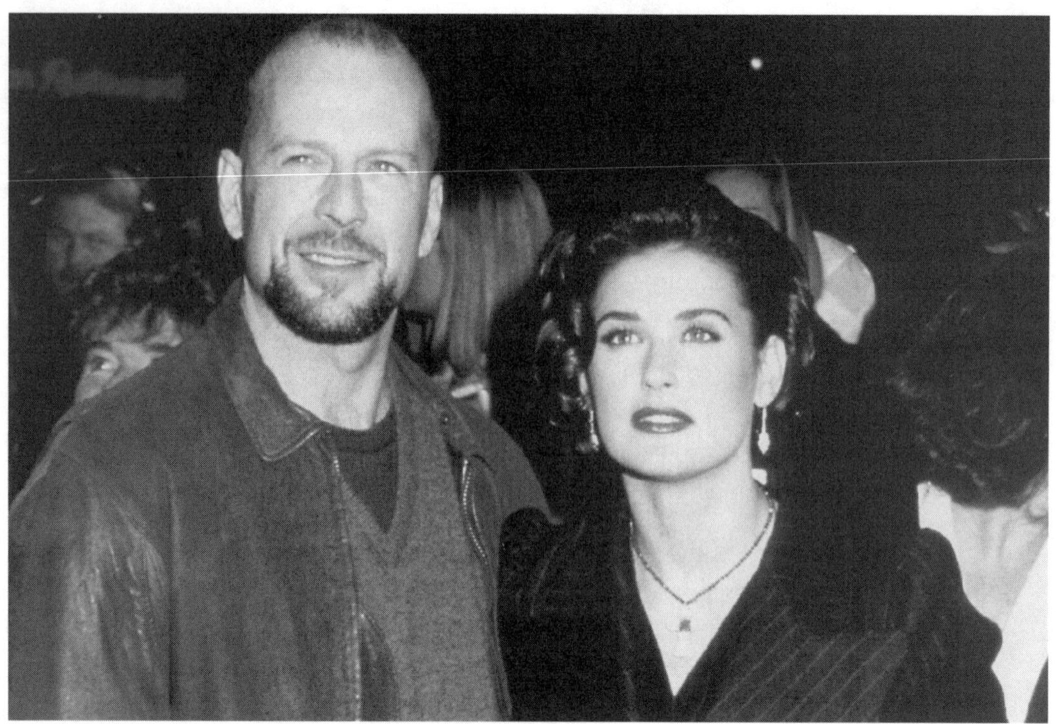

Demi Moore and Bruce Willis Ron Davis/Shooting Star

because the garbage had been picked up that day. They jumped out of the can with a video camera in my face. I just kept saying, "You were in my garbage can. You were in my garbage can." It just seemed so fitting somehow.

It is scary. I'm a girl. When you're alone at the house and you hear noises outside, it's kind of scary. People follow you home and you don't know if it's that or some kind of serial killer. It puts your heart through a lot of paces.

Demi Moore

Recently I went on vacation with my family. Wherever we went we had to watch for cameras. We're not able to be free because we're worried that they might get a picture, or I might have cellulite. On a more serious note, we really prefer for the children not to be photographed. Up until we let Rumer [her oldest daughter, Rumer Willis] do the movie, we've tried to maintain their anonymity until they made a decision of their own, as Rumer did when she asked to do *Striptease*.

Madonna

Photographers park in my neighborhood and follow me wherever I go, so I have to deal with those extraterrestrial beings following me around. Usually I just let them follow me—and hope that they don't get the table right next to me in the restaurant.

Pam Dawber

You hear the stories of so-and-so beating up the paparazzi outside the restaurant. Don't go to that restaurant! There are a million other restaurants to go to that paparazzi don't. You can avoid it if you want. "I can't go to the grocery store." Why not? It's amazing the number of famous actors I see in my grocery store pushing carts next to me.

Sandra Bullock

I don't want to constantly worry about leaving my house and having a line of paparazzi outside of my door. You want to leave your house looking like a slob. So you make adjustments, which I've definitely had to learn how to do.

Daryl Hannah

I walk into a premiere or a screening and I think, "Oh God, there's paparazzi. I'll just turn invisible." Then I walk on through. Then I see these pictures of me looking absolutely vacant. Completely vacuous. No wonder, because I've disappeared. I'm somewhere out there. My body is still present. It's a bad thing.

Sinbad

(To a gathering of photographers)

I want y'all's travel agents, because you get there before we get there. I just want to know who's doing your travel, because I want those travel agents. I want them working for me.

Lauren Holly

There was one night when Jim [Carrey] and I went out to dinner and they followed us. Then they were trying to follow us home and take pictures of us driving in the car and in order to do that they were driving in the opposite lane of traffic, causing other drivers to swerve off the road while they were trying to take pictures.

So what do we do at that point? Do we pull over in the car and give them their photo opportunity so that innocent people don't get killed? It's the most bizarre thing.

Robin Williams

The paparazzi follow me into the men's room. "Robin, could you hold it up? Could you make the puppet talk? Oh, you're having a movement? Oh great! IT'S LIVE STOOLS OF THE RICH AND FAMOUS! Oh no, watch out! Someone's had caviar. It's the proctocam! Guess who's colon this is? Is it Colin Powell? We'll tell you right after the commercial break!"

Vincent Perez

I'm in the gossip magazines these days and I hate that. They really give me a hard time, following me. I was in Spain, so suddenly I catch one at the airport. I was so happy and I took everything, the cameras, the films. The guy was trembling. He was shaking. I said, "Goodbye, thank you." I didn't hurt him. I just took his work with me. I was in a killing mood and he just let me do what I wanted to do.

Bruce Willis

It's always been just as hard to protect our [he and wife Demi Moore's] privacy. It's never been easy. The only answer we have found is to find a sanctuary for ourselves, to go somewhere where that doesn't exist. When we come to New York or Los Angeles we accept the fact that when you go out you're going to be the celebrity that you have called us. I never said I was a celebrity. I never said I was a superstar. I never said I was a mega-box office monster. I was just an actor. I wish that stuff had happened a little later. I'm still learning how to act.

Rene Russo

It's hard to deal with the criticism. I remember doing a satellite interview for *In the Line of Fire*, where they could see me but I couldn't see them. She said, "So Rene, what's it like when *People* magazine says...." and then she quoted the worst thing that an actress ever wants to hear about herself. It was a horrible review. With all these people there, it was like someone had just kicked me in the stomach.

Chris Farley

The criticism hurts me because I try to do the best that I can. If it's bad it just kind of hurts. I'm scared if people don't like what I do.

Geraldine Chaplin

He [her father, Charlie Chaplin] got a terrible, terrible shock when *Countess From Hong Kong* came out in London and got the most horrible reviews. I mean they slaughtered it. He never got over it.

Yoko Ono

The only time that I get really concerned now is when I read something that has venom in it, so vicious that you get scared and say, "I hope Sean [Lennon, her son] isn't going to be hurt."

Yoko Ono

The reason why we stopped doing all those rock 'n' roll avant-garde type things that we used to do in the beginning was because we were criticized so much that there wasn't a market there.

Jodie Foster

You have to disassociate yourself from this whole commercial end of it, unless you're making *Batman* or something. You can't have your self-worth dependent on it.

Ron Howard

You always hope that the good honest creative work that has gone into a movie by people who care about that first and foremost is not going to go unrecognized or be overwhelmed by other issues like success or failure. I don't think that people involved in a creative endeavor particularly relish being thrown into what's essentially a media-manufactured competition. The Academy Awards do it and everybody involved says it's great to win, but how can you really pick? It's a fabrication.

When you have a movie out in the summer, people look at the box office grosses like that's all that counts about any movie. Everybody wants their movie to be seen by as many people and make as much money as it can possibly make. We're all grown ups and we're in the business, but you don't want to only be thought of in terms of that.

It's impossible to separate the show from the business. I don't think you can start allowing that thinking to motivate you or guide your choices too much. In the end, what *Apollo 13* really represents to me is sixteen months of my life. First and foremost, if you're in a position to choose, you've got to choose experiences that are going to be interesting and represent you in a way that you'd like to be represented.

Quentin Tarantino

This weird backlash that hit me, I was kind of surprised by it. I expected backlash about my work. I didn't think anyone would give a damn if I did a sitcom. I didn't think I was going to get reviewed in the *New York Times* when I hosted *Saturday Night Live.* I never saw anybody else get reviewed for it. I thought I could have fun like everybody else. I didn't think I was going to be penalized.

Quentin Tarantino
Lisa O'Connor/Shooting Star

Siskel and Ebert did an episode of their show that talked all about my films. The last part of it was, "Quentin, you're screwing up. Stop being so bad in so many movies and stop doing all your junk and get back to what it is you do." It was a pretty mind-bending experience to be the guy that it was about.

One of the things they said is, I've been going on the Jay Leno show, not because I'm an egomaniac but because I'm trying to sell my movie, like everybody else is trying to sell their movie. And Siskel and Ebert said, "Quentin, don't go on the Jay Leno show and try to be a performer. If you're going to go on the show talk about movies." I'm sorry. I think they want me to go on and be funny. It's a talk show. I don't want to go on and be a boring director talking about boring director stuff. There's a little comedian guy in me. I want to go on and kill.

Robert Redford

You become a target. That's an unfortunate thing to deal with because you don't have any control over it.

Chevy Chase

I tend to get bad reviews and I don't know exactly why. It would be fair to say that what I do isn't easy, and maybe it looks easy. Maybe it looks so easy that they figure I'm doing nothing, therefore why give him a good review? Maybe it's fair to say that many of my movies are not particularly quality pictures. I can understand that point of view. I don't happen to agree. I think the world of my pictures. Well, not the world.

Chevy Chase

I'm not crazy about critics and they're not crazy about me. We both do the same thing, basically, which is entertain and edify. The difference is I don't have to take apart some guy, like a critic, in order to entertain and edify.

Geddy Lee

(Member of Rush)

It doesn't matter what we do. We are just perceived as being unhip. I think it will always be like that. That's just the way it is, for whatever reason.

Tim Robbins

I don't really read reviews. I'm aware of them. I'm aware that there are good reviews and I'm aware that there are bad reviews, but you just have to trust what you believe. When you see it you have doubts about some choices you've made, but you can never go back and there's no real point in laboring on it.

James Garner

I don't read reviews much. I can tell by audience reaction and people who talk to me whether they like the movie or not, or the TV show, or whatever, by how many people bring it up to you. I can tell much better than the press can tell, or a critic can tell about it. People are much more knowledgeable than the critics.

Kevin Spacey

I think nothing diminishes a work of art more than criticism. If a work of art comes from a true place, comes from a place of necessity, you don't need to ask anyone whether it is good or not. You know whether it is good or not. We live in a world where a lot of people make a lot of comments about things. That's fine. Someone may indeed have a very true and very true vision and opinion about something, but I think it's of a narrow field.

Paul Newman

I don't read reviews unless somebody plants it on my forehead and I can't escape it.

> *I came into the industry in 1961. I stopped reading reviews in '62.*
>
> *—Ann-Margret*

John Malkovich

I never read my reviews. Really, what can I do about it? They're not going to rewrite them. They're going to see it once and actually think that they know more about acting than I do, which would appear to me to be the height of arrogance. I'm sorry, but it's true.

Sylvester Stallone

I don't mind being criticized, but please, give me the answer. Tell me how to be better. It's like you saying to your kid, "You're stupid, go to your room." You have to say, "That was a stupid thing, but next time if you try to do it this way maybe you'll succeed." That's all I ask. If you're going to slap me with one hand, give me a kiss on the other side, okay, and I'll kill for you.

Shelley Long

When a review comes out and says, "You are a total piece of ka-ka. Get out of the business," when a frivolous piece of gossip appears in a periodical saying that you gave the most boring performance of the year or you were in the worst film of the year, these are zero days.

It's so personal. You can't read a review and have a critic say, "This is the most boring performance of the year," and not respond to that. I have feelings. I'm in this business because I have feelings, because I'm interested in other people's feelings.

Carole King

When a review is bad, no matter who writes it, it always bothers me momentarily. If the review is bad and it was written unintelligently and viciously and just to be extremely cool—as so many reviewers do, that's the "those that can do, those that can't review" school of reviewer—that's one thing. But there are some reviewers that can review, and it is those reviewers—whether it is a good review or a bad review—that I will consider very seriously what they have to say. If a reviewer gives me a bad review, and it was an intelligent bad review, I welcome that in a way, because it gives me an opportunity to question my work and see how I would have made it better. Sometimes I will not agree with the reviewer and say that's his or her opinion. And of course a well-written, good review is delightful.

John Malkovich

A certain amount of people are going to like you—almost no matter what you do—and a certain amount of people are going to hate you—again almost no matter what you do. If they draw comparisons to actors who have played the same role before, I don't really care. You know what? I've seen some of that stuff before and it was fucking shitty. The acting was hideous. I've seen plays like *The Glass Menagerie, Death of a Salesman,* absolutely sodomized by people who we think are good or famous. A lot of people like stuff that I could never watch, even for a second.

Brian Dennehy

Certainly many, many television critics are people who are not critics. They are not trained as critics. They have no particular training in literature, or comparative literature, or in understanding. They are people who, for a couple of years, are doing a particular job while they try to get to another job. "Sure, why not hire this person to be a television critic?" That seems to be the attitude. For someone like myself, who has spent twenty-five years training to be an actor, and who does work very hard in terms of literature and understanding, I resent the fact that someone who has no real basis in critical understanding is allowed to give a thumbs up or a thumbs down on my work, or anyone's work.

Henry Winkler

There was one reviewer on TV in L.A. who used to be an athlete, and he wasn't good at that either. It's shocking that these people review you and they have no idea what they're talking about, let alone the English language.

John Landis

You read these rants from critics, because they realize ultimately they're eunuchs. Orson Welles called them eunuchs at the orgy.

Tom Cruise

I can't control what people think or do. They're going to write whatever they want. It's up to me just to hope that people who meet me know what the truth is. I get up and read scripts, not the tabloids. Paul Newman said to me, "You gotta know what to worry about and what not to worry about." Newman is absolutely right. Forget it. Don't even worry about it. That is so low on the totem pole of priorities for me. It's like doing a performance for a critic. What? I'm going to alter my performance for a critic?

Keenen Ivory Wayans

In order to really be funny, you've got to be fearless. You can't sit back and worry about who is not going to like it. I do think that if you do something and you find that a large majority of people don't like it, then you've got to reevaluate what you've just done. But you've got to be fearless. Any of the great comics who've been out there have all been fearless.

Quentin Tarantino

It's about a career. It's about twenty-two films. People will like this one and people won't like this one. And maybe the one that gets kicked in the butt, twenty years from now it will be considered the best. That's happened to most of the film makers that I love.

John Landis

The Blues Brothers *is still referred to as a failure.* The picture made $350 million! It paid for my house and people are still saying it's a failure.

Richard Harris

I adored Wrestling Ernest Hemingway. *It was one* of the best movies I ever made. Then you read a critic who says, "Richard Harris is a poor man's Max Von Sydow" or, "He now looks like George Carlin." Have I worked for twenty weeks making this picture and four months preparing it to have my performance written off like that?

Janeane Garofalo

I would not want to be the person who has the name above the title. I don't think I could handle it if somebody said, "Finally they gave Janeane Garofalo a chance to carry a movie and we'd like to see LESS of her." I picture the sound bites. "She leaves you wanting less."

Dana Carvey

I think about Kevin Kline's reviews for *January Man*, which were really bad. Then ninety days later he had an Oscar in his hand. That probably can guide you through show business.

Steve Walsh

(Member of Kansas)

In Texas one time, a guy reviewed the show and said we just sucked. Then he started mentioning names of songs that we didn't even play. So I called this guy up at the paper and said, "Now you gotta tell me. Were you at the concert?" And he said, "No. Ha, ha, ha." I felt like going there and killing the guy.

Shirley MacLaine

The part that I think is really wrong and more self-defining of the journalists than me is when they review my work in terms of my metaphysical books. That is yellow journalism and really ticks me off. "Was she this in another life?" "Maybe she was channeling this." Some stupid bullshit like that. I don't like that at all.

Angus Young

(Member of AC/DC)

I remember once there was something in a women's magazine in England. They had an article with the latest pop idol, he was called "the boy the mums love." And then on the other page they had "the boy that the mothers hate," and it had a photo of me. It said, "This nasty piece of work is called Angus Young, from AC/DC." It said if your kids are coming home tattooed and swearing and suddenly they want to go out and purchase big amplifiers and bash a guitar and run around behaving like a maniac, blame this one.

Neil Tennant

(Member of The Pet Shop Boys)

The Sun *in England did an interview with us* and asked us our views on all sorts of different subjects—pop stars and films and clothes and TV—and then they only printed everything nasty we'd said. And then they said we were the rudest men in rock.

Hugh Grant

I'm getting better at divorcing myself from what's written about me. You just have to put yourself in the position of the journalist. How do you make a story out of things? Really, there are only two stories: Success or humiliation. There is a cruelty to that, but then it would be hypocritical of me to mind too much because I've always enjoyed that cruelty when it's focused on other people. I used to write book reviews in the *Daily Mail* and I can remember the temptation to write something that might not be particularly true or that might be cruel just because it was funny or a good line. I must confess that I did give in to that temptation once or twice. I get tremendous enjoyment from other people's failures and I'm a reader of the tabloid press. I enjoy other people getting taken down a peg, but it is an odd experience when that gets turned on you.

Andie MacDowell

I did write to Hugh Grant after all that, and I feel really bad because I have not mailed that letter. What I said to him is, "It could've been worse. You could've been dumped by Glenn Close." But it's all of a sudden become the center of his life. And it will be. It will never go away. It will always be something that some people are going to have to ask you about. But, as my manager tells me, I could use a little a bad publicity. I should go out and do something like that.

Johnny Depp

There's nothing strange about it. You have a little scrape with the law at a hotel and it's blasted all over the universe. You go out to dinner with

Hugh Grant and Elizabeth Hurley Ron Davis/Shooting Star

your girlfriend, it's blasted all over the universe. You buy a place to live and it's blasted all over the universe. There's nothing strange about it at all. I'm totally at ease with it. I'm comfortable. I welcome everybody over to my house for coffee and cheese and doughnuts. Yeah.

Rod Stewart

No one ever writes about the clever little twists that I put into songs that I'm so proud of. I get no credit for the songs I write. All they're concerned about is the women in me [sic] life, how much I drink, and how much money I've got.

Denzel Washington

When I was a kid, you couldn't hear or read about or watch what I consider to be heroes as much as you can now. You didn't have that luxury. The information machine was different in those days. You might have seen those people once a month, or a week, but you didn't know everything about them, what kind of clothes they wore, what time they went to the bathroom.

Denzel Washington

Information as we know it in this society now is controlled by less and less people. We all know the names of these guys—and it's all guys that control most of our information now. They own all the TV stations. Are we all in denial about the fact that maybe we're being led down a certain path? Am I being too paranoid?

Oliver Stone

The last thing I want to do is go on *Meet the Press.* There is that high priesthood that wants to control history and reality. They can be very ugly about it. They don't understand what a movie is—as opposed to a history book. But even their history books are skewed, as I've said in the past. I really have been one of the leading critics and skeptics of official history in this country. I remain so. I feel that about the *JFK* thing. I still think it's the biggest single act of disinformation that's occurred in my lifetime.

Ron Howard

If you're drawn to this business, you're probably a little bit on the eccentric side to begin with and there are certain pressures that sometimes push people to maybe misbehave. But I would think that if you looked at any profession and put it under the microscope the way entertainment, politics, sports, the way those individuals are, you'd find just as much eccentric behavior, or maybe more.

There are a lot of genuinely well-intentioned, good-hearted people with a lot of personal integrity at work in the business.

Jodie Foster

There is this misconception—it's a *New York Times* phenomenon—that somehow those people living in Los Angeles with their sunglasses on are these superficial people that only put out *Jurassic Park.* I'm sorry. It's not true. People that are in the film business, there are people that you don't like and there are people who are superficial and there are people who care about it and take it very seriously and want to make films that change people's lives.

Roseanne

I buy the National Enquirer *every week.* I think all the tabloids have totally impacted on the rest of the media, influencing everything. You don't know whether you read it in *Time* or the *Enquirer. Time* and *Newsweek* have absolutely no more credibility to me than *The National Enquirer.* Neither does the *New York Times.* They're all the same now. Society gets the television and the news we deserve. I love tabloids. I read every single one of them. I like the *Weekly World News* the most, because that's the one that has the alien shaking hands with [Bill] Clinton. That's the only newspaper that I trust.

Weird Rumors

One reason celebrities hold journalists in contempt is because they are frequently victimized by shoddy reporting practices. The most outlandish rumors are given credence in the press, often repeated endlessly until they take on the aura of truth. How many people believed that Jerry "The Beaver" Mathers was killed in Vietnam? Richard Gere and the gerbil? It's one thing to criticize a performance, but quite another to call the performer a pervert, a criminal, or a corpse.

Keanu Reeves

(On rumors that he is media mogul David Geffen's lover)

When I first heard about it I was playing *Hamlet* and it seemed funny. And then it got bigger and it seemed funnier. And then it got ridiculous. When it was supremely ridiculous my agent and my manager said I had to address it. So I did. I don't really care unless it starts to affect work or personal life. You know, where it's intrusive. But it's interesting. One of the things that I learned about it is if you don't address the press or media there seems to be a kind of animosity that can grow. And so it taught me that you have to share.

Robert Redford

I'm not a lonely man. That story that said I was has to do with the media and where it is today and the need to crystallize things into simple images. There's nothing I can do about that. The interview in *Esquire* was a much longer piece and it had to do with much broader topics. Sometimes in the editing down it gets edited in such a way that reshapes the point. I'm not either sad or lonely. What I did say, and maybe it was a mistake, was talking about sadness as an element in life that I accept. I accept it as a fact of life. And rather than deny it or shy away from it or try to go around it, I embrace it, in the work. I've found that to be a very dramatic and workable thing in the work that I've done, to embrace sadness. But there's a difference between accepting that as part of a process and being a sad person. I don't think of myself as a sad person, nor lonely.

Elle MacPherson

I really don't spend a lot of time reading my own press, because if I did I would drive myself crazy. All I can generalize and say is most of the bad things that you read about me are untrue. I have not slept with half of

America, though some may think I have. Because I haven't had time to. I would've liked to have, but I haven't.

Arnold Schwarzenegger

The things that I read about myself or about other actors—it's just hilarious. One day I get a phone call from my mother in Austria and she says, "What did you do to poor little Danny DeVito? I love this guy."

I said, "What are you talking about? What did I do?"

She said, "You threw him five feet through the air and they had to call Italy to hire Italian bodyguards and a judge ordered you to stay six feet away from him for now on."

And I said, "Well how will I do my scenes and act with him [in *Junior*] if I have to stay away six feet? And what are Italian bodyguards?"

She says, "There's a whole page in the Austrian paper and it's written up here all over the place."

Danny DeVito
Annie Liebovitz/
The Kobal Collection

Danny DeVito

It's so silly. None of this ever happened. Arnold [Schwarzenegger] and I are so close, it's crazy. One day my publicist called me and said, "There's this thing in the *Post* that they got from the *Star*, that you said something about this movie that he did and he picked you up." Then this Austrian magazine said he picked me up and threw me five meters. We got a big kick out of it. That's totally made-up stuff.

Danny DeVito

I was doing Taxi. *It was the first show* that Chris Lloyd ever did, we married Andy Kaufman to a hooker. Now, I had learned how to play the violin for *Goin' South.* So I said to Jim Brooks, "Maybe I should come out of the cage with my violin. I'll play my violin for Andy's wedding." So we did it. It was a really great show. Fabulous show.

Two weeks later in the *Enquirer* or one of the other papers there was a picture of me with the violin. It said, "Danny DeVito Gives Up Career as Virtuoso Violinist to Do a TV Show." This is the first year of *Taxi*. So Rhea [Perlman, his wife] and I cut it out, it was kind of cute, this whole story of how I used to practice four hours a day. Then the phone rings. It's my mother, God rest her soul. And she says to me, "I didn't know you wanted to play the violin."

Arnold Schwarzenegger

Many times my mother has called me up and said, "It's outrageous, your behavior!" And I say, "What did I do now?" And she will say, "Maria [Shriver, his wife] is pregnant and you don't even share this with me." I say, "Maria's not pregnant, maybe you know more than I do." And she says, "Don't you lie to your mother! I read it in the paper." Well, then it definitely isn't true.

Jason Alexander

The Enquirer *has one going right now* that says that I went in to tell Jerry [Seinfeld] that I couldn't do the show next year and that he and I blew up at each other and that we are no longer speaking. Usually in the *Enquirer* when it comes to me there's some hint of truth somewhere. This one was totally from Mars.

My mother actually heard that story—some radio station had picked it up and run with that one—and she went, "Did you yell at Jerry?"

I went, "Oh come on! When are you going to learn? It's been seven years now, for crying out loud. Don't believe anything that you read." She always thinks that I'm withholding information from her.

Danny DeVito

I've heard stories where people have actually paid other people to call newspapers and say they've seen screenings of movies that were bad, just because they wanted to sabotage the movie. That happens all the time.

Shelley Long

I get really discouraged by the negative gossip and the negative innuendos and accusations, many of which are completely false and fabricated. That's horrifying to me, but there's nothing I can do about it short of taking on major lawsuits, which some celebrities have. I give them a lot of credit because they end up spending a lot of money to do it. Generally in the business we've been told, "Don't comment on it." You just add fuel to that stinky fire. If you comment on it you draw attention to it. I hope the public understands that some of these ridiculous things we don't comment on because they're so ridiculous. If you talk about them you give them importance. If you talk about negative things you give them more power.

Annie Potts

When my last son was born they had me quoted in an article regarding the birth of my son, that he just "popped out like a little pea from a pod." Clearly their source was fucked because I labored over that for seventeen hours and he did not pop out like a pea. I hate the tabloids.

James Caan

(After an acquaintance fell to his death from his home)

What bothers me in those rags, those slimeball buzzards that they are, not in reference to me, but to this boy who has a family, all of a sudden he's a junkie. Where the fuck do they come up with that? "He was arrested before for robbery." All lies! But this kid has a family. He's not buried a day and his mom's got to read shit like that? Me, hell, it's part of business.

Liza Minnelli

I know my mother [Judy Garland]'s death wasn't suicide. I've seen the coroner's report. But it doesn't matter. They're going to write what they want to write anyway.

Vincent Perez

With Isabelle Adjani, that was awful. Everybody was saying in the press that she died. She was at home, very quiet, watching TV, and suddenly she sees this on TV because of a gossip magazine that started to create that. What about her friends and everybody surrounding her?

Jerry Mathers

I did not die in Vietnam. Actually, what they tell me is it ran on both wire services. At the time, bureau chiefs in major cities would scan casualty lists for people of prominence in their particular area to run a story. Something happened to either someone with the same name or a very similar name and they said, "That must be him." I had given away an Emmy that year to Gene Kelly for best children's movie. I was in the service at that time and I did it in uniform, so the story made sense to them.

Sean Connery

I've been reported dead twice now. The last time it was a mix-up because James Hunt, who was a chum of mine, had died. He lived near me in Spain. It was picked up by a South African station from Japan, but the Japanese pronunciation left something to be desired and it came over as "James Bond." They picked it up on the wires in South Africa and put it out. Then the French picked it up, and I have a lot of friends there. They were frightened to call my wife. Eventually one of them did.

He said, "Oh, terrible news."

And she said, "Oh, what?"

"I hear that Sean died."

"Oh, I don't think so. He's out playing golf."

Woody Harrelson

(It was reported that he had considered adopting the Islamic faith)

I never toyed with the idea of embracing any organized religion, other than the time I was a devout Presbyterian back in high school. I hate to have the truth interfere with a good story, though.

> *Let's make no mistake. I didn't throw up working on Apollo 13. Some people did. I was not one of the ones who did.*
>
> *—Kevin Bacon*

Ann-Margret

I have this big diamond ring that my husband gave me about sixteen years ago. One of those papers wrote that I had washed my hands, I had put it on a window sill, and a bird came and picked it up. Somebody was apparently sitting there and watching all this.

Uma Thurman

I read once that I was addicted to heroin living in some part of Eastern Europe. I thought, "Wow, that must have been some game of telephone."

The press just insists on some gamut of relationships, some of which are true, but many of which aren't. They don't get over it. You inform the press over and over again, "No, that's not the case." It doesn't matter. They like to write those things. They don't want it not to be true.

Helena Bonham Carter

You have to say that there's another Helena Bonham Carter floating out there. She's written about and she does all these things, when they deviate from the truth. When you see articles and the way they describe you, you can't identify. You've got to let it go.

Gary Oldman

This whole thing about Isabella [Rossellini] and I getting married, it was really invented. Then it just gives them a chance to say, "Oh, they didn't." "It's the on and off tempestuous relationship of Issy and Gary." I had the whole thing with Uma [Thurman]. "Hard drinking wild crazy party-loving Gary." There's a perception out there of me as this crazy, crazy, crazy guy.

James Caan

They had me fighting every other day. I was beating the shit out of somebody, beating my wife on the front cover—which was never true, of course. Retraction's on page eight.

Jason Alexander

There was one time when I was in *The New York Daily News.* It said that I and some friends had gone to Scores. We had possibly the most uninteresting time that I've ever had because we sat in the bar area, which is kind of away from the dancers. We drank a couple of Diet Cokes. We were there for thirty minutes and we left.

A: they thought that was a news story, and then they augmented the story by saying that I had gone back alone several days in a row after that and it was very confusing for the girls because they kept mistaking me for Kramer. We're so much alike. He's six-foot-four, curly hair. It's an obvious mistake.

It's the fabricated stuff that makes you go, "What's that all about?" It's obviously done with an eye towards the provocative and it's so unnecessary.

Demi Moore

Vanity Fair *said that Bruce [Willis, her husband]* has twenty-two assistants. Come on! What can he do with twenty-two assistants? Then the magazine said that a Disney executive supported that. Which executive? Goofy or Donald?

Liam Neeson

It's like a laugh. I've found myself in the past saying something to somebody and the next thing it's in print. These "friendships" I've had in the past, suddenly you see their names in heavy black print.

Paul Newman took the role of Michael Gallagher in Absence of Malice, the 1982 drama about a man who is wrongly implicated of misdoings in a newspaper article, because he related to his character. Said Newman, "90% of what's printed about me is false, made-up, or distorted."

Mary Steenburgen

They said we [she and Ted Danson] were getting married in December. We were totally intrigued to read that not only were we getting married, but they picked a date for us! We both figured out that when we don't get married in December—which we're not—they'll invent a big breakup!

Mary Steenburgen

When they write about our children it of course gets to us more than anything else. One of the tabloids invented a story that my son doesn't like Ted [Danson] and that he's so unhappy about our relationship that he's going to go live with his dad. This has no basis in truth. In fact, it's just the opposite. He loves him. And so Charlie was upset about this. We talked about it and Ted talked to him about it.

Ted said, "You and I know how we feel about each other. Let's just start there. Who else do you care about?"

And Charlie said, "I don't want my friends thinking that."

So he took the tabloid to school and in his little sharing thing at the beginning of class he read them this article. And not only did they get that wrong, but Charlie was very offended that they got his age wrong. Charlie's eleven and they said he was nine, which he found very offensive. So they went through it and the whole class had a discussion about how just because something is printed doesn't mean it's true.

Johnny Galecki

I had gone out to some restaurant or some club to see a friend's band play and Sara [Gilbert, his co-star on *Roseanne*] came with me. I ran into this photographer outside and he asked if he could take a picture of Sara and me. A couple of weeks later it showed up in the *Star* or one of them. I felt terrible, wondering what Sara was going to think. She knows me well enough to know that I would never try to set anything like that up and my relationship with Sara has always been very platonic. So I called and apologized and went on and on about this story saying we can't keep our hands off each other and you had your legs wrapped around me in this restaurant. And she laughed. She said, "Don't worry about it. It's much worse when it's true."

Uma Thurman

Katharine Hepburn once said, "I never care about anything that's written about me as long as it's not true."

Jodie Foster

There are autobiographical splashes in everything I do, but it's the truths and not the facts.

Cameron Diaz

Stories about anorexic models are totally, absolutely, to the highest extreme, blown out of proportion. I don't know any model who diets, in the first place. I don't know anybody who works out on a regular basis. All the girls that you see are just lucky because they have a quick metabolism. Besides that, modeling is physically demanding. You're never standing still when you're modeling. It's like being on the football field all day long. Models don't just drink water and only eat alfalfa sprouts. That is a total myth. I'm a cheeseburger junkie. I eat them every day.

Michael Douglas

I hear this thing about these calculated business decisions as far as pictures that I do. I always have to remind people that all the pictures, going back to *Cuckoo's Nest, China Syndrome, Romancing the Stone,*

Liam Neeson The Kobal Collection

Fatal Attraction, they couldn't get made at first! They took a long, long time and they were rejected by a lot of studios before they were made. After they became successful, writers would write about the formula and how obvious it was if it was a commercial success, but that wasn't the case at the time. It really is Monday morning quarterbacking. I resent that a little bit, when you're making pictures because you're impassioned from the heart and then someone says it's a calculated move.

Woody Allen

There are things that are written about you that are based on truth but nasty, and there are things that are written about you that are exaggerations, but there are many things that are written about you that are so silly you wouldn't know where to begin. It could just as well be space aliens.

For example, they said I was having an affair with Richard Schickel's daughter. Now, I didn't know he had a daughter. There are so many things like that.

> *Because we're in an information age, we live in an age of exaggeration.*
>
> *—Robert Redford*

Like I bought a palazzo in Venice. Now this thing has been in a hundred newspapers. I get calls from Sotheby's saying to me, "We know engineers who can help you with your home." It's been on television. They've done a half-hour show on *Hard Copy* or one of those things about my palazzo. I've never had any intention of owning a palazzo in Venice, nor do I own one, nor could I afford one, nor do I want one. These kinds of things are made up all the time.

John Malkovich

I don't know why people perceive me as being somehow outside of the Hollywood mainstream. I live in Hollywood. I don't have anything against anyone in Hollywood. I've received nothing but the nicest treatment by people in Hollywood. They've always been very fair to me. I've been able to make a great living from Hollywood, often doing things that I really wanted to do.

Michelle Pfeiffer

About every six months, or at least once a year, the English papers print that I'm moving to England. This has been going on for years. My dogs are in quarantine, the whole thing. I never ever even contemplated moving there. I like England, but no, no, NO!

Patricia Arquette

It's like being eternally in high school. There's always going to be some asshole making up lies about you or talking about you. It's like this public domain of gossip, but you never get out of high school. I try to teach my child these simple things, like don't talk about people behind their backs, don't judge people by the way that they look, and then I have all these grownups doing it. I don't know what to say anymore. It's like grownups should grow up, but usually they don't.

Charlie Sheen

Some of it is amusing. The blatant lies are annoying. Those can get to you a little bit. When you know you were somewhere with certain people and it's reported that you were elsewhere with somebody. If it's nothing damaging then you just laugh and walk away. If it is potentially damaging then they get a call from [attorney] Jake Bloom.

Wayne Newton

I can tell you that the accusations that were made of me will last me forever. Those will never be gone. The only vindication that one can get with that kind of trash is truly the courts and it took me seven years just to get them into court!

Johnny Carson represented at that time 20% of NBC's net gross. They were trying to re-sign him. The Aladdin was a deal [to purchase the hotel and casino in Las Vegas] that he wanted and in fact had. Because of

In 1976, a gossip item in the National Enquirer got the magazine in more trouble than the person they were writing about. When the subject, comedian/actress Carol Burnett objected to being described as rude, raucous, and possibly drunk at a Washington, D.C. restaurant, she sued for libel. Even though the magazine published a retraction a month later, admitting that the incident did not occur and expressing sorrow "for any embarrassment our report may have caused Miss Burnett," she still won her lawsuit. The judge found the retraction half-hearted and Burnett won a jury verdict of $1.6 million. The award was later reduced to $200,000, but Burnett remains a hero to famous tabloid press victims.

negotiations that he had ongoing at the time the people who owned the Aladdin declined to sell it to him and mine was a backup deal. They decided to accept my offer. We believe that NBC felt that if they could stop my licensing by virtue of tying me in with all this nonsense, then the deal would then fall back to Johnny Carson, which it would've. So they absolutely put a jacket on me, pure and simple.

NBC knew that the guy that they turned out to try and tie me into, they knew why I had called him. That was because of death threats to my daughter, after I had gone to the police and after I had gone to the FBI. I had simply called this guy because I knew he'd been in prison, he told me, because the threats were coming from the L.A. area. So I called him to see if he could find out who it was who was doing it, so I could turn him over to the cops. That's when they put that whole scenario together, where this guy had become a hidden partner in my acquisition of the Aladdin.

Richard Dreyfuss

I want to correct this. I only went down to the O.J. Simpson trial because I got a chance to go down to the O.J. Simpson trial. Wouldn't you go?

Ringo Starr

(On rumors that Bernard Purdie was the drummer on the Beatles records)

That's the biggest bullshit I've ever heard. Every couple of years Bernard comes out with, "I did it all." He's not in one photo, I might add. It's just crap. I hate to use words like that, but it's crap. Max Weinberg has offered him $250,000 if he can prove any of it.

Rosie O'Donnell

When I was in Grease, *there was a fistfight in the audience.* These four idiots from Queens decided to punch these two elderly couples in front of them, in the head, because they asked them to be quiet. The rest of the play they taunted these elderly people, "Are we too loud now?" I could hear them because I'm a comic. I'm used to listening to the audience.

So I am now livid by the end of the show. I bring up the little kid, we give him the t-shirt, we do the bow. I go, "You four people are pieces of shit. You're scum—and you should never walk into a theater again. Who do you think you are to punch somebody in the head? If it was up to me I would've thrown your sorry asses out into the street." I was livid.

The audience cheers.

Three days later, "Rosie O'Donnell's not only yelling at the producers, now she's yelling at the audience." This is what I'm reading in the paper.

Cybill Shepherd

The one false rumor I'd like to correct is that I'm difficult to work with, because I'm not. I have that reputation because if you stand up for your rights you're considered a bitch. Bette Davis said it all in this area and I love her two quotes on it. "If a man stands up for his rights, he's admired. If a woman stands up for her rights, she's a bitch." Also she said once, "If you've been in the business more than two years and you're not considered difficult you're probably not very talented."

Rosie O'Donnell
Ron Davis/Shooting Star

Debra Winger

I perpetrate reports that I'm hard to work with. I'm very proud of those. I work on them. I cultivate them. I don't mind any of that. It makes my life a lot easier. I have enough Christmas cards. It's really okay if I don't get any more. I don't make films to make friends. Relationships are great, but I'm not looking for everyone to like me. If you're an actor and you can only be sympathetic, you're going to have a very short career.

It happens to a lot of actors at a certain age. They become afraid to be disliked. They want so much to be loved. Maybe that's the reason that a lot of actors get into acting in the beginning. They are seeking approval and love. That can be a terrible trap. Maybe sometimes

I've gone too far in the other direction. Some of the things that helped me get free from whatever I was set up to be I no longer need. I think I'm not as tough as I used to be.

David Caruso

People say I'm difficult because it sells papers. There's an expression: "If you're foolish enough to hand somebody a stick they're going to hit you with it." The phrase that I say is: "Controversy is the new cocaine."

Arnold Schwarzenegger

The biggest misconception about me is that people think I'm a control freak. They think that in order to get things right for me I want to be involved in every little thing and tell people exactly the way things have to be done and that I have to have total control over it. The fact of the matter is I'm the most casual and the most loose person about all of those things, because for me most of it is improvisation. I don't make up a very tough schedule for myself. I improvise a lot. That's the biggest complaint my wife always has, "I never know what you want to do the next day. All of a sudden you say, 'Let's go to Hawaii.'"

I think people always think that way because it maybe sounds that way when they hear the German accent. But I'm like a puppy that's out there.

Dustin Hoffman

People say I'm a perfectionist. For the life of me I don't know what the word means. It's immediately pejorative. It's like you're going to be operated on and the doctor comes into your room and says, "Hi, I'm your surgeon and here's your anesthesiologist. I just want you to know that we're nice guys and we're not perfectionists."

Sean Young

I don't walk around thinking of myself as somebody who is difficult or somebody who is dangerous or somebody who is crazy. I don't perceive myself that way. That perception is floating around in some place that has almost no connection to me, except when other people give it energy, and that's about them.

William Shatner

(After being criticized in books by George "Sulu" Takei and Nichelle "Uhura" Nichols)

There had never been a harsh word between us. I thought George was terrific. I think he's terrific. And then I hear him going off about things. So I think either he's taken leave of his senses or he's selling a book. And as for Nichelle, last year I invited her to my house for Thanksgiving and she came with a friend of hers. We were kissing, holding hands, and being loving as two old friends. I don't know what's the matter with her. It seems very strange.

It's one thing to get on the phone and one friend says, "You said this," and you're privately on the line. But when they get on the national show and start talking about it, it's a little embarrassing.

John Landis

I never said that I would never work with Eddie Murphy again. Actually, Eddie said that. Then I got a call from Joel Silver, who ended up not making the movie, who said, "Would you do *Beverly Hills Cop III*?"

I said, "Hello?"

He said, "No, Eddie asked about you."

I flew to New Jersey and met with Eddie. He was serious, we made the movie, and actually had a very good time.

I have to tell you, when I made *Coming to America*—now Eddie may disagree with me about this—but I don't think he was a very happy guy. When I made *Trading Places*, he was just such a bundle of joy and energy and talent. It was just wonderful to be with him. Then seven years later he was not a happy guy. It's probably his family, but he's happier now, and it makes a big difference. He's got beautiful children.

Antonio Sabato, Jr.

I got filmed going out of a restaurant by *Hard Copy*. They said, "Here Antonio is getting into this car with his new girlfriend." It was my sister! I went out with my sister to dinner!

Rosie O'Donnell

When you're the most famous woman in the world, people are going to write stuff about you. When I first met Madonna, we were in Chicago shooting *A League of Their Own.* We went out to dinner at this place called Topo Gigio. She and I and that's it. We had dinner, we had pasta, we had tiramisu. We got home at midnight. I'm watching the news the next morning, in Chicago.

"Madonna flew to New York last night and had dinner with Donald Trump."

This was my first experience with the press announcing something that simply was not. When you read something about Madonna you have to realize her kind of fame comes along once a generation. She's as famous as Elvis Presley. Elvis, Michael Jackson, Madonna. You don't get much bigger than that. And who she is in real life has nothing to do with this image she has created, upon which society seems to vent all of its frustrations on.

Not to say that she's innocent.

Charlie Sheen

Just a couple of days ago on *Hard Copy* they said that I had a nice birthday party and my parents and everybody was there, a good family night, a sober night, they said. "But the real party took place the next day, when Charlie Sheen and all his buddies had a roomful of strippers and porn stars and there were adult films on all the monitors in every room of the house." I'm thinking, "No, this is absolute madness. I was at my house watching football with my friends! I've got twenty witnesses."

Liam Neeson

There was a house for sale in the town I grew up in, a town of about two thousand people in Ireland. It was always regarded as "the big house." It was up on this cliff. I vaguely remember my mother saying to me, "God, Liam, if you have the money you should buy this house. It's going cheap and it commands this view of the Irish sea. You can see Scotland in the distance." I said, "Yeah, I'll think about it."

So my mom obviously said to somebody that she told me about the house. The next thing was not only had I bought this house, but I was living in it—and Robert De Niro and various stars were coming in and we were having barbecues out in the back. This was held up by the milkman in the town who said, "Robert De Niro came to the door and picked up the two milk bottles." And he swears by it.

Mark Wahlberg

There were a couple of cool rumors about me—that I still tell my friends are true, of course. I think I was going out with Cindy Crawford, while she was married to Richard Gere. And I got in trouble for telling my friends that, because one of my friends is a priest.

Warren Beatty

Recently a lot of positive things have been invented about me. They're amazing, just amazing. I landed a plane. I invented a birthing tank. I rescued an old lady from a burning house.

Madeleine Stowe

(She's married to actor Brian Benben)

I heard the other day that I was living with somebody else. My girlfriend called me and said she was going to find out who that is. Interesting, since I'm pregnant. That would be quite a trick.

Juliette Lewis

You hear things from other people. "I saw Juliette at dinner the other night. She was talking to so-and-so. They seemed to be having a good time." So you have to make sure that between you and the person you're with there's major communication. If you're not really secure that stuff definitely gets in the way.

Angie Everhart

(Sylvester Stallone's ex-girlfriend)

Poor Julia Roberts was in New York and she dances with some guy and all of a sudden she's having an affair. What's so nice about that? There's nothing nice about that. That's the price that comes with fame. People are going to pry into your business. You lose a little bit of your freedom to be just like everyone else.

> *I never slept with Snow White.*
> —*Rob Lowe*

Julia Ormond

I find it very hard when I do go out with friends—and I have a lot of male friends and I enjoy male and female company—when you do go out, it's in the paper and you're romantically linked with them. I wish I did have this wonderful, full, romantic sex life, but I don't. That's hard too. It's not fair. I didn't get to do it.

Winona Ryder

Nothing that's ever been printed about me and my boyfriend has ever been true. I mean ever. Nobody knows anything. I made the mistake once of talking about my personal life, sharing it, because being in love was something I was excited about. My boyfriend did the same. That was like giving everybody permission to constantly attack us and constantly write about us. They just don't want it to be normal.

Julia Ormond

(After being asked if she was romantically involved with Harrison Ford)

I'm trying so hard to not freak about it. I understand the impulse to ask. It's such a known thing about the acting profession. A friend of mine sent me an article saying that we all behave like rabbits. It's not necessarily true.

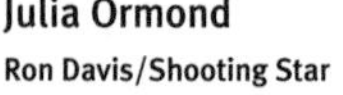

Julia Ormond
Ron Davis/Shooting Star

Robin Williams

(On rumors about the end of his first marriage)

It had nothing to do with the reality. And at the time I couldn't talk about it because when you're in the middle of a divorce a child is basically in a semi-hostage situation. You've got a kid who goes back and forth from house to house and you're trying to make it as pleasant a transition for him as possible, so you don't want to talk about certain things. Yet, when they pick on something that isn't true, implying that [his current wife Marsha] broke up our household, no, I'd been separated from my wife for a year. She wasn't even working for me at the time—and even when she was taking care of Zachary—I was married to my wife and she had a boyfriend. There was a whole other thing there. She came back to work, basically to be near Zachary, and I needed someone to work with me. We became involved after I'd been separated from my wife for a year. So it was a total fucked up chronology. And then there was a letter from the National Nanny Association. I wanted to write back, "Hey lady, wise the fuck up."

Richard Gere

You learn after a while there's really no point in my being upset here because I can have no effect on it.

Beset by persistent rumors of their homosexuality, married couple Cindy Crawford and Richard Gere took out a full page ad in April, 1994 in the London Times, at a reported cost of $30,000. It read: "We are heterosexual and monogamous, and take our commitment to each other very seriously." By July, the couple had separated.

Jason Patric

I was besieged by some of that stuff. There's a difference between truth and facts. I'd go nuts when all the facts were wrong, that you were somewhere and this happened and you said this. I wanted to rectify and challenge all those things. But now I've gotten to a place where I'll only fight for something that has to really do with the truth, not the facts that people put out there.

Linda Gray

When I was playing that alcoholic part as Sue Ellen on *Dallas*, people thought that's who I was. Then it got into the press that I was an alcoholic. Then it was picked up and I had to sue the London press. It got messy. I thought, "Should I even bother? Should I let it go?" But it was affecting my work. People weren't hiring me for things because they thought I would be irresponsible on the set and things like that. That was damaging to me as a human being. If they only knew the work I had done with my mother, who was an alcoholic. I really took a huge stand with my mother. We saw her through it, and all of a sudden that was reversed onto me because I did a good job playing an alcoholic. That was painful for me.

Charlene Tilton

One time they printed a story on Larry Hagman, a cover story naturally, about how he was always drinking and holding up production on the *Dallas* set. Every time J.R. took a shot of booze on the show it was always real. Well, obviously, none of that's true. What studio is going to put up with that? They ended up printing a retraction on the back page and an inch big, of course. Then I was out of the country and I saw this same story in a British newspaper. That's when it's really destructive. What if a British producer saw it and decided not to work with Larry because he thinks he has a drinking problem?

Kirstie Alley

Especially in regards to children and relationships, 99.9% of the stuff that's written about me is untrue. I've read that Parker [Stevenson] and I were getting a divorce at least six times a year for twelve years. I've read everything about our relationship that somebody could possibly say and there's never, ever been one iota of truth to anything that's been written —good or bad—about our relationship.

The dumbest part of it has been that I've said to my family about a million times, "Do not believe what you read, because it isn't true." I get a call at least once a month. "Do you really have cancer?"

"No."

"Are you really getting a divorce?"

"What have I told you a million times?"

"Did you buy a train?"

"NO!"

The dumbest thing I heard about myself was that I had bought a train and that I had shipped in yearly a thousand pounds of chocolate from Switzerland.

I've been sick and dying many times. The saddest part is my dad. He'll be playing golf and somebody will come up to him and say, "I hear your daughter's dying of cancer."

"Where'd you hear that?"

"*The Enquirer.*"

"Oh, I'll call and check."

I'm sure I'm going to tell the *Enquirer* before I tell my dad.

Mary Steenburgen

In spite of everyone's attempts to invade [her wedding to Ted Danson], they weren't able to. So they had to invent all kinds of other stories about why I didn't invite Carly Simon. The answer was simply that we didn't know her.

Ray Liotta

I've heard stories about people that I'm going out with—who I never even met! People make things up. I just don't understand the need for that. Watch a soap opera if you want to get off your life.

Matt Dillon

(On rumors that he sent three hundred roses to a Swedish model)

That's just a total lie. I don't even know who that person is. There's not one ounce of truth in that. I don't know who the person is and I never sent flowers to that person. Sometimes rumors like that can get you angry. What am I going to do? Somebody just makes up a blatant lie and puts it in the press.

Will Smith

The Enquirer *printed that I slept* with Karyn Parsons on my wedding night. I can laugh it off, but my newlywed wife didn't need to see that.

Christian Slater

Courteney Cox is a particularly wonderful girl, but we're just friends.

Antonio Sabato, Jr.

I hear rumors that I'm gay. I have nothing against gays. I'm not, but I'm not going to say, "I'm not." If they talk about it, fine. I mean, forget it. Might as well shoot myself in the head. There's just no way to get away from that. It's crazy.

Marlee Matlin

According to the Enquirer *I'm a lesbian.* I read it one day and my publicist and my business partner said, "So? Is there something you want to tell us?" I thought, "Oh yeah, I forgot that I'm a lesbian." No. It really upset me, because I had never been written about in that fashion. It was completely false and I thought, "Why do I have to defend myself in this fashion?"

My lawyers got into it, demanding a retraction, and the paper said, "No, sorry, it's true." We called them and said, "Seriously, honestly, it's not true."

And they said, "We have three witnesses who confirm that you were there. They took lie detector tests."

I feel sorry for these people.

Izabella Scorupco

(The latest Bond girl in Goldeneye*)*

I once read that I'm a lesbian. I'm not much for new relationships and I really have to find the perfect guy to fall in love. I didn't have a relationship for a while, so of course they started to write that I was a lesbian.

Dennis Hopper

All the people that do James Dean biographies seem to be homosexual. They all seem to be saying that he was a homosexual. Dean was not a homosexual. If he'd have been a homosexual he'd have been practicing in the streets. He wouldn't have been in the closet. He had a lot of friends who were homosexual, but all of us in this business do. The guy who was at UCLA with him and was his first biographer was gay. It's unfortunate that they've taken that tack with him, because that's not the guy I knew. The guy I knew tried to marry Anna Maria Alberghetti and then was in love with Ursula Andress.

I think Leonardo DiCaprio is the only young actor who could possibly play James Dean.

Ian McKellen

My career took a huge boost when I came out [as a gay man]. It was not because people's attitudes about me changed. I think it remained exactly as it was, with the exception of the thousands of people who wrote to thank me. But the boost I think came from my own self-confidence, the most necessary quality that an actor needs. I at last wasn't frightened to speak the truth to anybody in the world about that side of my nature. Not my life. I don't talk about my personal relationships. That's not the point. That is private. But the fact that I am gay, I'm very happy for it to be public knowledge and I don't deny it.

Woody Allen

Before anything broke in the newspapers with Mia [Farrow] and myself, every time I made a film people found connections between my real life and the film, which were very often totally fabricated and untrue.

Sometimes there might have been an insight, but most of them were untrue. When things happened in tabloids after that, it became an industry. People write anything they want about me, but it just isn't true.

It's not upsetting for me because the truth of the matter is I never read any of that. It has no substantive value at all. It's like if you've ever gone on vacation and you don't get your television and your newspaper for three weeks, or the papers strike, and then you find that for three weeks you didn't miss a thing. There's no real correlation between the millions of words written, and the millions of items, and the reality of life.

People ask me how was I so productive when all this nonsense was going on. I just didn't read any of it. I didn't care about it. My lawyers did what they had to do—and I stayed home and wrote and worked. I finished *Husbands and Wives.* I wrote and directed *Manhattan Murder Mystery.* I wrote a play for off-Broadway and I wrote *Bullets Over Broadway* and directed it. I wrote *Don't Drink the Water* and directed it on television. I wrote *Mighty Aphrodite.* I was focused on work and not picking up newspapers every day.

Woody Allen

I obviously don't hate adoption. I'm contemplating adopting a child now. I adopted a daughter and then was going to adopt another child when Mia [Farrow] became pregnant. People write anything they want about me, but of course saying that I hate adoption is not true.

When Mia first wanted to adopt, I was against it because I felt she had seven children already at the time. But once she adopted [daughter] Dylan I fell madly in love with her and thought she was great—and after that said, "If you want to adopt more, now it's okay with me, now that I have the fathering experience, I'm happy for you to adopt more." And then, as fate would have it, she became pregnant with [their son] Satchel. So it's completely untrue that I'm against adoption.

Woody Allen

Now the biggest misconception about me is that I'm sleeping with my daughter. There have been many misconceptions about me over the years, that I'm an intellectual, that I'm a workaholic. I'm not really a workaholic at all. I'm always watching ball games and going to the movies and playing my clarinet and goofing off. And I'm not an intellectual by any stretch of the imagination.

I was filming in Venice and someone stopped Soon-Yi [Previn, his girlfriend and ex-girlfriend Mia Farrow's adopted daughter] in the street and said, "How do you feel when your father gets all this attention?" Then two old ladies were walking past us in Paris and one of them said, "That's Woody Allen filming. He used to go with Mia Farrow and now he's sleeping with his daughter." Now I find that funny. We find that funny. But it's a big misconception that people have.

I think thinking people or more liberal people can understand what went on there and have some evaluation of it. But there are people who still think that Mia and I were married, that we lived together. They refer to her as "your ex-wife." It's an odd thing. I think that people—because they're not really that interested in my life—they'll always have a vague notion of, "Oh yeah, he's the guy who started going out with his daughter after he was married to Mia Farrow." That's a funny misconception about me and I laugh at it, but three years ago it was very harmful to me in my custody proceeding.

Michael Douglas

The sex addiction thing, that's still carrying on. I can't believe it. It just came out of the movie [*Basic Instinct*], which worked real well, and the time. I went off to rehab three years ago, that's for sure, but that's old news. It's like that Jon Lovitz thing, "I got an idea, yeah, that's the ticket." All of a sudden there it is, three years later. I'm looking at it again in a

When actress Mia Farrow discovered nude Polaroids of her adopted daughter Soon-Yi Previn in 1992 on the mantlepiece of her longtime lover, comedian/actor/director Woody Allen, she was furious. As she attempted to gain sole custody of the three children—two adopted and one natural—that they had raised together, the fight turned nasty. Farrow accused Allen of molesting Dylan, the daughter they adopted together.

While the allegations were generally believed to be unfounded, Farrow retained sole custody, depriving Allen of almost all visitation rights. Allen issued this statement to his children after the judgment: "I love you and I miss you, and don't worry, the dark forces will not prevail. Not second-rate police nor publicity hungry prosecutors, not judicial setbacks, not tabloid press nor those who perjure themselves nor all who rush to judgment...."

mainstream magazine. How or why? Just because you're a little lazy and it makes for an interesting spin.

Tony Danza

I was in jail. This was a while ago. I was sitting in the cell and a guy comes to me and says, "Hey Tony, you made the papers." It was a little bar fight and I thought, "Gee, what could it be? A little thing on the bottom?" Well, it was as if it had said, "America Declares War!" The paper said, "Taxi Star Seized in Brawl." And then on the side it says, "Westside Hotel Left in Shambles," as if I went room to room, "Hey, get outta your room, I gotta mess it up!" I couldn't believe it.

Johnny Depp

When I had that visit to the police station in New York City [after busting up his room at the Mark Hotel], I couldn't believe the media turnout. The next morning I saw one of those New York tabloids and I was on the cover—with the potential invasion of Haiti. It was me and that story neck and neck. I was absolutely shocked by that. I don't understand what was so fascinating about it. I can only say that I'm human and I was chasing a huge rat in the hotel room and I just kept swatting at it. I couldn't catch it and it just jumped out the window.

Johnny Depp

I'm all right. I've been accepted at the Day's Inn.

Tim Allen

After all those rumors, it was cathartic to write about my prison experiences. I could have written a whole book about just that.

Leonardo DiCaprio

Supposedly Marky [Wahlberg] and I went out to a club one night and Derrick Coleman was there and I picked a fight with him. We proceeded to get into a fight and then Marky came to my rescue and we all got into a brawl with Derrick Coleman, who is probably seven feet tall and three hundred pounds. Like I'd ever even look at him wrong!

Johnny Depp and Kate Moss Lisa O'Connor/Shooting Star

Sean Connery

This Barbara Walters issue has hung around for so long and it's quite wrong. She did nearly two hours of film and her sole intention was to get me to say, "Yes, it's okay to beat up women." She lifted it out of context, and I had explained to her at great length, but she was set upon getting me to say it's okay to hit a woman. What I had been talking about when this was lifted by her was a television program I had seen about battered husbands. What I had said is, "You can do a worse thing to a woman than give her a slap." I was talking about a relationship where a man can destroy a woman without putting a finger on her, so that she'll take months if she ever recovers from it. Taking away her dignity and damaging the whole persona of the person, that's what I was talking about.

But she lifted that out and said, "You said it's okay to hit a woman." I saw her after and she was terribly embarrassed. The response in this country was so enormous, you can't believe it. I'd be driving along and women would give me the finger!

Johnny Depp

One of the things that's really bothered me is that a lot of those tabloid magazines write fiction that my teenage niece and nephew read. Unfortunately, people believe the fiction that they read. It's been very upsetting to me because people have thought everything from the idea that I'm a mental case to the idea that I'm a drug addict or an alcoholic or a brawler or a brooding, angry, rebellious character. It's all these things that create this image. It's this image that I'm not.

Sarah Jessica Parker

My life, in so many ways, is open for discussion. It's no longer flattering or a compliment to be written about, especially untruthfully, in a paper. I really feel an invasion. I really do. In fact, I called a paper once and told them. I'm sure this guy had never heard from anybody he'd written about, but I said, "What you're printing is untrue. Stop it please, because it hurts. And it hurts my family."

My mom calls me and says, "My friend read to me blah, blah, blah."

I say, "Of course it's not true, Mommy. Don't believe it." But, you know, it's there and it's in print. It's hurtful.

Gary Oldman

I read in US *magazine* that I'm a lunatic. My mother reads that.

I think it upsets your family when they read that I'm an East End dropout. I don't come from the East End and I have B.A. honors degree in theater history.

John Goodman

I don't like a lot of the tabloid crap I've been reading lately. They've never written anything true about me anyway. One time they had a headline, "My Wonderful Wacky Wedding, by John Goodman." I haven't used wacky in a sentence since I was three years old, but they said I wrote the article. They've been trying to turn me into Hugh Hefner or something out of the Rat Pack and it bugs the hell out of my wife. Now it's starting to bug me, but there's not really a damn thing I can do about it. So I don't go out.

Pauly Shore

From my image, everybody thinks that I smoke pot and I drink beer and I screw all these girls and stuff. People don't know that I sit at home at night and read and drink herbal tea. It's like Superman taking off his glasses and turning into Clark Kent.

I want people to start knowing that I'm smart. I've always been smart. That's gotten me here. I want people to know that I write stuff, I cast stuff, I produce it. I'm smart.

Lukas Haas

I hate it when columnists degrade kids by writing "gonna" instead of "going to." An adult might have said "gonna," but they're going to write "going to." There are all sorts of words and phrases like that. That completely annoys me.

Melanie Griffith

(On reports that she was surprised to learn that six million people were murdered in the Nazi Holocaust)

When that happened I didn't know that it was six million people. Shoot me, sue me, I honestly didn't! I made a huge mistake, but I didn't know. I thought it was more like a million people. I don't know why I didn't know. Maybe I missed school that day. Maybe it's a big mistake, but I really got crucified for it. I'm not stupid. At the time it was just a realization that, "Oh my God, so many people." That's how I said it—and it was totally taken in a mean way.

Dana Carvey

People assume you're rich because you're in a hit movie. You must understand, it's not like you automatically have a little cash drawer at your house. "Gee, what did it do in Mongolia?"

Ozzy Osbourne

(The real story of why he bit off a live bird's head?)

It wasn't intentional. I'd been going to record company meetings and conventions for so many years, and I don't know them and they don't know me. They've heard of me through my involvement in the record business, but they don't know what I am about, what I am setting my body up to do. They put your record on to make it sound like they've been playing your record. So I thought, "I'll make this big impression this time with these two doves." So I threw one up and bit the other one's head off. CBS in Los Angeles from that point on called that room "the dove room." Which is a kind of a landmark, if you like. My statue.

Dustin Hoffman

Jack Nicholson did not take any more drugs than anybody else during that era of drug taking, yet he was the designated hitter. He took the hit for taking drugs. I mean, everyone was taking drugs in those days. Warren Beatty did not bed down any more—probably less—women than most of the stars at that time, and yet Warren Beatty had that distinction. Warren, for those people that know him, is probably as romantic a person as could ever be. He would follow an actress around for months. It became a project while everything else stopped in his life. Suddenly, he met her, found her, had a relationship with her, and lived with her. His reputation was distorted. That's the truth of it. I understand how it happens. If you're going to do an interview, what are you going to base your interview on? You're going to read the stuff that's been written before and what's been written before is written by people who have read the stuff that's been written before.

Dustin Hoffman
Yoram Kahana/Shooting Star

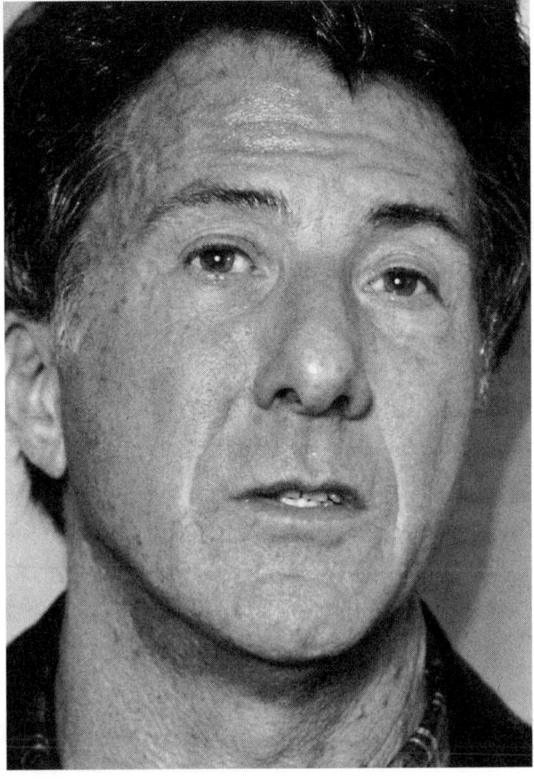

Richard Dreyfuss

The cocaine use that Julia Phillips wrote about in her book [*You'll Never Eat Lunch in This Town Again*] never happened. Never happened. But, let me tell you a quick story.

There's a story about a scholar, an academic, who is outraged at the idea that people could possibly believe that Homer wrote *The Iliad* and *The Odyssey.* This infuriates him, that people could possibly believe this. So he spends his entire career pursuing this and at the end of his career he in fact proves that Homer could not have written *The Iliad* and *The Odyssey.* They were written by another blind poet of the same name. Because as I was reading excerpts from Julia Phillips's book I thought to myself, "This never happened, but what REALLY happened is so much worse, that who cares."

Geraldine Chaplin

We never knew him [her dad, Charlie Chaplin] with his other wives, obviously, because we're all from the last one. When we did talk about it, the kids, "How many wives did Daddy have?," we could never quite figure out how many he'd had. This was before he'd written his autobiography and we didn't dare ask anyone in the family. We'd be slaughtered. But it was certainly something of fascination. And then when we heard that they were maybe very young girls, that was even more fascinating. You find the dark side of someone you love, especially a parent, and you're certainly quite proud of it.

Liza Minnelli

There will never be a book or a movie that will do justice to my mother [Judy Garland], because nobody knows the whole story. I don't. We all just know sections.

Nobody really wants to know how much fun she had, or how funny she was. She once said to me, "They don't care about that stuff. They like the drama." She said, "Let 'em take the drama."

Shirley MacLaine

Carrie [Fisher] got me at a Marvin Davis New Year's Eve party. I suppose that provides the environment to talk about anything. She said, "We're doing this picture [*Postcards from the Edge*] and I think you'd be very good to play the mother."

I called Debbie [Reynolds, Carrie Fisher's mother] the next day. I said, "What's happening here?"

"Oh dear," she said. "We've known each other for thirty years. I think you'd be wonderful playing the part, because you're funny. If you weren't funny, I would say no."

See, Debbie and I go back a long, long way. I was originally going to do *The Unsinkable Molly Brown*. She called me up and we had a discussion about it. "That part is so good, dear. You're going to get parts for the rest of your life. Do you think maybe I could do it?"

I said, "Debbie, if you really want to do this, great. I'm having some trouble with Hal Wallis and Metro anyway. You really want it?"

She said, "Yes."

I said, "You got it." So I think of this all as a wonderful karmic circle going here.

Chevy Chase

There was a book that came out that made it look like *Saturday Night Live* was a den of iniquity filled with drugs and fights and that it was an unhappy experience. It was a book that, literally Gilda [Radner] and I both cried when we read. It was so inaccurate and so hurtful. It was one of the most fun years of all of our lives. I will never forget that first year. It was that kind of spiteful journalism. There's a lot of bad will out there. I don't know what the point of it is. I guess it sells books. Those guys have actually gone out on talk shows as if they knew. They don't know nothin'. They talked to two or three people probably who were either fired or were no longer working there and told them stuff that wasn't true. It was just awful.

The only problem I ever had was with Billy [Murray] once one night, and that was over in a jiffy.

Sean Connery

They keep writing biographies—and I've never associated with any of them. People write things that they pick up from other biographies that were wrong in the first place. The facts are almost written in cement now, so they become a point of reference—and it's complete nonsense to the point where I had to take a statement to the press saying that I have nothing to do with them.

I don't get a penny out of it. I don't particularly want that kind of publicity, apart from the fact it's not true. So one's had to take a stand. Initially I was involved through the lawyers, because reams of it were wrong. They say to you, "I'll give you a proof and you can proof it." Then you're involved in writing it for them!

Hundreds of my friends get contacted and then they're phoning me. The work it gives my home is unbelievable.

Danny DeVito

I came out okay in Marilu Henner's book. She called me "sexy" and stuff like that. It's very good for my marriage that she didn't tell all the truth. It could be very difficult, because Rhea [Perlman] and I were together all during the *Taxi* experience. So it's good that she didn't tell all about the times that we fucked in the dressing room and stuff like that.

I'm only kidding, for crying out loud! Look at the look on his face! "Did I hear that?"

Shirley MacLaine

I read scandal magazines. I rarely pay for them, but I want to know what's happening. I'm rarely in them. I thought I was going to be the queen of the tabloids with this metaphysics, but it didn't happen. I'm intrigued as to why I'm not. I really tried to figure that out. I think I made it too legitimate. There wasn't enough that's sensational about it. And then my life is scandal free—except that I am a scandal. My love affairs are usually on the up and up. I don't care who knows what I'm doing anyway. My life is an open book, so what's the point?

Woody Allen

That stuff is all peripheral. That stuff, whether it's positive or negative, has no real substance. People that are flattering you or saying great things about you, or saying negative things about you, that's not the real thing. That's all press and talk. It doesn't mean anything either way. If you just work, it really works.

Luke Perry

(On rumors about Shannen Doherty and the cast of Beverly Hills 90210*)*

I didn't storm in there and we didn't have a party afterwards. It doesn't go down like that.

Shannen Doherty

Once people meet me they're very shocked and pleased to see that I'm not the absolute terror that I'm supposed to be. Otherwise I would be ripping your head off right now, wouldn't I?

I deny nothing.
—Elliott Gould

Isolation/ Alienation/ Sex

Hassled by fans and abused by the media, it's no wonder that stars often retreat into their own little worlds, keeping contact with outsiders to a minimum. Isolation inevitably leads to alienation. But how does this affect the artist? How can you reflect the realities of the audience when you've lost touch with their lives? When a schism develops between you and your image, it's even hard to stay in touch with yourself. For some people it's virtually impossible.

Sally Field

It's psychologically complicated. I know that psychologically you're deprived from getting human reaction. A bottom line basic human reaction is denied you and you are cut off from your fellow man. You have to work at it, but you're never really sure that it's there.

That's how people tell who they are. That's what human behavior is. I do something, you react, I perceive how you react to me, and then I form my image as to who I am. "Oh, I must be funny." "Oh, I must be terrible." And then your own dementia comes in and twists it and turns it and pokes it and pulls it down where you can handle it. You put your own twist on it, from who you are in your own personality and all your process. But celebrities are denied that, denied getting a real reaction. So then they have to desperately scramble around within themselves for contact, just for contact that's on a bottom level—you contact me, I'm a person, you're a person—that isn't about something else. It's a struggle. You're so isolated from having basic human needs answered.

> *A lot of doors have been closed to me because of fame and celebrity, but an equal amount of doors opened. If you ask about trading things for anonymity, if I would go back, the answer is an absolute yes.*
>
> *—Kevin Costner*

Natalie Portman

When my first movie came out [*The Professional*], people were excited that they knew someone who was in movies. They asked a lot of questions, but I told them that I really didn't want to talk about it, because the second you start talking about it, it puts you on a pedestal. That's really an uncomfortable place to be among friends.

Priscilla Presley

Before the Naked Gun *movies* I was totally unapproachable. No one would walk up to me. I felt like I had some sort of a disease.

Mary Steenburgen

I've been a friend of Bill and Hillary Clinton for many, many years. That has increased in terms of the importance of our friendship to both of us with this time, this very amazing happenstance of a friend becoming President. I think that it means a lot to them to be close to their friends who loved them before any of this happened. They know that my friendship with them is not about power, or any of those things. That's very meaningful to them.

Kirk Douglas

I don't think of myself as a "legend." I'm doing my thing. I kind of get a kick out of it. It took me a long time on the set of my last movie to say, "Would you mind calling me Kirk? You make me feel like one of those old guys."

Mary Tyler Moore

The only thing that probably keeps us from becoming chatty with each other is strangers' inability to treat me like one of their own, their need to talk about what Ted Knight was really like, and how does it feel to be asked for your autograph. Were it not for the self-imposed separateness that fans bring to a conversation there's no reason why we can't be comfortable with each other.

Julie Walters

The star treatment? I love all that. As soon as I got into the hotel I'd think, "Now what have they got?" The luggage is doubled.

Sophia Loren

I feel very nervous when they treat me like a star, because I like to be with other people. I like to mingle with them. But when I feel that they treat me like somebody else, very exceptional, I suffer very much. I really do.

Yoko Ono

My son Sean really wanted to go and shake hands with Michael Jackson at an opening. That was like a dream come true for any eight-year-old. Then some of the assistants suggested, "Well, shall we just call Michael Jackson's office and find out if Sean could meet him in private?"

Sean overheard that and said, "What? We're calling? No, no. We can't do that. That's rude." He doesn't want any special treatment. Of course, I would have been embarrassed to do that, too. So then he went through the normal route, just going up the stairs. And I didn't have the—I don't know—courage, is it? What you need to go there, big crowd and everything. So I asked Sean if he could go alone.

He said, "Fine." And that's how it happened.

Elton John

You have to live with it if you create the monster. We didn't set out to create the monster. The monster happened by accident. I flaunted it and enjoyed it. If you set yourself up in that respect then you must deal with it. You either deal with it or run away from it because it messes you up. And you don't go out at all. You get scared of your own publicity.

> *If I had known about the privacy thing, I might have made a different choice.*
>
> *—Richard Dreyfuss*

Shelley Long

I had to be ready to be seen at a time when I don't look my best, because I can't always look my best. That's hard for me because I also feel that I owe the public a certain positive image.

Christian Slater

I can relate to the guy who had a history and was hiding out, taking a break from everything and starting over. That's a romantic concept to me, abandoning a lot of insanity and starting over. Yeah, absolutely.

Madonna

Sometimes I feel isolated. I can walk around, but it's a pain in the ass. When I want to go out with a friend it's a question of "Do you want to deal with the flashbulbs going off in your face, too?"

Michael Richards

I've actually tinted the windows of my car. I start thinking I need gates. I need security. It makes it a little difficult riding my bike down the street. I have to wear a cap and sunglasses.

Mel Gibson

(After directing and starring as the horribly disfigured Man Without a Face*)*

I can identify with walking down the street, or going anywhere, and having people sort of crane their necks and do double takes as if I had a skunk sitting on my head, or had another head or, indeed, had a disfigurement. I know what it's like to receive abnormal attention in a public place. And I know what it's like to get the hell away from it, too, and shut myself up.

Sandra Bullock

There are people living on my street, I've lived there for two years, I've never seen them once. It's very easy, especially for someone who'd prefer to live that type of lifestyle and her job allows her to do that.

My house is my sanctuary. It's got everything that I ever possibly could need. If I never had to leave it, that would be great.

Elton John

You have to make sure you don't cut yourself off from the public, because it's the public who put you there in the first place. And there's no point in hiding the fact that you've had a hair transplant, or whatever. I never tried to hide facts from my fans. I always have this line about me, "Everybody knows everything about me, but knows nothing," which is true. I like it that way, but I certainly don't want to not go out. I can handle that side very well. I never used to be able to because I was very shy, but I'm much more confident now. If you don't handle it, then you run away from it. I enjoy the recognition as well, so that helps. Some people don't and they can still handle it by shutting themselves away, but that's not me. I'm not a recluse and I never will be.

Luke Perry

It dawned on me that people would notice when I went somewhere, but you can't let that hold you back. I'm not going to become a prisoner of what I think is a great situation, the fact that I've been afforded the opportunity to work as an actor. I'm not going to turn around and let that control me. And you know what? I have a lot of friends who are famous now, who were famous at one time, or who will certainly be famous in the future. Actors here in Hollywood, we know who's into being famous and who's into getting work. I would much rather continue to be a working actor than a famous one. The fame is a by-product of the work.

Carole King

I needed to get away. And when I did, being the type of person who does not do things halfway if there's an available extreme, I threw aside the city, vowing never to return. I went off into the wilderness. I lived isolated in a little tiny cabin, thirty miles from the nearest town for about three years. I taught my kids at home—and when they went back into the California school system they were ahead of their grade.

Sarah Jessica Parker

As I've become more well known, I've become more circumspect—and more philosophical. And maybe more monosyllabic regarding certain things. It's the new me.

I think there's a line, when you have been giving and open, and when it's abused you start becoming wary. And that's what I feel I don't owe. If I do an interview I'm agreeing to do an interview, but I just think I've become more wary.

Jack McDowell

(Baseball player and recording artist)

You get a different perception of yourself when people are throwing it back at you all the time. Then you become protective and then this weird dynamic happens that's really strange to deal with.

Mary Stuart Masterson

You can get swallowed up by all the things that are expected of you or the perspective that you lose on yourself, your own feelings, your own goals, your own life, really. It becomes larger and outside of yourself, like this big thing that has to be maintained, like an infrastructure. It's something that you have to work hard at, not losing your sense of self.

Robert Blake

I invented a Robert Blake character on *The Tonight Show,* which I did for twenty years, that America loved and Johnny [Carson] loved. It was 90% bullshit, but I'm not a stand-up character, I'm not a singer, so I had to do something. I was outrageous. It's easy for me to be outrageous. But my own self-destructive madness made me go sit there next to Carson.

It was a lot like that movie, *Network.* When I did finally start cracking up from working too hard for too long, they loved it. They said, "Hey man, the nuttier he gets the better. Maybe he'll cut his own throat on the show." They shouldn't have done that. Somebody should have come up to me and said, "Yeah Robert, we love you, but do you realize how badly you're hurting yourself now?" But they didn't. The more outrageous I got, the more they had me on. Johnny used to just goad me on.

You find out what people are thinking by actually wading among them. You can't just do it by sitting at home with a satellite dish going, "Hmm, that might work."

—Robin Williams

Robert Blake

It breaks my heart today when I see somebody cross the street when they see me walking down the street. It was not only something I did on *The Tonight Show,* but it was something I did a lot in person, too. I put up such a wall of tough guy that people always felt that they had to approach me with a whip and a chair and a piece of raw meat or they were going to get eaten.

Paul Newman

You develop a shield in front of you to protect your privacy and to protect that part of you that isn't public and is not up for examination. And I think that bleeds into your private life and you start putting up walls. It's an unfortunate part of the process. I've been there and I know what it's like.

Laura Linney

Once people see themselves as being "something," they start to close themselves off. They start to not go to the grocery store because they'll be recognized. They start to not talk to the plumber because the plumber knows who they are.

Ellen DeGeneres

You start putting yourself into a situation where you can't go anywhere and you have nothing to draw on anymore. That's what we're here for: to live and experience everything. If you stop experiencing you have nothing to draw on anymore. It's like, "You know, it's funny. My butler the other day said...."—like people are going to relate to that in some way.

Paul Newman Yoram Kahana/Shooting Star

Patricia Arquette

I feel ignorant. I used to have friends who are big stars, like Nicolas Cage or my sister [Rosanna Arquette]. We'd go somewhere and I'd whisper, "Everybody's staring at you." And they'd be like, "What? What are you talking about?" So people do that to me now and my friends say, "Those people are talking about you." It makes them a little awkward and I feel stupid, because I don't really notice.

Chuck Norris

[Sylvester] Stallone and those guys get harassed. [Steven] Seagal carries a gun on his hip.

Fred Williamson

I don't travel with an entourage. I don't need people around me. I don't need bodyguards. I don't need limousines. I don't isolate myself from the public. The image of being a pro football player and a guy noted for violent hits and a guy called "The Hammer" puts me in a unique position. As I was making movies and becoming more popular, the fans would come up to me in a mad dash—but then they'd stop three feet away and say, "Hello Mr. Williamson. Can I have your autograph?" There's no pulling, no tugging, no mobbing, because they don't really know what my reaction is going to be. All I really have to do to make that image work is to be who they think I am. If I don't break the image then they will never break through that image wall.

Larry Drake

People gave me a lot more credit than I quite deserved because I was playing Benny [on *L.A. Law*]. He was enormously lovable and they treated me like I was supposed to be lovable when they met me. I got credit for playing this guy, whereas Corbin Bernsen got extra disdain because he played Arnie Becker.

Peter Tork

I had pathological self value. I really didn't have any sense of it at all. I didn't get why. I thought I had been picked almost at random. I didn't have any sense of myself bringing anything except that character to the Monkees. What I thought they hired me for was that character, and I think to this day that that had a lot to do with it. I didn't recognize how that sprung forth from who I really am. I thought I was faking them out. I thought I was handing them a lie and they were buying the lie—and so how could I value myself?

Any time you compliment somebody and they can't take the compliment, what they're saying to you is, "You don't know what you're talking about." That's the message that anybody with low self-esteem gives back when somebody compliments them. Which is where I was. All that played into this fame thing.

And it plays backwards, too. The reason that I got into the fame game was because I didn't have any sense of value. I thought, "Jeez, if I can get the millions to love me then I'll be all right." I got the millions to love me—and it still wasn't all right. What a surprise. Ha, ha, ha.

Will Smith

Fame makes it impossible to stay in touch with the things that got you there in the first place. That's why it's difficult for me to do the music now. That comes from being submerged in it. That comes from all of your friends listening to rap music for twelve hours a day. In the streets of Philadelphia, that was the music of everyone that I associated with in the course of a day. On the basketball court, that's what you hear. You go in the house, that's what your brothers and sisters are listening to. You go to school, that's what all the kids have in their Walkman. So I was completely submerged in it. Now Bel-Air isn't the rap capital of L.A.

Quentin Tarantino

The biggest problem with the situation I'm in, is you forget to live the life, because events are just pulling you from day to day. The next thing you know, it's been three years and all you've done is gone from one set to the next, and why is my marriage breaking up? You've got to stop the ferris wheel—to me—constantly. You have to stop it every couple of months.

Uma Thurman

You give things up before you get them. You watch them go by like a leaf on a stream. In a way, there's motion and I'm moving in motion. I'm not activating so much.

Alannah Myles

Courtney Love's anger is almost like a leader for other people's anger, a touchstone, if you will. She's necessary in our culture.

Meg Ryan

I see a cultural or societal need for celebrities. I see that there's an idea of projecting an ideal on people who seem to be able to hold the projection. I'm not talking about me. You think of the idea of Robert Redford, the idea of Meryl Streep. They're sort of archetypical in a certain way.

Elliott Gould

I've had some great opportunities and great privileges, but it's important that you understand yourself. And to understand yourself, you have to accept yourself. If you don't accept yourself you can never understand yourself. Perhaps you can understand someone else's image of you.

Jack McDowell

It's amazing. It's a weird, strange, crazy thing. You just absolutely lose your sense of identity. There's this person that everybody thinks they know and they have an impression of and you kind of become that because you're expected to become that. It's a weird dynamic. It's a strange, strange thing.

Edward Furlong

When I've been online I see other people that are my name. So they say they're Edward Furlong. It's really weird. That's strange stuff.

Sammy Davis, Jr.

For a long time I didn't like me. I didn't like what I had made up. I became Dr. Frankenstein and the Monster. I was Jekyll and Hyde. I created both. Nobody told Henry Jekyll to go mess with those drugs and mix up this potion. Nobody told Dr. Frankenstein to go put this Monster together. They did it of their own free will, and they created something that they could no longer control, and subsequently it destroyed them. I was lucky that it didn't destroy me.

Tim Allen

Tim Dick [his real name] created all of this. Sometimes people—including myself—have a tough time figuring who's who. Tim Allen has become such a popular character that no one even cares about Tim Dick. Even Tim Allen. I feel like Mary Shelley. I've created Frankenstein, but I've become Frankenstein. Because Tim Allen has no past. It's only a persona that I've created as a comedian. I created him fifteen years ago. I made a guy on stage who isn't really me, but he's kind of a persona of me, a part of me, an accelerated me. But Tim Dick is actually the guy who created him. He's the brighter of all the men. He's the one who has the responsibility for all this. He's the one who takes the grief for all this. And here I am talking about him like he's not here. Ha, ha, ha, ha. I'm sick! Get me some help!

Tim Allen Bob D'Amico/The Kobal Collection

Clint Eastwood

I look at myself like another person. I always refer to myself as "he" when I'm with the editor in the editing room. I don't think of myself as Clint up there.

Paul Newman

They really think that that's me up there. That isn't me. It's somebody else, somebody some writer concocted and some actor dragged together and some director splashed up there. The director edited all the bad moments out and left the good moments and they think that's real up there. It really isn't. It has nothing to do with me.

Priscilla Presley

It's hard to put myself in perspective as to where the public is coming from with me, because there's been so much out there. I am confused. I don't even know what they're perceiving or what they think.

Richard Dreyfuss

I don't know. What is my image? People often say to me, "Well, you know the way that people look at you." No. How do they look at me? I would like to know what my reputation is. I would like to know how the world looks at me.

Winona Ryder

When people tell you what your feelings are or tell you who you are for ten years, you start to wonder if you're anyone at all. It's hard to have your personality dictated to you by the press and by people who don't really know you.

Ann-Margret

I've done forty films. I see them once, in a screening room, and that's it. I've never seen one of my forty films more than once. I don't know who that person is on screen. I never have known.

Sharon Stone

(On men who are attracted to her for her on-screen image)

They're validating something that I created. If it were a painting and they were standing in front of the painting going, "God, that's fabulous," I'd go, "Yeah, and I did that." That doesn't diminish me.

Madeleine Stowe

I don't like nudity, for the most part. I know that that's inconsistent with a lot of what I've done, but I don't like it.

Elle MacPherson

I don't have a problem with nudity. I never have. I was born naked. I'd like to be buried naked. It's a way of life in Australia.

Laura Dern

I became an actress first. I was never a face first. I was never a physical body first. I think people who were are trying so hard to prove themselves as something else, that it makes them feel really awkward when that keeps coming up. Since I was really thought of as an actress first, the sexuality that people are perceiving is really coming from my characters. I've met people who've seen *Rambling Rose* or *Wild at Heart* and they think I'm the sexiest woman they've ever seen in their life. Other people say, "Oh, you're really cute, but you don't look as good in that movie as you do in the other." Everybody's got a different opinion. But it's a quality as opposed to what I am. If I was a *Playboy* centerfold and I was trying to make it as an actress I'm sure I'd be extremely neurotic about it.

Sean Connery

"The Sexiest Man Alive?" It's very exhausting.

The guy phoned out of the blue from *People* magazine and said, "You've been voted the sexiest man alive." Well, what are you supposed to say? I just thought, "There's very few dead, I'm sure." He didn't see the fun of it.

Bruce Willis

It's no fun to be named "The Sexiest Man Alive." That's kind of a dubious honor. Brad Pitt is going through a time now that I think all actors who become movie stars, as opposed to just actors in films, go through. I think he's handling it very well. It's never pleasant. I don't know any actor who's gone through it that says, "Man, that was just the best period of my life, when people were going nuts about me and screaming and all that."

Paul Newman

It used to piss me off, sure. I mean, one struggles and works at one's craft and then that's the only thing that they have to say about you.

Mel Gibson

Being called "The Sexiest Man Alive?" I didn't think it was funny until they passed the title on to someone else. Then I laughed my head off.

Mark Harmon

"The Sexiest Man Alive?" It's pretty ridiculous stuff. I had so little to do with it happening in the first place. The only thing I agreed to do was an exit story from *St. Elsewhere* and that's what it became. I can't quite imagine taking that seriously, but you'd be surprised how many people do or did.

Have you ever thought about it? What does it mean? Do you remember voting on it? It's not like a poll where you go down and say, "I'm going to vote on this today." As far as I know, it's one person in a room somewhere who says, "Guess what. I'm going to mess up this person's life for a year."

When I first met Mel Gibson that's what he said. He was the guy before me and the first thing that he said was, "You poor fool."

Nick Nolte

Being called "The Sexiest Man in the World" almost cost me the job on *I'll Do Anything.* In the middle of a long casting process [to play a needy, not sexy lead character], *People* magazine decided that I was "The Sexiest Man Alive." So I called [director] Jim Brooks and I said, "Man, don't get *People* magazine. Don't look at it. Don't believe it. It's full of shit. I think Walter Cronkite's the sexiest man alive. Don't get a copy. I'll send you my copy." When I was in his office I drew a black tooth on the picture, put a moustache on the guy and crossed his eyes. He put that up on the wall. Eventually we got past that barrier.

And another thing. This "Sexiest Man Alive" comes off on only one picture, *The Prince of Tides.* You can't say that the guy in *Q&A* is the sexiest man alive, or the bum in *Down and Out in Beverly Hills* is sexy, either.

Rob Lowe

It has nothing to do with me. It's almost like they're talking about who they think I am, not who I really am. They don't know me. They see a picture of me or a movie or they see an interview with me, but they don't really know me. Now if my mother said, "Rob, you're really a hunk," then it might mean something to me. These editors, they don't know me. I take it as a compliment, but I move right on from it.

Robert Redford

I was not someone who grew up thinking of himself as a good-looking person. I was never referred to that way. The best I could hope for was cute. I was a freckle-faced kid with hair that was impossible and no one thought of me as good-looking. No one said that, so I didn't have that in my head. I entered the business to be an actor. Art was what interested me. I didn't know it was going to be in film. So when it happened and that reference came, I was of course flattered. I mean, who wouldn't be? Then it seemed that things got a little distorted and that made me nervous because I thought it might get in the way of the work—and it has sometimes.

Wesley Snipes

I didn't think I was a sex symbol until I got into the movies. Nobody else thought I was. Now, a woman came to me last night and she said, "When are you going to do some more movies where you take off your clothes?" Jean-Claude [Van Damme] and all of them, they want to do that type of stuff. I don't know if I want to put my booty up there on the screen.

Billy Dee Williams

Being a sex symbol has been wonderful for me, but it's also been a curse for me. I'm only allowed to go so far with it. There are a lot of people in this country who don't want to see a black man making love to a lot of women on the screen as a romantic image. It's very discouraging. It's stupid to me and it's always been stupid to me.

Christian Slater

Brad Pitt's got it covered really, so I feel pretty comfortable with that. He's the man on the mantle right now.

Jimmy Smits

When an actor starts thinking about an image, about "sex symbol" or any kind of tag that gets put on, you're in deep shit. Then you're basing career choices on some kind of image that you have to uphold? I don't come from there.

And I know that there is that dynamic through entertainment history, the "Latin lover." I understand what that's about, but I think it's very dangerous to play into that.

Tom Selleck

It's nice to win those "Ten Sexiest Men" things. I try to think about it as work and just be a little flattered, but if you get much past that it's a bad trap. If you buy the polls to begin with, you're in serious trouble emotionally when you don't win them, which is inevitable.

Being called a sex symbol has leant me a lot of perspective about what women talk about, about objectification and how it's belittling to yourself as a person. I find it that way. I sound like a Playboy centerfold now, don't I?

Every now and then it's vaguely neat, or vaguely flattering. And then you feel like such an idiot for being flattered.

—Ethan Hawke

William Baldwin

Many times, whether it be a male or a female actor, the actor is fulfilling a certain void, or a certain desire, or a certain fantasy for the viewer. You hear all these strange stories. I hear women when they see their favorite star, they almost physically get sick. They become so overcome with emotion that they almost faint, or throw up, or scream, or cry. It's strange.

Gary Oldman

(After starring in Bram Stoker's Dracula*)*

Being a sex symbol, yeah. I loved it.

Denzel Washington

People say to me, "Well, as a sex symbol...." and "How do you feel as a sex symbol?" I say, "I don't feel that way." The only time that that's brought up is basically when I do interviews. Nobody I know talks to me that way. I'm not saying you guys are the bad guys. I don't know. Are people telling you that? Is that what you're asked to ask? It's not who I am. I'm an actor who works at what I do. I try to be good at what I do and as a result of that I become what they call a movie star, or what they'll call a sex symbol. A couple of years from now they'll say a has-been. On the comeback. You know. The category changes, but that's not who I am.

Andy Garcia

The actor thing I take responsibility for. That's something I chose to do. The symbolic aspects of sex symbol, or whatever it is that they label you as, is someone else's doing. I don't take responsibility for that. You have to deal with it, though.

Pierce Brosnan

I don't see myself as a sex symbol at all. If you pay any attention to that or give it any credence then you're shooting yourself in the foot. I'm just an actor, just a guy. Do the job. I put a poster out, but that was in the days of *Remington Steele.* That was in my other life.

It's enjoyable. It's flattering, of course it is. But at the same time it can become a hindrance to your life. I am a family man. I have children, and I don't want it to interfere in their lives. I see already that it is a little bit with my twelve-year-old boy. It's a pressure when you're out in public. Then you have to protect them. I try and deal with the whole thing with humor.

Pierce Brosnan
Ron Davis/Shooting Star

Sarah Jessica Parker

I still don't see that sex symbol part of me. It feels like the biggest hoax I've ever seen pulled.

Robert Palmer

It confounds me. I'm not comfortable with my own appearance. I don't like watching myself on TV. I'm basically an introvert. I guess it's vanity that won't make me comfortable in front of the camera, not the opposite.

Patrick Stewart

I was not comfortable with this sex symbol thing at the beginning. Quite frankly, it made no sense to me at all. As it seems not to be going away, I've decided that the very best thing to do is to embrace the reality of it, and I'm beginning to enjoy it now. It still is as incomprehensible to me now as it was whenever this whole thing started. It's not any way that I have ever—even in my deepest and darkest fantasies—imagined myself to be. It's certainly something I hope to make good professional use of. It would have been nice if this had happened when I was nineteen.

Patrick Stewart

(On being considered a gay sex symbol)

I'm very flattered by that. Why not? Does it matter who thinks you're attractive and nice to be with? It didn't seem to do Tom Hanks any harm, although others brought this question to me when I was considering doing *Jeffrey*. I found it somewhat insulting that one would consider turning a role down for those very reasons.

There may come a time when I'm not enjoying myself, but right now I'm just enjoying the ride. If a good part comes along and they cast me because I look a certain way, I'll take it. I'm an actor. I want the good roles. I want to work with the great directors in the great parts. If it's because I look this way, so be it.

—Dylan McDermott

Belinda Carlisle

I don't understand the whole thing. I can see the glamour thing, but not the sex thing. I've tried to stay away from that. I don't feel comfortable with any sort of overtly sexual image. I have to be a role model. I'm a mother now.

Elle MacPherson

I don't think of myself as an object of lust for millions of strangers. I do my job. I enjoy it and try to control what I do as much as I can. That's as far as my thought process goes, to tell you the truth.

Madonna

The main thing I have in common with Marilyn Monroe is that we bleach our hair blonde and that she is a "sex symbol" or "sex goddess" or whatever. I relate to that in terms of that's how people see me, but I like to take the imagery of that and the preconceived notions of what a sex goddess is and turn it around and throw it back into your face. I can be a sex symbol, but I don't have to be a victim. I don't have to be fragile. My life is not consumed with placating people and being victimized.

Jeanne Tripplehorn

That's not me in the nude scene in *Waterworld.* I felt that it was a really gratuitous scene and it should be shot a little more creatively. It was kind of a standoff between myself and the directors and the producers. I think for a while they really thought I would capitulate and finally doff my duds, but I didn't. So when it came time to film it I said, "If you insist on doing this shot—if you're not going to be creative—then I have to pick my double. It's going to be my derriere there." And so I did.

We had three finalists. They were in a trailer. They said, "Jeanne, your ladies are waiting." So I walked into a trailer. They all had terry cloth robes on and they turned around. I said, "Ladies, drop." They dropped their robes and I was so embarrassed that I just went with the best one. I had derrierre instinct—and that's the one you see on camera.

Born Norma Jean Baker, Marilyn Monroe became Hollywood's ultimate blonde bombshell. Even decades after her mysterious death from an overdose of barbiturates, Monroe remains the personification of the term "sex symbol." Yet shortly before her death she told Life magazine, "I never understood it—the sex symbol. I always thought symbols were things you clashed together. That's the trouble. A sex symbol becomes a thing. I just hate to be a thing."

Jeanne Tripplehorn

Obviously, after having made Basic Instinct, *I don't have a problem* with nudity in the right context, in the right forum, in the right genre, in the right audience. *Waterworld* was a big summer movie and young people were going to be seeing it. I just felt they could be more creative and still convey the story.

Bridget Fonda

I go through periods when I say, "I'm sick of it. Never again. I'm tired of the weird feelings and the public perception that I take my clothes off in every movie." But I find that love scenes, making love in general, is one of the things in life that throws a wrench in the works. That's the only entrance of that promise that life is more than just workaday, that life has magic. That chemistry that happens is what confuses us all and makes us expect more, because we remember that magic moment. So I would hate for that to not be in a film. Every time I say, "Never again," then I realize how much that I want to see that element when I go see a movie. I get bored if that ingredient is left out. I love love.

Natasha Henstridge

When I read the script of *Species* I knew there was going to be nudity in it, so that was the time to back out. They didn't exploit me in any way. Sometimes you see movies and you think, "Why are they naked? What's the point?" I think the nudity in this case just defines the character a little more, the innocence of the character, at times.

Goldie Hawn

Nudity never bothers me. It's like words are just words until they're used improperly. It's how you use them that makes them bad. It's how you use your body that makes it unacceptable. The human body is fabulous.

Sharon Stone

Nudity by and large is uncomfortable. When you first take your robe off and then if you're doing the work, you should be much more worried about the scene that you're doing. It's a scene like any other scene that requires your absolute focus and concentration. Those scenes, probably more than any other scenes, can reveal your lack of focus and attention.

Judy Davis

You always see the woman's tits and then the guy always has a pillow in front. Most love scenes are designed to titillate the men. Which is interesting, because a lot of women go to see these films, too. So then you have to think that maybe they're designed also to titillate the producers who are working on the film.

Jada Pinkett

Sometimes directors and studios get all into showing the nudity and forgetting that it's about the sensuality and the passion. Then it just turns into sex and there's a difference. Now you don't have a love scene anymore, you just have sex.

Allen Payne

Filming a love scene is the worst. And with the kind of career it looks like I'm going to have it's probably something they'll have me doing often. So I have to prepare myself. "Here we go with this part of the movie again. Awwwright." I hate it.

Amy Brenneman

Like anything, it just takes a long time to get it on film. So you end up being touched for fourteen or fifteen hours. Your endorphins are worn out. I get very, very punchy.

> *You're in a bedroom somewhere trying to create some intimate fiction and there's a roomful of strangers with audiovisual equipment monitoring your every move and breath. That's truly unnerving.*
>
> *—Charlie Sheen*

Nick Nolte

The tendency was, in the love scenes in *The Prince of Tides*, just when it got very hot Barbra [Streisand, his co-star and director] would cut. Like the actress was saying to the director, "Get me out of this." Love scenes are probably more difficult for females than for males simply because film is male-dominated and a female is being asked to perform with a lot of males around. She needs a confidante to get through it. The actress usually has a relationship with the director. A lot of people think that it's the actor the actress has a relationship with, but it's not really true. The actress has to have the director to give the freedom to expose the feminine mystique in front of all of these males. It was kind of interesting that the actress wanted to cut when the director knew it should have gone on.

Barbra Streisand

A shy actress got in the way of the director. She screwed the director by yelling "Cut." I know I probably should have gone on, but you could say that the director was really there and thought she got enough. I did get very shy. I thought, "My God, how could I be making love to him in the corridor here with my crew watching?" The director was sensitive to the actress by knowing she was getting slightly embarrassed and she cut for her.

Michael Douglas

My position has been, because there are more men around on the set, the actor's responsibility is to take care of the actress a little bit and assume responsibility there, in terms of protecting her. It goes with the territory. It's like doing an action scene. It's better sometimes than having to do dialogue.

Vincent Perez

Love scenes are not my favorite scenes. You feel like a piece of meat at the end of the day. It's a bit depressing, in fact. You can't touch. You can't do anything. I'm always behaving like a gentleman, covering my partner and just trying to make her relax.

Everything is so precise when you do a love scene. There is no improvisation. The camera is following your hand and your movements.

Sophia Loren

I never thought of myself as a very beautiful woman, because I have many defects in my face. I have a long nose, I have a big mouth, but maybe the ensemble of so many irregularities makes me a person who doesn't look like anybody else. I go out from the banality of being the perfect beautiful face and the perfect beautiful body.

Milla Jovovich

From my modeling experience I've come to think that beauty is just so benign. Your parents made your beauty. You had nothing to do with it. I take it more as a compliment when people compliment my writing or my music or my acting. That's something that I created. But beauty is more like, "My mom and dad are over there, so why don't you go thank them." It has nothing to do with me.

Deidre Hall

Part of the job of being an actor is having an instrument that works, that instrument meaning your body. Obviously, if you gain weight, it's a problem. If you lose weight, it's a problem. If you're prematurely gray. There are all kinds of problems that will defy the believability of your character. Aging is always a sensitive question. We're the fantasy people. I'm certainly on top of what's available to me in the cosmetic business, whether it's bleach or collagen or whatever. That's part of their fantasy. It's part of our job to maintain the best appearance that we can.

Elle MacPherson

Someone might want to come up and meet me because I'm beautiful. That's not a problem. What follows is the problem. But it's never a problem. It's always an advantage. I get to meet wonderfully interesting, fabulous people. I meet a lot of boring people, too. That's life. It's not any worse just because you're beautiful.

And believe you me, I'm pretty hard on myself most of the time. I wake up and look in the mirror and I certainly don't think, "Thank God you're so beautiful." I think, "How are you going to go out and convince everyone that I'm something that I really don't feel I am today?" It's not like I'm just accepting that beauty thing is a part of me. I have to deal with it myself every day.

Catherine Deneuve

The problem with physical appearance is, before I didn't think about it. I could get ready in fifteen minutes, despite everybody thinking that I'm a very sophisticated person. Today it's a little more of a problem. It takes a little longer. I'm a very speedy person, so it's a little boring.

Paul Newman

I really hate a person like Marlon [Brando], because he's gifted. He truly is. I've always felt that I was very lucky because of my appearance. It's always been very hard for me, but I can understand how someone as talented as Marlon would feel that it's a waste of time, because he really didn't have to work. I always had a tremendous amount of envy for the natural athlete, the natural mathematician, the gifted politician, the person with natural social graces.

Greta Scacchi

Another aspect of Deborah [the character she plays in *Country Life*] that I can relate to, is that she makes an impression on people, everyone around her, that colors their reactions to her and their attitudes to her. She can't convey and express easily and naturally who she is, because everybody has a preconception about her. That's the cross that she has to bear.

Nicolas Cage

It's hard for a famous person to talk about the problems of being famous. I have friends who are famous and I have friends who are not famous. I can talk about it with my famous friends, but I can't talk about it with my friends who aren't famous because they get upset. "What right do you have? You can drive a 427 1967 Stingray because of that." But they don't know what it feels like to answer a million questions about some movie you made.

Brendan Fraser

It's easier to speak with people who have had similar experiences. If I want to grouse about something, I can't necessarily go to one of my actor friends who hasn't perhaps had the same experience. "Oh, gosh darn, I've gotta go and talk to all these reporters. They're gonna fly me to New York and pay for all my food." They don't want to hear about it. It's tough to find a peer group sometimes, but there are a few actors who are pretty cool and who—believe it or not—have had similar experiences and lend a real good shoulder to cry on.

Elliott Gould

I went to meet Elvis [Presley]. I brought Joey Walsh with me. We went to see him at the International. We went backstage to see him. He was expecting me. His father and the Colonel were there. I left Joey with them—and we went as deep into his space as possible. And he said, "You're crazy."

I said, "I'm not crazy. I'm scared, just like you. And they're not going to let us stay alone together."

He said, "Why didn't you and Barbra [Streisand] stay together? You were two of my favorite people."

I said, "Elvis, listen to me. You can't do any more for Elvis. They're never going to let you be free, Elvis. Come out with us and act. You can be anything you want to be. Come on out with the spirit. Leave yourself here. It's not going to be any different, because they don't know any different—and you don't care."

But he couldn't. He was a prisoner.

Catherine Deneuve Ron Davis/Shooting Star

Jack McDowell

A lot of people make comments like, "It's worth it because you've got the money." Yeah, I've got the money, but all the money does is allow me to hide myself as much as I can and do things in different ways, because you can't really do things the way you used to do them.

Alicia Silverstone

I do feel different. I feel really judged. I feel like if I don't feel good that day I can't say that because somebody's going to say, "You look great, you're beautiful." But I don't feel that way. It's almost like people don't let you be who you are or feel what you feel. You're supposed to feel what they want you to feel and what they think you are. It's hard. I'm just an actress.

Kate Winslet

It's a real shame actually, when you aren't familiar with famous movie stars, it's so easy to categorize them as part of another world in a way. You think they're glamorous and incredibly wealthy, having this easy time and just being wonderful actors. Of course, that's not the case. They're still people. They're still real people.

Bruce Willis

There's the work I do as an actor—and then there is everything else that surrounds being a celebrity. And all that stuff is truly horseshit. It's so unreal. Oh, man. It's just unreal. It doesn't have any resemblance to real life at all. What, that I am somehow more important or what I have to say is more important because I'm a successful actor?! I still don't understand it after eleven years. We'll probably be talking ten years from now and I'll be saying the same thing.

Juliette Lewis

I still refuse to acknowledge the fact that I'm famous. I don't acknowledge it. I don't take it personally. When I get recognized in person, it's like recognizing a painting. I'm just that painting. I'm the person who painted this painting, so I'm it. I'm the object of what they saw on the screen.

Jack McDowell

It's like that public figure is somebody else that I can almost more readily talk about. It's like two different people, but people don't get that when they see you on the street. You're THAT PERSON. But in your own head you're not THAT PERSON.

Is it in your own head, or is it how people see you? Who are you? Are you the person that you think you are, or are you the person that every single person you're going to come in contact with thinks you are? Who's right and who's wrong? What's true and what's not true? It's true to them. It may not be true to you, but is that because that's not you or is that because that's not what you want to be? There are so many weird dynamics that happen with that.

Ted Danson

You get trapped into thinking you have to walk around as other people's image of you, as opposed to doing and being who you are. I'm an actor. I'll paint myself purple for a part. But if I have to be concerned about you in my everyday life, then life becomes very unpleasant. So does growing bald concern me? It used to. Not anymore. Does it concern me that it concerns you? Not really. But how you think about me when I act concerns me hugely.

Dylan McDermott

I want to maintain who I am. Sometimes with fame you can't always do that. You get stripped of your identity somewhere along the way and people's projections of you become who you are. I know that it's a very dangerous thing, in terms of my own psyche.

I see a lot of people and what happens to their work after they become famous. It's always the early years that people are really good. Later on they become a caricature of themselves. I've thought about it a lot, what happens to people and why they aren't as good as when they began. Certainly fame is locked into that somewhere.

Elliott Gould

Now I can understand why I made myself so unpredictable and acted so outrageously in the face of reality. To give myself every opportunity to define me—and me every opportunity to define myself—before someone else did. The key to all of this is that I realized, in relation to that, that you are what the other person thinks you are, whether you like it or not. But that's their problem. What do you think? Most of us don't know.

George Harrison

I see pop stars being teenagers. It's funny when you get known like that. I know that there are people far older than me doing it, but it's a funny business. I don't see myself as a pop star or a filmmaker or any of those things. It's all part of me. Just like being a gardener on occasion. I'm a gardener, too, but I'm not really a gardener, either. I play with a guitar, write a few tunes, make a few movies, but none of that's really me. The real me is something else. You have to figure that out. The real me is the same as the real you.

Rod Stewart

The public, they're the ones that put me there anyway, I think they deserve to know what I do a certain amount of the time. Most of the time I'll share my life with the public, but no one ever gets that close to me. No one ever knows really what ticks inside me.

By definition, the same flaws that are in other people are in me. To be surprised that I even have them, you have to be a joke of a person.

—Kevin Costner

Richard Dreyfuss

I never let the world in to me for a good number of years, probably because I was afraid that the world would say things I didn't want to hear. So when I had the accident, the metaphor I've used is that God flipped that car over so that he could attract my attention and talk to me. I think what happened after that was I was able to listen better—and let the world in more.

Mary Tyler Moore

Part of the reason I wrote [her autobiography] *After All* is to say through the stories you share, "Look how similar we all are. You may not have had these specifics, but you have had the general emotion and feeling and fear and confidence and relationships that I have had." The more we are able to see the similarities along with the differences, the healthier we all become. You because you read my story and I because I get feedback from you.

Julianne Moore

I'll be walking around Westwood or somewhere and then I'll hear the following week that somebody said, "Oh, I heard you were in Westwood with a blonde girl and somebody else." And I'll go, "Yeah, I was in Westwood with my friend and my sister." Then I'll realize that they saw me but I didn't see them. That's strange to me. This is somebody that I don't know, but they know me. So there's a sense of being displaced.

Olympia Dukakis

I've spent more time alone since I've become popular in films. When I started to have children I decided I wasn't going to travel. There was a theater that I was involved with, I taught at NYU, and I did little film roles. For a while there I did a soap, but I did all these things at home. And then this happened and now I live out of a suitcase. I'm very alone in many cities and that's very interesting, what happens to you and what you start thinking about and what you start rerouting.

Gary Oldman

New Orleans for two nights or a week's holiday is terrific. When you're in New Orleans for nine weeks, and then you're in Dallas for ten weeks, you want to jump out the window.

Warren Beatty

The difference between acting/directing/producing/writing and just acting is the difference between masturbating and making love. It's a lot more fun if you're not alone.

Artistic Limitations

While fame opens many doors professionally, it often pushes you through the wrong ones. Today's stars must struggle to stay in touch with whatever it was that made them famous in the first place, but they also must struggle against the forces that want them to stay so true to the past that there's no chance to grow. One way or another, the pressures just to keep working are immense. Those who continue to crank out the same kind of product are soon taken for granted or written off as one-note wonders. Others get pushed into the wrong projects just to cash in on their popularity.

Christopher Reeve

Because I had box office clout from *Superman,* Karel Reisz, the director of *The French Lieutenant's Woman,* was forced by my agents of the time to seriously consider me for the part that Jeremy Irons wound up playing. I remember looking at him and realizing that he was being forced to see me, that this was politics, this was economics. I told him I shouldn't be doing this and he said, "I'm so relieved to hear you say that." We stayed and had a lovely lunch. So I actually had too much opportunity, undeserved opportunity, just because I happened to be in a hit.

Michael Keaton

If I were in Chris [Reeve]'s position, I'm not sure I would have done the second *Superman* movie. But that's easy to say. In fact, I probably would have done it. But, gee, that would have been scary, because you can see what could happen there. I was fortunate that I had done a bunch of movies before I did *Batman,* and a pretty wide variety of roles. But in Europe and a lot of countries overseas that's all they know me as. They know me as *Batman.* But so what? How tough is that?

I didn't do the third *Batman* movie because I'd done it twice, and I thought the first time I did it pretty well. So when I added it all up my

In 1989, Michael Keaton starred in Batman, one of the top-grossing movies of all time. Three years later, he reprised the role of the Caped Crusader in Batman Returns, another box office smash. But Keaton walked away from the most successful film franchise since Star Wars rather than put on the cowl again in 1995's Batman Forever. He was succeeded by Val Kilmer in the third blockbuster in the series. Then Kilmer stunned Hollywood by walking away from the role, apparently agreeing with Keaton that becoming too closely associated with the superhero character was not in his longterm best interests. The bat ears will be worn next by George Clooney, the heartthrob of the TV hit E.R. for the fourth installment in the series, tentatively titled Batman and Robin.

heart said, "Not this time. Time to move on. Keep going. There are too many other things to do."

Sylvester Stallone

There is a necessity now I think to really do what I do and not shirk my responsibilities. We all have strengths and I'd been avoiding mine for years, trying to take it into different directions. Even though some of the efforts were well-intended, they didn't work out that well because they did not deliver what I really am. I represent a certain school of thought or lifestyle or political belief, or at least my characters do, and I've got to stay with that.

Arnold Schwarzenegger

I have the same emotions as you or anyone else. The only thing is, when you have done so many action films as I have done, emotions normally don't have much room when you do a *Predator* or a *Terminator.*

Studio executives especially try to throw in a lot of stuff, even in action films, in order to sell extra tickets, but it doesn't work. They want you to have emotions, or to have a love scene. You're going to run through the jungle, this predator is hunting you down, he's killed twenty of your guys and you're next—and now you're supposed to go to the girl and say, "Let's have a little nookie behind this tree here."

Robert Redford

You do what you want to do in the best way to do it, but it gets harder and harder to do the work when the surrounding baggage gets so heavy. I wish there was a way to cut that free or to jettison it, but I can't control it. I can't control what's going on on the set if suddenly people are coming around with cameras and taking pictures. They're taking pictures of me and suddenly it's more about me than the film. So you do the best you can to avoid it or hide from it.

Mike Love

(Member of the Beach Boys)

People have a certain aural picture of what the Beach Boys are or should be. It's a strong definition in the minds of millions of people. Whenever we've departed too far from that very successful formula, people will reject it. They'd really rather have a "Pet Sounds" or "I Get Around" or "Don't Worry Baby."

Adam Sandler

When I go to the Improv now, I don't feel like I can just go on stage and try new jokes out. I get a little self-conscious up there now because I know people are expecting something from me. I'm nervous about trying new stuff out. Fame's affected me in that way.

Ron Howard

There was a time I feared I'd never be anything but Opie [his character from *The Andy Griffith Show]* and then *Happy Days* came along. Then I was afraid I'd never progress beyond that in people's minds. Now I seem to have this relationship with people, this history, particularly with American audiences, which is something I really value. I wouldn't change it at all. I'm proud that the shows still play and that they've found a place in our society. I don't feel it's any kind of limitation, at this point.

Mary Tyler Moore

Both Laura Petrie and Mary Richards [her characters from *The Dick Van Dyke* and *The Mary Tyler Moore* shows] are so very much a part of me and so much the rock solid foundation of everything I do, everything I have done from that point on. I'm very grateful to them. I delight in talking about them, and as long as people will allow me to do other roles and judge me as an actress rather than a personality, there's room on the Earth for all three of us.

Mary Tyler Moore

Robert Redford did say that the only thing that gave him second thoughts about casting me as Beth in *Ordinary People* was the television persona. He was nervous about people saying, "Oh look, there's Mary Tyler Moore and she's not being funny." Finally he believed I was right for the role and he went for it. The same thing was the case with *Whose Life Is It Anyway?* when I did that on Broadway, which was a straight dramatic role. People said they came in expecting to see "Mary Richards Goes to the Hospital."

Keenen Ivory Wayans

Once you establish an expectation for an audience there's no way to disregard it. Anybody who does is just asking to fail—and anybody who does, does fail. The times that people go, "I want to be dramatic," it just doesn't work. So you do become your worst enemy. Once you say, "This is what I do," trying to do something different becomes difficult.

Chuck Norris

I often wonder why my movie *Hero and the Terror* didn't do too well. I guess the character I played was a little too subservient. He wasn't that strong image character that people go to see me do. It was like John Wayne doing a light-hearted good guy type instead of the tough two-fisted guy.

Unfortunately, you get categorized, and when you move out of that category many times the films don't do well, even if they're good films. Clint Eastwood's a prime example. Movies like *Bronco Billy* and some of the other movies that I thought he did very well as an actor in just didn't do well because they didn't see him as that particular type of a character.

Clint Eastwood

I like to think that audiences are looking for something new. Just to come back and do a repeat of something I've done before might be appealing, or might not. Probably not. What I've done before is constantly out there on TV and video and cable. For my own satisfaction I have to reach out and find new elements of storytelling to get across.

Howie Long

When I want to go see Clint Eastwood, I don't want to see *Bridges of Madison County*. I grew up on Clint Eastwood.

Clint Eastwood

Some people still think of me as Dirty Harry. I'm sure everyone thinks of Harrison Ford as Indiana Jones. Whatever you're best known for doing, you're stuck with. And I've made some sequels to those films, so I have no one to blame but myself.

Sigourney Weaver

Ripley died in the third Alien *movie* because I wanted to free her and not allow her to become some kind of joke. I made the decision. I am sure that the people at 20th Century Fox think I'm a dope. I had this franchise in my hot little hands. I also wanted to be free of her. I felt that I could not make a great movie anymore.

Charlton Heston

You could make the argument that Paul Newman and I—who are almost exact contemporaries, he came out just a year or two before I did—could have exchanged careers. Just as Paul became the quintessential twentieth century urban American man, as Bill Holden had been before him and Humphrey Bogart before him, early on I began to play guys who wore funny clothes and came from different countries and lived in different centuries.

Keenen Ivory Wayans
Nikki Vai/Shooting Star

Paul Newman

I think there are a lot of wonderful actors out there. It's just sad that they don't get a chance to stretch their wings as frequently as I did.

Sally Field

I seem like somebody that you could know, that you could live next door to. Sharon Stone seems like something else—and not that. I don't have the things that she has, so when you're looking to cast Miss, Mrs., or Ms. Ordinary Citizen, Ordinary Mother, Ordinary Person, I'm at the top of the list. If you want Miss Sex Symbol to Die For Drop Dead, no, maybe not. I could do that, though!

Susan Sarandon

My representation was not happy about me suddenly going to play moms because they were afraid I wouldn't be able to come back. There are not very many lead parts that are moms in this country, or people who still have their sexuality. In this industry you are stripped when you get to a certain age, or when you have kids. Even Anne Bancroft was just barely older than Dustin Hoffman in *The Graduate*. She was like thirty-five and he was thirty. Sally Field played Tom Hanks's love interest in one movie [*Punchline*] and then she plays his mother in *Forrest Gump*.

Robin Wright

All of the actresses go through this. You're dying to do a role which is playing a retard or something. "No, absolutely, you're too pretty. You have to play the sister who's a debutante." Forget it.

I heard an inside scoop story about producers in a production meeting, saying point blank, "We cannot have her because she is not beautiful enough. She's ugly. You've got to have beautiful people on the screen because nobody wants to look at an ugly person." And if you look at it, all the stars are pretty. Yeah, it's very irritating, but I'm sure it's very irritating for the not-so-attractive people who are brilliant as actors. They're not going to become stars and people who have looks are not going to get the opportunity to play real meaty roles.

I remember in school, they thought you were a bitch because you were pretty. And I was so shy. So I was a bitch. There you have it.

Anne Archer

I don't mean to be patting myself on the back, but I think I was too pretty, frankly, when I was younger. Now I can play a lot more things, more interesting women.

Paul Sorvino

The most discouraging part of my career came in the last few years. It has been extraordinarily painful for me to be characterized as a slow-moving goon. To be thought of, even perceived as I walk down the street, as a Mafia boss. It's so antithetical to my nature, so little a part of the way I see the world, and the kind of person, father, and citizen that I am. That's a world so foreign to me and yet that's the world with which I have become so identified. And that's the world in which I have been encapsulated for my work.

Leonard Nimoy

There is no question that I will go to my grave being identified most strongly with the character of Mr. Spock [from *Star Trek*]. They will write, "He was best known for Spock," or "He was most successful playing Spock," or "He was so strongly identified with Spock that he could not...." That's the way it is. I've learned to come to grips with that. There have been times when I was frankly rather impatient with the press on this issue, because it's a fairly easy quick-grab handle. "Leonard Nimoy, he of the pointed ears...." Give me a break.

Brent Spiner

I don't think I'm any more typecast from playing Data on *Star Trek* than, say, Harpo Marx. He went on to do wonderful Shakespearean roles and all sorts of things, didn't he?

Surely I'm going to be identified with this part forever. I'm not sure how good or bad that is.

Matt Dillon

Especially if you start as young as I did, I think that sometimes audience's perceptions of you—or the industry's perception of you—is different. You get pigeonholed that way. If you start as young as I did, you're naturally going to grow and learn a lot. Where I make the transition, it's like they don't want me to grow up.

Mariel Hemingway

I think because Manhattan *was such a success* that people saw me as that cute young girl. It didn't matter what I did. People would say, "You were so cute in *Manhattan*" and I would say, "Thank you, but I'm thirty now. I've got to grow up."

Also, for me, being Mariel Hemingway, I'm stuck with this celebrity name which I hate. I'd rather have my married name, but now I'm stuck with Hemingway.

Mariel Hemingway

I think originally the name was very helpful. After *Star 80,* there were some years it was difficult. I could always meet somebody, but I would realize halfway through the meeting that I was here for that reason.

Elmore Leonard

Once I hit the best seller list after writing all those books, I'm going to continue to write that kind of a book.

Walt Parazaider

(Member of Chicago)

We were opening for Jimi Hendrix, and I was sitting next to him on a plane one night. We just started talking, and we got pretty real. I said, "Are you happy with everything that's going on?"

And he says, "No." He says, "What really bugs me is I've gotta keep spitting out my hits, night after night, in front of all these people that really don't listen. I'm not complaining. I know you've gotta do this. This is what I worked for."

I said, "Well, what would you like to do?"

"I'd like to take my old lady and play every South Side bar across the country with my guitar to get back in touch with really playing again." He looked me right in the eye and said, "Someday you'll know what I mean, because you're headed there, and you're going to be there a long time. Don't let it make you crazy. And remember, give the kids a break along the way."

From that little piece of advice, we had everybody from the Doobies open for us, Seals & Croft, the Pointer Sisters, whoever, because of that little piece of advice. I thought it was the most human thing—and at the time I wasn't really comprehending all of it. But all these years later I understand. You can get real complacent.

> *It's like being a painter and being given two colors. "Here are your two tubes of paint. You get red and blue. That's all you get. Here's your canvas and for the rest of your life you get to use red and blue." I don't think I'm unique in that. Most actors today feel that way.*
>
> *—Bonnie Bedelia*

John Cleese

I seem to have a lower boredom threshold than most people. The great thing about *Fawlty Towers* was that when I finished those twelve I said to Connie [Booth], "I don't think we should do anymore," and she said, "Neither do I." We'd done it.

The Pythons didn't feel that back in '73. I didn't even want to do the third series. Then they said, "Let's do just seven." And when we'd done seven they kind of leaned on me to do thirteen. By the end of it I'd really had it. I felt that I wrote two original bits of material in the last year. That was pretty depressing. I remember when we were going on the Canadian stage tour saying, "I really don't want to do them anymore. I'd like to do the movie next year, but we have done the TV show." Two of them didn't like it at all. In fact, I realized later, they were the two who I think were a little worried—quite unnecessarily—about whether they'd make a reasonable living once Python broke up. Of course, a year later they found that they were making more money than they had with Python and then they didn't dislike me so much. There was a certain amount of antagonism for about a year because of my desire to stop, but I had to.

Keith Carradine

I did a pilot for a TV series last March which did not get picked up, thank goodness. I only say thank goodness because those people I know who've gotten into that game say that it's really the golden handcuffs. You can get very rich and be in this gilded cage for years. It can be very frustrating and very confining.

Robert Blake

I spent my life making a silk purse out of a pig's ass. That's the mistake I always make. I just shouldn't have done *Baretta.* You don't go from *In Cold Blood* to *Baretta.* You do a series on the way up, or on the way down. The whole goal in life is to avoid doing a series. Doing a series is the rectum of show business. It has the least to do with acting or art or dignity or self-respect.

James Garner

I made $500 a week playing *Maverick* the first year, $600 a week the second year, and $1,250 the last year. As a matter of fact, I made $92,000 I figured once, when I was under contract with Warner Brothers for about four years—and I paid $100,000 to my lawyers to get out of it. So I lost $8,000 during that period.

Patrick Stewart

I was very concerned, during those first five days when I was trying to make my decision [to star in *Star Trek: The Next Generation*], that it would be some kind of stigma on my career. I was afraid that after a while the show would become an albatross around my neck and that no matter how successful it was, I would never be able to do anything of any real interest because I would always be classified as Captain Picard. As a result of that real fear, throughout the last four years of the series I worked with the people who work with me very deliberately trying to create a parallel career to *The Next Generation* and to look for little bits of work—it wasn't easy to do because the series took up ten months of the year—that would let people see that I was in fact an actor with a range and not just an icon in a space suit.

That's the irony. If you're identified with a character you're successful with that character. Double-edged sword? Yes, but it is success. It's like saying, "Would you rather not be sixty years old today?" What's the alternative? The alternative is dismal failure where you have no identification.

—Leonard Nimoy

Tina Louise

Gilligan's Island was only three years of my life, although it's been on the air forever.

Alan Young

I quit the business for a while after *Mr. Ed.* I had to get off the horse—and I have not got off of him yet.

Rob Reiner

When I left All in the Family, *I was a television actor* at that time. In those days, this was 1978, there was a snob thing that went on in films. People in the film business looked down on television people. They didn't let you into that exclusive little club. It was very difficult for me to make that transition, especially since they were throwing just piles of money to continue to do the character that I had been doing on *All in the Family.* It's tough enough to become successful, but once you do you've got the rest of your life to live.

Steve Martin

Especially with television stars, because it's such a sudden rise and it can so suddenly be over, sometimes they get identified with one role and that's it. Their life is over in a way, at least that part of it.

That's why I went into movies, actually. I was doing the stand-up and I knew that that could only go so far. I had more to do.

Dana Carvey

I can't do any observational comedy anymore, where I go, "You know, like, when you're driving your car...."

"You suck, Garth!"

So I'll just do all the different characters. Or I'll just go into Church Lady for twenty minutes.

Salma Hayek

I was a very successful actress in Mexico. I had a very comfortable life. I was very, very famous. I was an overnight success and I was very young. I knew that that was threatening my craft as an actress, and I left that comfortable life to come here and put my feet on the ground and work and work and work on my stuff. To get to know myself, I had to get away from all that and really dig.

Meat Loaf

The Bat Out of Hell album blew up on us and got real big real fast. People didn't know how to deal with it and people didn't know how to take it. It was nerve-wracking. Then the pressure got put on Jimmy [Steinman, the songwriter] and we started to argue a bit about the next song. I thought it sounded too much like *Bat Out of Hell.* I didn't want to go in that direction and Jim's going, "That's what they're wanting."

Peter Frampton

After the Comes Alive *album* the pressure was so great. There was so much thought that went into writing, as opposed to letting it happen. That can be dangerous. Then you manufacture a song as opposed to letting it come out from the heart.

David Bowie

I made a solemn decision—sob, sob—to not perform my older songs again after 1990. As an artist, I think it's important to make radical decisions for one's self to prevent complacency building. It's an adventure.

Crystal Bernard

I'm the girl next door. I remember going to this club after the *Wings* Christmas party one year. I had on this very short see-through black lace dress, with garters and boots. To me, this spells whore. I was as sexy as I could possibly look. We went into the VIP room and here I am thinking, "I look hot." My girlfriend and I are having fun, then the first guy who comes up to me says, "What are YOU doing here?" There's no way you can get away from it.

Leslie Nielsen

O.J. Simpson is so much bigger than life today. I think the hardest thing in the world would be to put him into a comedy. Whenever he's on the screen you would forget the jokes and think about other things. So I don't expect that O.J. would be included in *Naked Gun* number four.

Uma Thurman

When you meet someone who has a very intensely preconceived notion about you because of what you do, it's a hurdle you have to climb over in order to be really interactive with another person. You're not any of that list of clichés that they think you are. Maybe you're some of them, but maybe not in the order that they think you are.

Uma Thurman
Ron Davis/Shooting Star

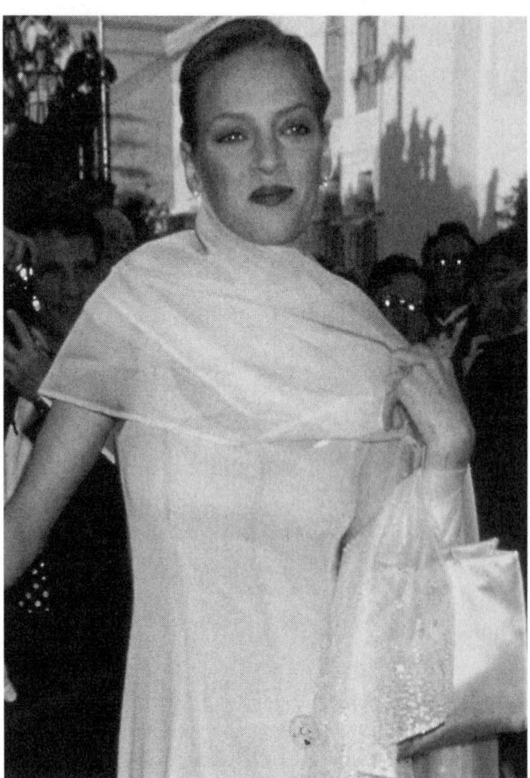

Rob Lowe

It's really difficult to break into what you want to do. It's been a fight. People perceive my career as being blessed—and it's not the case. It's been a real fight to get the roles that I want.

Jean-Claude Van Damme

You have to fight for a relationship. I had dinner with Oliver Stone. I showed him that I have something different—like the fact that I can smile. When that happens, they'll know that I can do more than action films. This way we have fun and slowly build a relationship. That's what Arnold Schwarzenegger did with James Cameron and Paul Verhoeven. Look at Sean Connery. It took him ten years—and he's a good actor. You have to convince people that you're something different. You have to insist, because you become an image in Hollywood.

Elle MacPherson

Generally there is a whitewash that models are dumb. That's totally understandable. I can understand why people would think that, but they confuse youth with being stupid. Models are usually young girls. They possess no more or less intelligence than anybody else at sixteen years old. I've never come across any difficulties in my business—maybe I'm too dumb to see them.

Natasha Henstridge

Sometimes household names like Cindy Crawford who are doing movies now, it's a little bit difficult on them just because they're well-known models and people think of them to be models. Luckily, I wasn't at the top of the top of the modeling world.

Tyra Banks

No matter how much you don't want to be a model anymore, the modeling world still keeps on pulling you. "She's a model/actress." Andie MacDowell and Rene Russo, they still have these model attachments to their names. It's kind of hard to get away from it. I think if you do a good job in the movies you can be taken as a serious actress as well as a model, but if you do a bad job you look like an idiot.

Elle MacPherson

Modeling and acting have absolutely nothing to do with each other. When you model, it's a relationship between you and the camera. When you act, it's a relationship between yourself and another character—and the camera is an observer.

The actual skills that you have inbred in you after modeling for all these years are so far removed from the ones that you need for acting that it's not normal to make the transition.

Cameron Diaz

Everybody hates me and I don't care. I paid my dues, regardless of what anybody thinks.

Kim Basinger

Once you fight the "model/actress" stigma, you're always fighting it. I think it's just a shallow way of looking at it, because I had to get out of Georgia and that's the way I could make money. When I found out I could make money that way, it was better than waiting on tables. It wasn't the happiest time of my life, because I didn't feel I was good at it. I didn't have patience. I wasn't in love with the mirror. I found it very stifling, because I really wanted to be an actress, or be in music.

Tia Carrere

I got my record deal and released a record. That's a lifelong dream for many people. I got it through a movie called *Wayne's World.* Now from that record I can move into another type of record and notoriety of movies, and it feeds each other. The problem is getting taken seriously as a recording artist. Like Madonna, "She can't act."

Sharon Stone

I'd like to think that my audience has a sophistication that lends itself to move beyond a simple Pavlovian response. I like to feel that I have more to give them than an imitation of a thing that they've already seen before. I feel that as an artist it's my responsibility to continue to push the boundaries of thought of the audience. We see actors and artists who do the same thing all the time. They make a hit and then they make that thing until they're sixty. More than the intensity of the sexuality of some of the roles that I've played, I identify with the risk-taking element of things. It's much more thrilling to me to take the risk of playing something new than it is to just do the thing. And if you're really, really in the mood for the thing, rent the other one. It exists already. I'm not taking it away. But I want to do more. I want to try more. I want to be more of an artist than I was the year before.

Daryl Hannah
Ron Davis/Shooting Star

Nick Nolte

When actors succeed in a certain role they think, "I've got to succeed again." I'll repeat. Then you're repeating. That kind of thinking does happen. That's the trap.

Bruce Willis

As an actor it's your job to try and expand your range, especially in films. In TV you can get away with playing the same thing over and over. It's an episodic thing. I think TV burned that out of me. I was so sick of playing that guy. I played David Addison for sixty-seven hours of TV, which is the equivalent of playing the same character in films thirty-two times. It's like doing the same movie thirty-two times. After four and a half years, I was just sick of it.

Michael Mann

Something that may be flattering but is also kind of a nuisance are some of the aspects of being what you call a star. For actors in general, and particularly these two men [Robert De Niro and Al Pacino whom he directed in *Heat*], a very important part of it is taking in. Taking in the experiences on the street. Taking in aspects of life that you see. Some of that, fame gets in the way of that. And so the avoidance of it becomes a very important part.

Clint Eastwood

You spend all of your life learning to act by watching other people. Studying other people. When you're a young student you go into restaurants or saloons and study people and their characteristics. But once you're a noted figure you're the studyee and not the studier. That becomes a problem. I think that's where a lot of people shut down. That's the end of their growing period. I'm trying not to let that happen.

Christian Slater

I got a chance to do a little directing recently and one of the things I loved was that I got to be in the observer's seat again. That was a lot of fun. I got a kick out of watching people do their thing. Usually I'm the one that's being observed. That's one of the things you miss, being able to walk around and be a normal human.

Daryl Hannah

To be a really good actor you've got to be able to go around and observe people. Just to watch human behavior, you learn everything from watching people. If you can't, because everybody's watching you, that's kind of bad.

D.B. Sweeney

I like getting a good table at a restaurant, but I also like walking around and not having anybody notice me, so I can observe people that I might want to consider when I'm building a character. You take pieces of people that you see and if people are looking at you it's harder to observe them.

Denzel Washington

Earlier on in my career it was easier for me to be an actor, to go out in the field and go and observe and learn who it is I'm supposed to be. Now when I go out in the field I'm the one being observed. Part of my job now is sneaking around and trying to observe without getting observed. It distorts the whole deal.

I remember Meryl Streep saying in an interview, "It's really hard to be the focus of the attention because you can't observe." I thought, "My God, that's so true!" When I go to an event and people are looking at me, I feel funny because I feel like I want to just watch. I want to be looking at people. I want to be observing. That's very frustrating.

—Annette Bening

Don Rickles

I went to the American Academy of Dramatic Arts. I auditioned, was accepted, and graduated there. I'm very proud of that. I did some acting, but what paid the bills was doing the jokes and making fun. So that's what I stuck to. There was a period when movies were coming pretty strong for me, but then I developed this style and it became more and more apparent that the insult, insult, insult thing—"The Merchant of Venom" and all these titles they gave—was working. Producers started to go away from me because my image got so strong as the comedian that they said, "Oh no, he'll never make it in the movies."

Rosie Perez

I don't mind being "the girl from New York." But sometimes you want to do something different. You don't want to eat vanilla all the time. Sometimes you want chocolate ice cream with sprinkles on top. You just want to do something different. You want to stretch and grow. You want to please yourself and see if you could pull it off. If you keep on doing the same thing, you become bored and it isn't fun anymore. I need challenges in my life, in every single aspect of my life.

Anne Archer

After Fatal Attraction, *sometimes you do a character* that everyone loves so much and is so big that everybody thinks that's who you are, and they can't see you as anything else. I've really had to fight and go do other things to try and get away from it.

Johnny Depp

I was hearing a lot of things like, "He only plays the oddball. He only plays these strange characters." So I suppose I started to get sick of the label of being just thought of as just the oddball.

Robert Downey, Jr.

I don't like being eccentric anymore.

Michael Palin

Anything that you do well, you're likely to be asked to do again and again and again, whether it's doing Monty Python or Shakespeare in the park. It's very easy to be typecast. In the roles that I get offered, there's a certain Python stigma attached. They tend to think of me to do comedy roles, whereas every now and then I wouldn't mind something more serious.

Eric Idle

On my tombstone I think it will say, "Say no more."

Woody Allen

I think I should limit the amount of movies that I'm in. I should direct other people, but I should limit the amount I'm in because you get very tired of my character if you see it too much. It's nice to see it every three or four films—or maybe even five or six for all I know.

Daryl Hannah

One can only take so much of playing the one-dimensional girlfriend part.

Luke Perry

If I had my way about it, I'd be playing a one-legged Irish transvestite in the next movie.

Mary Elizabeth Mastrantonio

You invest time in New York and you invest time with acting coaches and you beat your head against the wall. You don't think about much else, really, for several years. Then you get there and you realize a lot of that was unnecessary because what they really want is somebody who is strong but really vulnerable and not too threatening, who the men can probably get a leg over. I hate to say that, but I don't get it. I thought I signed up for a different course.

Madeleine Stowe

I'm finding it increasingly difficult to be supportive, to be the supportive woman. There's no purpose in it. It's not active. I'm not talking about supporting roles. I'm talking about being the reason for two men to have a fight. It's stupid. It would make me soul sick to have to go to work and do that.

Robert Blake

When I came back they sent me scripts and most of them were cops. A good cop and a bad cop. An old cop and a young cop. A girl cop and a boy cop. A straight cop and a gay cop—and who cares? I just don't want to go back leaping from building to building again, doing all that shit that I left because of.

> *I'd like to do something where I get the guy, instead of the kid, or the girl. I'd like to have a sexy part, before my legs go.*
>
> *—Bette Midler*

Clint Eastwood

No one's looking to read their own epitaph, but I don't want them saying, "Well, he did twenty westerns and twenty cop dramas and that was his career."

James Caan

Left to their own devices, after *The Godfather,* I'd have been playing Sonny Corleone for the rest of my life. It used to be if there weren't nineteen people dead on page ten the script didn't come to me.

Gary Oldman

They don't go, "Harry Met Sally?—Gary Oldman!" They don't do that. They go, "Charles Manson?—Gary Oldman!"

Edward Furlong

I'm proud to be part of the *Terminator* series, but a lot of times people go, "Hey! It's the 'Terminator' boy!" That's my name sometimes.

Laraine Newman

It's a desirable thing to be on any show that's successful or a "hit." Hopefully, most actors feel that they want to get an identity onto themselves after that. If they're successful in other things, that's what happens. The previous accomplishment falls away like the stages of a rocket.

Bronson Pinchot

When you don't hear, "Oh, I miss Balki," that's a great thing. In 1979 I had hair out to here—like everybody else in the room—and you don't want to hear somebody say, "I miss your big hair." The hair's gone. It's just boring to hear that.

My mother makes this incredible eggplant Parmigiana. She makes it once a year so that we root for it. If she made it every night nobody would want it and she would lose her eggplant primacy.

John Turturro

People see you do something, then they want you to do the same thing. They want the same thing. People say to me, "You play ethnic parts." Well, my face is such that I could play a lot of different ethnic roles. Films are based on your face.

Hayley Mills

You get a bit trapped into the same sort of thing. At one time it was a serious problem for me. I kept on being offered the same kind of parts. They were all fifteen and I was now twenty-three. I thought, "This is ridiculous."

Charlene Tilton

Dallas *was such a strong show* and the character of Lucy was a very definite character, so it's been a problem reeducating people. I've grown up since then.

Matthew Broderick

If you have success as a boy something, people think of you that way or want to try and keep you there. So whether I will ever be as successful as an adult actor as I was as a teen I don't know, but I will keep plugging away.

Sally Kellerman

People associating me with "Hot Lips" in the movie *M*A*S*H* stayed strong for a lot of years. There were a couple of years in there when I was still a brat and would go, "Ugh!" A lot of proving I'm not just "Hot Lips." Those were the silliest moves I made. Now if they remember me at all I'm thrilled.

Alan Alda

I've gotten successful enough to have my own stereotype. That's really climbing right up there to the top.

I think people have combined the fact that I played a doctor who tried to save people's lives on *M*A*S*H* with something that they saw of me when I was out campaigning for the Equal Rights Amendment. They put those together and made me Mr. Compassion. And I am compassionate. I probably am decent and nice, whatever that means. That's all true, but I'm also other things.

Robert Conrad

I never punched a guy that didn't have it coming. I never went out of my way to be a brawler. The women that I've known I cared about, even if it was only caring about them for an evening.

Gene Kelly

We were given complete creative freedom in our musicals. Even when I did straight pictures, of which I did quite a few, I still didn't feel any compunction about anything. Censorship was the only thing that they pushed on. They were afraid of the Catholic Church and the Legion of Decency.

Fred Williamson

I had three rules that Hollywood just wouldn't adhere to: I've got to win the fights, you can't kill me, and I've got to get the girl at the end of the movie. They weren't going to let that happen, so I went to Europe.

In America they pigeonhole my films. No matter what film I make, they try to call it "Fred Williamson's latest black movie." I'm an equal opportunity employer. I beat up white people, yellow people, pink people, red people. Whoever's a bad guy is who I beat up. Even if I'm the only black person in the film, they still try to call it a black exploitation film. When they do that, it limits the market, it limits where they play it. In Europe, my films play in action theaters, where Clint Eastwood films play, so consequently my audience there is much broader.

Dustin Hoffman

(On his reputation for being difficult to work with)

You get stuck with something and it lives for the rest of your life. It's like being on trial in public. It doesn't matter whether you're declared innocent or guilty. You will be looked at in a different light for the rest of your life. I am no more or less difficult than any actor with power—meaning you're not afraid of getting fired if you disagree—that I've ever known. You don't hear about them.

Helena Bonham Carter
Ron Davis/Shooting Star

Kenneth Branagh

That's the last thing that I am, I think to the disappointment of some people, is some walking dictionary of Shakespeare's works. I'm a practitioner, I've done a bit now. But that's about what it represents.

I do think it would be nice to wear a pair of trousers in a film, rather than tights or leather pants.

Ian McKellen

I never liked being called a Shakespeare actor, as if that's the only thing that I could do. It's a shorthand. It's a journalist's way of reminding their readers who Ian McKellen is. I don't deny that I've enjoyed doing Shakespeare and done some of my best work doing Shakespeare, but I've done just as many new plays and quite a few movies.

Helena Bonham Carter

It's just pure typecasting. They think I have certain physical things, what the ideal Victorian woman looked like, which I'm sure wasn't the case. It's just the ideal one's ended up on the portraits, i.e., that I'm pale and look fragile and malleable, and had long hair at one point, and anemic looking. That's what people's idea of a period heroine looked like. It certainly has been frustrating for me.

Ellen Barkin

I was offered one victimized woman after another. Gabriel [Byrne] said to me once, "As soon as you read where it says she cries, you have to turn it down." It was true. Every part I'd get, eventually I'd get to the point where I'd break down and cry.

Christopher Walken

Movies are so expensive to make that if you do something that's effective you might get asked to do it again. It's a business. When they hire you, they want to know that you can do THAT. "Let's get Chris, he'll get the girl." Maybe not. But, "Let's get Chris, he'll do something else." Maybe.

Bronson Pinchot

After the first Beverly Hills Cop *I think I really truly* could've just worked steadily forever doing snotty maître de's and people that were snooty and all the rest of it. I said no. I would really rather scrape wallpaper than keep doing the same thing.

Esther Williams

I once asked, "Is there any chance that you can think of me for a picture out of the water in a good straight role? I'm only in the water ten minutes. That other eighty that make up the movie I'm talking and moving around and I've got twenty changes that are all dry."

One executive producer—he must have expected me. He had the grosses from my last movie and by that time I was in the top ten. He said, "If it ain't broke, don't fix it."

It was okay. I got used to it. John Wayne must have got used to being in a cowboy outfit all the time, too. I came to the conclusion that that's how you got your name above the title. You were in your own niche. There was nobody else who could do my movies.

David Alan Grier

I don't get offered anything but comedies. But before *In Living Color* it was just the opposite. My agent would tell me, "They don't want to see you because they don't think you're funny." In this business you constantly have to redefine yourself.

Mel Brooks

I will win the Academy Award. I will win it because I will direct a dark, serious, philosophical, or political treatise—and I will win the Academy Award just for changing speed on America. They will never respect me directing a comedy because they don't respect comedy.

Roger Daltrey

The legendary status of The Who is obviously something that I have to work against as an artist. It's very difficult to work with it, because everything that I do gets compared with it—which is ridiculous. People ask me, "What do you think of your work compared with what The Who did?" I think The Who is one of the greatest rock 'n' roll bands ever, so I would have to say that I think that everything compared to what The Who did is inferior. So it's a stupid question to ask in the first place.

Tim Curry

Here I am, a moderately articulate person with some experience of the world, and more often than not there is still a photograph of Dr. Frank N. Furter [his character from *The Rocky Horror Picture Show*] affixed to almost anything that I have to say, largely because it's another way of getting a pair of legs and suspenders and garters onto the pages of a family newspaper to astonish and amuse. That gets pretty old after a while because it's sloppy and it's cheap and it's unsparing. But so is fame.

Sean Connery

It's thirty-three years since I first played James Bond. I'm certainly not going to fight it for another thirty-three years. So there's a certain inevitably about it. I used to get much more upset about it because I couldn't see the fairness in it. I was around at the time of the Beatles — and there were four of them to deal with it.

George Harrison

I always really enjoyed performing in our early days, before we got too famous. We [The Beatles] used to play clubs all the time and it was fun. It was good because you got to play and you got to get quite good on the instrument. But then we got famous and it spoiled all that. We'd just go round and round the world singing the same ten dopey tunes. Then you'd have a few weeks off and you didn't want to know about the guitar.

George Harrison

There is definitely a thrill, when the band is all together and it all is working, you can't beat being in a group. But the effort to put a band together, rehearse all the tunes, then you have to go out on tour for months to justify the expense, I don't know if I want to do that. I'm not going on a Spinal Tap tour.

Anne Bancroft

I was asked to do an awful lot of older women and younger men after *The Graduate.* I always turned it down. Had that relationship been in a great script I wouldn't have turned it down, but of course it never was. It is a little difficult to break out of that. I mean, here we are, twenty-six years later, and we're still talking about it. So it makes an imprint. In a lot of directors' and producers' minds that's probably who they think I am.

If you can't fail then how can you possibly develop as a communicator or as a creator of anything? We are locked into a DEEPLY unhealthy notion that somehow you've got to succeed all the time. An appalling notion. Any painter or writer will tell you that that is no way to proceed. One of the things that will kill off a decent actor, especially a young actor early on and they will never recover from it, is too much success. It's disastrous. You stop being criticized, therefore you stop challenging yourself. You then can't afford to fail because there's too far to fall. I've seen that happen to a lot of young actors in America.

—Emma Thompson

Julianne Phillips

They're not going to hire you because of who you've been with [she's divorced from Bruce Springsteen]. Usually it hampers you, I think, because they see you as a certain type. They see you for who you're with. You may get to a certain spot, but you're not going to get any further.

Jack McDowell

(Baseball player and recording artist)

I haven't heard P [Johnny Depp's band] or Dogstar [Keanu Reeves's band], but it's weird because they act for a living. So it's like, "That's fake." That's the first thing everybody says. "It's an actor being in a band. So is he acting like a guy in a band, or is this something he really feels?" That's got to be frustrating if they really care about what they're doing musically.

For me, everybody that's seen me play knows that I'm a freak on the field and absolutely mean what I'm doing, so that's easy. I've always been truthful. Never tried to act or try to create some kind of cartoon character for myself.

Wesley Snipes

I made some adjustments in my managerial camp that afforded me the opportunity to be a bit more open [to taking smaller roles in quality projects]. People have wanted to put me into this whole leading man star type of category and it closed me off from doing good work and keeping my skills up.

Madonna

When you're a celebrity or an icon, you're usually allowed to have one personality trait, which is ridiculous, because a person is made up of so many things. I am strong and I am vulnerable—and I am a million things in between. Like everyone.

Going to Your

One of the greatest challenges of stardom is not letting it go to your head. Everyone is telling you how great you are. You have more money than you know what to do with. Beautiful people want to be with you. Who wouldn't get a swelled head? So pampered celebrities often take on the qualities of vain and spoiled children. Once someone starts believing the hype, look out!

Henry Winkler

Fame is not a normal state of affairs for the human being. It takes a lot of strength and a lot of patience and a tremendous amount of reality checks to live through something like being The Fonz [his character on *Happy Days*]. But if you get caught up in it, it will eventually cut you in half.

Ozzy Osbourne

I began for a while to take Ozzy Osbourne home. John Osbourne [his real name], that's the other one of me, is a pretty laid-back guy, but there was a while there where he wouldn't let me go. I was Ozzy Osbourne all the time—and he gets real tiring, man. He's like the proverbial animal madman. Anything, he just goes over the top. There comes a point where you have to say to yourself, "Hey man, you're getting into the danger zone."

> *When you're in a movie they treat you like you're four years old and give you whatever you want. On some level it's really wonderful and gratifying, but on another level it's rather disturbing. I'm sure you've spoken to movie stars and wondered: How do these people survive without their babysitters?*
>
> —Eric Stoltz

Jeanne Moreau

Is there a toxic element to fame? It all depends on the way you drink the brew. There is a sort of fame where you can become a victim of your fame. You can be eaten up by your fame. You can have distorted self-esteem that deals more with vanity. But if you take fame as an acceptance and as a reward for your work, that doesn't mean that you are a victim of your fame. On the contrary, fame is given to you, then you feel responsible. You owe something excellent to the people who've recognized you.

Richard Harris

Wouldn't it be very stupid if I were to say I didn't believe my clippings? It has to affect you. Yes, you're inclined to be somewhat impressed by yourself, that you get so much coverage in the press. Everything you do is highlighted. You're bound to feel impressed with yourself, aren't you? Yeah.

James Garner

You really have to watch it, that you don't get carried away and think you're as good as everybody says you are. If you listen to what you people said, if people start listening to their press, they're in a lot of trouble. Most of the time it's good—and then the first time that you do a little bitty thing wrong the same people are going to cut your legs right out from under you.

Kevin Spacey

I think it's best for an actor not to be aware of his or her virtues. If you want to try to keep a candor and an innocence about the way that you go about working, it's the reason that you shouldn't read reviews.

Julia Roberts

I don't question the reasons for my success. I'm not curious about it. I don't need to know that and I don't concern myself with that.

Laura San Giacomo

I really try not to read too much about what people think of me. I'm human. I can be infected by that. And I just try to keep as neutral a perspective as I possibly can about the way my life looks, because that's just how it looks. There's really nowhere to get to. Everybody feels like there's somewhere to get to—even Michelle Pfeiffer feels like there's somewhere to go. So we all have somewhere to go, but it's about being present in the moment so you can do what is given to you to do—and do it well—and then move to where you need to go to next.

Celebrity gets out of hand if you allow it to get out of hand. I take it all with a very large grain of salt—and with the knowledge that as quickly as it came it can all disappear. Popularity is a very fickle thing—and in most cases transitory.

—Jason Alexander

Chubby Checker

I invented disco. All the music that's come around since "The Twist" is all "The Twist." They said, "Chubby, why don't you do disco?" I said, "How can I do something that I already invented?"

It was very painful watching people do my dances to somebody else's records and not knowing that Chubby Checker had anything to do with it. That was probably the most painful thing in my life. I would hate for musical history to continue without people knowing that Chubby Checker did what they're doing first.

Fred Williamson

I think I'd be a part owner now if I played football, the kind of money that Dion Sanders is making now, and he couldn't carry my jockstrap. He's making $32 million. I'd be part be owner. Jim Brown would probably own two teams.

Madonna

I don't think any artist can sit there and go, "I'm the best painter." "I'm the best songwriter." I think once you get into the arena of competing with people, then you've lost the essence of what you're doing.

Sammy Davis, Jr.

I don't think that I'm the greatest entertainer who ever lived, like a few other people think. I think I'm a good pro. I lasted longer than a lot of other guys. "Gimme the spot and get away from me." But to think that you're the best that ever lived? Get outta here. I never thought that in my worst egomaniacal days. I thought that I was damn good, a superstar, you know. But the greatest? Get outta here.

Berry Gordy

Your fame comes because of your accomplishments. So you must realize that your accomplishments are not you, they are only your accomplishments. Where people get into trouble is, they think they are their accomplishments. They rise above their accomplishments and when they look down on their accomplishments they're miserable. "I'm paying too many taxes, my life is horrible." They end up miserable, treating people like shit.

Quentin Tarantino

I take my work very seriously, but I don't take myself too seriously at all. You have to keep it all in perspective and also remember to live a life.

Jason Alexander

It has a lot to do with the perception of yourself as being powerful, when in fact you are not powerful. It is the things that you provide that are powerful. A lot of young actors really make that mistake. What is being admired is the fact that you play these attributes, or you play someone who has these words, or this mind. Even leading men, there are a lot of great looking guys, who, if they drive a truck, don't get the kind of adulation they get if they're Brad Pitt or Tom Cruise. That does not make you powerful. You are in something that's powerful. These guys then try and go off and recreate that power in their lives and it doesn't exist. They go, "What the hell is wrong here?" It just screws everything up.

Robert Downey, Jr.

In becoming a pretty well-known actor, there's a lot of temptations and a lot of tendency to just revel in the status and not necessarily get back to the work, and to want the approval of others as opposed to that sense of accomplishment which is really between you and God.

Robert Blake

In 1968, Dustin Hoffman did *The Graduate.* Warren Beatty did *Bonnie & Clyde.* Jack Nicholson did *Easy Rider.* And I did *In Cold Blood.* None of them had to go have a life on *The Tonight Show.*

Dodd Darin

You either loved Bobby Darin [his dad] or hated him. There was no in between. The arrogance, brashness, cockiness, turned people off. A lot of people said he was the most hated man in show business. Then you have to understand where it came from. It came from the ticking clock. He had to make it in the time he had.

In early July of 1995, rising star Hugh Grant was arrested by police for engaging in a sexual act with a prostitute in a car parked off Hollywood Boulevard in Los Angeles. This $60 misdeed generated headlines around the world for Grant, and the prostitute, Divine Brown. Critics wondered if Grant had quashed his growing career and ruined his nice-guy image. His subsequent appearance on The Tonight Show with Jay Leno—Grant's first public appearance since his arrest—brought Leno his highest ratings ever. Grant's next film, Nine Months, released just a few weeks after the scandal broke, grossed nearly $70 million in the United States alone.

David Birney

The temptation is to care more about the fame than about the work. The work is, of course, what it's all about. If you don't have a good grip on that, and a strong sense of who you are, what you're about, and what you want to have done when they put your hands across your chest in the box, then you can get into trouble. And you see it all the time in the entertainment business, people who are frightened and panicked because they're not famous this fifteen minutes.

Anthony Hopkins

It's good to have some self-doubt, because otherwise you become so vain and conceited, but it can cripple you. You've got to find confidence somehow.

John Malkovich

People have a slight tendency to feel that people became actors because they have exhibitionist tendencies, which may be true on some level. But I think some people perhaps became actors because they had an overwhelming need to hide. I may fit into that more. Perhaps. I don't know. Maybe.

Elliott Gould

I had harbored my pain in fear. I covered that with layers of pride. But I'm also proud inside, in relation to Mom and Dad. I don't want to be too proud. Someone said it's the first deadly sin. But I buried my pride very deep because I was a little ashamed, being that my Mom and Dad didn't really know how to care for one another.

Wesley Snipes

I've developed some bad habits from doing movies. I saw some friends on stage, and I was sitting there thinking, "Can I do it now? Can I be as convincing and as powerful as I was before I started doing films, now?" I don't think I can, but I'm humble enough to say, "I'll go back to class and break all the bad habits I've learned from film, so I can re-establish my strength for stage." There's a big difference.

Man, with action movies a lot of times I can roll out of bed, learn my lines in two minutes, and then go and say it like I've been practicing it for two or three months. That's a bad habit. After it's over with you can't even remember the lines you said. All those bad habits will not work on stage.

Julia Roberts

My mannerisms and whatever I do is spontaneous and unaffected. It will not be controlled by what people think or say, or what they like. If somebody tells me they like something I probably won't do it anymore.

Martin Sheen

You can very easily begin to believe something about yourself that is totally untrue, but it's nurtured by success and attention. You've gotta be real careful. You've gotta be grounded.

Michelle Pfeiffer

My feet are almost always planted. I've always considered it to be so, almost to a fault. If anything, I've had to work to be lighter and not so serious and take things a little more in stride. That's just my nature, to be really rooted to the ground.

Tyra Banks

I was really excited when I had all this hype around me, but at the same time my mom—she's my manager—she'd always say, "Don't believe the hype. It's all crap. They'll love you now, but when you get your wrinkles they're not going to love you anymore."

Anna Chlumsky

My mom helps me a lot with that, keeping me on ground, saying, "Anna, you're not that great."

Earvin "Magic" Johnson

I'm just Earvin. "Magic" sometimes, but Earvin most of the time. My wife, my mother, my father, and my family, they all keep me on the ground. I know just as fast as you have it, it could be gone tomorrow.

Earvin "Magic" Johnson and his wife Cookie Ron Davis/Shooting Star

Shirley MacLaine

It's funny. I've always been considered "the stable one" in Hollywood. A taskmaster, but there's never any temperament with me, or outrageous ego trips. Tough? Yes, but not those things. And yet I'm the one who's writing about all these things that seem to be unstable or unsane [sic].

> *According to the late Cary Grant, "When you become famous, you don't change, but everyone around you does."*

Natasha Henstridge

It's hard because now all my friends want to ask me everything about it and I'm like, "NOOO! Please, I've answered enough questions." I just try to keep it in the back of my head as much as possible, because if I start to think about it and think about what could become of it, it'll drive me crazy.

Debbie Gibson

I have to know that for everybody who loves what I do there are an equal number of people who hate what I do and just want to slap me in the face.

Michael Palin

The only way to enjoy fame is to remember what it was like when you didn't have it. That's very, very difficult, but I try not to take it all for granted. I'm not one to ring up restaurants and say, "It's Michael Palin here, give me the best table." I would get someone to do that for me, but I wouldn't do it myself.

Bruce Willis

We [he and wife Demi Moore] just make fun of our celebrity all the time. We break each other's balls all the time about being famous and about being big shots. Our friends do the same thing and that really keeps us from believing it too much.

I never wanted to be the actor who believes the things that are said about him. I've seen guys like that, who read everything and walk around like they're some superstar. I've always been kind of embarrassed by that title.

Elliott Gould

Al Pacino said to me once, "How can I go to a basketball game with you?"

And I said, "Who do you think you are? Forget about who you think you are and come to the game with me." Both of us being New Yorkers, I said, "I take the subway still. I walk in the streets. I'm the same with everyone."

It's one of the gifts, one of the bonuses that I've been able to acquire in relation to how painful it's been to go through the process without understanding what the world is and what business in the world is—and even our products.

Elisabeth Shue

You have to be connected to your real life in order to experience life that then can be translated into the parts that you play. If you stay in that show business world there's an emptiness that invades your soul. It's important not to experience it too much.

Kermit the Frog

I'm a very simple frog. When I'm not working I go back to the swamp. I don't let the Hollywood thing get to me.

Tom Arnold

It's weird how you get used to things that you never thought of doing before. You have to travel in a private jet. You get used to that, to having your own bed and your own stuff on this jet. I can't sleep on planes, never could, but I could sleep on that one. You suddenly have to have that. How else are you going to travel? There's no other way, you think. It just gets really scary about what you have, and what you are going to need, just to be okay.

Jack McDowell

(Baseball player and recording artist)

You do change. You have to change. I can't be the same exact person I was a long time ago because it doesn't work that way. I changed in a lot of ways—and I think that's good.

Mary Stuart Masterson

Some people feel twice as insecure, the more famous you get. Some have delusions of grandeur. It does screw with your perspective a bit. If anything it makes you more hungry for real connection with people.

Fred Williamson

I'm a hero in life. The movies only exemplify what Fred Williamson stands for anyway.

Paul Hogan

I have virtually replaced the kangaroo as the image of Australia. I don't know whether to be grateful or not.

Michael Palin

The Monty Python *television shows* are still playing. People are talking about it being like *I Love Lucy*. That's a very weird feeling. It's like being already pronounced dead, "but the shows will live on" sort of feeling. That's a curiously eerie sensation.

Michael Richards

Jim Carrey and I go all the way back to the days when we used to stand out in front of the Comedy Store hoping we could get that Saturday night slot because they paid double. That would've been $70 a night. Then you see Jim the way he is now. I talk to him, I say, "Are you okay? Are your feet on the ground?" He goes, "WOOOOO, MAAANNN!!! WOOOOO!!!"

Henry Winkler

It's very heady. You can easily start to believe that you're more than you are. They make you believe that you're very special, that all of a sudden you've grown inches. You're handsomer than you were. Your hair is golden blonde and flowing. It's a very seductive thing. Maybe one of the great lessons of life is how to maintain your equilibrium.

John Landis

Alfred Hitchcock was nominated for an Oscar fourteen times. The quote from Hitch was, "The Oscars are trivial bullshit—unless you're nominated."

Ellen Burstyn

I kept trying to get this sentence out of my head. "I'd like to thank the members of the Academy...." It was just running like a mantra through my mind. I kept trying to get rid of it and it wouldn't go away. I remember I got in my car and drove up to Santa Barbara and sat and watched the ocean, to not be glued to my radio, but I just sat there thanking the members of the Academy.

Salma Hayek

When I was a soap opera star in Mexico, the closest you can get to being President is to be a soap star in Mexico.

Patrick Swayze

If you live through the initial stages of fame and get past it, and remember that's not who you are, is this hype, if you live past that, then you have a hope of maybe learning how to spell the word artist.

Anthony Hopkins

I'm aware that I'm an immensely successful actor now, but it's been such a good steady journey through my life. I'm not world-weary, but I've been there, done it, bought the postcard, bought the t-shirt. I'm not cynical about it. I can't really grasp it. I see my name above the name *Nixon.* I'm aware of it, but I can't really take it in. I think it's the safest part of one's consciousness, because once you start believing that you are different then I think you're in big trouble. You see it happen with younger actors because they can't cope with it.

But as I've gotten older I've realized it's only a moment in the sun. It's a communication job and I'm good at it. I'm no longer modest. I'm very good at what I do, extremely good at it. And I like that. I like saying that about myself because I've paid my dues. I can say it with all confidence because I'm a craftsman and an artist. I'm glad it's worked out, but I can't go beyond that. I'm very, very fortunate. I don't know what the combinations are, but there is such a thing as destiny or fate, and I have had the most remarkable life, the most remarkable career.

Woody Allen

I've always felt that we give artists too much leeway, that we tolerate their cruelties and their narcissism and their temperament because they're artists, when in fact we shouldn't. This started in my life during the McCarthy era. We have a tendency to make allowances for artists because they're in some mystical realm. "He's a terrible guy, but he can't create unless you give him that leeway." I don't believe we should excuse artists that way. I don't believe you should ever judge an artist's work by his life. I think you can be T.S. Eliot and be an anti-Semite and a great poet at the same time, but I don't think you should excuse artists in their life being for bad people just because they need that to create, or claim they do.

Christopher Reeve

A famous person can be unkind, uncharitable, selfish, ungiving with friends, non-responsive, and be indulged in it. Then the famous person loses self-respect—and that can be very damaging. Normally in any human transaction there's a fair give and take. I've gotta bring fifty—you've gotta bring fifty. That equilibrium gets upset with fame.

Ozzy Osbourne

I lost my values in life. I didn't know how to say, "Is that one cheaper than that one, or do I really need that one?" I'd just grab it and get it. I began to become an animal. I had no respect for anything or anybody. I didn't have the time of day for anybody. I was just the king bee, you know?

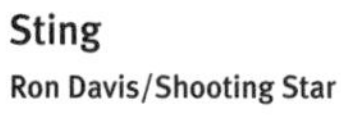
Sting
Ron Davis/Shooting Star

Mary-Kate Olsen

When we [she and twin sister Ashley] were filming *It Takes Two* we had this little thing. Whoever got our names wrong had to pay us two dollars.

Val Kilmer

I don't read the reviews. The first play I did, I and my classmates wrote together in school. It went right down the toilet because we got good reviews—specifically because of that. We were right out of school and all filled up with these ideals. [The former *New York Times* critic] Frank Rich says, "Yes. You may live." Everyone came in to act after that like they were standing on tables, putting their hands out. It was awful. I decided that when someone likes you, from what I experienced, it's the worst thing for the play. You're going to have to forget it anyway. If someone says, "I really love that moment," and you're really loving getting to that moment, then it's really bad.

Sting

How could you replace the feeling of walking out onto a stage in front of thousands of people and all of them basically saying as one, "We like you. We approve of you." That's not something you could do without really.

Warren Beatty

I have a friend from Tennessee whose father is an orator in the Tennessee State Assembly. He said, "The greatest gift that God can give a man is to enjoy the sound of his own voice. The second greatest gift is to get somebody to listen to it."

Richard Gere

Any creative act, whether it's hitting a baseball or acting or solving a mathematical problem, I think all of those things connect with a higher energy. What they have in common, I would think, is your lack of ego. When you connect a baseball with a bat, it ain't you doing it. It's out of the realm of me and my ego. It's true when you write a poem. It happens outside of me and my needs. Acting is the same.

Laraine Newman

Being famous on Saturday Night Live *was a double-edged sword* because we all have a tendency to compare ourselves, and not all of us on the show were as successful as others. That was very tough. It was almost like children fighting for the love of one parent and it being obvious that one was not the favorite child. I wasn't the only one who felt that way. At times we all felt that way. Whatever it was, it wasn't enough. The stakes were very high on that show. It's only after working on that show that I've realized what a brutal atmosphere it was there.

The famous people that I have met, whether they are actors or rock stars, depending on their level of fame and success, oftentimes feel that they have a right to do whatever they want—as long as no one finds out. As long as the press doesn't find out they are morally beyond reproach. I'm waiting to become much more successful so that I can start acting like a complete idiot, too, and take advantage of some of these great things.

—Eric Stoltz

Shaquille O'Neal

I'm not in this to compete with Michael Jordan. I'm just in it to have fun, to take care of my family, and to take care of opportunities that come my way.

Wesley Snipes

If I end my career tomorrow, I don't want there to be any questions as far as me being an actor goes. I don't want any of that, "Oh, he's just an action guy." "He's just a sex symbol." None of the garbage. It's just straight up, "Yo. He was one of the better American actors, period, point blank, bar none." I don't want to hear nothing after that. I want to play Michael Jordan when it comes to it.

Marlon Wayans

To me, an ego is your self-devil. Ego is the worst thing in the world to have. It just doesn't work for you in life. It's not good to have an ego. I try to be egoless.

George Michael

The most impressive thing about Prince's career is that at the beginning, when no one wanted to know anything about him, he wouldn't give interviews.

William Hurt

Ego is a muscle. You're either in control of it or it's in control of you. I always remember that Greek tale about the son of the man who guides the horses of the sun across the sky every day. He warns him not to take the horses out until he's ready, but the kid says, "Oh, I can do this." And he gets up there and he falls out. Or Icarus. If you're in control of fame, it can do a lot, but you have to have a lot of restraint. I think that's tough for anybody to learn. And I think living in our time, I don't think this is a time which demands that we go to the deepest and most delicate and most sensitive and most profound and wisest in us.

Elliott Gould

What is fame? Not to take it too seriously or make it too significant, what it means is your work has been recognized and you have made people outside of yourself aware that you are somebody. It's a great calling card, as long as it's not misused.

Vanity and ego has to be accepted, has to be focused on, to see what it is. Start to absorb it. Keep it someplace, in a museum. Keep it someplace behind glass. To be aware that that's what happens to us when we think we're more than we really are.

Charlton Heston

You've got to believe you can do it. When Rod Laver stepped up to the service line serving for the last point in his second Grand Slam, he didn't think, "Maybe I can't do it." He thought, "Give me those goddamn balls." It's the difference between vanity and ego. To be vain is to think, "I am the best there is. This performance is the best performance anybody can ever do." It's ridiculous. It's bullshit. Ego is thinking, "I can do it." You have to believe you can do it, or you really can't.

Dennis Miller

I always view people in show business as kind of needy, not heroic. Why would you put your esteem in the hands of strangers if you weren't a very needful person? I know I am. I just don't think it's a place for heroes. I don't watch movie stars and think they're heroic. Real life people who do a lot of things and never get accolades for it, they're heroic.

Jason Alexander

I got an honorary doctorate from my alma mater last year. My thesis was basically about if you define success by fame you've got a bad definition.

I remember having a conversation about a show with a surgeon one time. The guy actually said, "My opinion doesn't really matter because I'm just a surgeon." I thought, first of all, that's insane because you were in the audience. You put something out, it's for an audience and an audience will make it live or die. But second of all, to be in a position where a guy thinks he is less valuable because he's a surgeon and I'm making movies, I tried to explain it to the guy. There comes a time in everyone's life when essentially they're going to need a doctor. There's never a time in anyone's life when they need an actor. It's a complete luxury item. Please don't devalue yourself along those lines.

And yet people do. It's a measuring stick. You either have it or you don't have it. If you don't have it you're not as good, not as great, not as important. All those definitions are incorrect.

Jim Carrey

What happens ultimately is that you end up working so much that you're "on" much more than normal—or than should be allowed. I don't really have a problem relaxing. It's just that when you're living a real exciting career life, after you've created all this wonderful whimsical stuff, you go home and taking the garbage out is difficult. It's like walking on the moon and then having to go home and wash your car.

Kevin Pollak

Only my girlfriend complains about that from time to time, that I should calm down. I actually like turning it off in a huge way. I think that's one of the reasons why I enjoy acting so much, because it's in such short bursts. Then you get to go sit for nine hours while they set up the next shot. You still get the incredible rush, that performer's high, without having to be funny for an hour.

Mick Ralphs

(Member of Bad Company)

At the end of the day, when you put your instrument away in its case and the tour ends, you go home to your family and your house and you're just like anybody else. You've done your job. It's like you finish work at the end of the day. You go home. I know so many musicians that when the tour stops, they've had it. They can't go home. They fight with their wives and they want to know when the next tour is. If you tour a lot and you don't ground yourself every so often, then you can just live this life as long as there's a next page. When the pages stop, suddenly that's it. There are so many guys in the business you see in bars around L.A., telling you, "I was on the road with so-and-so and my wife's left me."

Tom Hanks

My joke, the first time I won an Academy Award, was if you're nominated and you don't win, everybody pretty much forgets it after a week. And if you're nominated and you do win, everybody pretty much forgets it after two weeks.

Richard Dreyfuss

I made lots of money betting against myself the year *Duddy Kravitz* came out. They said, "You're going to get nominated." I told them no and I told them why—and I made a lot of money.

I made a lot of money betting that I WOULD win the Academy Award in 1978—because I just figured it out—and I made a lot of money.

And then I made A LOT of money betting the next year that you could not tell me who won the Best Actor Oscar the year before—when the answer was me! [Dreyfuss won the Oscar for his performance in *The Goodbye Girl.*]

I don't know that fame in and of itself is toxic. If it were, Frank Sinatra would be dead. Fame in and of itself can't quite be a permanently fatal toxin. What I think is true is that toxic people seek fame. It's very rare to be really famous and healthy. The most healthy people wouldn't get involved in fame, I don't think.

—Peter Tork

Eddie Murphy

I hear, "Are you still down? Are you still a real brother? Did you forget where you came from?" Since I was nineteen, I've been in the public eye. I was born into the projects. There's no way I could forget who I am.

Judge Reinhold

When you work with an actor who's very insecure, misbehavior comes out of that. It's a by-product. People get angry and freaked out and temperamental because they're scared. I think that happens more and more.

Samuel L. Jackson

I think I'm a very normal person that has a very extraordinary job. As long as I don't start to think of myself as an extraordinary person who has a very important job, then I'll be able to carry on and live my life the way that I live it now. My mother still feels like she can hit me when she feels like it.

Wesley Snipes

It's a real problem, because on one hand people want you to be great and they always go around and say, "You're wonderful, you're great." But then when they get in a personal one-on-one relationship with you the first thing they say is, "Oh, you think you're all that! Who do you think you are?"

"But wait a minute. That's part of the reason why you're here! That's one of the things you said when you first met me. 'I love your movies.' You didn't say, 'Wow, you have a great mind. Your spirit just overwhelms me.'"

How do you balance that?

Bruce Willis

The less importance I give it the easier it is to be gracious about it.

Kevin Spacey

Looking at the amount of infotainment that we have in this country, we observe a lot of people who become famous. I think that there's just an extraordinary and unfortunate amount of arrogance out there. One movie and people think pretty terrific of themselves.

Wesley Snipes
Fotex/Shooting Star

Henry Winkler

A lot of people became stars and filled the holes they never took care of, the stuff in their personalities they never worked on, but they filled it up with air. They filled it up with cotton. They hide behind this ability to be more important in the world, but then they're more important for two or three minutes. There's a whole life to live out there. I don't want to be isolated from walking down the street or going to the theater or riding on the train and just being. That other way to live is full of shit. The other way to live is not the way to be on this Earth.

Elliott Gould

We think we're something special. We think we're better than anything else. And we ain't.

Steve Martin

I always believe that people who are difficult celebrities were also difficult unknowns.

Toadies, Leeches, Sycophants &

There are small armies of people who will quickly surround celebrities and insulate them from the real world. Good managers or agents or publicists might perform invaluable services, but they have their own agendas, too. Dependent on their stars financially, frequently taking a percentage of their earnings, their advice is often colored by considerations other than what is best for the health and happiness of their clients in the long run. Then there are the other members of a star's entourage, friends, relatives, personal assistants, etc., who perform the service of a court jester. No wonder it's so hard to stay grounded.

Treat Williams

Unless you've been through it, it's very hard to explain what it does to the psyche. Unless you're very, very strong you really begin to believe that when people are all listening to you, that what you have to say is terribly important—and it just isn't. You don't realize that they're just people doing their jobs. If they weren't getting paid they might not be there in the room with you listening to what you have to say, what you think is so fascinating and charming.

Eddie Murphy

All the people that used to be around are guys I went to high school with. It was no deeper than that. We used to laugh all the time, reading "his entourage" and all that. I went to high school with these guys. Hey, I got famous and made some money and went, "C'mon, let's go!" I was in my twenties. We were having fun. My life was really like that scene in *Trading Places* where my character finally went, "Get the fuck out!"

I now have the power to get movies made. Just because I can doesn't mean I should. A movie has to be a combination of an organic entity and a binary entity. It has to exist for a very specific reason, meaning that a story is so good that it has to be told. You don't have to go back very far at all in the history of my crass industry to realize that there were plenty of products that were made solely on vanity that never should've seen the light of day. They just weren't good stories. It's as simple as that.

The power that I have now is that I can ally myself with good filmmakers who want to tell good stories. It's true, I probably could go out and make any movie a reality if I wanted to. There are people out there who will be happy for me to do anything that I wanted to do. That's not any reason to have those movies made. I've been lucky that I've had my butt kicked enough in the motion picture industry to know that that is true. My joke is that I've made twenty films and five of them are pretty good.

—Tom Hanks

Rick Wills

(Member of Foreigner/Bad Company)

It can be very strange when you earn lots and lots of money and you're not from that sort of background. You're not trained in having lots of money. You just suddenly acquire it. Everything goes mad for a while. Then the tax man catches up with you and you find out what reality is again, quickly. You can go through hell for a while. And you find out who your real friends are because everybody likes to attach themselves to whatever the latest successful thing is. So it can be quite painful at times.

Anthony Edwards

When people make so much money off your work, they want to tell you what you want to hear. You know they're doing that and you don't want to be in a place where you go, "Jesus, these are the only people in my life. Do I trust them or I do I not? Who am I?" Trying to balance all that out is a perspective trick.

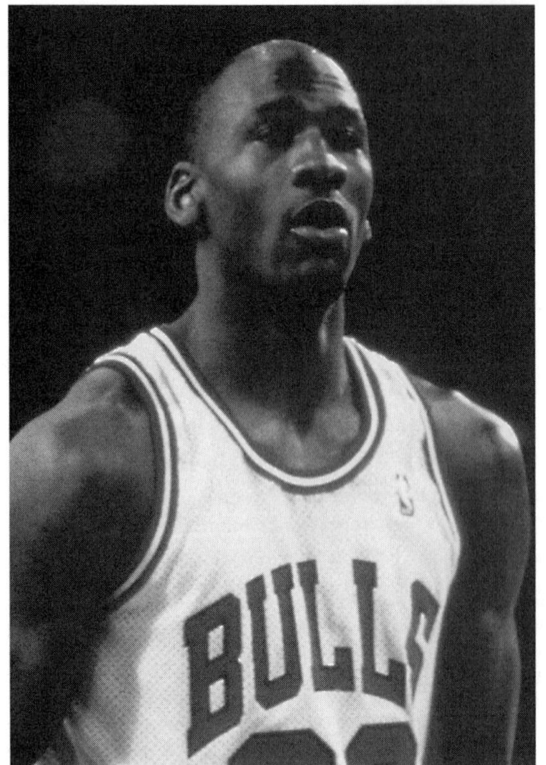

Michael Jordan
Maggie Mitchell/Shooting Star

Michelle Pfeiffer

I just don't have a clue what's commercial. I'm an idiot when it comes to reading scripts. There are people who are really good at it and they'll say, "Michelle, I'm telling you," and I'll go, "WHAT! Nobody's going to go see that. That's the worst thing I've read." I just don't have a clue. Look, if I read something and I could tell this was going to make $300 million, I'd do it in a second. Are you kidding? But I think, "Nobody's going to go see this—and it makes $300 million."

John Landis

The famous William Goldman quote, "Nobody knows anything." Of course it's true. Therefore, if you have a big hit, they go, "He must know." So they all come rushing to you and finance what you want to make. The ultimate example of that is Steven Spielberg. He's the only one who could have gotten *Schindler's List* made.

Bo Derek

After 10 came out I could do anything I wanted. It was not a battle. Literally, we were in the Orient and people were flying in with projects with suitcases full of money to try and get me to do something. And all I had to say was, "I'd like to do a Tarzan movie and I think I'd like to produce it." That's about as hard as it was for me.

At this particular moment I've got a lot of freedom. If I want to make a film about that bottle of Evian on the table, I probably could.

—Hugh Grant

Michael Jordan

I've never looked at the acting industry that much, but when the opportunity to star in a movie came up my kids really wanted me to do it. I thought it would be a great opportunity. I get the opportunity to play myself, and if I can't play myself I can't play no one else.

Ethan Hawke

I did this movie, Reality Bites. *I sang one song* and people asked me if I wanted to have a recording contract. I wrote this little piece for myself like a lot of people write things and I made the mistake of giving it to some people not really knowing what I was doing. Then some people got interested in publishing it and I realized that I actually didn't want to have it published. That was kind of awkward.

Paul Reiser

They actually came to me and said, "You wanna write a book? [*Couplehood*]"

And I said, "Why?"

"It could be fun and you could talk about things that you don't get to do on the show."

So I started writing and as I was doing it it came into shape.

The irony is, I know nothing. The audacity to write a book. I have no answers. I don't even know what the questions are.

Rita Rudner

Viking Press called me up and said, "Do you want to write a book [*Naked Beneath My Clothes*]?" I said yes. It wasn't like I had a burning ambition, like the first time I saw a pencil I said, "Yes! That's me. I want to write a book!" It's funny. I wanted to make it like my act only it's longer and there's no cover charge and you don't have to sit next to people who are drinking and smoking.

Tim Allen

I was so embarrassed to write a book [*Don't Stand Too Close to a Naked Man*] because I read a lot. As my mother said, I don't think she meant it this way, but she said, "Who are you to write a book?" And I took that to heart. Who am I? But John Grisham, he's not Edgar Allen Poe. There are books on how to raise tomatoes, for God sakes. That's my justification. Anybody can write a book. That's the freedom of the press. And as long as I was going to do that, I wasn't going to write just a joke book, which is what the publishers wanted.

I thought, as most people do in my position, if I could come out with these steps, maybe if you read these steps you don't have to step in these same piles of blankety-blank that I stepped in to get where I was. That's why I put my prison stuff in and some of the more personal stuff.

Robert Blake

People talk to me about writing books all the time, but it's such a pain in the ass because writing is very difficult. I could write a whole book about just *The Little Rascals.* How do I put this sixty years of madness between two covers? If I start talking to you about just my relationship with Buckwheat, I could be here for a week, because nobody knows Buckwheat. I'm the only person on the planet today who's alive. Buckwheat was my closest and dearest friend. If he was alive today he would hate America for the clown that they've made out of him. He hated that guy he played on the *Rascals.* Hell, I could do a book on Buckwheat, let alone *The Little Rascals.*

Kim Basinger

I worked on an album for almost a year. I wrote much of it and it was an urban record. I was just unhappy making the record and I turned around one day and said, "What am I doing?" I made a very wrong choice of trying to fit in an area of music I don't belong instead of being who I am and following what I'm about. Why was I going into this street level, pounding on the drums kind of stuff? Maybe I was overwhelmed at the time by the Janet Jacksons, Whitney Houstons, and Madonnas. We had all the album covers and everything. Thank God I stopped the albums from being distributed.

Shaquille O'Neal

I'm sure when the hip-hoppers first heard I was coming out with an album they were pretty reluctant to buy it, but I think I do a pretty good job with the music.

Eddie Murphy

The music is the easiest thing to do because there are no expectations there. Musically, it's like, "He's a comedian, so surely this music is going to suck." So I just go and write whatever I want to because they are expecting it to be lousy. The challenge and the risk is every time I get in front of a movie camera.

Keith Carradine

After Nashville, I had a top ten record, it's true. Then I did my second record and it sold 80,000 copies. It was interesting, because I thought it was a much better record than the first one I'd done. After that record Asylum Records disinvited me to stay on.

Woody Harrelson

I put together this little band and everybody just wanted to Go! Go! Go! And I just wanted to say, "Whoa!" I don't want it to be like it was with my acting career. I spent a lot of time just desperate and hungry and driven. "I must succeed." Then I found myself getting successful and it was like, "What was I pushing for? This is hollow. It doesn't fill me up." It's not like it was a bad thing, but it's not the thing that's going to make me happy. So I'm not going to jump into this music thing, which is something I value a lot, and be concerned about anything but being up on stage for that two hours performing.

Yoko Ono

Whenever we watched Citizen Kane, *you see how this guy* is trying to push this girl into singing and they hire an opera house and she's supposed to sing and everybody's saying, "Oh, what a terrible voice." We were laughing like crazy. You know, 'cause it looks like John and me. John saying, "No, you're going to sing that. Sing!" And nobody wants to know.

Laurence Fishburne

The first time we mounted Riff Raff *[a play he wrote, directed, produced and starred in]* in Los Angeles, I put up my own money to do it. I figured, "Hey, why should anybody else give me money to do my thing if I'm not willing to take a risk myself?"

Paul Hogan

To fund my movie Lightning Jack, *I floated it on the stock exchange.* There are 5,680 small investors, many of them I know personally or are friends, relatives, or neighbors. I'd rather make money for them than I would for Sony or Time Warner or some other joint conglomerate. But then there's the fear of lynch mobs.

The stock writers that underwrote *Crocodile Dundee* made a fortune for themselves and their investors. They've been around ever since and sensed the opportunity and came to me. But the structure of film investing has changed. The only way to do it was to float it on the stock exchange. It's never been done anywhere else in the world because normally, when a company goes public, they've got a factory and an idea of a sales record. All they had was an idea, Paul Hogan and a comedy-western called *Lightning Jack.*

The minimum investment was $2,000. The maximum is me. I'm the biggest investor in it. You put up your money in good faith, but my money is where my mouth is, too.

Johnny Depp

At a certain point you have to come out and live your life the way you want to live it. I don't want to answer to anybody. I don't have to explain myself to a single soul on Earth. That's my reality.

There have been advisors here and there who have said, "Why don't you do some big blockbuster type of thing? We know that this film is going to be a massive hit. Do it." I can't do that. I'd feel ridiculous. It wouldn't be about the work and that's really what I'm in this for. My agents think I'm a little weird. But they also know that I was in a television series for three years and I was really miserable and hard to deal with. When you're miserable you're not very nice to people sometimes.

Ethan Hawke

There's absolutely no encouragement to learn things and get better. There's a lot of encouragement for things like, "Do you have what it takes to go big?" All of a sudden it's a competition thing. Do I have what it takes to be in a $40 million movie that I wouldn't like to begin with? Well, why would I want to do that? Why should I feel flattered? You don't want to be ungrateful, but that doesn't mean I have to do the movie.

Nick Nolte

A young actor came to me one time and said, "You know, Nick, I'm way up there, but I'm just repeating the same story over and over. How do I find something new to do?"

The only answer I had was, "You ever think about just waiting for three or four years?"

And he said, "Oh, I can't do that."

I said, "Well, then you can't mature." Maturity comes with age.

Robert Blake

They paid me $250,000 to do *Judgement Day,* which I thought was a fortune. I found out that it isn't. People were getting four or five hundred grand for a movie of the week. But it's okay. It's all Monopoly money anyway. You see how I live. I'm a little cracker box house here in the [San Fernando] Valley. What are you going to do with it? You put it in your estate someplace and somebody spends it after you croak.

Nick Nolte

How much money can you make? How much money do you really need? Do you not—if you make X millions of dollars then elevate your lifestyle into that, and do you not then have the same economic insecurity you had when you only had five bucks? There's not one of those guys with multimillions of dollars that I know of in this business that is happy. They're miserable. Money becomes the standard of value.

Elton John

You can't become a slave to money. If money dictates your life and you spend years trying to save money, for what? You could die. You could have a heart attack. You could be knocked over by a bus. You spent all your life trying to save money being unhappy and living in a place you don't want to and all of a sudden, POW, you're dead. Great fun. That's ridiculous.

> *At the end of the day, all money gets you is a better place to watch television. If you're humiliated by your work, what's the point?*
>
> *—Dana Carvey*

Peter Frampton

You go along with everybody's advice, which is: You've gotta take advantage of the success. Nobody had sold that many records at that point [after *Frampton Comes Alive*], apart from me. So why was I asking them? Nobody else knew. In fact, I was the most experienced person there was. So I should've gone with my gut instinct, which was to take time off at that point.

Ann Miller

They had a hundred people in the MGM publicity offices doing nothing, day in day out, except publicizing their stars. Their starlets, too. Today they don't have that. Today someone like Robert Redford has to go out and hire his own press agent. Can you believe that? I find that very sad.

When you were under contract to a studio, they watched your makeup, they watched your hair. There was somebody there grooming you like a race horse or a French poodle every five minutes. You had your gowns designed. A stuffed figure was made of your body, or maybe three or four of them. They had one when you were thin, when I would rehearse real hard I'd lose a lot of weight. Then I'd start shooting, I'd start eating. I already knew the dance routines so I could relax a little bit, and they had a stuffed figure that was a little heavier. It was wonderful. They watched everything. And the publicity was incredible.

It was hard on some of the stars because Mr. Mayer was very strict and he wouldn't put up with anything that wasn't nice. If anybody cursed in a room in front of a lady he'd get up and knock him down.

Mark Wahlberg

The most important thing I can say to anyone on the brink of stardom is be true to yourself. Try not to lose that, because once you lose yourself you're working for all these twenty percenters around you that don't give a shit about you. I had a lot of people involved in my life at the time who had different agendas and different goals. They saw that I had a certain marquee value and they tried to use that to their advantage. When I got into the driver's seat of my own career it was like I didn't even have a license to drive, but I figured if it's me who's gotta go out there, at the end of the day I might as well control my destiny. If I'm gonna crash at least I drove the car. I don't want to be a passenger. Usually the only seat that's got an airbag is the driver's.

Clint Eastwood

I've been advised against almost everything I've ever done at some point.

Marisa Tomei

The thing that is most prominent in my mind right now is to trust myself. That's when you get off course, when people give you advice, or I think someone knows better than I do, or I think I'm not experienced. That never really winds up working out for me.

Eric Stoltz

Sometimes you feel distanced from people because of this support system. Sometimes I'll work with actors that I literally have to say, "Let's get away from all these people and just talk about the scene." I don't function well with hangers-on.

John Landis

When you work with a superstar there's added baggage, those nine guys standing over there. And you have to pay for these six guys over there. That's universal. That's the superstar package.

Sean Connery

I talked to Wesley Snipes about all this and I told him to have a really good confidante and a very good lawyer. I told him that any deals that he's making, he should assume the worst of the partner and the partner should assume the worst of him. Get it all out before, instead of saying, "Oh, we went to school together," or, "We played ball together." Disaster.

Robert Redford

Business managers, consultants, and lawyers all clog the process, just like what happens in the legal system. It takes such a long and hard time to get from the idea to the inception that sometimes it's almost not worth it.

Ben Cross

When Chariots of Fire *won the Oscar,* there was a great danger of it all going to my head and not being able to cope. I suddenly acquired all these deep and meaningful relationships with these people that I didn't know at all.

Had fate decreed that I was going to have an explosive and lasting career in Hollywood, there was a very great danger of me turning into a first-class asshole.

Robin Givens

Our heroes aren't really allowed to be people and experience things in life and the difficulties that people experience. Even if you have problems, oftentimes your problems aren't addressed because you're exempt from those problems and we want to put those problems someplace else. We have to remember that heroes are human beings. Just because you can play basketball well doesn't make you exempt from being human. We overlook flaws in our heroes, or else we magnify them.

James Caan

I was stuck [with a gambling debt] for $12,000 at a time in my life when that was like $12,000,000. There was no fucking way. Then I had friends who

Robert Redford The Kobal Collection

said, "Don't worry about this marker. We'll tear that up." Bullshit. I paid it. If you're gonna play you gotta pay. My dad always taught me that. I worked and I paid it off. Now, with football, I bet because I want to be right.

Tom Arnold

Fame can be very toxic to people with personalities like mine, recovering alcoholics or practicing alcoholics. It just isn't conducive to being healthy because it's all about keeping your ego in check if you're going to survive—and yet in this business to survive you need ego. With the fame comes a lot of ego. Everything you feel about yourself negatively is amplified incredibly. Your shame is spread out among the whole world. It literally kills a lot of people.

Jennifer Lopez

Everybody thinks that you're the one that changes, but it's the way people treat you that changes. You see them looking at you weird. It's like, "Why are you looking at me weird?" I'm still Jennifer and I'm still the same and my mother's still Lupe and that's the way it is. Why are you freaking? People have a thing. That's why we make the money we do, I guess.

Wesley Snipes

To be able to criticize, you've got to be able to bring something to the table. When you're living in a glass house, don't throw no stones. You can talk about me all you want, but how clean is your house?

Mary Stuart Masterson

Fame has made me question myself. It definitely at times has made me insecure about myself. It creates a weird kind of guilt. In friendships it's hard to be away so much. It's hard.

Julia Ormond

It's pretty difficult to keep a sense of reality in this business. You start with an agent, the person who gets you work. As things build up he says, "Julia, I'm getting too many phone calls every day about publicity. I can't do it. I haven't got the staff to do it and it's not fair on my other clients." So you get a publicist, and then your friends go, "Eeeeww, a publicist."

David Spade

Friends from growing up, there's a fine line for them. If they're ever nice to me they might feel like they're kissing my ass. So you get both ways. They're kind of mean to you sometimes, or they ignore you. It's hard to play. It's so weird for everyone, me included. They know I bought a house and they haven't yet, so there are little things that are weird.

Bruce Willis

Just about all of my friends join with me in mocking my celebrity and making fun of the fact that other people think that I'm some sort of big shot. I'm not a big shot. I don't behave like that. I never walk around like a big shot. I've seen people who think they are big shots and I've always been embarrassed to be around them. So I'm always getting busted on it. My friends keep me honest in that way.

Rod Stewart

I'm very lucky because many people when they get up high in their career they've lost contact with their old mates. I haven't, but you know you can never please 'em. If you don't buy 'em a drink, they think you're being tight. If you buy 'em a drink, "A round of drinks for all the boys on me," they think you're being flash. So you can never win. Generally speaking they know how to cut me down a peg or two, which sometimes I need that to be done to me.

Elton John

I don't have a lot of friends in the business because I'm not really interested in their style of behavior and I don't want to talk about music

Elvis Presley surrounded himself for more than two decades with a group of men he called "The Guys." Known elsewhere as "the Memphis Mafia," they could be distinguished by one uniform piece of jewelry: a lightning flash with the initials TCB, which stood for "Takin' Care of Business." They were responsible for protecting "the King of Rock 'n' Roll" by keeping the outside world away, caring for him when he sank into drug-induced stupors, and protecting his life with a sometimes maniacal vigilance. The pay was often surprisingly low for these bodyguard/confidants, but the perks were good. Occasionally they would get large cash bonuses, fancy cars, or other gifts—and they always got all the drugs they could handle.

all the time. There are other things in my life besides music. I have lots of friends, but all my friends are people nobody else would know.

Eddie Murphy

I have this reputation for always having ten bodyguards and always having a leather suit on. It ain't like that. This is what it is. I'm in a business dominated by white people. So during business hours I have to travel in totally white circles. I have my relatives and friends who are my staff. Now people are always saying, "It must be hard to find genuine friends being so famous." No. I keep the people who I grew up with and went to school with all around me. They have jobs and they do things for me. It's not like a boss/employee relationship. It's like I always have my family with me. That's how I travel. I can walk into a room with my brother Charlie and my brother Vernon and my cousin Ray and one security person and they say, "He showed up with bodyguards, entourage, and hangers-on." That's just somebody else's trip.

Leonardo DiCaprio
Ron Davis/Shooting Star

Jason James Richter

People do treat you differently. Not really my friends, people who know me don't treat me much different, but people who don't know me and meet me for the first time and find out I'm the kid from *Free Willy* stick to me like flies. They never go away.

Leonardo DiCaprio

I've got my friends right now. I don't want to get any more.

Bo Derek

Everyone around you instantly loves you, but wants something from it, from your situation.

Kirk Douglas

If you have fame, if you have money, people want to be near you. A lot of times I see some billionaires. People want to pick up the check for the billionaire! You feel that some of that money is going to rub off on you. Nothing is going to rub off on you! But we all have that tendency. That's understandable. When I meet Elie Wiesel or somebody famous like that, I'd like to get close to him. Fame is like a flame that attracts a moth.

Flea

(Member of the Red Hot Chili Peppers)

A lot of musicians that get real famous have this feeling that everyone that's dealing with them wants something from them.

Mick Ralphs

(Member of Bad Company)

It's strange how people appear to be well-meaning and they're not. They're after something that you've got. You always think that they want your friendship, but they don't. They want what comes with your friendship, the money, the fun, the parties, the free ride. When you're not selling records and your wife's left and they're all gone, then you suddenly realize that maybe you don't have any friends.

Luke Perry

Ever seen the movie Cool Hand Luke? *Eggs? There's a scene* where he's tried to escape for the second time. They bring him back and he's all beaten up and nobody wants anything to do with him. Everybody wants something to do with you when you're on top, but when you fail nobody's there. I saw that happen in that film and I knew that will happen to you in your life.

Peter Frampton

When the big one hit, when the live album [*Frampton Comes Alive*] hit, we accelerated my work schedule. I didn't think it was possible, but we actually worked more than we had before.

It wouldn't have seemed too good for these guys that were all paying themselves very nicely and helping me spend my money and counting into a mirror, paying me in a mirror, if I had taken six months off. Did I get my point across? There were a lot of people spending my money, that I can't go into for legal reasons. I should be a lot wealthier. It's very difficult when you've got a family of managers to support.

James Caan

I had made a lot of money, but it was taken from me, unbeknownst to me, which I guess is not an uncommon story.

Sean Connery

It's very difficult to measure trust. You either trust somebody or you don't. I've mistakenly trusted and been screwed more times than a hooker.

George Harrison

(What is his most precious Beatles memory?)

I think just being ripped off by all those people, those publishers and managers and stuff. What did I learn and what do I carry with me today? An empty wallet.

Mick Jones

(Member of Foreigner)

That's one of the things that people don't realize. We are vulnerable. Artists seem to be easy prey. A lot of people zero in on that and take advantage of it. It's such a time-consuming thing that you really don't have time to think about business too much. It just goes against the creative thing.

Carole King

Fame brings leeches and sharks who see you as something commercial to attach themselves to and treat as a piece of meat rather than a human being with feelings.

I've worked at having a balance in my life, a place to which I could escape when those types of pressures became overwhelming.

Natasha Henstridge

I have people taking care of the "business" and I do the "show." That's how I like it to be. I don't know a lot about the business, so I just hire people to do that for me.

Anthony Quinn

John Gotti's an acquaintance, but I was friends with Frank Costello. I'll tell you a story about Frank Costello. I was making a picture in New York called *Across 110th Street* and United Artists pulled out of the deal one day. I had $3 million to make the picture—suddenly I found myself with no money. I was having breakfast with Costello every day. He was about eighty years old at the time and he saw I was very, very depressed. I told him it was nothing, but he said, "No, no, I feel it. You have a bad dream or something?"

I told him that I got a notice from the studio and I don't know where to go for the money. I need a million dollars. And he says, "Aaaahhh, enjoy your breakfast. I'll give you the million."

I said, "That's wonderful of you, but I can't take it. I have to sign a contract. What happens if you give me the million? How do I pay you back?"

"You'll pay me back whenever your picture makes money. Don't worry, don't worry."

"But suppose I can't pay you back?"

"Hey, we shake hands and that's a deal."

"But suppose I can't pay you back?"

"Send me back the hand."

Tom Arnold

Arnold [Schwarzenegger] gave me some financial advice which has paid off very well. Stuff I didn't know. You're afraid to ask people stuff in this

At thirty-five, Yolanda Saldivar considered herself Selena's closest confidant. After all, Saldivar had launched the beautiful young Tejano singing star's fan club, served as her personal assistant, and even ran the two Selena, Etc. boutiques located in Texas. But when Selena's father, Abraham Quintanilla, Jr. accused Saldivar of embezzling $30,000 from the fan club, things soured. On March 31, 1995, at a Days Inn in Corpus Christi, Texas, Selena argued with Saldivar. Saldivar pulled out her legally purchased .38 caliber hand gun and fired. The twenty-five cent bullet ripped through Selena's right shoulder blade, slashed through a main artery and killed her. Saldivar ran to her red truck and held a gun to her head, keeping police at bay for more than nine and a half hours. Finally, exhausted, she gave up and was taken into custody.

In October 1995, the jury rejected Salvidar's contention that the shooting was an accident and convicted her of murder. She was sentenced to life in prison and faces at least 30 years behind bars.

town. "Do you pay a percentage for this and that?" Finally I felt comfortable around him and I asked him a whole bunch of questions that I'd always wanted to know—and I made changes in my business.

Yoko Ono

If I become paranoid at all, then that's very unhealthy. I can't live that way.

The source of energy that we have is power of love, power of truth, power of knowledge. Maybe John [Lennon] and I had power of love and power of truth, but power of knowledge? I don't know how much we had. It's nothing wrong in having knowledge. The more knowledge you have is power.

I should trust, not with a certain simplemindedness, but I should trust with a full understanding.

Elliott Gould

Now that I understand the politics, now that I understand the world and life in the world, I can play respectfully and I can choose for myself. I don't have to hurt myself anymore and I don't have to allow myself to be taken advantage of—although I choose to retain the privilege to allow myself to be taken advantage of. I don't want to be closed. I want to stay open. But now I can listen, and I also know how to hear a little bit more than I could hear before.

Robert Blake

I need an agent who believes in my dream for the third act of my life. Agents want me to do a TV series because they make a couple of million dollars a year if you do one. I need somebody who will be strong when I'm destructive, when I say, "Oh, what the hell. Why don't we do this series?"

I want somebody to say, "Hey! What happened to your dream, schmuck? You want to do another series? Go get another agent."

Martin Lawrence

The only agent I need, baby, is God. I know what I want to say. I know what I want to do. I'm a positive, strong, black man. I don't need nobody else to feed it to me.

Chazz Palminteri

I have a lot of confidence in myself, and I really like myself a lot, so I feel like if I wasn't famous somebody would like me anyway. I hope that doesn't sound weird. That's from my mom and dad, who gave me a lot of respect for myself. So if somebody's nicer to me because I'm famous that's all right, because if they really got to know me they would like me anyway.

Jonathan Taylor Thomas

You just have to take everything in stride and take this whole business with a grain of salt. It's put up on a pedestal and it's made out to be things that it's not, so if you buy too much into it then you'll totally get lost and caught up with it. But if you take everything for what it really is and what it's really worth, then you're much better off.

Some kids have a paper route. I go to the set. That's how I look at it. It's just a different job.

Stephen Baldwin

Hollywood's weird, man. There's an energy here that just brainwashes you. So I live in Arizona, 'cause I'm already weird enough.

The Family Burden

In most cases where stars are relatively successful in minimizing the toxicity of fame, strong family roots are in evidence. When it comes to diaper changing, it really doesn't matter how famous you are. But how do you keep those family ties strong when work takes you away from home for months at a time? The demands of stardom are tiring and time-consuming, like any powerful position in society. Juggling work and family is tough enough for anyone, but try it under the magnification of the spotlight. Similarly, parent/child and other family relationships are always complex. How can the singular rewards of fame be shared with loved ones?

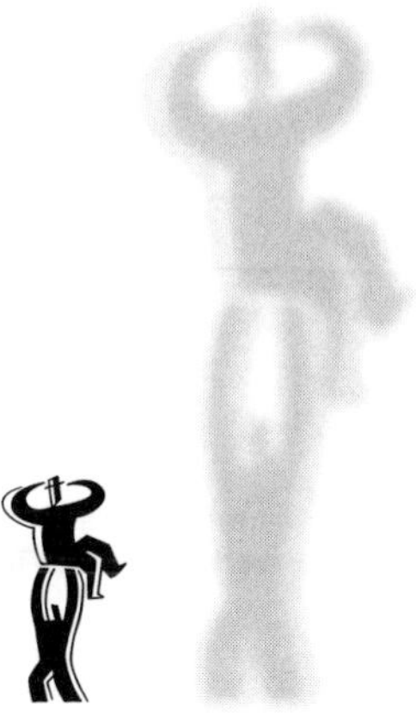

Meryl Streep

No matter how rich and famous you are, if you're a working mother you're always pulled to the limit. I think everybody knows that. People probably think, "You have sitters and someone to cook," but you're always feeling that you're late for one appointment, inadequate in this, coming up short with that, and it's a stretch and a strain. It's something I have to deal with every day. But I couldn't live any other way because I couldn't live without either dimension.

Joanne Woodward

If I had really wanted a big, big career, maybe it wouldn't have been possible. I suspect I could have. I started off fine. But I then chose to have children. I turned down an awful lot of things because I didn't want to go away. I didn't want to leave Paul [Newman, her husband]. I didn't want to leave the kids. I don't like to fly. I had any number of reasons why I didn't do things and still don't do things.

I believe that you do make choices between the nurturing side of your life and the professional side. It's not physically possible in the universe to be two places at once. You can't be home and at work at the same time.

—Kate Capshaw

Robin Wright

It's the location. Do I want to go to Aruba with the two kids and the nannies? That's the only thought you have now. The exhaustion.

Meg Ryan

It's hard for every woman with children. There's nowhere to go for advice about it except to your peers. We're all going, "Well, what do you do?" It's such a vamp, such an improv. On the one hand you feel that you need to do what you do that makes you you, and on the other hand you have this other love and this other responsibility. One has more weight than the other so fast.

Phoebe Cates

I asked another actress, "How do you do it? You're working so much. I see you everywhere and you have children."

She said, "I hire good people."

I thought, "That's really honest."

Nastassia Kinski

My daughter was burned and I wasn't there. The nanny did something really stupid. So you have to have people that you really trust, great people for your kids, because you're not there.

Alannah Myles

You have to love it with all your heart and soul, because you're deprived of a happy home life. You're deprived of child-rearing. You can't seem to mingle them both with a successful career, unless you're lucky enough to find a man who will do all of the above for you, which is pretty much nonexistent in the 1990s. Being in it for the money is just going to put you where I wound up—and it's not a happy place.

Dennis Miller

You ever feel like you were being a phony with yourself in your life? I'm saying one thing, I'm trumpeting the fact that I'd like to pull back, and yet I'm taking these movie roles. I finally just had a talk with myself. I said, "Listen, man. You're a parent now. You don't have much time. You should stay at home more." So that's what I'm going to do. I'm going to stay at home with my kids.

John Travolta

I would like a little more time with my son [Jett], because at this point I've chosen to work more and that frustrates me. I miss him when I'm on the set. Trying to schedule free time has been a little hard lately. I basically had a week off last year and I'll get a week off this year.

John Travolta Lisa O'Connor/Shooting Star

Kirk Douglas

Michael [Douglas, his son] took a year off to catch up with his son—and I admired him for that. Jesus, I wasn't catching up with anybody, including myself. That's why I wrote my autobiography, *The Ragman's Son.* It was a chance for me to catch up with myself.

Chevy Chase

If I have to be gone, three weeks is the outside. Then they either come to me for a week, or I come home.

Gabriel Byrne

Over the last eighteen months, since I've been separated, I have chosen small roles in movies where I can do my parts in just ten or fifteen days and I'm gone. I've made that very deliberate choice, because I chose between my family and my career. I don't want to be on location and in hotels and in airports for nine months out of the year.

James Spader

There's a certain amount of the year that I want to devote to the making of movies. Then the rest of the year I like to devote to my family and my friends and my life outside of it, which is very vital to me, and quite full. I'm not an actor who has ever gone right from one film to the next. I do this just when I have to—and then I don't.

I've never worked for free. Like on *The Music of Chance,* they had a very small budget, but I went to the director and I told him, "I'm dying to do this film, but I haven't done a film in a little bit because I've been running around with my family and playing with my kids. I'd love to do this film, but I've got to pay my bills, too." I don't mind going to somebody and saying, "Okay, this is how much money I need to pay my bills for the next six months. If you pay me that, I'll do the film."

Matthew Modine

I was gone out of the country for six months [while filming *Cutthroat Island*]. I'm married and I've got a couple of kids. Six months is a long time to be away from a five and a ten-year-old. I've been playing catchup, but you can never make up the time that you're away. It's gone —and gone forever.

My father was very sick, also, and I was desperately trying to finish so that I could get home to be with him. My father passed away in July.

Elliott Gould

My great ambition is to be a great-great-grandfather. So that the children of the children's children's children and I can share this conscious faculty, and then, as Mr. Gershwin said, "Who could ask for anything more?"

Gabriel Byrne

Melissa Mathison [Harrison Ford's wife and the screenwriter of E.T.*] had a very good quote* in a piece that I read. She said, "I don't want to be on movie sets writing about kids. I want to be at home with my kids." The real pressures of a married actor's life come when you have to go away for nine weeks and leave your kids, who are standing at the side of the road saying, "Bye, bye, Dad," and you're trying to say, "I'll be back." When you're sitting in a hotel room in Denver at eleven o'clock at night flicking the channels, that's when you really have to pay for being an actor.

Sting

The kids share our work, because they have no choice. I make records at home with the kids around me. My work isn't a mystery to them.

Sally Field

My kids are very critical about my work, but they're usually very smart about it. And they don't comment anything on *The Flying Nun.*

Diane Venora

If your work is priority, your relationships will always suffer. And if your children are priority your marriage will always suffer. So whatever you pick first is going to affect everything you do, whether you're a doctor, a lawyer, or an Indian chief. Whatever drives somebody. Picasso's life was his work and everyone else filled in secondly.

Geraldine Chaplin

We lived in a hotel for a long time and then my mother [Oona O'Neill], she was then pregnant with her fifth child, and she said, "Charlie, I'm not going to have this in a hotel." That's when we got our house.

She was disowned by her own father [playwright Eugene O'Neill] when she married my father [Charlie Chaplin]. They never reconciled. I never met my grandfather. I wish I had.

Lynn Redgrave

The intensity with which my father [Michael Redgrave] would submerge himself into a part was actually quite frightening when we were kids. If he was playing a tragedy then you stayed well away from him, and if he was playing comedies then it was songs 'round the piano.

Jack Lemmon

I did come to a realization when I was very young. I think into my thirties I had been totally self-absorbed—and maybe you have to be in a high risk profession like this. But I just did not have room in my mind and in my emotions for a hell of a lot beyond me and my acting career. It began to change when Chris was born, my son who's now over forty. I began to start thinking about the environment and the kind of world he's going to grow up in. Before that I was fighting and clawing and trying to make a career in a high risk profession, thinking so much about myself.

Phoebe Cates

Parenthood is a little easier on the father, when it comes to work. The mother really gives up more. I know that will set some men screaming, but that's definitely true. It's definitely true in my case. He [husband Kevin Kline]'s more careful about what he chooses as well, because he likes to spend time with his son and with me, but it's really the mother who the baby wants the first few years and it's more important that the mother be the constant.

Mary Elizabeth Mastrantonio

I do believe there's a double standard. It's somehow easier for a woman to follow a man. How do I look at my husband and say, "I know you're a free thinking individual with an incredible will and an incredible mind—and I'd like you to come sit with me again for four months in a hotel while I make a movie." He can't have the babies. That to me is the most difficult thing, because you don't know if you're trading one for the other.

Dennis Quaid

Her [wife Meg Ryan's] career has really skyrocketed since she had Jack, our son. Maybe I should have a baby.

Warren Beatty

I'm surprised that people were surprised that I wanted to have a child.

> *I have to confess, it's pretty hard to juggle this career and motherhood. I like my baby better than I like my job.*
>
> *—Bette Midler*

Michael J. Fox

Being a father helps me with my guilt feelings, that I've had all this success and other people can't have it, and I should feel bad about it. But most people, with the obvious sad exceptions, can have kids. That's much better than any professional success, family success.

Sophia Loren

For me, marriage is something sacred and family is the most important thing in my life. A woman must love family and must make it a constant thought, especially if you have children. That's the only thing you really have to think seriously about. It goes without saying that my family comes first, as you have seen lately. I'm not in many pictures anymore. I'm very pleased with it. It's my first choice.

Charlene Tilton

I went back to work on *Dallas* four days after I had my daughter, Cherish.

James Spader

Luckily, the actor in our house is sort of a lazy actor who likes to work maybe one film a year, at the most two if one of them is a small role. Geographically, it can get tough. *Stargate* was the first film where the whole family didn't all transplant to wherever we were shooting. It was great when we all transplanted. It was tougher being in Yuma all by myself and wanting to put my kids to bed every night and them wanting to see Papa.

Joan Armatrading

It sounds flippant, but I really haven't got the time to have a family. At certain points you have to decide, "Do I want to have a family or do I want to do what I'm doing, which takes an awful lot of time?" Friends of mine, who are in the music business as well, have just decided that they want a family. So straight away, because they want a family, it seems that both of them, their careers have had to stop because they do this work that takes them away.

Bill Pullman

Tom Hanks on the Academy Awards thanked his wife [actress Rita Wilson] and kids for giving him the time. Some people mocked that, but they give up all of their time with you. That's a gift.

Rita Wilson

I never see Tom [Hanks, her husband] reading a script, working on his lines, or working on his character, and yet I'll see him gazing, glazing over, and he's not in the room. I'm talking, "andthenwewentdown youcouldn'tbelieveit," and suddenly he goes, "What?" I know that that's how he's working.

Tim Robbins
Nikki Vai/Shooting Star

Rita Wilson

Home is wherever we are. We [she and husband Tom Hanks] go on location with each other and we bring the family. We're very strict about doing that. We make sure that that happens. I know a lot of people don't do it that way, one person stays home and all of that, but I really believe that the family is where the family is, not where the house is or where the school is.

Tim Robbins

I don't like to direct too often. While I was finishing *Dead Man Walking,* my son said to me, "Daddy, directing takes a lot longer than acting."

I said, "Yeah, you're right."

He said, "I don't think you should direct too much."

I agree with him. He's six.

Susan Sarandon

Eventually, when I finish directing my family I might direct a film. I've been offered directing jobs. I just do not have the kind of time to give a year of that kind of obsession. Maybe I'll find I want to do that when everything falls and nobody wants to hire me for the kind of stuff I want to do.

Christine Lahti

It's really difficult to balance motherhood and my career, especially the directing thing. I could not direct a feature for a while. My twins were only a year and a half when I directed a short film for Showtime. I realized that being a director you have no life. As an actor I don't work all the time and there's a lot of down time even when I am working. I've always been very selective about what I do, so there are always many months out of the year when I do nothing but be a mom.

Ron Howard

I really don't want to take two or three weeks away from my family or my primary job [directing] and do what for me now would be kind of a lark, to do some acting. But one day, maybe when the kids are raised, I would kind of like to do it.

Robert Downey, Jr.

I thought that in some ways my dad [director Robert Downey] was an absent father, but he'd be there for every Christmas. He'd go out of town a lot, but he was pretty much there a lot more than most dads. Now that I do have to leave town sometimes and go places, I go, "Wow, it's really hard to be there all the time for your kid, no matter what." I guess what's important is the quality of time when you are with them.

Faye Dunaway

They say that quality time is better than quantity time, but I don't agree. I think quantity is a lot better. The quantity of time that I spend with my fourteen-year-old son tells me who he is. If I come in and spend five minutes a day, I don't know who he is. It's when he's not watching me. It's the ongoing moments, the little things.

Having said that, I get a lot done. I know how to work very fast. I do three or four things at once, which actually I enjoy doing. I like being very busy. I think that's the definition of stardom, really. It's energy. It really is.

So I hope I haven't done badly. We'll see. As Jackie Onassis said, "If you don't do a good job with your children it doesn't very much matter what else you do."

Diane Venora

If your child is two years old and hasn't seen Mommy in two days while you're on a press junket, that's okay. But if that continues over a long period of time you're going to pay.

Sigourney Weaver

Last night, after I went home after forty TV interviews, I had to construct a long story for my daughter. I thought, "This is the only important part of my day and I MUST find the energy to do this." She's the first priority. That's the hardest part for me as an actor now, making sure that I can really do my work and at the same time maintain a proper presence as a parent. I feel guilty all the time, especially when I'm enjoying myself.

Dana Carvey

"Daddy play? Daddy play? Daddy play?" That's great when you've just flown in, you're jetlagged and it's 5:30 in the morning. "I wanna Daddy play."

Pat Benatar

Chrissie Hynde talked to me when I first had a child about touring. She said, "No big deal. You take the nanny. You go. Nothing." It's really no big deal, because you spend most of your day doing nothing and you work for a little bit during the soundcheck in the afternoon. Then you do the show at night. You do some publicity during the day. So you have many hours when you do nothing. Now we do nothing as a family.

Alannah Myles

You can't place your sole expectations of personal fulfillment in Grammys and million sales and money. You can't curl up with a Grammy at night and kiss it goodnight and say, "Honey, will you love me tomorrow?" It's pretty vacuous. You have to find your source of fulfillment in places that are beyond the materialism that that world provides.

Jason Alexander

The important thing is that you go home and there's somebody there who thinks half as much of you as those people do as you're coming out that stage door. If that's for real, then you've got something.

Arsenio Hall

The simple things, like taking my mom to lunch, that's important. When you're experiencing a certain kind of success and working all these hours, you can't just give Mom the credit card and say, "You're on your own." Sometimes it's about being there, it's about love. I had some things in my life that I had to straighten out. My dog was looking at me like I was one of the gardeners.

I try to keep my home life and my business as far apart from each other as I can. I don't want to exclude anybody, but there are times when I'm doing my job that it's uncomfortable for me not just to have my wife but to have anybody from my personal life there. I think you'd be a fool to say, "Honey, we're shooting the big love scene today. You want to come down?"

—Luke Perry

Gary Oldman

You have to sacrifice a lot of family and friends. You have to be quite single-minded and at times very selfish. Then in a strange kind of way it eats in on itself. The more successful you get, the more you're flying here, there, and everywhere. You're never at home. You're never with your family. You're always on the road. You live out of a bag in another hotel room. That's the killer. "Another fucking hotel room."

Michael Crawford

Home is really in my Delsey suitcase. I live in that suitcase.

Joan Plowright

Of course it's more difficult to be a parent in this business. I don't think you ever get rid of the feeling of guilt.

Annie Potts

I've noticed, especially with my older son, when he was with me at work he would never call me Mom. He would always call me Annie, to distinguish that I was a different person there. I always thought how weird that must be for him.

Martin Short

I found this note on my mirror when I got home last night, because I'm rehearsing a play right now. "For Daddy only." It's from daughter Katherine, eleven. "Dear Daddy, I miss you. I know you're not in another country, but I miss talking to you. It's kind of like you're not here, because I only see you for fifteen minutes in the morning. I understand that you have to do your play, dot, dot, dot, Oh I don't know. I hope you're having fun doing your play. I hope you do really well tomorrow night. See you soon." Isn't that cute?

I expect that one day my children will write a book, "Damn You, Daddy, Sir." That can't be helped. They'll need money and I understand that. If I had left them more [money] they wouldn't have written it.

George Lucas

A director gets up at four o'clock in the morning, works until midnight, seven days a week, and doesn't have any life. After I finished the last *Star Wars,* [*Return of the Jedi*] I had a daughter. I have three kids now and I spend a great deal of time with my kids. So I'm raising three kids, running three companies, and making movies at the same time. That's hard to do when you're a director. You can kind of manage it when you're a producer.

Denzel Washington

It's easier to balance my family and my career now because I'm older. I'm not an "overnight sensation." I've been slowly moving up the ladder. I've learned a lot about life and one of the things I've learned is to keep it simple. What I do is not rocket science. I go to work in the morning. I get off in the evening. When I open the door at home they could care less that I've talked to you. They want to talk about their homework, or whatever. My job is to be there for them and to listen and help them with the homework—and to put out the trash.

Madonna

I suppose I have a bit of an obsession with motherhood and mothering because I didn't have a mother. All my life I've wandered around wondering what it would have been like if I would have had a mother. I think I transfer those feelings onto other people, so I try to be the mother that I never had to the group of people that I'm working with. I instinctively am drawn to people who need mothering so that I may live out this fantasy that I have about what it must be like to have a mother.

Madonna

I definitely see having a child, yes. I don't think you have to be in a longtime relationship with a man to have one though. But that would be nice.

I'm looking for the chicken before the egg.

Catherine Deneuve

Having children out of wedlock made life difficult. If I look back, of course, it's not the best choice for my children. But it was not a decision I made before. It's something that happened that I had to deal with. Sometimes today when I hear women talking about having a child and living just by themselves with the child I'm shocked, really deeply shocked and upset. Because I know what it is and I cannot think that someone would think of raising a child by herself from the start. To me it's shocking. It's so selfish.

Jodie Foster

Having a child is a big, messy, great, human process. I feel like I either will or I won't in my lifetime. I don't feel this, "I am nothing unless I have children," like women do perhaps at a certain age. I don't think I'm nothing if I don't have kids.

Denzel Washington
Ron Davis/Shooting Star

Paul Reiser

I never put anything really totally personal in my work. I don't know who it was that said once that the most personal stuff is the most universal. So whenever you do talk about stuff that's really small, whether it's sexual or emotional or hygienic, everybody knows. Everybody's had a thing in the shower. Everybody's been in bed naked with somebody else.

When I wrote my book my wife had first right of refusal. "Anything in there you want me to cut, it's gone. Unless it's really funny and then to hell with you."

> *I don't talk about my family specifically too much or have people photograph in my home because I feel that it's asking for trouble. They are private moments. I don't want to give them away.*
>
> *—Susan Sarandon*

Esther Williams

You finished a movie and the whole publicity department moved into your house. Three months after you had a baby, that baby better look good, because it was going to get its picture taken. Portraits. They figured the redness should go and they should get some of the wrinkles out and stop peeing in people's faces.

Tony Curtis

Lew Wasserman was my agent. When I started in pictures in '48 he said to me, "Tony, it's going to take you ten hard, heavy years to become internationally known." So I put my head down and for ten years I made pictures, three a year. I didn't stop. I never thought about it, whatever marriages, whatever. After ten years, Lew was right. Every country in the world knew me.

Richard Harris

It's impossible to make a marriage work. The reason that I'm so friendly with my two ex-wives is because I say to them, "It was my fault." There is no dividing here. I always say it was 100% my fault. Number one, it was the job I was in. Number two, I was wild. I said to my ex, "You had all the hardship. You brought them up. I had all the fun."

I'm a better friend than I was a husband.

Gene Hackman

You don't realize until years and years later how selfish a job this is we have. In order to do it well you really have to commit to it, and in order to commit to it, you leave family outside of it. It's very difficult for families to get into the brotherhood of filmmaking. Years down the line you realize what it is that you've done to people who you care a great deal about. I have a lot of regrets about that. In the end, what does film mean? I like the idea that I was successful in my career, but there are things that are maybe more important.

Nicolas Cage

Being away on location seems to be the way my life is going. I can't be there as a father as much as I want to be there. I think my relationship has lost some closeness because of that. It's just something that I can only hope that later in life will be rekindled.

Beau Bridges

My dad [actor Lloyd Bridges] was starting to travel a lot in his work when Jeff [Bridges, his brother] was younger. I took his part in some situations, like teaching Jeff how to throw a ball and a lot of those things. So, the sibling rivalry thing never happened.

Kiefer Sutherland

I have had very forgiving children. I had them when I was very young. Your natural reaction when you are young and you are given this authority is to think that you're going to be a good father and have a strong hand in raising them. My oldest daughter, especially, has been the most forgiving. As I started to become a little more open to what they actually wanted to do, they became a lot more receptive to me as a father. It's a never-ending education.

Lauren Bacall

I fulfilled my real life, but I did not fulfill my acting potential because I put my real life first. I did everything backwards. I screwed up everything. Next time, when I come back, I'm going to do things a little bit differently. I haven't done a lot of things I feel I can do.

Salma Hayek

My love scene with Antonio Banderas in *Desperado* is pretty hot. There were no body doubles, but I'm telling my father that some of it is body doubles, and some of it they erased part of my clothing with the computer the same way they erased the cables when I jumped from one building to the other. The action stuff was a blast. It was the love scene that I had trouble with.

Dennis Quaid

When you make a sexy movie like *The Big Easy,* even before you have kids, you say, "My mother's going to see this." It's either your mother or your kids you have to think about. You've got to be an orphan without children to do it without guilt.

Laura Linney

My family is understandably stunned—as I am. "My God, there's my daughter running through the jungle with a gun in her hand."

Dean Roland

(Member of Collective Soul)

My dad watches MTV all the time. He's a preacher, so he's never been into MTV at all. We got him a picture-in-picture television and now he keeps the corner picture on MTV all the time waiting for our videos to come on.

Ron Howard

My mom is Mrs. Lovell in *Apollo 13,* the grandmother in the nursing home. My dad came to me and said, "Looks like you wrote a part for your mother."

I said, "Gee, I didn't. I wasn't thinking of her for that."

He said, "Well, she'd be good in it."

My great concern always, is I love working with my family, but I want them to excel. It's far too important to ever cast anybody who's not going to excel. I will have to admit that I put my mother through a very extensive audition—and she got the job. She earned it. I took the tape back and showed it to other people. Everybody was saying, "Just give her the part, Ron. It's okay."

"No, no, no! I want you to look at this tape and tell me what you think." I even had other women come in and audition.

Garry Marshall

A lot of times I hire relatives. A relative is safe. You can always yell at a relative. It has worked for me in the past, not to have to worry about the other person and concentrate on your star, because that's who is giving you the performance that is going to be memorable.

Carl Reiner

What father ever understood his kid? I never understood Rob [Reiner, his son]. He came from a different generation. I came from a Depression. He came from a rich household. How do you understand your kid? Our kids were even harder to understand because they changed the rules in the 1960s. We had whole different rules about ethics and morality, what's right and wrong, country and motherhood. All of a sudden they're burning flags.

Alan Young

My dad used to work very hard to make five dollars a day and he saw me making six dollars a day in radio. He said, "Son, you keep up with this talking business because lips don't sweat."

Carl Reiner

It's funny. Rob [Reiner, his son] is so honest that when he's interviewed, he tells it all and people think that we're enemies or something. We have been very close for a lot of years and still are.

Eric Roberts

My mother and I have only spoken once since I was fourteen years old. So I was an adolescent and a young adult without a mother. Then I met Lee Grant on *It's My Party* and we bonded. To cut to the chase, she's now basically my surrogate mother. I would call Lee for anything and everything. Lee is my mother and I got to choose her.

James Earl Jones

My father and I can be friends, we still talk, but to be father and son it's too late. It's hard for him to acknowledge that. He wants to reap the benefits of being the patriarch. I say, "No, it's too late. You didn't pay anything in. You can't take anything out of the bank." He hates it. He says, "How dare you?! You can't talk to me that way."

Lauren Holly

All of a sudden friends or more distant family members that you don't usually spend time with want to be a part of every social occasion. You don't want to hurt anybody's feelings, but it's like, "Since when did you come to dinner every Friday night?" That's sort of weird.

Or if one of my close friends was having a birthday party, do we go? That always comes up, because all of a sudden we become the focus of attention when it's their birthday party. You have guilt about that.

Sharon Stone told the Los Angeles Times that she watched a television documentary about the Beatles with great interest. She was especially struck by a part in which Ringo Starr talked about how he knew the band was getting really big when members of his own family started treating him differently. "I was really identifying with that a lot," Stone said.

Jimmy Smits

Some people in my family relate to me from their perspective of Hollywood and what they think the business is all about. It comes out as a nervous kind of thing.

James Earl Jones

My relatives don't know how to handle my fame. There was not supposed to be anybody successful in the family. It wasn't supposed to happen. So when it happened it was like, "What are we supposed to do with it?"

"I need a new roof for my house."

They assume I'm rich. They'll say things like that because they don't know what else to say. I don't even go to family reunions any more.

Anfernee Hardaway

(Plays basketball with the Orlando Magic)

My grandmother raised me and I talk to her every day, her and my mom. She never lets me stray away from where I came from.

Tyra Banks

People that start treating me like a princess I try to cut off. I have people in my family saying, "Oh no, wait! She can't do that." Like this Christmas, it was, "Go fix her plate for her. She's a princess. That's supermodel Tyra." It makes me sometimes not even want to be around some family members because of that. That's how I shield myself, not being around that type of energy.

Julie Walters

My mother never was one for paying any compliments, but she used to say things to other people. Like we'd be walking along the street where I live and I'd feel her edging me over and then she'd bump into somebody on purpose. "Oh, this is my daughter, Julie. She's just completed a film with Michael Caine" as if he'd been some sort of extra in it. She did it in that way, so I figured she must be proud. And then she died in 1989 and I found all these cuttings that she'd kept. I never thought she kept anything like that. She never showed any interest.

Mary Tyler Moore

I grew up feeling that I was not valued. I was a poor student and I was closed off myself to pretty closed off parents, so that became self-fulfilling. But as I began to emerge as a source of pride and conversation between my parents and their friends, it became a center for us. They never were self-conscious with me, but I knew that they were proud of me. And I knew that they were pleasantly surprised that the kid who said, "No mother, I'm not going to take typing because I don't want to have to go to work as a secretary," gosh, maybe was right after all. Maybe it was right for her to be taking those dancing classes instead.

Although while I was writing my book, having to write it in long hand, I regretted having taken that stand.

Julie Walters

My mother did come to the premiere of *Educating Rita.* She came the wrong way up to the theater. There was this barrier and all these policemen because the Duke of Edinburgh came to it. And she said, "EXCUSE ME! WILL YOU LET ME THROUGH! THAT'S MY DAUGHTER UP THERE!" The policeman took the barrier down, but I think he thought she was a madwoman.

Liam Neeson

It's great going back, but it's lovely getting away again.

Talia Shire

When I was in drama school, Stella Adler would look at me and say, "You should take a course in Chutzpah I and Chutzpah II." What she meant was, however the arrangement of siblings in our family was, I didn't know how to manage a career. Certainly there was this one dynamic sibling becoming very famous [her brother, director Francis Ford Coppola] and it made me waffle terribly. I wasn't coming out of Yale like Meryl Streep. I was coming out very doubtful about it. So when people talked about nepotism, that was very rough. [Talia got her big break when her brother cast her in *The Godfather*.] It was tough within me, because you never want to exploit all the people you're going to meet. If you're tending to meet lovely people coming through friends, you can't say, "Hey, would you consider me for this job?" So you feel very bound.

> *I get mistaken for my brothers all the time. I have a lot of fun with it. They say, "You were great in Sliver, can I have your autograph?" And I say, "Go to hell, you bastard." Then they walk away going, "That Billy Baldwin, he's such a prick." He does it to Alec, too.*
>
> *—Stephen Baldwin*

Eric Roberts

My sister [actress Julia Roberts] and I disagree on a couple of key family issues like all brothers and sisters do. I love my sister. I'm very proud of my sister. I would love to take credit for all of it, but I deserve none of it.

I've never been jealous of her for a minute. I've been unhappy for her at times, like in her marriage [her brief marriage to singer Lyle Lovett failed], but quite frankly, under the circumstances and considering where she comes from, there isn't a better job that could have been done with her young life thus far. If she ever needs me for anything, anytime, anywhere, I'll be there.

Pat Conroy

My sister won't talk to me. When Mom was dying, she said, "I hear you're writing a book about us." That was *The Prince of Tides*. She said, "You can't write about me."

"I will say this as kindly as I can, but I don't let people tell me what I can write about."

"You cannot steal my life."

"There is this unfortunate aspect. We're brother and sister. Your life is my life."

So we have not spoken since Mom's funeral.

Randy Quaid

Doing True West *was really like therapy* for us [he and brother Dennis Quaid], doing it on stage every night for six months in front of three hundred people. Personally, we weren't like the characters in *True West,* but a lot of the same dynamics of their relationship were working in Dennis's and my relationship. We came away from there much closer to each other.

Emilio Estevez

There was a period of my life where I was really rejecting the family, going out on my own, creating my own name, my own image, separating myself. Every time I saw my name in print there was "Martin Sheen's son" afterwards. So I've done pictures with each one of them [his dad and his brother, Charlie Sheen]. I've made amends. Now I'm moving on. I probably won't make a film with either one of them until we're all in our sixties. It's not in the stars.

Mel Gibson

My sister was getting her hair done one day. She was sitting in a chair and I came up in conversation and this lady was slagging off on me. She didn't like me very much.

So my sister is sitting in her chair and the lady doing her hair said, "This is his sister."

And the lady turned to my sister and said, "I don't like your brother."

So my sister said, "Oh, I don't like YOUR brother."

And the lady said, "You don't know my brother," and my sister said, "You don't know mine."

Growing Up

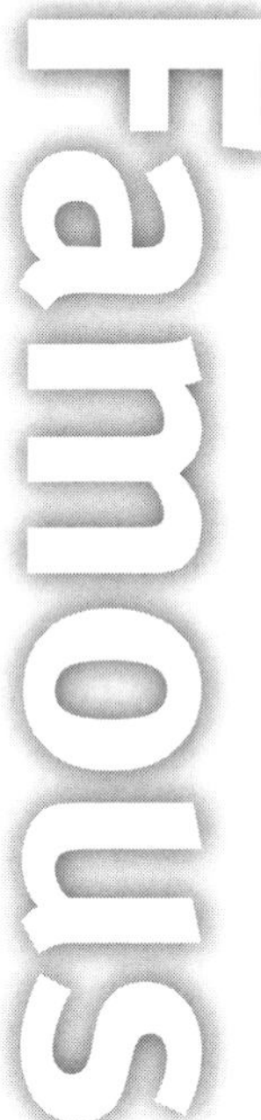

Let's say you keep your head screwed on right, you keep your career moving forward, and you learn to deal with the problems of fame. What about your kids? The reflected glare of the spotlight can be the most dangerous of all. How can you protect them? And what about the child star, who has to figure it all out while dealing with the normal traumas of adolescence? Fame is toxic enough at adult strength.

Melanie Griffith

I got this doll that was a replica of my mother [actress Tippi Hedren] that was in a coffin from Alfred Hitchcock for my birthday. Nice, huh? I think he was very strange. That's a strange thing to send to anyone, much less a five-year-old little girl. I never played with it. I just put it away.

Keith Carradine

I would see him [John Carradine, his dad] on television. In fact, I saw him killed on a *Navy Log* in 1954 and my grandparents spent days trying to convince me that it didn't really happen, because he was away.

Isabella Rossellini

I'd come home and mother [actress Ingrid Bergman] was there saying, "That stupid journalist met me for five minutes and is going to write about me." I was glad to step out of journalism.

Jennifer Jason Leigh

(Actor Vic Morrow's daughter)

I was always very introverted. I read a lot. With my friends I would act, because that's how I came out of myself. That and years and years and years of therapy.

Deborah Harry

(Member of Blondie)

Fame is never like your fantasies. It's always different. I think had I come from a family that was in the business I would have had a better perspective about it. I think that a lot of kids that follow in their parents' footsteps that are in the entertainment business have a real healthy point of view about it, because they know what the business is about.

Mary Crosby

I feel very, very strongly about this. Being a celebrity's kid either goes one of two ways. You either become a mess or you become very strong.

The questions aren't any different. "Who am I? What am I? Where do I want to go with my life?" All of those things everybody has to deal with. The only difference is, if you're a celebrity's child you have to deal with those questions earlier. If you don't establish a very strong sense of your own identity, people will project on you what they want, as so-and-so's son or daughter.

Growing up as Bing [Crosby]'s daughter is something that I am very proud of. I love being his kid. I am from good stock, as they say. I am proud to have his genes and the genes of my mother in my body. I think they make me strong and talented and good. On a more personal level, it was great because Daddy had always had boys and he never had a girl. He didn't know what to do with me as a girl. It was terrific. He taught me how to play baseball and how to hunt and how to fish. I am, to this day, an incorrigible tomboy. And we got serenaded with "White Christmas."

Joely Richardson

(Actress Vanessa Redgrave and director Tony Richardson's daughter; actress Natasha Richardson's sister)

As children we always traveled with our mother. If she went on a job we'd up and move to L.A. for a few months. We loved that. That was really fun, to be allowed to experience all these different places.

Vanessa Redgrave

I admire them [daughters Natasha and Joely Richardson] very much. You have to have a lot of courage to be an actress or an actor today.

Paul Newman was known to tell his friends that he lived in fear of that telephone call that will come in the night, "telling me that something has happened to Scott." By 1978, Scott Newman, who was tall, green-eyed, and as handsome as you would expect, was beginning to come to terms with his life in the shadow of famous parents. The twenty-eight-year-old stuntman/daredevil was moving beyond his feelings of inadequacy in relation to his idolized dad. He joined Alcoholics Anonymous and was seeing a private therapist. But he reportedly still drank and, bothered by the aches and pains of stunt work, he took a variety of painkillers and illegal drugs. The combination proved lethal.

Scott died in his sleep—and his devastated father finally received the dreaded call.

Joely Richardson

It is difficult if you have a parent who is controversial. [Vanessa Redgrave has been an outspoken supporter of Palestinian rights.] Obviously if someone is very controversial there will be lots of people who will be pro them and lots of people who will be against them. If people attack your mother, for whatever reason, it's a painful thing. Also, it means that people are always asking you about it, because controversy is interesting. But it's not your business to be a spokesperson for someone else.

Jeff Bridges

Beau [Bridges, his brother] was basically my teacher. He's eight years older than I am. He taught me all kinds of stuff. We used to rent a flatbed truck and get some scenes together and play the supermarket circuit.

Beau Bridges

My brother [Jeff Bridges] was about sixteen and I thought it was a good time to get his feet wet. When you do stuff like that you really get in touch on a very gut level with what it is to put on a show. You come in and you check out the law first, see where they are. You go up to the policeman and say, "We're going to put this little show on. We don't mean any harm. Let me know if we become a hassle," so they don't bust you.

Jeff Bridges

My father [actor Lloyd Bridges] encouraged me, not in the way of a typical show biz parent, but he always made it available to me. One of the toughest things is getting your foot in the door and that was kind of handled for me. No problem. If ever there was a little kid in *Sea Hunt,* he'd say, "Hey, you want to do this?"

I'd say, "I don't know."

He'd say, "You'll get out of school."

"Okay."

Beau Bridges

My father said things like, "Just go with the truth. Keep it simple and try to speak out of a place of truth inside yourself—then you really can't go wrong."

At Christmas time and Thanksgiving, the children would always put on a play for the adults. That was something that always used to happen and continues to happen now with the new kids coming up.

Lloyd Bridges

Osmosis, I guess. They [sons Beau and Jeff] were around. They hear all this talk about the theater. They're always performing something, my grandchildren. My wife encourages all that. Beau's got a couple of younger children that I think are going to be actors. About half of them. I've got a dozen grandchildren.

Hayley Mills

(Actor John Mills's daughter and actress Juliet Mills's sister)

My parents didn't push any of us into it, but it would've been surprising if we hadn't been drawn into it. It's the family business. You know that your family would be rather happy if you did join the family business.

Mia Farrow

(Actress Maureen O'Sullivan's daughter)

My father discouraged me. He said he never saw a happy actress. And I guess he ought to know.

Anthony Quinn

I discouraged all my kids from becoming actors. It's the worst profession in the world. The rejection hurts one so much.

James Garner

I've tried to keep my daughters out of the business. As a matter of fact, the youngest one worked for me on the crew of *Rockford* for one summer when she was going to USC. She wasn't any good so I let her go. Now she's a songwriter in Nashville.

Samantha Mathis

It took me about four years to convince my mother [actress Bibi Besch] to actually let me go into the business. If anything, she discouraged me. She would drag me onto the set where she was working at 4:30 in the morning and stick me in the back with the crew guys. She was concerned that I was caught up in some sort of glamorous idea of what it would all be, so she tried to educate me in terms of what it really is like to be doing it.

Isabella Rossellini

My father [director Roberto Rossellini] was a little concerned about my going into modeling, acting, forget it, he would have been very concerned —because actors don't work. They are unemployed.

Lloyd Bridges

It would be difficult if they weren't talented to dissuade somebody. But fortunately they [sons Beau and Jeff] cut the mustard.

Martha Plimpton

My mom [actress Shelley Plimpton] certainly did not want me to do it initially, but she knew better than to try and keep me from it because I was a very forceful child. It just happened by osmosis, because my mother was working at the time with a woman named Elizabeth Swados, who was then casting a play that she asked me to audition for. Certainly had my mother not been in that play, I would not have been in the one following. On the other side of the coin, it certainly doesn't make it any easier or more natural.

My father [actor Keith Carradine] was not really an influence.

Keith Carradine

When I made my decision that acting was what I wanted to do, my father [John Carradine] was both supportive and cautioning. He said, "It's a lousy profession. There's no security. But if you must do it, it's in your blood." He said, "Get yourself an education. Get a good liberal arts degree, so you have something to fall back on." I'm not sure what he meant by that. I don't think you can do this if you have something to fall back on.

Melanie Griffith

My kids know how tough it is in the acting business. They've seen me work. They don't think it's glamorous at all. But they like the finished product, so there's a problem already. I can see it.

Melanie Griffith

I didn't want to be an actress. I didn't understand it. All I knew was that my mother [Tippi Hedren] was away and she was in front of the mirror a lot.

Campbell Scott

(Actor George C. Scott and actress Colleen Dewhurst's son)

No one ever believes this, but I really had no interest at all in being an actor. For me when I was a kid, it was my parents' job. They went away to work and came back. Then I did some plays when I was in college. For me it really started from reading, from literature. That's where I spent my childhood, just reading a lot, and the next step is expressing it.

You see nepotism in any business. Often it's because that's what the kids know. Or through osmosis they begin to understand how to enter those worlds and maybe they're comfortable there.

Emilio Estevez

The biggest misconception of our family was that we grew up very privileged and we had certain things handed to us because our father [Martin Sheen] was who he was. For the most part growing up, my father was a struggling actor who did a film every now and again in between guest shots on all those Quinn Martin productions. If you know anything about growing up in the home of an actor who's waiting for the phone to ring, sure we were close, but it was by no means a privileged upbringing.

Cecilia Peck

I didn't grow up in Beverly Hills. I was born in Santa Monica and grew up there. My father [Gregory Peck] quite deliberately didn't want us to grow up in a mansion and behind iron gates. We didn't have a lot of privileges

Melanie Griffith Ron Davis/Shooting Star

or trust funds or any of that. I always had summer jobs when I was in high school. That was quite conscious on his part and I'm grateful for that, too. It's easy to begin to take things for granted if you grow up like that.

Samantha Mathis

Because I grew up in the business with a working actress who's not necessarily a star but who's always made a living, she always raised me with a very grounded mentality about it. To not take it all too seriously, that it's just a job. I remember that.

My grandmother [Austrian actress Gusti Huber] was very similar. "Don't pay attention to the good reviews. Don't pay attention to the bad reviews. Remember why you're doing what you're doing and stick to that. Don't get caught up in all the fanfare and all the hoopla. It can lead you down some bad roads."

Carrie Fisher

I read my book Postcards from the Edge *out loud* with my mother [actress Debbie Reynolds] and the line that bothered her was, "You want me to do well, just not better than you." She said, "Well that REALLY isn't like us!" The feeling of being a kid of anybody powerful is that the way for them to remain powerful is to put them always in a position of them giving you advice.

Look at my ex-husband. How do you be Paul Simon's father? "Well you know what you should do on this album...."

Jamie Lee Curtis

One key piece of advice my father [actor Tony Curtis] gave me was, "Don't ever forget that this will last forever." I don't think I paid attention to that.

Laura Dern

(Actor Bruce Dern and actress Diane Ladd's daughter]

My father's advice was more business-oriented. Things like, "Remember this is a conglomerate, and soda companies decide who goes in a movie. Your ego's got to stay out of it because the bottom line is most of the time it doesn't have to do with talent. You can't take it personally.

People are in this business to make money." It really helped me a lot. The emotional side and the personal side I dealt with a lot with my mom, but there are so many other levels that can really mess people up in this business that helped me understand a little better.

Bridget Fonda

My favorite thing to tell the press about what my aunt [Jane Fonda] has said to me is, "Oh, don't pay too much attention to the press." I've had some painful times with that and she's been really generous and kind about it.

Matthew Broderick

He [dad James Broderick] did plays a lot. Summers we would follow him, to get out of New York City. I watched him endlessly—and he was wackier than you might think. I think he's known by most people as the dad in *Family,* which is very far from what he was like, even what he was like professionally.

Actress Sarah Bernhardt spoke of fame in Memories of My Life. "Those who know the joys and miseries of celebrity...know...It is a sort of octopus with innumerable tentacles. It throws out its clammy arms on the right and on the left, in front and behind, and gathers into its thousand little inhaling organs all the gossip and slander and praise afloat to spit out again at the public when it is vomiting its black gall."

Geraldine Chaplin

I felt that his [dad Charlie Chaplin's] commitment was to his family, but that's, I suppose, because he was a very clever man. In Switzerland, he had his family and he had his work. He'd get up in the morning and he'd go down into his working room. He'd sit there with a paper and pencil, or he'd write music. He'd work all day long. When he stopped working he died. That's a fact. He wrote a script that was never done because they wouldn't insure him. Then he wrote the music to all his silent films—and when the music to the last silent film had been done there was nothing else. He immediately went into a decline. And then he died.

Michael Douglas

You never get used to being famous. I'm fortunate because I grew up second generation [his dad is actor Kirk Douglas], but I hate to see the toll that it takes on one's family, one's wife, one's kids. Kids have to go to school. They have friends. It puts more pressure on everything. Not only do they have to accept your career, which is pretty demanding, but then they've got to take all this other stuff. They didn't ask for it.

Michael Douglas

Whereas in acting you're trying to define your own character and yourself, obviously half of your genes are your dad's. Dad did Dad better than anybody else. So early on you were scared when you'd see yourself behaving in a part like your father, because you could never do it to the extent that he could do himself. So you found yourself either playing sensitive young men roles or ducking away. That's why I think second generation kids are late bloomers. They take a lot longer to define themselves.

Ben Stiller

(Actor Jerry Stiller and actress Anne Meara's son)

It's definitely an issue. I spent many hours of therapy talking about having famous parents. It is weird when your parents are famous. That's why a lot of children of famous people have a tough time getting it together. You are constantly seeing people be extremely nice to your parents and doing favors for them. They're very established and you're trying to figure out, "Where do I fit in? What do I do? Who am I? Is it okay if I'm not famous?" A lot of times it's not. You want to emulate your parents and if your parents are famous you go, okay, I'll be famous, too. If you want that and it doesn't work out, then it can be a problem. I never thought about doing anything else.

Kiefer Sutherland

My father did The Dirty Dozen *when I was being thought of,* so he was famous when I was born. I knew that my dad's fame was special. Then again, I didn't live with my dad for very long. I didn't have to deal with it a lot. That's how I knew it was special. When other kids found out my dad was Donald Sutherland it was important to them. It takes away your self-identity for a while.

Carl Reiner

Rob, when he was born and started to grow up, we knew he was a very bright kid who had very strong opinions about what was good and bad.

Very strong. You couldn't shake him. And he's been proven right. Everything that he's done in movies I have applauded, not because he's done it, but because I loved it.

Rob Reiner

The difficulty is not so much in getting your father to approve of you or think that you're good. The difficulty with someone who's famous and well-respected is to find your niche, the way you would do it, separate and apart from him, and to feel good about how you're doing it separate and apart from him. When you're a young person starting out, you're compared to your father and he's accomplished already. In my case, I'm nineteen years old, he's forty, forty-five years old. He's already had a lot of accomplishments. They're not comparing me to the nineteen-year-old Carl Reiner. So with that looming above you, you have to fight and find the thing that will identify you and separate you out from your father.

Michael Douglas
Russ Einhorn/Shooting Star

Jason Gould

(Singer/actress/director Barbra Streisand and actor Elliott Gould's son)

I was a very shy kid. I wasn't comfortable with being the son of famous people. That's why I'm pursuing an acting career. It's a way of overcoming my shyness and getting to know myself better and facing my worst fears, being judged and compared.

Sage Stallone

I was brought up with the boxing thing since I was four or five. My father [Sylvester Stallone] wanted me to learn self-defense. I stopped for a little while, then *Rocky V* came up and I started up again. I've loved it. I've been in a couple of fights outside the ring, not major. I guess I've done a little damage. Sometimes kids want to fight with me because I'm Sly's kid. "Hey look, Stallone's kid! Yo!"

They think I'm gonna be like, "Hey, I'm Sage Stallone, pretty cool, Rambo's kid." But he's just a normal father to me. I love him. It's hard being his son sometimes. At school sometimes people make fun of me and they make fun of my father. I ignore them, or go, "What does your father do?"

Isabella Rossellini

All my past has intimidated me. I didn't become an actress until I was thirty-one, after I succeeded on TV in Italy, and after I succeeded in modeling. That gave me enough courage, but I think I was pretty wise. If I had started at eighteen it wouldn't have worked. I would have felt I had failed as a person.

Liza Minnelli

When I was doing Best Foot Forward, *which is the first show* I ever did, I was leaving the theater one night and I overheard two women talking to their husbands. One of them said, "Well, I thought Judy Garland's kid was just great."

And the husband said, "Well of course."

The other woman said to her husband, "I don't know. I didn't think Judy Garland's daughter was so good."

And the husband said, "Well of course."

That's the "of course syndrome," and that's what you have to not pay any attention to and keep your own through line going.

Bridget Fonda

I went through it in college. I felt that it was debilitating for me to always feel that I was being compared to, or someone expected me to be as good as, which was incomprehensible to me. You can understand debilitating when you're eighteen years old and they're expecting you to be as good as Jane Fonda. It's not like they're expecting you to be as good as somebody else who's eighteen, which is hard enough as it is. But to be as good as somebody who's already done *Coming Home,* or *Klute,* I mean please. That was really hard.

Geraldine Chaplin

I always knew, from the very beginning, that my father was the most famous man in the world. I used to cash in on it at school. "Allow me to copy your exam and I'll take you home and you'll get to meet Charlie Chaplin." That's how I got through my studies. My mother used to say, "You've got these strange friends." They'd always be first in the class, these plain girls with glasses. I was just bringing them home so I'd be allowed to copy their Latin exams.

Liza Minnelli

Being Judy Garland's daughter is dramatic and people like the drama of that.

Dodd Darin

I was a reckless kid. I was the typical Hollywood troubled kid. Beer, drugs, cars. I went through that. Didn't have my dad [singer Bobby Darin]. Mom has had a long battle with anorexia and alcoholism. We both fought our battles and made it through.

I just had turned twelve, four days earlier, when my dad passed away in December, 1973.

> *I always had a fantasy that I would like to have a normal life, like the one I saw on TV in Father Knows Best, which I think destroyed a lot of people.*
>
> *—Carrie Fisher*

Gunnar Nelson

(One half of the rock group Nelson)

When my sister Tracy was asked about her family when she was starting out in acting, she only thought it went back to the "Ozzie & Harriet" thing and my father [Rick Nelson] and then to her. But my Grandma Harriet said, "Oh, no, no, no, no. It goes way back." My Grandma Harriet's father, Roy Hilliard, was a Shakespearean actor. His parents were vaudevillians. Their parents were circus performers, all the way back down the line. It's like seven generations of Nelsons.

Matthew Nelson

(Gunnar's twin brother and the other half of Nelson)

It was our tenth birthday. We had just written our first song. Our parents told us that we had a dentist appointment on our birthday and we had to wait after school to get picked up. So we had an awful attitude. My mother actually picked us up—and she showed up about an hour and a half late. To a ten-year-old waiting at school, on his birthday, for a dentist appointment, we had really stinking attitudes. She drove us to this place and said, "Go on, get ready for your fillings." We walked into the hallway, bitching and moaning to each other, and we looked in this room. Our musical equipment was set up and our father [Rick Nelson] was waving to us from the control room window. We recorded that song. It was so bubblegum, it sounds like Alvin and the Chipmunks. June and Ruth Pointer came in and sang backup vocals, though. They were friends of my dad. We didn't even know who they were.

Pam Dawber

The kids absorb what the parents put out. If the parents think show business is the greatest, most exciting thing in the world, the kids are going to absorb that. If they treat it as a job, the kids are going to see it that way. Our child knows that his dad [actor Mark Harmon] has played a policeman and a farmer. He knows that his mom has played Mindy. He happened to see an excerpt of a TV movie that I'd done where I fall from the side of a building. He started to cry—and it made me realize that this is not good for him. That was just on a morning show. "Oh look, Mommy's on *Regis!*"

Natalie Cole

Perhaps because of my father [the late Nat "King" Cole]'s legacy, I am committed to doing quality stuff. I've tried to do the commercial stuff for commercial purposes, and every time I do that with the wrong intentions it just screws up. It does not pay off for me. And that means sacrifice, perhaps not being as big as Madonna or somebody like that, because that's just not where I really want to be. With all of that kind of success, there's a downside to that, too. There's a lot of sacrifice to be made.

Pam Dawber

Mark [Harmon, her husband] comes from a show business family. His sister was married to Ricky Nelson at the height of that. He knows what it does, how phony it can be, and the damage that it can do if you take it seriously. What should be taken seriously? It's a job that you do. You make a lot of money. It's fun. If you have a good experience, that's as important as it should be.

Bridget Fonda

My family has always been inspirational, but sometimes a little daunting, especially when I was just starting out. There are some big shoes to fill and you feel everyone is watching you. You're not going to step out on stage for your first time and be as good as Aunt Jane. It's surprising how many people say that acting must be in my genes, that I must have been born able to do it. The reality is that it's a very awkward thing getting up in front of people. Well, for me anyway, because I'm shy. And I found out later that my grandfather [Henry Fonda] was the same way.

Anjelica Huston
(Director John Huston's daughter)

I was one of those children who dressed up a lot and spent a lot of time making faces in the mirror. I remember putting on plays for my unfortunate parents. I think it was in the blood. My grandfather [Walter Huston] was a very good actor. He died two years before I was born so I got to know him in movies. When I first saw *Treasure of the Sierra Madre* I thought that was my grandfather. Later on, in my twenties, I saw *Dodsworth* and I said, "Ah, that was my grandfather." He had many incarnations and I always liked my grandfather's choices. Although he was a tremendously good-looking man he liked to play bad and old character parts—and that's what I'm interested in.

Bridget Fonda

I have my big relationship with my grandfather [Henry Fonda] by watching his movies over and over and over again. I love his work. I respect him. I'd give anything if I could have that conversation about acting with him, but at the time when he was still alive I was really unformed in this. I was very stubborn and pig-headed that I wanted to do things my own way. And now, of course, I would really enjoy that conversation.

Bridget Fonda

I didn't know my grandfather as well as I would have liked. He was very quiet. I used to like to watch him paint. I have to say that the way he painted had a lot to do with the way that he acted. I think I learned something in a strange way from that—that you start with the finest wash

Bridget Fonda Yoram Kahana/Shooting Star

and just build and build and build. His watercolors were exquisite and had such a reverence for the subject. He did it exactly as he saw it, but he saw it in a more burnished and wonderful way. He would see each little water spot on an apple as a little beauty mark. That's sort of what you want to do with acting. You want to take reality and you want to have it be true, but you want to celebrate the things about it that people often wipe off or take for granted.

Paul Sorvino

It's common to look at the offspring of the well-known with disdain and jealousy. [Daughter] Mira encountered it. She went for a year without booking anything. And she was the same actress then as she is now, I assure you.

Sophia Loren

People expect always more and more and more from children that have important parents.

Mary Crosby

We were raised with very good manners from day one. My mother said, "Your father wants perfect children and by God he's going to get them." We knew he was special. Children are the most intuitive people on this Earth. They know better than anybody what the differences are, how people treat other people, and if maybe they treat one person differently from another.

Keith Carradine

People expect you not to be very good, that the only reason you're there is you're sliding in on someone's coattails and you probably don't have much to offer. But they're forced to see you because of some political thing. I certainly sensed that in the beginning of my career, a very definite serious doubt when I would walk into a room. "Okay, here's another one." It was challenging.

I was pretty defenseless when I started out. Having grown up the son of an actor people expect you to know what you're doing. And I really didn't. The first time I was on a movie set I was utterly clueless. I was also emotionally very naive and very wide open when I began in this business. I had some things said and done to me early on that were devastating.

Meg Ryan

How am I going to keep my son Jack from the excesses of Hollywood? Dennis [Quaid] and I think about it all the time. We just don't know. We can't get over the fact that we can barely relate to our own son's experience even up 'til now. He's the son of celebrity people and that's not like anything that has ever happened in Dennis's life or in my life. We think, "Where should we live? How can we protect him? What are going to be his concerns?" There are some really healthy children of celebrities, but then there are some real tragic cases of not making it. It's very scary for us. He's three. All we can do is take it as it comes. I'm really nervous about him being a teenager.

Dennis Quaid

He's just not going to have the same childhood that I did. He won't live on a block and go down the street and go down to the grocery store.

People coming up and asking for autographs from us [he and wife Meg Ryan] is just going to be a normal thing for him. I don't know how that's going to affect him.

Meg Ryan

(What if Jack wants to be an actor?)

No way. Just no way. Imagine being a teenager and being an actor at the same time? When he's eighteen he can do what he wants, but no way will I be the person who encourages that.

I unfortunately have been around child actors. Even if the kids are tough and the parents are good, the place is toxic. There's a lot of pressure. There's a lot of dementing attention. And that's on the set, I'm not even talking about them being famous people. There are five hundred people doing their bidding. If you're a kid and there are five hundred people doing your bidding, I'm sorry, something's going to mess up.

Jodie Foster

I don't feel that the film business is some kind of Gothic monster which swallows you up and is such a horrible place to live in that you immediately become a poorly adjusted, misspent youth. For me personally, it's been really instructive and informative. It allowed me to have relationships with grownups at a young age that I never would've had any other way. It allowed me to travel places and to come in contact with different groups of people that I never would've known. I just thank my lucky stars that I was in the film business when I was a kid. I don't know who I would be without it.

Alan Arkin

My son Adam used to call me up and ask me how I felt about this performance or that performance. I loved that role in his life. I was very happy about it because it was very comfortable between us. He seemed to feed off that. It made me feel useful in his life. Then about four years ago he was doing *I Hate Hamlet* on Broadway. He was in previews and he called me and he said, "Dad, I need your help. I'm drowning. It stinks. I'm

Meg Ryan The Kobal Collection

doing terrible work and the play stinks." I went to look at it, to try and give my fatherly advice, and he was brilliant, just brilliant. I went backstage and I couldn't do anything except say goodbye to a son and say hello to a colleague. It was a bittersweet moment, watching this little boy disappear.

Campbell Scott

As professionals, I've always been able to look at my parents as completely separate entities from "my parents." When I was a kid they were just my parents, like everybody's. Then when I became a professional I even worked with my mother [Colleen Dewhurst] a couple of times before she died. I was able to absolutely separate it—and learn from them. They're both very talented. My mother was very supportive, eventually, like any mother would be.

Jamie Lee Curtis

I'm a ham. I've been a ham since I was a little kid. The fact that I'm an actor and my parents [Tony Curtis and Janet Leigh] were actors, maybe there's a genetic thing.

Gary Busey

My son, Jake, said to me, "Dad, I don't want to go to college. I want to play drums in a rock 'n' roll band and play guitar and record and act." I said, "My God. That's what I did."

Matthew Broderick

I was wild sometimes as a kid. I can remember a lot of times having to wait outside in the hallway until I got a hold of myself. When I was like five we had library cards in my school and I remember I wrote "actor" under the space for profession. I think I always assumed that's what I was going to be. I don't know why I thought that. You know my dad was an actor [James Broderick] and maybe it was just that simple. I thought I'd either be an actor, a baseball player, or a fire engine, according to my parents.

Gary Busey

My son, Jake, played my son in *Straight Time,* when he was five years old. Myself, Kathy Bates, and Dustin [Hoffman] are in the scene. I'm going through withdrawal. It's a three page scene. Five years old, his hair back with Vaseline, he wanted to be in the movie. But today he said, "I'm only going to do this scene once because I'm drawing trucks."

So we do the scene. Everything was one take. We're driving home. Jake is still drawing his truck. "Jake, you were fantastic today. You inspired the cast. We did everything in one take. That was beautiful. What do you think of acting now?"

"I think it's the dumbest thing I've ever done."

"Why do you think it's so dumb?"

"Because Dad, all you do is pretend, except you play like you're not pretending. I would rather be drawing a truck."

So here's Dad going, "God, What can I do to bring him over to my side?" I say, "Let's go by Lucky's market and get some Spam and take it home and carve dinosaurs out of it."

"Yeah!"

Thank God for truth and imagination.

Gary Busey

After Straight Time, *I told my wife,* "He [son Jake] has got the goods to do what I'm doing, but we have got to figure out how to do this. I don't know how to take a child actor through the works and let him have a childhood." I don't know how many child actors have transferred to adult actors.

We put the money, instead of tuition, into good acting courses. And he built a truck from the ground up for off-road Baja racing.

Robert Blake

The camera saved my life. If I hadn't gone in front of the camera I'm sure that I would have been a terrible criminal. At that, I was a criminal in my teenage years, but I would not have survived. My father wanted to be a movie star—and he was nuts. The only decent thing he ever did was kill himself back in the fifties. He wanted my brother to be a movie star. They hated the fact that I was successful and wanted to kill me for it. But I was an extra on *The Little Rascals* and I realized that if you spoke they paid attention to you. And if you did it good somebody hugged you. And if you did it really good you got praised. That was my life. I was not an abused child because somebody put me in front of the camera and exploited me. On the contrary, they not only didn't exploit me, they never got me an agent, they never got me a manager. They discouraged me from working. They still wanted my brother to be a star. I stayed in front of the camera in spite of my family, not because of them.

Daniel Stern

When I was directing Rookie of the Year, *I was searching* for the boy to play the lead in it. My son Henry was perfect for the movie. I coached his baseball team and we love to play baseball. Actually, the character's name was Henry when I got the script. I kept going, "Oh, this is perfect for Henry." I was getting to a point of anxiety that I wouldn't find the kid, so I said, "Henry, read this for me." Henry read it, and he did really well. So I brought him in to the casting agent and asked her to read him, because I couldn't be sure I wasn't prejudiced. She came out and said he was incredible, the best kid we'd seen. My wife and I talked about it and we decided he shouldn't do it. If any situation would have been right for him to be in a movie, it would have been that. I was there. I could protect him. But even so, the end result for me and my children was that he would be tainted in a certain way. If the movie was successful there would be an oddness to his school life, as I perceived it. And if it wasn't successful his feelings might be hurt, so I wasn't going to put him in that position. He understood that, actually.

Tom Berenger

I've always tried to keep my kids separate from the business. I really, quite honestly, do not want them in the film business. I don't want them living in Los Angeles. I don't want to hear whining about the business. I don't want to hear shop talk. My teenagers aren't really into it, but I have a younger daughter who's a little scary. She's like living with Shirley Temple. It's frightening. She wears costumes, makes entrances. She's dramatic. I catch her doing English accents because she's watching *The Parent Trap* with Hayley Mills.

Ron Howard

I would definitely not want my kids to be child actors. My experience was a good one, but it's kind of an anomaly. Kurt Russell had a pretty good time with it. My brother Clint, he enjoyed it. But my parents are fantastic. The only way it'll really work is if the parent is willing to provide a tremendous amount of supervision. It really helps when the parent knows something about the business. Kurt's dad is an actor. My mom and dad are actors. They were able to provide a unique quality of supervision and could also interact with directors and other actors and help us avoid a lot of bad habits—and continue to teach us to act. A lot of kid actors don't learn the fundamentals. Neither my wife nor I are willing, or able, to focus that kind of time and energy and supervision—especially with four kids—on one kid at a time while they pursue a career. Also, I hate to see them put into a position where they're going to be compared to Opie.

Connie Selleca

I would not for a second let my child live in this adult world and be a child actor. I have a friend who's doing it now and I've tried every way I could think of to discourage her from letting her kid do it.

Tommy Rettig played Lassie's young master, Jeff Miller, in the original Lassie television show from 1954 to 1958. As a young adult, he was arrested several times on drug charges and was alleged to have grown marijuana on his California farm. Rettig went on to publish three computer books, but he remained a staunch supporter of the legalization of marijuana until his death in 1996, at the age of fifty-four.

Kevin Bacon

I would not encourage my kids to go into the business. I wouldn't mind if they went into it. I'd be happier if they went into it behind the scenes. There's only a handful of people who really are successful at what I do. It's a very tough, tough life. You get beaten up a lot. There's a lot of disappointment and a lot of insecurity. I don't encourage anybody to go into it.

Certainly not a child actor. I would definitely not allow that. Not while they're in my house.

Kyra Sedgwick

In regard to the reflected glare of the spotlight on the kids, I think we've only scratched the surface on how hard that's going to be. I think it kind of stinks in a way. I worry. I know it's going to have an effect.

Annie Potts

When I'd been away and had my oldest son with me on location, people would be especially nice to him. When he got old enough to be savvy I remember him saying, "Boy, these people sure are being nice to me."

And I said, "Yes, they are, and I hope you thanked them for it."

He went, "Tell me something Mom. Are they being nice to me because they really like me or are they being nice to me because of you?"

I said, "I'm sure it's because of you," but that's a weird thing for kids. I wish they didn't have the burden of that.

John Travolta

(What if his son Jett wants to be an actor?)

Man, I wouldn't hold him back. My problem is I'd be one of those pushy stage mothers. "Okay, show everyone how brilliant you are!"

> *So many young kids are thrown in by their parents and they really don't care about acting. They're doing it for their parents.*
>
> *—Dennis Hopper*

Sean Connery

When they offered him [his son Jason] the role of Ian Fleming [in *Spymaker: The Secret Life of Ian Fleming*], he called me up and told me about it. I said, "Is it a good part? Is it well written? Is he a good director?" He said yes, so I said, "I think you should do it." He was more concerned about it than I was.

Christopher Walken

I was put in show business. My father was a baker. We lived in Queens, a ten minute subway ride from midtown Manhattan, where television was born in the fifties. There were ninety live shows every week. My mother, with dozens of other mothers, we'd get on the train, we'd go in and we'd do these shows. It really was fun. I personally saw Howdy Doody being dragged from the dressing room when he was strings.

I have two brothers and we were all in show business. They used a lot of kids on television in the early fifties, really more as furniture. It was a nice time. I consider it better than going to Harvard. When I got to be about eighteen and I thought about what I wanted to do for a living, I really couldn't do anything else.

Keenen Ivory Wayans

As little guys, my brothers saw their older brother doing something. It becomes real to them at that point. It becomes tangible. So it becomes one of the choices they could have made. Marlon and Shawn were born comedians. They were a team when they were four and five years old. I would come home from Los Angeles, or even when I was in college, and they would have routines worked out for me.

Marlon Wayans

Keenen was the pioneer and Damon followed and showed us that Keenan wasn't a fluke. Then me and Shawn and Kim were like, "Hey, we can go out there and make some money, too." But Keenen showed us that it's not just a dream, that it can become a reality. Until a dream becomes reality, it's just a dream.

Shawn Wayans

Keenen is the president. He's like Papa Bear. He's like the second father. Our parents raised us as a close-knit family. We didn't have money. All we had was each other.

Samantha Mathis

I grew up around it from the time I was born. My mother's an actress. My grandmother was an actress. I was raised by my mother, so I was shuttled off to locations and theaters and acting classes from the time I was born. I actually did a commercial with my mother when I was six months old, her first audition back after she had had me. They wanted me. She said, "You don't get the baby without me." So we did some kind of softener commercial. It's been a huge part of my life since I was conceived.

Jamie Lee Curtis

That's something that everybody wants to make into an issue. You want to think my parents [Tony Curtis and Janet Leigh] were abusive. Richard Lewis used to do this very funny imitation of my father being a parent as he was sword fighting. "I'm sorry, honey, I can't play Barbies with you right now. I'm dueling Kirk Douglas." People like to believe that celebrity parents say things like, "Mommy can't be with you tonight because she's going off to a premiere." That's just a bunch of crap. Being an actor doesn't mean you're a bad parent. It doesn't mean that you don't care about your family. The demands on you in your personal life are different than they are if you're a doctor, but believe me, how many doctors are terrible parents because they're never there?

Being a parent is a weird juggling act—and nobody does it right. Everybody does it wrong.

Keith Carradine

Here was this Shakespearean actor [his dad, John Carradine] who, in the fifties, to feed his children, did a lot of horror movies. That's mostly what he's known for. I think it sort of broke his heart. He was really a Shakespearean at heart. So I grew up in this atmosphere of classical literature and classical music, but at the same time he didn't take us around with him. He didn't take us to movie sets. He kept us away from that. We knew what he did. We knew what his profession was. I was mostly made aware of who my dad was by the parents of my schoolmates.

Natalie Cole

My sister and I used to sing a lot at home. Every Broadway show that came by we knew all the words, but I never thought that I had a voice until very late. I would say I was almost twenty before I thought that I had a voice that was even decent. When I was younger I thought my voice was terrible. There were times when Dad would sing crazy songs to us, not serious stuff. He wouldn't sit around and sing "Unforgettable," or things like that.

I wasn't looking to be an entertainer. That was Dad's job—and Dad was good at that. I was going to be a doctor. I just took it as a kick and I found out that I was up against a lot of pressure and a lot of expectations that I had no intentions of living up to. Yes, I was "the daughter of...," but that was it. I really couldn't understand why everybody made such a big fuss over me.

Roger Daltrey

(Member of The Who)

I've got a son who played in a band in Sweden. He's Swedish. Had him by a Swedish girlfriend I had. He played in a band, but he wasn't brilliant. He's my boy, but I have to be honest. There are a million as good as him out there.

Campbell Scott

People are going to think what they want to think. People will make judgments and label you almost immediately, just so that you fit into their framework. There's no way that you can fight that. If you're the foreman's son on the carpenter job it's the same thing. It's just not quite as visible, but still as affecting to your life, if you really want to be a carpenter.

Ed Begley, Jr.

It serves no purpose to think about the negatives, people comparing you to your father [actor Ed Begley], people mention your dad endlessly in ways that begin to rattle you. So I found a couple of big pluses to it all. Like when you go on a job interview, if they have something to talk about, like, "Before we get started, I worked with your dad in the Philco Theater and we did a play and it was so wonderful and blah, blah, blah." And then perhaps the biggest plus of it all is that they remember you. Whether you're Liza Minnelli or Rob Reiner or Ed Begley, Jr. or Carrie Fisher, they don't go, "What was that guy's name again?" That helps when you're getting started.

But ultimately the important thing to realize is that nobody is going to risk a $500,000 budget on a half-hour TV show or a $40 million budget on a movie by giving any part of any size at all to somebody that can't do the job. You can get the foot in the door, but you better have some good product to sell after that.

Cecilia Peck

One thing that happens is you can start to assume you're special without ever having earned it. It's something really to be careful of, to think that things will always happen easily and doors will open graciously. You don't get anything for free. You can't take anything for granted. If anything, you have to work harder because people are skeptical, thinking you're not really talented or dedicated or serious.

On the other hand, people almost unanimously respect my dad [Gregory Peck], so in most cases they're predisposed to liking me, or thinking that maybe something good has sprung from that tree.

Sage Stallone

In the future, when I get out of school, I'll probably be starring in a couple of films and I'll be directing some films and maybe writing or producing some films.

Geraldine Chaplin

Every door was open when I decided I wanted to do movies. Everybody wanted to see, "Oh, Charlie Chaplin's daughter. Maybe she has a little bit of talent. Let's see her." I didn't have to fight to get auditions.

Jason Patric

(Actor/playwright Jason Miller's son and actor Jackie Gleason's grandson)

I was aware of the theater at an early age, like a dentist's son is aware of that drill going on. It certainly deterred me in the sense that I didn't want to attach myself to a shadow or somebody's reputation. I had to figure out what I wanted to do on my own. But it was something I was aware of. I changed my name because I didn't want any associations. I also wanted to personally have all the achievement or failure on my own shoulders. Patric is my middle name and it's a family name back in Ireland.

Geraldine Chaplin

He was horrified that I would cash in on the name. He thought that was dreadful. I said, "I'm not going to change it."

Brandon Lee

If I had changed my last name to something else, you don't think you guys would find out that I was Bruce Lee's son and ask me about it anyway? Then you'd just be asking me, "Why'd you change your name?"

Cecilia Peck

Sometimes I think maybe I should have changed my name, but I didn't, therefore I can't deny it or pretend it's not who I am. It is. Besides I love my family.

Sam Robards

(Actress Lauren Bacall and actor Jason Robards's son)

You keep trying to hammer away the best that you can. If something happens, it happens. If it doesn't, it doesn't. My name is what I was born with. If it helps get me in, great, but once I'm in there it's me. No one's going to do you any favors in this business. If you have what they think they can use, then they'll use you. If you don't, they won't. It doesn't matter what your lineage is.

Lauren Bacall

Having me for a mother and Jason Robards as a father has hurt my son, Sam, more than helped him. It's always about identity. Are you Jason Robards's son? Are you Lauren Bacall's son? It's a fight for identity, I think. It's that much more difficult to rise above and prove their own talents.

When Sam told me he wanted to be an actor I told him, "It's a life of rejection." When it works it's great, but most of the time it doesn't.

Mary Crosby

Being a celebrity's kid doesn't help your career. It does open doors. When I came to L.A. at eighteen after he had died, I had my SAG card and I had my agent. Those are things that are very difficult to get. Those doors were opened, but once those doors are opened it's up to you to get the job, because nobody is going to hire anybody based on what their name is or whose kid they are.

In the case of *Dallas,* it worked against me. The producers were very worried about Bing's daughter, "White Christmas," Minute Maid, doing all these horrible nasty things to J.R. Would the public accept it?

Lynn Redgrave

In England when I was growing up, nepotism was a really dirty word. There were people who wouldn't see me for an audition just because they didn't want to play favorites. They went too far the other way. "No, no, I know Michael [Redgrave, her dad]. I just must not show any sort of privileged treatment here." One didn't get a chance to get an interview that someone out of the blue might have got.

If you get up and are a Redgrave, everybody expects you to be either terrible "Ha, just trading on the name," or brilliant. Of course, the reality is as you begin, you're a beginner.

Brandon Lee

I'm intrigued by the continuing interest in my father [Bruce Lee], twenty years after he passed away. To this day he still adorns the covers of most of the martial arts magazines published here in the United States and other places at least half the year. His impact is obviously still being felt. As far as how that affects me, I chose this career. I could've been a framer or a plumber or a bartender. I knew what I was getting myself into. I don't really have a problem with my father. I'm proud to be his son. Right now I don't have that wide a body of work behind me, so it doesn't seem that unnatural that people like you would want to talk to me about him.

There are times when it has been difficult to be the son of my father [martial arts legend Bruce Lee]. It's a very dangerous thing, when you start to make your decisions based on what you think someone else's perception of you is.

—Brandon Lee

Robert Blake

My son Noah is an actor. I don't do nothing for him. I don't put down Martin Sheen or Donald Sutherland or whoever's helped their kids, but I know the best way I can help Noah is to do nothing for him. I break down every once in a while and I give him advice, but only about acting teachers or what I think acting might be about. But I've never made a phone call for him. This is a very small town and I have a lot of friends in it. I could call some director who's doing some series, but I never did. So whatever he accomplishes, good, bad, right, or wrong—and he's made a lot of horrendous mistakes—is his.

Emilio Estevez

The only time I asked my father [Martin Sheen] to help me out, he flatly refused. I was incredibly cross with him and didn't understand why. He said, "You will later on in life." In fact, I did.

Bruce Willis

My oldest girl [Rumer] is just starting to get a little taste of what it is, but we don't live in Los Angeles anymore. There's going to come a time when

Lauren Bacall The Kobal Collection

we can't keep it from them anymore, but I'm all for letting kids be kids as long as they can be. In Los Angeles, by the time kids are ten or eleven years old they know everything.

Dennis Quaid

We have a place in Montana, but we really live in L.A. Montana is nine months of winter and three months of house guests.

Robert Redford

I grew up in Los Angeles. That was enough.

Harrison Ford

There's this place called Los Angeles and we all know it's not a great place to live, if you have other options. So I moved to Jackson, Wyoming. I wasn't fleeing Los Angeles. I just no longer had to live there in order to do my business. I'm able to continue to do my business and bring my kids up in a terrific place.

Tim Robbins

I don't see any reason in becoming insular. I'm not overly friendly with strangers. I live right in New York City where you have to live with it every day. You see everything right in front of your eyes. For me, that's the most important thing, that there's always life going on around you and different faces to look at and different experiences to have. Having children, also, walking around the streets is incredibly educational for them. I grew up in New York City and I knew very early on the difference between someone who was poor and someone who was going to try and use you in some way. Prejudices leap out because we don't have enough information. I think there is less of that in the city. There are so many lessons to learn for children about humanity and about what happens when a whole bunch of people are mixed into one pot.

Annette Bening

My kids I worry about, and I don't know how to handle that. My daughter is becoming aware. "Why are those people taking our picture?" How do I describe it to her and how do I make it okay? How do I help her handle the fact that she's going to have attention that another child wouldn't have, given who her parents are?

Kyra Sedgwick

I'm going to keep my shirt on. I think that will be helpful. Imagine my boy going to school and hearing, "I saw your mom's timmies last night on video." That's too much.

James Earl Jones

When I walk down the street, my thirteen-year-old son does not understand, never has, the handshakes and the autographs. He says, "How can you have so many friends?" A serious question for him.

Lorraine Bracco

My daughter [with actor Harvey Keitel] is at peer pressure age. She goes to public school. I'm not going to be an idiot. I'm involved. Those kids know me. I'm a cool mom with a cool job. That's how we describe it. There are problems when your mom is a movie actress, but she says, "Look, I'm not my mom, I'm me." We've taught her really good things, to be strong, to be herself, and not to be in anyone else's shadow. It's a lot of work.

My favorite thing is all her friends are Siskel and Ebert now. "Oh, I liked that movie." "What did you do that one for?" It's very funny.

Robin Williams

You try and make it as normal as possible. That's why I live [in San Francisco]. People say, "How normal is it living in San Francisco?" This place is not Hollywood. It has a whole different sense of dealing with the world. They know who I am, but they don't care. The children go to school, I took Zelda into class the other day. A little kid walked up and went, "Oh, the actor."

Kate Capshaw

I can't control how other people will perceive my children [with Steven Spielberg]—and they are perceived differently—not because the children do that, but because when the children go home their parents see the class list. "Oh, you know who Theo's dad is?" or "You know who Sasha's dad is?" "Did you know Sawyer's dad?" They become burdened with that. I can't protect them from how other people perceive them.

Yoko Ono

In the beginning I was very, very caring about it and I thought, "We have to hide him [son Sean]." Then he started saying, "Well look, Mommy, I want to go to school." Now John [Lennon] and I had decided that he would not be sent to school unless he himself would start to want to go to school. But then how am I going to send him to school? First of all, I want to hide which school he is going to. So I made a great effort to get a car that looks innocuous and he would ride in an innocuous car to go to school. But the minute he started going to school the photographers were following him with telephoto lenses. Of course, immediately everybody knew which school he's going to. But you just can't keep him in a box. And also, this situation is probably not going to be over for a while.

Demi Moore

People may want to assume that I've chosen this and that's fine but my family hasn't. My children haven't. When I have *Hard Copy* trying to photograph my yard and I have *Enquirer* photographers in the front of my house, I think that that's infringing on my rights and that does make me angry.

My children don't have an anonymous life, but I feel that they have rights as individuals to have as much anonymity as possible until they choose for themselves.

Kirstie Alley

We were just in New York and we were watching a parade. I hate it when I have my kids on my shoulders and there are twenty photographers in your face. My oldest is three years old now and he'll ask me, "Why is he doing that?" And I'll think, "Exactly." They don't like that part of it. I don't think anybody likes that part of it.

Robin Williams

Yesterday my wife Marsha walked out of the hotel with the kids and there were three photographers. That kind of scares them sometimes. "Why do they want pictures of us?" They know that they want pictures of me. They don't like that. Zelda will hide. Cody is like, "Is this my good side?" And Zachary is like twelve. He's like, "So?"

Nicole Kidman

I think you get used to it for yourselves [she's married to Tom Cruise], but when it's in relation to your children that's when I tend to get not so used to it. You really see an invasion in their lives. If someone comes up and flashes right in their faces or pushes them, to me it's so upsetting. It's kids, little kids. You don't do that to kids.

Belle is only two and a half, so she doesn't really have a sense of it. Sometimes she'll look in a magazine and go, "Mommy!" But sometimes she'll look at other people and think it's me as well.

Kelly Lynch

When my daughter was really little, whenever there was a blonde lady on TV she used to go, "Mommy!" Sometimes it was somebody I really didn't want to be and other times I'd go, "That's right, that's me."

Mariel Hemingway

It's very weird. TV mommy. I turned on the *Today* show and my daughter said, "We can watch your commercial if you like, Mommy."

I said, "No, we don't have to watch my commercial."

She said, "No, it's okay, you probably want to see if it's okay. I'd like to watch it. I think it's very funny that you're on TV in the morning."

She doesn't have a normal mom and she doesn't know it's different. Of course, she also goes to school in California where everybody else's mom is on television, too.

Liza Minnelli

That's what was amazing about people who grew up in Hollywood. Everybody's parents [her parents were Judy Garland and director Vincente Minnelli] all went to the same factory. They all came home at the same time. Everybody's family was famous, so you never realized that these were—in other people's eyes—extraordinary people. I had no idea until I moved out of Hollywood how special the people that I grew up around were. Like Uncle Frank [Sinatra] and Uncle Sammy [Davis, Jr.]. I still call him Uncle Frank—and he still reacts the same way he did when I was four. "Hiya kiddo. How are ya?"

Annette Bening

I remember being in New York with my little girl. She wasn't even two yet. In New York it's hard because we stay in hotels and they know we're there. If it's just me, I can handle it. It doesn't bother me. But somebody invading my kid? So I remember, we would spend some time trying to sneak out. She would of course be aware that I was saying, "Okay, are they out there?" So this one time we were at a friend's building. We were coming out. It was late at night. Nobody knew we were there. She could barely say the words, but she said, "No photographers." She was already used to people chasing her around and being in her face. That's kind of troubling. So far I've been able to handle it pretty well with my kids, but I think as they get older it's going to become harder.

> *I'm in show business. My baby ain't.*
>
> *—Arsenio Hall*

Michael J. Fox

We had to chase a few people out of Cedars Sinai when my son was born.

Daniel Stern

I want to look at the dolphins at Sea World with my kids, then another kid wants to know how I got the brick in the face in *Home Alone*. It's like, "Could I tell you that later?" On the other hand, that's part of my job. My kids say, "Couldn't you ask him about the brick when I'm not here?" They like to have me on the time that I'm with them. That's not their favorite thing either, but they like that I'm an actor. They love me working in the movies. They love to come with me when I'm working on the movies. I always tell them and they understand, "There's a price to pay and we've got a really nice life and that's part of your job, too."

Bill Pullman

It's a little problematic when you're with your kids and there's so much attention on who you are. That's the most awkward part of it. I try to diminish that in front of them. I don't want to eclipse them.

Alfre Woodard

It's really, really inconsiderate when they don't think that a child is a person. You have to make sure that that child is given his self-worth by not switching channels when they're talking to you or you're talking to him. When someone interrupts me when I'm with my children, I just say, "Excuse me. This is my daughter and we were talking." I try to get that person to say "Excuse me" to her so that she understands how you approach people also.

Very early on she said, "Why is that person talking to you?"

I said, "Maybe they saw me on the television and they wanted to talk to me."

And she said, "Well we don't want to talk to them now."

Kyra Sedgwick

We're [she and husband Kevin Bacon] walking along the street and we're having our moment with the kids and someone comes up and asks Daddy for an autograph. It's really weird. They'll look up at the stranger and they'll look up at Daddy and it's an invasion, no matter how you slice it. It feels like, "God, he's not just mine."

Bill Pullman and his wife
Lisa O'Connor/Shooting Star

Timothy Hutton

If we're out having dinner and someone comes up to the table, I can see the look on my eight-year-old's face. "Oh right, this is a part of dad's life." His mom [Debra Winger] gets it all the time, too.

Catherine Deneuve

I have been able to keep my children out of the spotlight, but not the troubles of it. Being a woman working, sometimes away, doing that kind of profession, I've been very protective, but on the main thing you cannot protect them. You have someone at home, but when you raise children and you are doing films and you have an image, children have got to live with it as well.

John Cusack

I think all the kids who are child stars end up to be either junkies or serial killers anyway. I just don't think you have a shot. It's just too sick. It's just horrible. It's so rare when they are able to get out of it. Being fifteen or sixteen is a lot different. I got my first role in a movie when I was sixteen and a half. I started in the theater at fifteen. Most of my childhood was totally normal.

Jason James Richter

I was like eight, nine years old when I moved here. I'd never heard of a gang before. In Hawaii the gangs are surfboard gangs, "Hey, get off our beach!" Los Angeles is whole different ballgame. It's scary for people who aren't from here. Some of my family is from Oregon and they think, "How can you live down there? It's so crazy and dangerous."

Well aware of the problems associated with child stardom and trying to protect her privacy, a young actress and her parents decided to adopt the stage name of Natalie Portman when she began acting in films. While acting in such films as Heat and Beautiful Girls, she continued to be an A student at a public high school on Long Island. After turning down a very lucrative offer to play the title role in Lolita, her mother told the New York Times, "I don't want her to have some sexual scene at the age of fourteen that she may not experience in life until she's seventeen."

Christina Ricci

(After playing Wednesday in The Addams Family *movies)*

When I walked down to the cafeteria in school, they'd shout, "Hey Wednesday!" That was annoying as hell.

Natalie Portman

I didn't tell anybody at school because I didn't want anybody to act differently. Some kids have asked me for my autograph—and I said no. That's ridiculous. We're equals. Autograph means that someone's above you. If someone on the street asks me for my autograph I'll say yes. It's just quick, sign it, bye, never going to see them again. But when you're with someone every day, I don't want them to say, "Wow, she's a movie star." I want them to say, "Wow, she's a really good student."

Natalie Portman

Sometimes I go nights without sleeping because I'm up doing my homework because I had a premiere to go to the night before. It's the price you have to pay.

Henry Thomas

When I was ten or eleven, after doing *E.T.,* I knew more about the business than most people. You get into a frame of mind and a way of thinking that is in some ways cruel to children, having to think on a cutthroat level.

Edward Furlong

I thought it was dumb for people to talk about the court situation and my custody stuff. It really had nothing to do with my business. It was nobody else's business that didn't know me. It had nothing to do with my acting. I just get mad when people release that stuff. Showing me on the news coming out of the courtroom and me having to sneak out of the courts when the press was there, it's talking about stuff that's kind of personal.

Daniel Stern

The hard part of being in show business for kids is the perception of failure. Why would you think that a kid failed? They didn't fail. If a movie bombs, is Macaulay Culkin a failure? No. He's a wonderful, sweet, sweet kid, who's in his adolescence now. He's certainly not a failure in any way.

Macaulay Culkin
Nikki Vai/Shooting Star

Macaulay Culkin

I have chores. I have to walk my dog and take out the garbage, things like that. I go out with my friends. I like to go out to electronics shops.

Jamie Lee Curtis

The place that highlights Macaulay [Culkin]'s stardom is doing press. The actual day-to-day working, he has a responsibility. Nobody can do it for him. Nobody can make him do it. He's a good actor. He's a professional. He shows up.

He does his work. He goes home. And quite frankly, it's so easy to say, because he's such a huge star, that you can attach some sort of attitude problem to him.

After the release of the film E.T. Drew Barrymore became the most famous seven-year-old girl in the world. Despite the fact that she came from a long line of acclaimed actors, Drew had trouble dealing with all the attention. Her fellow students taunted her with shouts of "Phone home, E.T.!" When she didn't want to talk about the movie, she was branded a snob.

Within three years, Drew was smoking, drinking, and using marijuana. A few years later, in the first week of 1989, the headlines blared: "E.T. Star at Cocaine and Booze Clinic—at 13!"

Kieran Culkin

(Macaulay's brother)

If my pickup is at 7:30, they wouldn't start my hours until I got to the set. Like if it took a half-hour to get there, at 8:00, they'd start it then. I'd work for ten hours, until 6:00, and then I can go home. Then they can't have me back on the set for another twelve hours. They can't go earlier than twelve hours. It's a twelve-hour turnaround, they call it.

I'd rather be in regular school than on a movie set.

Patsy Kensit

I started as a child by sheer luck. My mom's friend was involved in the British end of casting *The Great Gatsby*. They were looking for a little girl to play Mia Farrow's daughter. She said to my mom, "Please, we don't want to go to a stage school. Patsy will be perfect. It'll be good for me. Bring her along." So we went and I got the part. It was in the summer holidays and mother would get to see Robert Redford, so she thought, "We'll let her do it this once."

I just kept doing things in the holidays. It was like a hobby really. It was never a career. And in England it's not such a big business as it is in America. You hear such horror stories about kids who grow up so fast and become so screwed up. It wasn't like that. I never talked to the press. My mother would never let me. I never went on television to do interviews. I had a normal childhood, believe it or not.

Jerry Mathers

I started working when I was two years old. I can even remember the Ed Wynn show I did when I was two years old. I had a diaper and a big ten gallon hat and guns on. It was a barroom scene and Ed Wynn was behind the bar. I would come up and a guy would put me on a bar stool. I would pound on the bar and say, "I'm the toughest hombre in these parts and you better have my brand." Then Ed Wynn would go into a commercial for Pet milk, which was one of his big sponsors. Once I did that I was hired all the time by all the other live shows.

People have memories of when they were two and three. Mine are very, very vivid because what I was doing was going on shows in front of live audiences. I was working with Spike Jones. I used to be the little boy who would come out and pull on that checkered coat that he had while all these people in the band were shooting guns off and clanging together trash can lids. I worked with Ray Bolger on his show. I remember him singing to me. By the time *Leave It to Beaver* started I had done about a hundred and fifty TV shows and about forty movies.

I worked with Alfred Hitchcock in *The Trouble With Harry.* That was Shirley MacLaine's first movie. I was about six then. I did two movies with Bob Hope. I had a very small part in *The Seven Little Foys,* playing Eddie Foy, Jr. in the fire scene. The first time they set it up I was supposed to be watching backstage as Bob Hope performed as Eddie Foy and a fire broke out. They started the set on fire and it got away from them. The only person who could get me down was Bob Hope. The stunt man couldn't get to me, so Bob Hope actually climbed up the ladder and grabbed me down.

Lukas Haas

My life has definitely been different than any of my friends' lives. From anybody's life. I haven't had the same life as anybody has ever had. I can know that for sure.

I'm very self-conscious when I'm with my friends at home. It's kind of embarrassing.

Kirk Cameron

Sometimes I felt like I was missing out on life, hanging out with all my friends, being a kid. You live in such an adult world at nine and ten years old. It's real tough when people put so much importance and stress on being the cutest kid on the block. One of your teeth falls out and your agent has a fit. It gave me a false sense of reality, of what life is really all about.

Dean Stockwell

Being a child actor set me apart and I didn't really want to be set apart. It was very strange. I was pretty young, but I was aware that I had a contract. My parents split up when I was six and my father wasn't around. It never occurred to my mother that she could break a contract. She was a simple woman from an Italian family. We were locked into these seven year contracts at MGM. But when I graduated high school I had a certain sense of independence then and I quit. I just traveled around the country. Changed my name and did odd jobs for five years. And then I went back. There was nothing else I was prepared to do. I had no training for anything else. I'd spent nine years out of my first sixteen doing that.

Sarah Jessica Parker

I know what I missed, being a child actor. I missed a good, consistent education. There were certain social skills that I didn't possess. I was very good at conversations with adults and interviews for jobs and auditions. I felt comfortable in that environment. When I went to high school after I left *Annie,* I didn't know the currency. That was scary.

Jerry Mathers

The adults that I was dealing with on *Leave It to Beaver,* their jobs depended on me being happy. If I was there and I was unhappy, they might not be working the next week. There were eighty people on the set who were in some ways surrogate parents. We used to build boats and build parachutes all the things that kids do, except I had the top technicians in Hollywood building me a little boat because one day I happened to be walking through the set and I saw a piece of wood that was kind of pointy on one end and said, "Oh, I'll build a boat." The next thing I know the curtain department was making sails. They were painting it in

As a child star under contract to MGM, Elizabeth Taylor was a very pampered girl. When a small blemish appeared on her face, she was whisked off to see a top dermatologist. When she coughed, a full examination was ordered. After time, Taylor began to expect this type of royal treatment, as befits a movie star. As she wrote in a letter to her mother when she was about fifteen, "I realize that my whole life is being in motion pictures. For me to quit would be like cutting away the roots of a tree—I'd soon wilt and become dead and useless."

the paint department. They had a guy who was a whittler in the woodworking department carving little cannons and things like that.

Patrick Dempsey

It's been hard growing up in front of everybody and being out there, but at the same time I've learned a lot and I've had a lot of opportunities. Now I'm really enjoying it. The press junkets? I really hated doing them because I was just insecure about talking about things. When you're young you're trying so hard just to sound intelligent and be a certain image that you come off as an idiot. Now if I don't know something I'm just going to cop to it.

Winona Ryder

Not only was I going through the normal changes that a young woman goes through when she's going through adolescence, but I was reading about it and watching it. I didn't understand why people were interested. I really did feel like everyone was picking on me, when it was just their job—as pathetic as the job is.

Jodie Foster

I had different problems than other kids had. Some kids live too much, they're out there doing stuff. I had to struggle to have a real life as a real person. That was something that was real important to me and I hope that kids growing up in the business take to heart. If you want to go to college, go to college. If you're talented, you'll be talented when you're fifty. You have to live your life.

Jonathan Taylor Thomas

I prefer to be the Ron Howard, or the Jodie Foster. I think that's the path that I'm taking and it's set up now. What you do now definitely has an impact on your future. I'm getting good grades in school. I'm keeping a lot of balls in the air. It's a constant juggling act. I want to definitely go to college, Northwestern or Yale, if I can get in. I'd like to become a director or a producer/writer, but I want to stay in this industry. Yeah, those are the people I aspire to be like, the Ron Howards and the Jodie Fosters who have basically grown up in this industry and are now extremely successful and the best in their craft. But there are a lot of pitfalls.

You can fall into a trap at every turn. You can get caught up in this whole industry because it moves so fast. If you put all your eggs in one basket, if you focus everything in this industry and all of a sudden it's taken away from you, you have absolutely nothing. I concentrate on getting a great education, the best I can get, and I read a lot. I do other things, so that if this ever goes away I have something to fall back on. I think that's what happened to those child stars you don't hear about any more, they had nothing to fall back on.

Jerry Mathers

I had a private tutor when we did *Leave It to Beaver.* I probably had one of the best educations that anyone could possibly buy. It was like the English royalty of the last century were raised. I had a one-on-one relationship with a teacher. If I didn't understand something, she knew it. I couldn't hide in the back of the class. I was always a little bit weaker in math, so we spent a lot more time doing mathematics and a lot less time in English and literature. Because of that I went to Berkeley, where I got a degree in philosophy.

Ariana Richards

I've actually never been to a real high school. I get independent study at home.

Thora Birch

I couldn't imagine myself as an office worker or a secretary or with a nine-to-five job. When you grow up in this business I don't think it's easy to change into a normal life. Once you're in, you're in, and it's hard to get out because of the attention. I wouldn't want to lead a normal life because I want to be somebody and do something. I want attention. I'm an attention hog.

If they chew me up as a kid, fine, I'm adult now. If somebody gets chewed up as a kid, hey, you still have your whole life. You can become whatever you want. Well, not really.

Diane Lane

Now I can put on the makeup and do the worm-to-the-butterfly metamorphosis and play the actress part. People want that. There's a persona to being an actress. But that took me, I mean, that could put anyone into the shrink's office, especially if you're fifteen, sixteen, eighteen years old going through that, realizing that the job is to have a persona. I'm still trying to learn that.

Jonathan Taylor Thomas

My mom and I, before we make decisions, we both sit down and talk about them, because our decisions are going to affect our whole family. We make sure that we're all pleased with what we're going to do—and then we go about our business.

Kirsten Dunst

My mom has been with me all my life, taking me to auditions and everything. She's given up half her life for me. I love her for it. She actually was a painter and owned an art gallery with her sister before I was born and a little bit after.

Fred Savage

When I was doing The Wonder Years, *my dad* still lived in Chicago. He commuted back and forth. The worst part was not being able to see my dad as much as most kids did.

Samantha Mathis

I was in such a hurry to grow up when I was sixteen. I was just thankful to be out of high school. I've always felt more comfortable around adults, growing up on sets and all of that. I really feel that the older I've gotten, the younger I've gotten. I was so intent on being an adult when I was nineteen and now, at twenty-five, I'm letting that go.

Christina Ricci

I'm still fifteen and I'm still going through my awkward stage. When you're an actress people expect you to be perfect all the time, but I'm just fifteen. I'm not even fully grown yet. Sometimes I wake up in the morning and I look like crap, but you're not really allowed to be like that. The pressure with that is kind of weird.

(Do teenage boys act weird around her?)

No weirder than they do around anyone else.

Virna Lisi

My first kiss, it was in my first film. I never kissed anyone before. In that film there was a very innocent kiss. I had my partner in front of me and it was necessary for me to put my arms around him. I was arching my back away from him and the director pushed me near the man, but it was impossible because I was so frightened to touch someone and kiss. They made fun of me for years after that. [The movie was *Naples Sings.*]

Anouk Aimee

Me too, my first kiss was on screen. For me it was very difficult because he had a spot. I didn't want to kiss a young boy who had spots. I said to the director, "I cannot kiss him."

"Why?"

"Because he has spots."

He said, "It's impossible, it's for a film."

I said, "Yes, but I never kissed a man. I want the first man I kiss to be without spots."

Ann Miller

I grew up on the screen. I'm really a child of Hollywood. I was thirteen years old when I got my contract with RKO, a seven year contract. They weren't hiring minors and I had to lie about my age.

When somebody finally told the head of the studio that I was only thirteen, he faced me down with it. I went to Ginger Rogers, I was crying, and she was my friend. We were both from Texas. She said, "You get on the phone and get a fake birth certificate right away. If you don't you're going to lose your contract."

So I called my father, who was an attorney, mother and dad were divorced, and he came up with that fake birth certificate. How he did it I'll never know. But that age has haunted me down through the years.

Belinda Carlisle

The kind of fame and success that the Go-Go's had for about a year there —and when you're that young—I was eighteen—there's no way to prepare for it. It always—99% of the time—will screw you up somehow. It did all of us. We all dealt with it in our ways, and for the most part it wasn't good ways. It's a heavy thing. I think about Shannen Doherty, being young and having that kind of fame. I feel bad for her. It's a hard thing to handle. It's a horrible thing to have to handle if you can't handle it.

Rene Russo

In modeling, there's a cliché, "She's dumb beyond beautiful." Listen, when I was seventeen I did not have it together. I was naive. I was an idiot, okay? The thing that infuriates me is we're talking about seventeen-year-old girls. They're children. They look like they're twenty-five and twenty-eight and they're not always together. They can't always carry on the most intelligent conversation.

I was a high school drop out. They made me up and put me in front of a camera. I looked twenty-seven when I was seventeen. I remember sitting at a dinner party when I was seventeen and one of the people who was probably about forty-five turned to me and said, "Do you know what your problem is, Rene? You're ignorant." In front of an entire dinner party! Give me a break.

Shannen Doherty

I don't think anybody allowed me to grow up. They didn't look at it objectively and say, "You know what, this girl got on the show when she was eighteen and a half years old. My God, let's cut her a break. Of course she's going to go out there and trouble may come her way because of who she is." Instead it was like this fleet of piranhas attacking me and putting me out there for a feeding frenzy.

Jonathan Taylor Thomas

Seeing my face on all those magazine covers is kind of odd. You get into the business and it's not something that you ever expect. It comes out of the blue. One day you're walking through the store and there they are. It's different. It's something you have to deal with on a regular basis. Not all kids, but generally people in this industry have to face that at some point.

John Landis

(He directed Michael Jackson's "Thriller" video)

Poor Michael. From the time he was a kid he was pushed out front. It's almost impossible to survive those circumstances.

Jonathan Taylor Thomas

It gets more and more difficult as time goes on. I still go out. I go to the movies with my friends. I go play sports. I love fishing. I'm a fairly private person and I'm lucky that the things that I like to do generally don't involve a lot of groups. I'll have one or two friends come over, things like that. I don't like being in big groups. I don't like hanging out at malls or that sort of thing. I like being in the outdoors, being in the open. I'm fortunate that I'm a person who likes privacy and being alone sometimes, also.

> *What happens to a kid when he's thirteen years old and his face starts breaking out? Everyone goes nuts and doesn't want him anymore. How do you tell a kid that nobody wants him because he isn't cute anymore?*
>
> *—Kirk Cameron*

Winona Ryder

Coming of age in the spotlight sucked! I hated it! It's probably the most dangerous thing about this industry, to put children through that. The only way it can happen successfully is if you have great parents who aren't putting pressure on you and are protecting you. I was lucky enough to have that, but I think that I suffered—and I had it great. A lot of kids I know didn't have it so great and REALLY suffered. I went through a couple of years when I had the hugest identity crisis. I didn't know who I was. I just wanted to be who people were writing that I was. I was reading about myself going, "That's who I am, I guess." It was really awful and hard and painful.

No kid should have to worry about getting a pimple that's going to cost $300,000 to shut down shooting for a day. No kid should have that kind of pressure of him. High school is bad enough, remembering your locker combination. Skin in high school is bad enough. I remember once working with a kid who had a pimple and they couldn't shoot him because it was big. The camera crew and the director were making this huge scene about it in front of this teenage boy who was just dying of humiliation. It's not funny. It was really awful. I don't think he'll ever get over that day.

Winona Ryder Van Redin/The Kobal Collection

Looking for Love

Love and romance can bring the greatest joys into anyone's life. And the greatest sorrows. Fame can certainly make one more attractive, but how can you be sure if your new honey loves you or your image? Is it the glamour and riches that turns them on? In turn, the partner of a celebrity faces fears of abandonment while inheriting a disproportionate burden of domestic responsibility. Maybe it makes more sense to snuggle up with someone equally famous, but what happens when they go off with someone who has even more starpower than you?

Eric Stoltz

When you're an actor, your relationships are constantly fraught with temptation and danger. [His girlfriend, Bridget Fonda] thinks that I'm surrounded by predatory co-stars and I think that she's surrounded by predatory co-stars. The people we work with are all charming and rich and handsome and talented and beautiful. And often completely amoral. I can name four or five different actors or actresses who feel that they are above and beyond the rules of society and have no respect for anyone else's relationships. They are charming people, box office people, but most actors are dogs and predatory and will fuck up a relationship if given a chance.

Mary Steenburgen

(She married two of her co-stars, Malcolm McDowell and Ted Danson)

What's dangerous about what we do is when we're on a movie set time is suspended. We're not taking out the trash. We're not cooking dinner. We're not yelling at the gas company because they didn't fill the gas tank. Whatever it is that you're dealing with in life you're not doing. You're on location. You're staying in a hotel. Somebody makes your bed. Somebody lays your clothes out. Somebody fixes your hair. You're basically a big baby. If you fall in love in those circumstances, you have to be very careful to ask yourself how real is this? How much reality is this based in? Because there's such a degree of unreality about a movie set.

Ellen Barkin

I am not a believer of that myth about your husband going off to make a movie with a beautiful co-star. I'm sure lawyers have affairs with lawyers and doctors have affairs with doctors as often as actors do with actors. Yeah, it's slightly more intimate when you're in a bed kissing somebody, but it is, after a while, a part of your job. I don't think the obstetrician gets turned on every time he does a pelvic exam.

Roger Daltrey

I've been married twice. I was married very early on in the Who days. It was a conscious decision: Either I stuck with the band or I stayed married. There was no way in those days it would ever have worked.

Kirk Pengilly

(Member of INXS)

It's a marriage, being in a band to start, and it's always interesting when new girls come on the scene. It must be the most stressful thing that they can go through, because not only do they have to get to know and go out with the particular guy, they also have to go out with the other five guys as well—and their girlfriends and wives—and get along with them all. I really pity that sort of situation.

Bryan Adams

I kicked a girlfriend out of my life because she was driving me crazy. She couldn't understand that I really, really wanted to devote my life to this. She wanted me to marry her.

Clarence Clemons

Marriage and rock 'n' roll are incompatible if you make it incompatible. Some people want it to be incompatible. When I got married, we came down off that mountain and said our lives would be one. Her responsibility to my job is just as important as my responsibility to that job is. She deals with me and I deal with it. We work it out together. She goes with me on tour and we love each other.

Keenen Ivory Wayans

You go home after living your love scene fantasy out on the set and you go, "Hey baby, that's just acting. That's just the business. You have to be able to deal with that." You know, you get your rap on. She didn't buy it, though. That's part of being with someone in our business.

Paul Reiser

Finishing this book, Couplehood, *was weird.* I was writing this book at night and on weekends. My wife would say, "You want to go do something?"

"I'm writing the book."

"Are you going to come to bed?"

"I'm writing a book about loving couples! Can't you see I'm busy!"

Natalie Cole

I don't know that the music business is hard on relationships. I think life is hard on relationships. I think that's a poor excuse.

If you hook up with somebody who's got the kind of job that you really wish that they didn't, it's not compatible with your lifestyle, then just don't hook up with that person. But if you really love that person, you just adjust. The music business allows people to excuse themselves from having to adjust.

I do feel that I need to be with someone who can adjust to my lifestyle, because I travel. Literally, I'm just not home a lot. I don't know a lot of men who would want that kind of relationship.

> *Marriages work or don't work in every walk of life. An incredible amount of people have marriages that fall apart. The reason that people perceive actors as not having them work is because every time they get a divorce it ends up in the newspaper. I don't think necessarily there's more of a precedent for it happening any more in the entertainment industry than any other industry. Maybe I'm wrong. I don't know.*
>
> *—Kevin Bacon*

Forest Whitaker

Professionally, I'm really happy with the progression of my career. Personally, it's difficult for me. I'm not home very much. It's difficult on my relationships. It's difficult because I want to see my family. I want to be with my friends. You can't have quality relationships like that.

Bonnie Bedelia

I haven't had as much romance in my life as I would like. Movies are romantic. My life hasn't been. I'm at a loss with questions of this nature. I have nothing witty or funny to say and I don't want to sit here and discuss pain and loss.

Linda Fiorentino

I haven't had a boyfriend for the last year. It's funny. Men will think that I'm going to say no to them. "She'll never go out with me. She wants a movie star or some rich guy." That's just what they perceive. Men don't approach me. So I have to be the aggressor, I guess.

Glenn Close

I really don't know how men perceive me. I hope they're not afraid of me. I think I've scared the you-know-what out of a lot of men just because of the roles I've played, but I'm really not a frightening person, ha, ha.

Juliette Lewis

It was so tough to have a public relationship with Brad [Pitt]. The person you love is on the screen and millions of people can have whatever they want of that person in their mind. They can have their romance. That bothered me. Brad was fine. It was other people that bothered me.

Marisa Tomei

It's hard to have relationships anyway, whether you're famous or not.

Nathan Lane

Right now I don't have a personal life, but as soon as I do you'll be the first one I call.

Esther Williams

Fernando Lamas said to me, "I really would like to marry you, but could you stop being Esther Williams?"

I said, "That's a really interesting question." I've been Esther Williams since I was twelve years old, when I started competitive swimming and became a name on the sports pages and then on the marquee. I said, "Could you stop fooling around?"

He said, "I don't know."

"I can stop being Esther Williams easier than you can stop fooling around, obviously."

Saving his Argentinean pride he said, "Yeah, I'm getting tired anyway." [They were married for twenty-two years.]

> *I did my first movie with Bette Davis. And you know what she said to me? Oh, it just haunts me. I wonder if it's true, maybe she's right. She said, "You can't have a relationship and a career. You can't have both."*
>
> *—Rosanna Arquette*

Dennis Quaid

There's no competition between us [he and wife Meg Ryan]. She's a woman. I'm a man. We're not up for the same roles yet. We're best friends. The business doesn't really enter into our relationship. I do love working with her, though. We've made three movies together.

Luke Perry

When it's exploding and all the stuff is going on, you don't really have time for any relationship. It wasn't what I was looking for anyway. It wasn't my bag. I wasn't ever going to get married. I was the most eligible bachelor walking.

Jada Pinkett

Career comes first. That's right. I had a boyfriend who said, "Would you ever give your career up?" Not right now. The only way I would ever give my career up is for a family—and I don't plan on having a family until who knows when.

Halle Berry

I don't think my husband [baseball star David Justice, now her ex] will ever get comfortable with seeing me kiss a guy on screen. I tell him, "You might want to close your eyes for the next five minutes." It's hard. I have to respect that and try to make him feel better about it, because I know if it were me I don't know if I could take it. I honestly don't know how I would react. That's why he can't act. He can't do that.

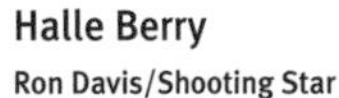
Halle Berry
Ron Davis/Shooting Star

Cameron Diaz

I didn't know Jim Carrey very well at the time we had to do our kissing in *The Mask.* It was quite an experience. Jim and I kept looking at each other laughing like little kids. "We have to kiss each other, hee, hee, hee."

"Do you have Binaca?"

"I'll take some if you take some."

Sandra Bullock

I got asked so many times, "What was it like to kiss Keanu Reeves—and how is it different than kissing Sly Stallone?" Do you want the graphic details? Do you want technique? What is it that you're looking for?

Tia Carrere

Pauly Shore is a better kisser than Mike Myers. Mike was very nervous about it and I knew Pauly before, so I think that added comfort. Mike was a little afraid of the whole thing. Very nervous, very tense. I don't think I'm going to run away from my husband for Pauly, but I'm not going to say that watching me kiss another gentleman is a wonderful thing for my husband to experience.

Bridget Fonda

(On shooting love scenes with boyfriend Eric Stoltz)

Eric likes to tell everybody that we really did have sex that day. "Everybody in the whole crew joined in."

It's a lot easier. You feel a lot more comfortable. You're never comfortable, but you're eliminating one of the uncomfortable factors, which is the fact that you have to be intimate with somebody who you don't know, who you always have to be polite to. You're always trying to figure out if that other person is okay, and you're covering yourself, and you're trying to be funny. That and the crew usually makes the whole experience incredibly strange.

Meg Ryan

It was so awful to do that love scene in *Flesh and Bone*. I kept saying to Dennis [Quaid], "Don't kiss me, because if you really kiss me we'll never be able to kiss again." It's the most impersonal thing you can a ever do, a love scene. It's like gymnastics, or some kind of strange choreography.

Dennis Quaid

Love scenes are always uncomfortable, no matter what. You've got five electricians over here with beer guts. It's a little less uncomfortable with her [wife Meg Ryan]. The good thing is when we go see the film together neither of us have to shut our eyes.

Arnold Schwarzenegger

Love scenes are not difficult—except that there are always a hundred people standing around watching you. Everyone tries to help you the day that you do a scene like this. Usually you can never find them anywhere. You need somebody from wardrobe and you have to go on a search, but that day they're all around.

Jamie Lee Curtis

My husband [writer/director Christopher Guest] and I have been married more than ten years. When you're not married and your partner is not married then you might enter into some serious lip lock, but when you're working with an actor who is married and you are married you no longer invest in the kiss. Because screen kissing is all about almost doing nothing. When you see people who you know and they're actually having an affair and they're slobbering all over each other, it looks gross. It's not pretty to watch. A screen kiss, when it works, is almost very benign and simple. My kissing Arnold Schwarzenegger in *True Lies* was very chaste and absolutely done with complete decorum and understanding that we're both married people and this is just part of our job.

Deidre Hall

As a performer, you know what makes your co-star goosy. Things to do that give them chills, involuntarily. Of course, we don't do them.

Eddie Murphy

Nobody's really doing it under the covers. You get embarrassed for the other actor and you do little things to make her feel comfortable. Between shots you help them cover themselves up. There's no way you can really get into it, with lights and crew everywhere, and her boyfriend is over there and your girlfriend is over there. Then the director's saying, "Make it look like you're having an orgasm."

James Garner

It is tough for a woman to see her husband in bed kissing a girl, and whatever, all day long. They worry about that. Some young girl, they can get jealous. My wife trusts me—poor fool, ha, ha, ha. No, no. I've always been very considerate. I've never tried to put her in a compromising position through that.

Luke Perry

I've been in situations where I had to do a love scene with a girl and her husband or her boyfriend sat right offstage there. It doesn't bother me at all, "Hey bro, you're in the audience. Tough." But some people have problems with it. I wouldn't inflict that on somebody else. By the same token, I know people who have done films where the director is married to the actress. My God, what are they thinking!

Demi Moore

Love scenes are the most difficult thing I've ever had to do in my life. I particularly hated it in *Indecent Exposure,* because Woody Harrelson is my husband [Bruce Willis]'s friend. Woody kept looking at me saying, "I'm supposed to look at you like you're attractive? You're my friend. Oh no." And [director] Adrian Lyne is saying, "Just go lie in bed together for rehearsal."

Deidre Hall

Soap stars are all very familiar with the part of rehearsal that says, "Okay, here's the love scene." I remember meeting Peter Bergman at an awards show, shaking hands and realizing, "Whoa, we're in bed soon."

We walked onto the set. I was in a little skimpy thing. We had a little talk. "I'll put my arm around your left shoulder. You grab my thigh."

"If you lift me this way, I can then roll over on you."

"If you kiss me this way, I can then pull my head back and moan some."

"I'll turn this way, you turn that way." It was choreographed in the corner of the room.

Laura San Giacomo

When I was doing Nina Takes a Love*r and* The Stand *I kissed* four guys who weren't my husband [she's married to actor Cameron Dye] in the span of three months. It was truly ridiculous, but he was really great about it because he knew I was coming home.

We met on the set of *Miami Vice.*

Patsy Kensit

It's horrible actually. It's the most unnatural situation you're ever going to find yourself in. Totally unromantic. There are thirty guys standing around. It's hot. You've got to lie a certain way. It's not at all what it seems on the screen. Also, I met my husband when I was sixteen and he's the only man I've ever really known. It's so peculiar being in a bed with someone other than my husband.

Jada Pinkett

It's real tough to have a career and a man in your life. That's why I'm single. With the traveling and the ego thing that becomes involved, it's very difficult for men to have a woman that's doing films and have other men out there talking about, "Oooo, Jada Pinkett." It's hard. I understand. It's going to take a strong man to really be able to come over here and deal with what I got.

Halle Berry

When I'm kissing my husband or my husband is holding me, those feelings don't compare to what I feel when I'm kissing Jimmy Smits or Eddie Murphy. It's not the same thing at all and I'm not confused by the difference.

Laura San Giacomo

It's intimate, but there's an element to it that's still acting. You meet, you become so close, you lead this little mini-life inside of your life, and then you go off. Something's really been exchanged. It is real and true and honest, but it's also within the situation that has been given to you by the writer. It's you amplified through what this character is and what this situation is. There's that safety. You can be as honest and as true to who you are through that medium and you're still acting.

Sandra Bullock

When those days come to shoot love scenes, you get very excited. When you're teamed up with a person that you genuinely like as a person and they happen to be really, really good looking, you don't go, "Oh my God, I have to kiss this person. How am I going to get through this day?" You go, "Oh great! I get to suck face with somebody who's really cute—and it's

legal!" That's what I thought at first. But when you get to the day it's always panicked. It's never romantic and you're never swept off your feet. It's always very technical.

But, there's always a moment, and sometimes it's not when you expect it to happen. It's always when you least expect it. I'm counting the beats, "Okay, we're supposed to kiss for two beats, then I say my line, then they want another kiss for four beats." I'm going, "One Mississippi, two Mississippi, three and break." It's like choreography. Sometimes you have your experiences with actors who feel that it's their job to get as far down into your throat as possible. You're like, "Excuse me. I like you, but not that much."

Gary Oldman

It's a strange job, where you meet someone for the first time at ten o'clock in the morning and by 11:30 you have your tongue down her throat.

John Ritter

It's that wonderful thing about acting. "Hello, this is Monique, she will be your bed slave this morning."

"What was your name again?"

"Monique."

"Hello, Monique. That's a very lovely birthmark."

What a lot of people don't know about love scenes and acting—at least when I'm around—is it's pretty funny. If somebody's really shy, then you take it seriously.

Laura San Giacomo

Some actors do fall in love with their leading ladies. From my own experience, I always call it "significant other." This person becomes extremely important to me and we become significant others for this film because I can't do it without this person. We usually become really good friends,

Sandra Bullock Ralph Nelson/The Kobal Collection

but then I have my real life and my real marriage. So it's a love, but for me it's not falling in love. It's better than friendship, because it's more special.

Laura Dern

There are times when you have, when you have great affection for somebody, and if they're playing your boyfriend or your lover in a film the affection might become flirtatious because that's the dynamic of the relationship. When the film ends you want them to be your brother forever, but it has nothing to do with a romantic relationship. I've seen so many marriages break up because of absurd summer camp flirtation. Then the movie ends and the man turns around and his wife is gone. Inevitably it's better to wait until your heart is clear.

Laura Dern

I'm a person who is always open to her emotions, on a movie especially, because they're heightened. You're working and you're laughing and you're crying. That's why my cardinal rule is if at the end of a film you still have feelings for somebody, then develop a relationship. But I couldn't start an affair on a movie and continue that while I'm working. It's too complicated.

> *There is a great bonding that you experience if the work is intense. If you're waking up every day at four in the morning and going to bed at nine at night and you eat all your meals together and you're at your worst and your best moments for eighteen weeks, you're either going to walk away with some very close friends or some real enemies.*
>
> *—Laura Dern*

Natasha Richardson

If you're opposite somebody who you have to fall in love with on the screen—and you don't like him and don't get on with him—you still have to do a convincing job of falling in love with him so that everyone believes it. That's what we do. We act. We pretend. It's the same with Liam [Neeson, her husband] and me. We just act.

Nancy Travis

You're working fifteen or sixteen hours a day and it becomes all about sweat and did you do your homework. You cease to see how gorgeous they are. And remember, I'm seeing these guys when they come in at five in the morning before they come in for makeup.

Jean-Claude Van Damme

You can't fall in love doing a love scene because when you start to kiss, they tell you to stop. And when you ask what happened, they tell you that your nose needs more shadow. Then they'll tell you to stop again and again. It looks good on camera only because all those shots are cut together.

Deidre Hall

Love scenes are harder than crying scenes. They're harder than hysteria scenes. They're harder than children scenes. They're not harder than shower scenes, however. I've done several of those.

Love scenes are hard because there are no marks on the bed. Marks are what actors use to know where to stand and where to sit and where to cross to. So you never know exactly if the camera can see you. Now add to that you have your eyes closed. You're making love trying to feel the light on your face, trying to make sure that the slip is around your bosom, trying to make sure that the lines are being said because you can't see your co-star who's mumbling, "I love you, I can't live without you," as you're trying to say, "Take me now, honey, take me now." It's working without a net.

Madonna

It is hard to pretend to make love to someone you don't know that well.

Kimberly Williams

I was dating someone for two years. We'd go to premieres together and he'd get pushed aside. I hate that. You have to find somebody who's okay with that, who has enough self-confidence to be able to realize that that's a stupid part of the business.

The harder part of it is the schedule. Like right now I'm doing a movie in Texas. I don't know anybody in Texas, and if I met somebody in Texas, in seven weeks I'm going to be in L.A. again, or somewhere else. I hope that I can find a way to make it work eventually.

Cathy Lee Crosby

Being on the tennis tour sucked. Every week you go to another tournament, another tournament, another tournament. There weren't a lot of guys. You can't, as a girl, have a relationship and expect a guy to travel around the circuit with you. And you're certainly not the type of person who, every week you're going to find a guy in each city and have a relationship. It didn't make sense to me.

On March 16, 1995, Easy-E, a co-founder of the gangsta rap group N.W.A. and one of the biggest stars in the rap world, announced that he had contracted AIDS. His hospital logged ten thousand calls of concern shortly after, the most frantic of which were from ex-girlfriends and one-night stands. Ten days later, he died, at the age of thirty-one. In South Central Los Angeles there was an 80% increase in requests for AIDS tests.

Chris Farley

I want to get married and have kids, but I'm not in one place that much.

Alicia Silverstone

I don't feel like a dream girl. It's nice, though. A part of me wishes I got that sort of attention in my real life. In my real life I'm just this weird dorky girl who hangs out with her dog.

Chris Farley

I've gone out with some girls that sure are pretty and I can't believe it because some of the gals in high school I dated looked like me in a wig. It's kind of strange that these girls are talking to me now.

Martin Lawrence

(Asked if he has to fight off women now?)

I don't fight off too many. I wasn't always the finest brother in the world. I take what I can get now.

Elijah Wood

My older brother told me, "Stay away from women," and I'm taking it to heart. I'm staying clear. It's kind of like a museum where they have those really cool paintings. They're behind the glass and you can look at them, but you can't touch them. That's what it's like with girls. I can get myself into trouble. And also it's hard because I'm an actor and girls might not like me for who I am. That's hard to deal with.

Pauly Shore

I haven't even had one normal girlfriend since this whole thing went down, someone who I know for sure loves me for me. These girls generally love me after they get to know me, but then I also think that there's this one little thing in the back of their head saying, "He's not as popular as he used to be," or "He's not buying me what he used to buy me."

Shannen Doherty

I really picked bad men. I picked men who were opportunists and were looking for press and looking for extra money. I don't know very many ninety-two pound girls who can actually beat up a one hundred and eighty pound man. There were quite a few lies out there. It was mind-boggling to me at the time, but I understood later when their bank account was $60,000 richer.

Mary Stuart Masterson

The more relationships that you're in that end, the more you realize that you should be trusting your instincts from the beginning. First impressions usually tell you a lot more about a person than they would tell you about themselves.

Alicia Silverstone
Yoram Kahana/Shooting Star

Chris O'Donnell

When I was back at Boston College we'd go out to bars and there would be a lot of girls who would hang around just 'cause I was in films. After a while you'd get confused 'cause you think maybe you just have a pretty good rap. Then we went to Europe to do *The Three Musketeers* and I remember going to bars in Vienna and trying to talk to girls. They'd just look at me and walk away. It's a little blow to the ego, but it was a good experience, I guess.

Johnny Galecki

It's tough to approach people sometimes because you don't know exactly why they're looking at you or why you've met eyes with this person. If it's a girl, you don't know if she's looking at you maybe because she saw you on *Roseanne* last night or maybe because she might think you're attractive. It puts a buffer in between maybe having a conversation with a nice person walking down the street.

Lukas Haas

There are younger girls at my school who just know that I'm in the movies so they have a crush on me. Or girls who live in Austin, they see me somewhere, then they write me a letter saying that they like me. Or just fan letters from people that I don't know, with pictures. Then they want you to send naked pictures.

Thomas Ian Nicholas

I get all this fan mail from these girls and they're like, "Oh God, THOMAS!" What makes me leery about it is they're writing to Thomas Ian Nicholas, also known as Henry Rowengartner, also known as Calvin Fuller. They're writing more to what I've done than to me personally. They don't know me.

Julia Ormond

People bring a wall down in front of you. And you start to question what is it that this person is interested in or intrigued by. You fear that once they get over the star thing they'll be crushingly disappointed. "You're normal?" "Yeah."

It's something that it's up to you to a certain extent to deal with. You have to say, "I don't want to be treated like that." I don't want to relate to someone in a different way than if I was still in drama school, or how I have done in the past. Somebody has to be very levelheaded to be with somebody in this business. And secure.

Ethan Hawke

What starts to happen is your ability to make a first impression gets less and less and less and less as people start to have a preconceived notion of who you are and what you're about. That's a really weird thing to get stripped of. It separates you from your peers in a negative way.

Christian Slater

It's still possible to find romance. I've found some pretty incredible relationships and shared some pretty amazing love with some people. I don't think the celebrity thing has totally gotten in the way of that.

Glenn Close

You go out with your own kind. I love actors. I call them "my people," people you don't have to explain your existence to.

Marlee Matlin

Dating actors gets competitive. Coming home and saying, "My agent got me this." Then he says his agent got him that. It was a lot of BS. Some of the actors that I dated were very nice. Some of them were complete jerks. A few of them had let their acting personas get into their mindsets and into their lives. That wasn't something I wanted.

Kim Basinger

The very first week he [husband Alec Baldwin] came to California for the first day of rehearsals [for *The Marrying Man*], his car broke down in the parking lot of Morton's and I had to take him home. He asked me if I wanted kids. I said, "Uh oh." I was very, very relationship shy. He was very set, cut, and dried, once he met me. I thought this guy was crazy and psychotic. And then I found myself falling in love with him.

We wanted to get married for a long time. After I said yes, he said, "This is it. I really need to know. I need to do this." So he flew back to New York—I had to do *Wayne's World* in California—and he did everything. He did the whole wedding. The only thing they did ask me was what colors I liked. I was like, "For what?" I was in a daze. He always said to me from the beginning of our relationship, "I just want some good memories." After the wedding I said, "This is truly a memory."

Belinda Carlisle

A deejay in Los Angeles called me and said there's this guy, Morgan Mason, who wants to meet you. He worked in the White House and went out with Joan Collins. I said, "I don't think so." People kept telling me this guy wants to meet me. I'm sure Joan Collins is fine, but I don't think anybody who went out with Joan Collins would necessarily be anybody that I would get along with. Especially somebody who worked in the Reagan White House.

I went to a party one night and he was there and he came up to me. We were introduced and he walked away. I said, "No one walks away

from me," but he did anyway. I ran into him a couple of days later and he threw me his card and said, "If anything comes up, give me a call."

I had friend call him and say she was me and ask him out. He called the next day. He was a completely different person. We went on the first date to see Hall & Oates and went to Trader Vic's afterwards. We fell in love. I moved in with him the next day.

Catherine Deneuve

When you work in films you work with different people in different places. Sometimes you are not going to see them again for a long time. Even in France, sometimes I will not see someone again for years. There are some actors that I got very friendly with on a film, but I never tried to maintain a relationship. Actors are like gypsies. You cannot have a long relationship with an actor.

It's hard to have a relationship in this business. It's a really transient business. It's easier sometimes if you have somebody who is in the business and understands the constraints.

—Jeanne Tripplehorn

Shirley MacLaine

Marcello Mastroianni was always going through his clandestine affairs from European city to European city—and so was I, usually with married people. So we were trying to avoid any curious eyes, but we would always run into each other and go, "Oh, hi. Who are you with this year?" Finally we met to work together and reminisced about that. We never had an affair together. We weren't attracted to each other, but we were always interested in who the other was attracted to.

Mary Stuart Masterson

I got married very young. If you chalk up my divorce to anything it would be a lot of years on the road, a lack of what I felt was roots, or home. That doesn't actually explain it, nor will I sit here and explain the relationship, but I think that a big part of the relationships not working is the traveling.

Kim Basinger and Alec Baldwin Lee Salem/Shooting Star

Joan Armatrading

I'm not married. I haven't got time to be married. I'm too busy. I'm on tour for six months. Some have been eight months. Then I'll make a record, do promotion stuff, and I'm very lucky if I've got a month at home.

Helena Bonham Carter

You've got to work at keeping certain friendships throughout this very disjointed lifestyle. I live with my mom and dad so I keep on coming back to that. As far as old romances, well, you know, it's a bit erratic. At twenty-eight, I think it's okay. Work has definitely been a priority and that's how I've led my life so far.

Salma Hayek

I haven't been able to have a life for a long time. The last boyfriend I had was three and a half years ago. There's something wrong with me. I'm very focused. I'm very determined. I'm doing something that is so hard to do that no one has done it since Dolores Del Rio, when the movies were silent. It takes that much dedication to cross over from Mexico to Hollywood. But I think one day very soon I'm going to do one movie a year and I'll get to do hobbies the rest of the time.

Juliette Lewis

Leo DiCaprio and I were in New York making movies at the same time. Since he was up there and I was up there, we went out once. A few times he would be at the same place I would be at so we would see each other on and off. But just for the record, I haven't been with anybody famous since Brad [Pitt]. I'd prefer not to be with somebody famous unless we're truly going to commit and we're going to be together for a very long time. I don't want to have a string of famous people.

Laura Dern

The younger ilk of actors that don't have a set relationship, it's harder. You're on movie after movie and locations. There's new people around. It's just like summer camp or high school.

Chris O'Donnell

Al Pacino told me, "Don't date an actress." I'm sticking to it.

Ray Liotta

Poor Kiefer [Sutherland] and what he had to go through [when Julia Roberts called off their wedding]. I worked with him on *Article 99* and I think that's why I've stayed away from going out with actresses.

> *If you're looking for love, show business is the wrong place to find it.*
>
> *—Peter Gallagher*

Pauly Shore

I've been quoted as saying I don't like women, but in the article I talk about women in this town [Hollywood], not women in general. Those are the girls that I am surrounded by because I'm in show business. I would like to say, "Hey, you know what? I want a girl who's got a job and she's got a brain on her head and she works from nine to five," but I don't meet those girls. In return I get with these girls who need something. What they need is someone to live off of. My last three girlfriends, those are the ones that I fell in love with. I had one girlfriend shoot herself in the head and that was a very, very heavy thing for me. Just because this girl does porno or *Playboy* or *Penthouse,* does that mean she's a slut? Does that mean she's dirty? Does that mean she isn't as nice as us? No. That means she got involved with something that is wrong, but she wasn't strong enough. I don't judge people by what they do. If you're a heroin addict, a junkie, I'm not going to turn my head on you. This is a human being we're talking about. Someone who has some feelings that are sadder than your simple little life. Those are the girls that I've been dealing with. I don't want to go out with them any more.

Tea Leoni

Well, there was an upside to playing a nymphomaniac on TV. I'm not married any more.

Michael Douglas

The national divorce average is a little under 50%. There's probably more pressures on us in terms of a lifestyle, being away for periods of time. It's hard to have relationships. For the record, Diandra and I are separated.

We're quite happy to talk to each other almost every day. A lot of love. Sadness, but no grief.

Elliott Gould

We [he and ex-wife Barbara Streisand] started out together. But I had come up through the ranks. I was a chorus boy. I was trained in certain things. I don't know that Barbra was trained, except that she was brilliant. But it's one thing to be brilliant, it's another thing to come out here and live. To live and go with life.

We're still friends, great friends. We fight. We don't see much of one another, but our son Jason is my best friend.

Madonna

It was a great disappointment that my marriage [to actor/director Sean Penn] didn't work, but I'm not paralyzed by it.

Lauren Holly

If Jim [Carrey] and I didn't make it, and I was sad about it and I was eating chips in bed and watching talk shows and telling my friends how horrible I feel, it would be sad that I'd have to see it on the news, too.

Sondra Locke

It's not my nature to throw stones, but the problem is when you don't do that a lot of preconceptions get out there and nobody knows what goes on. You end up on the rough end because you're the unknown. You're the enigma. Having lived in Clint [Eastwood]'s shadow, nobody really knows very much about me. If they think anything, they think of some of the characters that I've played, which are very different from me. You find yourself in a bind. On the one hand, you're very quiet and private and you don't want to put yourself out there, especially at such a painful and awkward time. On the other hand, it doesn't seem to do you any good to hide out, either. It's a Catch-22 situation.

Sondra Locke

I got the opportunity to play some wonderful parts and I enjoyed it, but I didn't really get the credit that I would have gotten most likely if I had given those same performances in films with other actors, because there's a certain stigma going along with the fact that, "Sure, she's in this film, but they live together." You don't really get the credit for having the other abilities that went along with it. It was okay for me at that time—and still would be okay with me today if things were being handled a little differently. I was very much in love. We had a wonderful life together. We had a wonderful time working together, but it's also quite obvious that I'd lost my own separate identity.

Tom Arnold

Being compared to Roseanne might be the bad part of getting divorced from her, but I had five years of being in a family, with the kids and everything, that was very rewarding. I feel blessed to have that opportunity, besides the professional stuff, which was incredible, too.

Other Hollywood stars have had divorces and went on with their lives and married other people or done whatever. You might not even remember who they were married to their first time. I don't think that's going to happen here, but it might. That's all right though. I was married to her and it was great. It was an honor to be in that family for five years.

Kenneth Branagh

(Commenting on his breakup with wife Emma Thompson)

You take one day at a time in these situations. It's been a challenging year all around. The situation personally that I'm involved with is extremely, staggeringly sad, as I'm sure it always is. It has the added factor of, to some extent, being under the media spotlight, of being subject to media curiosity. What one does is attempt to protect the very personal side of it. We've never talked in any kind of intimate detail about our personal relationship up to this point, so it's no surprise to anyone that we're not

Kenneth Branagh and Emma Thompson were considered to be the golden couple of the British cinema. He was "the next Olivier," directing well-received film versions of Shakespearean classics, while she earned an Oscar for Howard's End. They had triumphed together in such films as Dead Again and Much Ado About Nothing by some observers. But by the end of 1995, with his A Midwinter's Tale and her Sense and Sensibility being released, the marriage was over. Branagh and Thompson issued only a terse public statement, stating, "Our work has inevitably led to our spending long periods of time away from each other, and as a result, we have drifted apart."

going to start opening up about things that are entirely to do with us.

I can understand the curiosity, but at the same time people I think understand that there's a point that beyond which it's just not possible to talk about these things. It's one's own problem. It's happened to a trillion people. They have to get on with it. We're blessed with all the cliché things, good health currently, financial independence, a lot of things that people don't have in these situations that make life incredibly difficult. There are no children involved, etc.

There's no point in going on about "our pain," and all the rest of it. It's ours. It's no more special than anybody else's. It's sometimes a pain in the ass to be watched in that regard, but it just is what it is. People would pay to have our problems.

Kenneth Branagh

There are specific factors involved. Long separations and all of that, I think that's probably the principal factor, in fact. There's always a price to pay for the privilege of being offered extraordinary opportunities workwise that separate you, where choices get made that I'm sure have some kind of price to pay in your very personal lives.

Diane Lane

(Divorced from fellow actor Christopher Lambert)

Time spent away is time swept away. You have so much to make up for when you get back together that after a while it becomes more work than spontaneity.

Lauren Holly

It's hard to make quiet time, unless we're [she and Jim Carrey] in a vault somewhere. I think two people really need that. Whereas some people's focus on a relationship may be on things like being less selfish or more generous or whatever, our focus is usually, "We need to find two hours that's quiet and private." We're master planners and scheduling maniacs. It's bizarre, but necessary.

Kenneth Branagh and Emma Thompson Ron Davis/Shooting Star

Lauren Holly

When we don't get to see each other, Jim [Carrey] writes me messages with a bar of soap on the mirror in the bathroom.

Ellen Barkin

(Separated from husband Gabriel Byrne)

I don't think it's impossible for actors to be married to each other. The only thing that makes it difficult is the logistics. Am I upset that my husband is gone all the time and doesn't have a job? Sure, but I'm gone all the time, too.

Rita Wilson

I suppose it could be insane for some people, but Tom [Hanks] 's very levelheaded and I am very levelheaded and it's important to us to create and keep a balance between our professional lives and personal lives.

On July 29, 1981, five hundred million viewers worldwide watched live television coverage of the royal marriage of Prince Charles to Lady Diana Spencer. "Di" was the lovely heroine in a fairy tale concocted by the media, and embraced by people everywhere. But the marriage was real, not a fairy tale, and everywhere the prince and princess went, cameras did too. Their personal troubles were announced and analyzed, and the fairy tale lost some of its glow. The world was stunned in December, 1992 when the royal couple officially separated, amid accusations of infidelity. In December, 1995, Queen Elizabeth asked them to divorce. On February 28, 1996, Diana issued the following statement to the press: "The Princess of Wales has agreed to Prince Charles' request for a divorce. The Princess will continue to be involved in all decisions relating to the children and will remain at Kensington Palace with offices in St. James's Palace. The Princess of Wales will retain the title and be known as Diana, Princess of Wales."

The story garnered front page headlines worldwide. Magazines featured cover stories of the divorce, analyzing what it means for Diana, Charles, and the British monarchy—and reminding everyone that the dream was just that, a dream. In the March 11, 1996 issue Time magazine commented: "One thing no longer alive is the dream that dies so hard. Charles and Diana are two people who stumbled into a fantasy fervently embraced by millions. She embodied it; he was swept up in it, much against his will. When the so-called fairy tale began, all Charles wanted was more of what he already had: a comfortable life of conscientious royal duty, shooting, polo, painting pictures—and a nice quiet double standard. But people may never forgive him for puncturing their dream...The divorce announcement, however muddled, only served to reopen the scrapbooks of memory, reminding people of the fairy tale that was too good to be true."

Winona Ryder

If a relationship is real and it's strong, fame can hurt it, but it can't destroy it. But if it's not meant to be, then, yeah, it does have a damaging effect.

Jean-Claude Van Damme

(Now married to his fourth wife)

If you're a star or she's a star, you need a very strong husband or a very strong wife. The guy is always traveling and you have all those people following you and you're famous and you're a sex symbol, so the woman who's married to a movie star has to be very stable. It's difficult to find a stable woman these days, or a stable guy. Like the old fashioned woman, like my mother, she's stable. Sometimes it's difficult because people get very insecure. I don't know why it happens, but it's very hard for a woman and a man to have that very stable attitude.

Alec Baldwin

People were totally expecting my wife [Kim Basinger] and I to be together for the run of the movie we did first and split up.

Geena Davis

(Divorced from Jeff Goldblum)

I think getting written up in the tabloids bonds you together even more. We [she and her husband Renny Harlin] have a lot of friends in the business, celebrity couples even. From the time we spend with some of our friends and the view that we have, we can't believe that they can weather some of the things that happen.

I don't know what it is. I guess for some reason as soon as two celebrities get together it's, "Oh! We've got to start writing about it! Create some thing about it!" Somehow it's like a magnet for attention.

John Leguizamo

Marriage is wild. I thought it was this perfect land of happiness and joy. Wrong! After you say you do, you don't for a long time.

Roger Daltrey

(Member of The Who)

"You just go and have a good time," my wife says and she means it. If I went and had a really good time with a lot of chicks, or whatever, if she

didn't know about it, she'd not be worried about it in the least. But the fact is, why bother? I've got the best one at home.

Tim Robbins

(Asked if he will ever marry Susan Sarandon, with whom he has three children)

For your sake? It's not in the foreseeable future. It's not something that's important to us. I think we're really committed to each other. Why spoil a good thing?

Eric Stoltz

(Asked if he will marry long-time girlfriend Bridget Fonda)

That's none of your business.

Goldie Hawn

As far as I'm concerned, Kurt [Russell] and I are married. I love him. I've told him I love him in front of all my children. We've all exchanged our vows, but I have a problem being married twice before, knowing that doesn't mean anything. You have a ceremony, you get married, and everyone's euphoric for a while. Then life begins. The only different thing is the state suddenly has a say about what you do and how much money you have to pay that person if in fact you fall out of love. I personally don't want to give the state that power. And God is inside of me, so I don't have to prove anything to him. I just don't understand marriage at all at this point.

Richard Gere

I don't believe that human love really exists. Our concept of love is very small. I keep wanting to have glimpses of Big Love. I feel that is possible. But our love is very much about attachment. That is how we can crawl over homeless people and allow people to starve. Our love is about things that belong to us. We have to grow beyond that.

Bruce Willis

Our [he and wife Demi Moore's] marriage is like a lot of people's marriages. We have our ups and downs. We argue. It's not like you get

Richard Gere Takashi Seida/The Kobal Collection

married and then life is okay. It's a little garden you have to tend all the time. You have to pay attention to it. It helps us take time off from the films. The film world is not like real life at all. It's an illusion. To get out of Hollywood and to get away from that is a nice thing.

Brian Benben

(Married to actress Madeleine Stowe)

We've [he and actress Madeleine Stowe] been together for so long and since we were so young. I was I think eight when I met Madeleine. We met in Sunday school, I'll never forget it. [They actually met while making *The Gangster Chronicles.*]

Look, the only thing that keeps people together is wanting to be together. And if you really want to be together you get on the phone, you travel, you never let more than a week and a half or whatever go by, or try not to. We've been able to spend time together on our [Texas] ranch. For the first time in about five years we've had a block of time together. You do what you can when you can. You travel a lot and you get on the phone a lot.

Phoebe Cates

About five years ago we [she and husband Kevin Kline] decided that we were not going to work at the same time, because we felt that the separation was really destructive. So we don't. We've stuck to it—and it's hard, harder on me, because he gets offered much better parts than I do.

Kirstie Alley

We [she and husband Parker Stevenson] have a rule that we're never away from each other for more than three weeks. We don't believe absence makes the heart grow fonder. We've been married for twelve years and we've always had that rule.

Dennis Quaid

We're best friends [he and wife Meg Ryan]. We make each other laugh. We're not like anybody's dream couple, that's just too much responsibility. In fact, we were offered the cover of *Newsweek* magazine as "The New American Family." We said no. We don't want to be any symbol for anything. That's like Jinx! Jinx! Jinx!

We've done three movies together, so we're taking a little break from that. Maybe in another time in our lives, we'll see what transpires. We're not actively searching for anything to do together. We don't want to be Hume Cronyn and Jessica Tandy yet. We'll save that for the later part of our careers.

We just have a thing where we're never separated for more than two weeks at a time. Like when I was doing *Dragonheart* in Slovokia, she was doing *French Kiss* in Paris. That's just two hours away and I'd go there every weekend. Jack would stay with me, then he'd stay with her. You just work it out. Most people work fifty weeks of the year, they go off early in the morning, they come home tired at night and just want to zone out.

Natasha Richardson

Just because a couple is together doesn't mean they have chemistry. If Liam [Neeson] and I do have chemistry together that's a plus—and it's something that has to be carefully protected. There are a lot of people who ask us to do a lot of things together. They'd have us do everything together. We're really overly careful—to the nth degree—that we have to pick exactly the right projects. Maybe over the course of the years we will want to occasionally work together and I want to preserve that. I don't want to be in a movie with Liam and have them write what they wrote about Warren Beatty and Annette Bening in *Love Affair.*

Warren Beatty

I got extremely lucky when I met this person [Annette Bening]. It was immediate. I had seen Annette's work in movies and I thought that she was the most versatile and pound for pound the best actress in movies. I was very interested in working with her.

We met for *Bugsy*. I hadn't known her before that. When I met her I knew immediately that this was a significant event in my own life.

James Garner

I met my wife at a friend's house. She was there in the backyard and I said, "Woo-eee, what a pretty girl!" I said hello and that was about it. Then a week later there was this rally for Adlai Stevenson at the same house. She was there and I asked her to go out to dinner with me. We went out to dinner that night, and the next night, and the next night for thirteen or fourteen days—and got married. Two weeks. It's lasted for forty years.

James Garner

In our two week courtship, we did a lot of talking. I pointed out the situation of an actor and the pressures that come to bear. You don't have to know somebody for a long, long time. When you get married it's a two-way street. You have to be considerate of the other person. We've both tried to be considerate. I think that's what's held us together.

Robert Downey, Jr.

I was in a relationship with Sarah Jessica Parker for a long time. I guess mostly what happened is if you're both working all the time then you just never see each other.

My wife Deborah started working quite a bit as an actress right about the time we first met. She was starting to get big parts, but one morning she just said to me, "You know what? I don't want to do this anymore."

I said, "Why?" and she said, "Because I don't like it. I don't like getting up at seven in the morning. I don't like having to be made an object of people's desire that I don't know. I just want to be with you."

I swear to God, it just changed my life. I was like, "I can't believe you're saying this. I love you."

Kyra Sedgwick

Kevin [Bacon, her husband] and I have a lot of the same values. Once you pick your priorities and they're pretty clear everything else falls into place in a simple way. Logistically, with the different locations and packing up the [two] kids, we're almost always together. I know it's hard to believe because we both do work a lot, but we hardly have ever worked at the same time. It only happened once. It was a huge mistake and we learned our lesson, when he was doing *The Air Up There* in Africa and I was doing *Heart and Souls.* It was a nightmare, but it was a wonderfully clear message. Apart from the fact that it's really hard on the kids, we just don't like being separated for any length of time.

Kyra Sedgwick

If anyone told me I was going to marry an actor, I would've told them they were completely insane [she married Kevin Bacon]. And probably vice versa. But you know, it was just so clear that he was the right one, so quickly. I was only twenty-one when I met him. I was twenty-two when I got married and twenty-three when I had my first kid.

> *Kyra [Sedgwick] and I joked about when we had our fifth wedding anniversary, we called it our "Hollywood Gold Anniversary." Five years and you're making a real commitment out here.*
>
> *—Kevin Bacon*

Patricia Arquette

(She's married to actor Nicolas Cage)

There are these people who are watching you and want you to fail, sometimes even making up stories about your failure which aren't true.

Roger Daltrey

(Member of The Who)

I'd like to reach my golden wedding anniversary. In this business, that would be quite an achievement. I don't know whether anybody's done that yet.

Winona Ryder

It's extra pressure because you're being watched and written about. Everyone's saying that I'm engaged when I'm not. Some tabloid printed it and now you find out who really reads the tabloids because everybody in the world thinks it's true—and it's not true. It's irritating.

Jon Bon Jovi

I'm used to people looking at me and saying, "That looks like Bon Jovi." That's cool, but this was what they'd say, "That's Bon Jovi and that's Diane Lane." Wherever we went, whatever we did, two is more obvious than one. It got in the magazines and her friends are calling her up saying, "What are you doing out on the road with a rock band?"

Justine Frischman

(Member of Elastica)

It's difficult at home because the guy I go out with is very well-known in Britain. We have tabloid press hanging around. It's actually a real joy for me to come to America because I haven't got that kind of thing around my neck. It's not nice having photographers hiding in your garden, which we've experienced, and people interviewing the neighbors on the radio.

Uma Thurman

It's just a pain in the neck. The truth is, though, it doesn't matter what's written. Your private life is always your private life. The coverage never reflects your private life. I can guarantee the public that.

Christian Slater

Those tabloid headlines about me, that stuff is really make-believe. Anything you read, some of the people that I'm dating in those headlines are incredible. I wish I were dating them. I'm not.

Sylvester Stallone and Angie Everhart
Lisa O'Connor/Shooting Star

Angie Everhart

Just because Sylvester Stallone is a mega-famous guy our relationship was in the tabloids. Everybody has had a relationship and broken up and got back together at least once in their life. Unfortunately, because he's a mega-star, it's in the press and it was publicized. We broke up for our own reasons. I think of it as a great experience. I genuinely and deeply loved him. Things sometimes don't happen the way you want them to happen.

Sylvester Stallone

It puts a lot of pressure on relationships. A LOT of pressure on relationships. It's going to go quicker. It's going to burn brighter. And it's going to fizzle faster because it's on a fast track. They'll want you, perhaps because you represent a good meal ticket. "Hanging out with him I get free publicity." There's a lot of suspicion and reticence about being brought into a whole new group of strangers. You have this mistrust. Then you say, "I don't want to walk around mistrusting people." So you open your heart up and you get taken advantage of. "Nice heart, let me try eating the liver now."

Glenn Close

Who do I ask to escort me to something without ending up on Page Six or in the *National Enquirer*? Now when I ask somebody, "Would you take me to this?" I have to say, "You may end up in the newspapers. Are you ready for that?" It can be a real pain in the ass.

Madonna

(Asked if any man could deal with life in the reflected glare of her spotlight)

Could you?

New Responsibilities

With fame comes power—and with power comes responsibility. There are responsibilities to the people you work with, to use your fame to promote your projects. You may have gone into show business to escape being a salesman, only to find out that they don't call it show BUSINESS for nothing. You are held to a "role model" standard of behavior that even Mother Theresa would struggle to live up to. There are also responsibilities as a citizen. We all have those, but celebrities quickly find that their ability to attract the media can be exploited for whatever cause captures their fancy. Whether or not that's a good thing is another story.

Ron Silver

If you're lucky enough to have your voice be a little louder than others—and by that I mean they're sticking a microphone in front of me and not my mother or father—if you can use it to do some good, what you perceive to be good, I think it's an okay thing to do. There is a caveat. You have to take a little time to be informed about the issue and that you do care about the issue and not just mouth off as a mouthpiece for some cause that's using you. If something is very personal and you feel strongly about it and you take the time to find out about the issue, I don't see anything wrong with it.

To me the only reason to have any sort of power in any field is to confer a voice on people who don't have power. There are a lot of disorganized people out there with little resources that can't be heard. If you feel strongly about something that can be helpful to them, why not use the opportunity?

Barbra Streisand

It's horrible what they're doing to the environment and upsetting the balance of nature. It breaks my heart. So I started a foundation, the Streisand Foundation. I started it a long time ago when I established a university chair in my father's name. It's called the Streisand Chair in Cardiology to study cholesterol and congenital heart disease. Then I supported a program about the study of men and women at USC, sexuality and intimacy, men and women in a changing society, because I want to understand how the women's movement is affecting men and relationships. Then, with the One Voice concert, I gave those proceeds to helping the environment, anti-nuclear activities, and civil liberties organizations. We support a lot of good groups.

Gore Vidal

A celebrity endorsement doesn't change any votes, but it raises money. If you can get Barbra Streisand to sing for you, you've got $5 million. That's what it's about. I don't think that any American much cares to plumb the shallows of Charlton Heston's mind and follow his advice.

Ted Danson

I have a neat solution to the living in a fishbowl part of being famous. I use this analogy because I have kids. A bunch of adults all turn around and focus on Johnny, who's five years old. In about five seconds Johnny will spin out and become this obnoxious, crazed person because of all this adult energy pouring into him. That's what it's like being a celebrity. Everybody looks at you and focuses on you and if you just absorb it you become an obnoxious, crazy person. But if you deflect it and use that energy to do something else, it saves you, plus you can do some pretty interesting things with all that energy. That's where the American Oceans Campaign comes from, which is to preserve and conserve the oceans. The trick is to not take all this celebrity stuff personally.

> *Asking me to comment on politics is a bit like asking a pitcher for the Orioles to talk about physics because he throws a fastball.*
>
> —*Robin Williams*

Jane Fonda

I am not interested in spending time talking to a small group of people who can afford $50 or $60 tickets to the theater. I'd rather do television. I'm interested in communicating to the largest number of people possible. I'd rather be a television reporter than a theater actress.

Harrison Ford

I'm a private person. I do those things that I feel strongly about as a private citizen. I don't believe in celebrity spokesmen. I think the quality of a lot of very important issues and debates are being debased by the fact that the general population is deciding what side of the question to come down on, on the basis of what celebrity all-star team they most admire. I think it does great disservice to us all.

Sting

Not every performer has to be politically active. I'm not saying that. But those of us who do feel that we can make a difference ought to. The difference we can make is focusing media attention on a particular issue. That's what we're good at. We're not field activists. None of us can say we're experts in anything but playing music or focusing attention. So that's what we do. Of course, whether people respond to that or not is up to them.

Ally Sheedy

I can't say that because I'm famous I'm not going to make my political views known. I'm not going to be quiet about things because I shouldn't speak as a famous person. I don't think it's part of being an actor to go on picket lines or go marching. It gets confused. But I feel a personal responsibility, because I know that a lot of young people follow my movies and read interviews like this one. I can't say that it's been anything but beneficial to me to be involved in raising money for shelters for the homeless or feeding people. I think it's important to be concerned about other people in your society.

Robert Redford

People essentially want to come out and see what you look like, more than what you were having to say. You accept that fact, but you seize the opportunity to try to make a point about something that you believe in. Then you have to fight the elements that are going to try to discredit you because of the power you can command by gaining a platform.

By the way, I'm sympathetic to some of those people. Some people commit their energies and their lives—a lifetime of hard work—to try to get their point across and someone like myself steps up and gets the platform in a broader way in a few minutes. That's got to be frustrating. So I always felt the need to be doubly sure about what I was saying, to really know my facts, to have them well-researched and to make sure that I was speaking from a conviction that was supported by fact. That was a good education for me. It made me toe the line a lot more than just saying, "This is ridiculous," without knowing why.

Eddie Murphy

I always get bent out of shape when someone expects an entertainer to put your politics on front street, to use your visibility for politics. When people get a connection to an artist, it's for entertainment value. You don't want your artists to preach or tell you what to do.

Forest Whitaker

It's a difficult position because as minority artists, people are watching you. There are not many role models, so what you do is important. You try to govern yourself accordingly, but then it gets frustrating at times because you want to make choices like any other actor. You want to be able to play any character you want, just out of interest.

[Al] Pacino can play *Scarface*. A black guy plays a character like that, maybe comparable to what Wesley [Snipes] did in *New Jack City*, there are certain connotations that come about. That's unfortunate.

Eddie Murphy
Ron Davis/Shooting Star

Blair Underwood

As a black actor, I have to at least consider the ramifications and the implications of any character I play. Sidney Poitier told me something very interesting. He said that with what Denzel [Washington] and Wesley [Snipes] and Danny Glover and Morgan Freeman and all these actors are doing now, we have more variety than when he came along. He didn't have that luxury. But there should come a time—and why not now?—when we should be able to play all kinds of different roles. He had to be dignified and positive with everything he did, so that we wouldn't have to in our generation.

Sidney Poitier

Being a role model is a burden, yes. It has been. It is no longer. It cannot now be a burden because times have begun to change, at least in the direction that I think that they should be—and that pleases me. But there was a time when I was the only guy out there and that was burdensome, of course. I couldn't carry the dreams of so many people. It is better carried now with fifteen guys in the game.

Cheech Marin

The great thing about being Latino is we're all standard bearers, because it's like there ain't.

Salma Hayek

I would love for the Hispanic people who live here, who don't think that they are as good as some other people, to see that I can sneak in. Then they can say, "Maybe we can do it, too." The Hispanic people are minimized by their own Hispanic people. I hope that maybe something that I do can empower them.

Will Smith

Black audiences respond to their film heroes differently than white audiences respond. Denzel Washington was telling me that he feels a little more cramped. In the cinema blacks haven't had as many heroes as the white community has had in films, so what happens is everybody who makes it through is carrying the torch for the black community.

Denzel Washington

People ask me, "Speaking for the African-American community...." I don't speak for them. I don't call up forty million people and say, "What do you think I should do?" or "How do you feel about this part?" Doesn't work like that. Can't work like that.

Spike Lee

It's not gratifying to be called "the preeminent black filmmaker." I've been pushed into the position of being the spokesperson for black America. That's not something I'm comfortable with. Anytime something happens, press from all over the world call and ask, "So what do you think about the riots in Teaneck? What about the Korean boycott?"

Richard Dreyfuss

I speak political views that are basically in the majority of the community that I live in. It's not like I'm speaking always from a rebel or outcast point of view. There are some points of view that I have that are not mainstream, but the fact that I'm political has less to do with my profession or with my community than it has to do with my being a citizen. I speak out because I feel like it's my civic duty to speak out. But I don't speak out and find myself in total opposition to Hollywood's mainstream political philosophy because Hollywood's mainstream political philosophy is pretty liberal.

Rob Lowe

When I was eight years old I was selling Kool-Aid for McGovern.

Arnold Schwarzenegger

I think it sometimes is a fantasy when people talk about that in Hollywood people will put you on a blacklist if you have a different political view. One of the advantages in having a liberal-minded town like Hollywood is that they are open-minded. They understand that people have different points of view.

Same thing with my in-laws. I may be politically conservative, but socially, I may be very liberal a lot of times.

Phil Hartman

Performers tend to be liberal overall and really identify with the common man. When a Republican administration is in power, we tend to attack their policies and big business and special interests and so on. When Democrats are in power, it tends to be more along the lines of personal attacks, womanizing and drinking and weight problems. We agree with their policies, so what else can we do? In fact, we're much meaner to our own kind than we are to the opposition.

Sinbad

I have a rule of thumb. If that family was sitting in front of me, could I tell this joke? I tell comics, "If Michael Jackson was sitting here, would you tell that joke?" It's such a chump way of doing it, if they're not in your face. It's like shock jocks in the morning on the radio, they don't have to face people. But if the artist is in the studio selling the album, it's, "Man, I love your album!" But you just dogged him the day before.

Richard Dreyfuss

When we were making Close Encounters of the Third Kind, *the [Ku Klux] Klan was marching* in Mobile. I found out about it and I sent a statement to the Associated Press wire. The statement said that under the Constitution of the United States and the Bill of Rights the Klan had every right to march in Mobile—and under the same Bill of Rights I had every right to say that they were pond scum. And I did. They read that on television and within five minutes there were death threats against me and they sent security guards to my house. I was sitting in the living room with security guards with sixteen gauge this and .357 that and attack dogs. They were just hired to protect this human. They didn't know why.

So we're talking. I'm in my bathrobe and we're shootin' the shit. And this one guy goes, "Yeah, I've been in the Klan for about sixteen years." That's literally what happened. He was holding a fucking shotgun.

I said, "Excuse me," and went to the phone and called the producer. "Can I get the fuck out of Mobile for a while?" So I was sent to New York for a week.

Ian McKellen

I use my celebrity in a very limited area, which is in subjects on which I consider myself to be an expert. As an actor I've seen at close quarters the way that the arts are funded in the United Kingdom, the way they function, and the way the nation relates to them. I feel it's quite proper, on occasion, to make clear my views, when I feel things are going wrong or think they're going well. I'll put on as much pressure as I have, because I know often the main players, the people of influence, to point out what I think needs to be pointed out.

Ian McKellen

The other area in which I'm an expert is as a gay man. There I work with many others in trying to change those old-fashioned laws in the United Kingdom which disadvantage lesbians and gay men considerably, and treat them as second-class citizens. Beyond that my voice is shut. I'm a vegetarian, but I don't go on about it. I don't like nuclear weapons, but I don't go on about that. There are other people who have studied those and other issues that I am interested in with a great deal more care than I have. But on gay issues and on arts issues, there I speak out.

Anne Archer

I think I was the first actress to ever speak out publicly and say, "I'm pro-choice." Women were afraid—and anyone in public life was afraid, probably because of the violence connected with the issue. I wanted to help Planned Parenthood, which I feel does a tremendous amount of good.

I had an abortion. That's public knowledge. It's been published in a book and in magazines. I don't think that anyone understands the issue unless they hear the personal stories.

Mary Steenburgen

The celebrity part of it has to be used very judiciously. I don't think that anybody in the whole world should vote or believe what I believe just because I'm an actress. I think it's a privilege to have access to the media. You should ask yourself very carefully if what you are saying is what you really believe, and be careful about the way you say it because you have access. I have a respect for the fact that it's a privilege to be able to say to people what I believe. But I was extremely active, politically, before I ever made a movie. So, for me, to falsely stop doing things would've felt very strange. With the birth of my two children came an increasing desire to be political. It didn't follow to me that you would be careful about their house, the school they go to, the clothes they wear, and their safety, and not extend that to the world that they're inheriting.

But I've also learned in the past few years to say no to things that I'm not so sure about, or that I just don't have the time to do.

Ron Silver

I'm more concerned about uninformed journalists and politicians who have a daily forum for voicing their opinions. And in a political sense, they're passing legislation and they're captives of certain interests and they're as misinformed as anybody else in this society.

There are a lot of similarities and dissimilarities between the political process and acting. The dissimilarities are rather obvious. A politician, in order to be a successful politician, has to negotiate and compromise. An artist, quite often, has the opposite job, to maintain a vision and not be worried about reconciling contradictions. People are contradictory. We all feel one way and act another sometimes. We have conflicting emotions and a lot of ambivalence. Politicians can't do that. They have to vote yes or no. They have to make decisions. Actors don't really have constituencies, they don't have to worry about competing interests. So there are a lot of dissimilarities.

The similarities are obvious, too. They both depend on communication. They both have to use the media to express themselves and persuade a wide variety of people. So there are a lot of things that are very similar. On the other hand, for politicians there's a lot of power there without much sex. Most actors have sex without much real power.

Al Pacino

There are parallels between politicians and actors. You're in the public eye. You are watched. There's a lot of media today. Everything you do is looked at and I guess that's with politicians, too. But they have it on a daily basis. It takes a certain kind of hide to cope with that every day.

Clint Eastwood

I enjoyed being Mayor of Carmel immensely. I was very glad it was only a two-year term when I got a year and a half into it.

Richard Dreyfuss

I don't get stung by people saying, "Oh, what does an actor know?," because what does a commentator know? And by the way, it's hard for them to pull that off after Ronald Reagan was President of the United States.

Richard Dreyfuss

I certainly don't preclude actors from politics because of Ronald Reagan. I don't look upon the Reagan years as a failure for the acting community. And I certainly don't preclude that from my future.

I would have contempt for anyone who said that actors should think twice about going into politics. I doubt that Paul Newman goes to bed every night wanting to be a Senator from Connecticut, but saying, "I don't want to take advantage of my celebrity," I doubt that that's true.

Robert Redford

I used to get, "What does he know? He's an actor," until Reagan got elected.

Dana Carvey

Chevy Chase met up with Gerald Ford at some golf thing a year later and Ford said, "You cost me the election."

Sammy Davis, Jr.

The mistake I made was hugging Nixon. You don't hug the President of the United States. That's bad taste. Shake his hand firmly, but I'm demonstrative.

The friends who had pigeonholed me as super-liberal, they were the ones who were disappointed. I had a few people who I cared about who hung in. Shirley MacLaine was one. Martin Luther [King] was another, or I should say Mrs. King. Jesse [Jackson]. Shirley flew to Vegas to ask me, "Why'd you do this?" She cared that much.

Phil Hartman

As satirists I know sometimes we really ruffled President Clinton's feathers. At one point we made some fun at Chelsea's expense and Hillary got very upset. She said so in the press and our people backed off. I think we did cross the line in a couple of instances.

Michael Keaton

I think the whole [Presidential] campaign looked to Hollywood too much—and took advice. Here's the two truths. The one truth is: You do have to know how to work the media to get elected. The other truth is: That's not what it's about.

Goldie Hawn

I had wonderful time having dinner with President Bush. I'd love to have dinner with him again. I didn't discuss one political thing with him and he was a happy potato that I didn't.

Arnold Schwarzenegger

In my resignation letter to President Clinton, I made it very clear that although I stepped down as the chairman of the President's Council on Physical Fitness, I would not stop with the fitness crusade.

Arnold Schwarzenegger Ron Davis/Shooting Star

Robert Redford

I'm fed up with electoral politics. Absolutely. The emphasis on power and money has taken away a sense of community. We have a kind of disease. It's not a political sickness. It's a soul sickness. We have a system that is so constipated it virtually cannot move.

Ron Silver

(Why not run for political office himself?)

What? No sex and no power. The worst of both worlds. No, the only reason I'm not interested is I'm afraid of losing whatever influence I may now have if I actually do become a politician.

Alec Baldwin

(Will he run for office some day?)

No, no. That's another public lie. When I get out of making movies I'm going to go do something else, like run an ice cream store or something. Kim & Alec's.

John Hall

I have friends who tell me I should go into politics and run for some kind of office. But I've got a friend who's a Congressman from Connecticut who says, "Keep playing the guitar, you reach more people that way." He wants to be Dan Rather.

Robert Redford

The Candidate *was a film about the cosmetics* of how we get people elected in this country, rather than what we do to get forth a position or an ideology or something to do with issues. It was all about image and looks, on the assumption that that finally was maybe what the country was most interested in. So nothing's changed there. The only difference is it's gotten so low. There's virtually no buffer between what someone will do to effect an image and the truth.

Robert Redford

There was never a time when I thought I should go totally political and leave the business behind. There were times when I went extremely political for stretches of time, but never leaving the business behind because this is what I can do best. I also think, particularly now, I can have more effect exactly where I am. This is not a system that would invite the best in the land. We can see some of the best people quitting because they are so frustrated with the system. They're beginning to say, "Wait a minute. Life is only so long and you have so much energy and resources to commit to it. If you're going to be frustrated by a failed system that's decrepit and corrupt, forget it." That's the way I felt a long time ago. Plus the fact that I like to have too much fun.

Jonathan Taylor Thomas

Running for public office would be kind of interesting. I think I'm in a more powerful position right now, because I think politicians nowadays, I don't know how much power they actually have. I'm in a good position right now where I can accomplish a lot and help a lot of people. As long as I'm doing that then I'm comfortable where I am.

> *I don't think that I'm the great savior of the community. I think if I create one job people should be grateful. Everybody wants me to be the savior of the community. Everybody wants Bill Cosby, Magic Johnson, anybody famous, the neighborhood is like, "Y'all should do something for us." Looking back, nobody had done anything for me.*
>
> *—Ice Cube*

Vanessa Redgrave

I would not have the work I have today, I would have been silenced, if not for the fact that my rights have been protected by many artists—most specifically and most to the forefront Jewish artists. It's important that people know that. Everybody knows that I've got certain political views, but perhaps not many people know who's defended my right to have the political views I have. Every time there's been an attempt to blacklist me, artists have come to my defense, because we're all too concerned with blacklisting and its implications for society and for artists and art. Some of us remember, I certainly know the history all too well, of what happened to art and artists, and Jewish artists of course in particular, under the Third Reich. We know what happened under Stalin and the period of Stalinism. And we know what happened to art and artists in the McCarthy period. What we all have in common is that we just simply will not allow this to happen in so far as any of us can do anything about it.

Tim Robbins

I've never felt more alone in this country than during the Gulf War. [He and Susan Sarandon spoke out against it.] I called a lot of friends, tried to get them to come to a protest rally, but people were just frightened off. I was warned that it might not be good for my career, but we felt we had to go. When I went, I was very happy I went. It validated, for me, a lot of feelings I was having at the time.

Susan Sarandon

The Gulf War made it pretty clear that you could get in trouble for speaking out. I never felt as frightened about having an opinion as during that time. But there are people like Harry Belafonte who's been active for years and years and years. Ossie Davis. There is a tradition of involvement. Ed Asner. Martin Sheen.

Lloyd Bridges

I had to appear before a Congressional committee and explain to them that I wasn't a member of the Communist Party. I was surrounded by quite a few people who were members because I was going to the Actors Lab. Some of the members of the Communist Party were members of the Actors Lab, but they weren't politically involved really. They just wanted to do something for humanity and that's what the Communist Party seemed to represent at that time.

I was cleared then, but I hadn't worked in three years. It was necessary that I had to do something. Most people thought that if you got cleared you must have snitched on somebody, because they wanted names all the time. As a matter of fact, John Wayne and Ward Bond weren't happy with my testimony because I hadn't named anybody. So Dore Schary, the head of MGM at that time, a wonderful liberal guy, broke the spell for me and gave me a part as Spencer Tracy's first mate in *Plymouth Adventure.*

I had worked on the picture for about a week when they got a call from Ward Bond, who said, "He's going to have to clear himself." They had some committee that would strain all the people and give them a clean bill of health. It was a little embarrassing to do that, but I was desperate—and it was kind of interesting to see how he operated. So I went and convinced him apparently, so that I was able to go back in the picture. It wasn't a very good picture, but I had at least broken the spell.

Lloyd Bridges

A lot of good writers, actors, and directors bit the dust because of that character McCarthy. I've always felt that Larry Parks would still be here. He was my close friend. I stood up for him as best man when he got married. He went through hell with all of that. It wrecked him, ruined him. He was at the top of his career, too.

Kim Hunter

Because of the blacklist I wasn't able to work in film or television for five years, for signing civil rights petitions and protesting lynching of blacks for no reason down in the south. Those were all on my list. I was in a Lillian Hellman play. That was on my list. The first thing on my list was attending a World Peace Conference at the Waldorf Hotel in '47 or '48. I suppose there were some Communists there, but there were four hundred American sponsors, including Albert Einstein.

Susan Sarandon
Ron Davis/Shooting Star

Alan Alda

They think that your life is bounded by the parts that you play.

A very good illustration of that was when Judy Holliday was brought up in front of the House Un-American Activities Committee. She didn't want to answer their questions—and she didn't have to do what everybody else did, which was refuse to answer the questions, because she knew she'd get put in jail for that. So she played her character and they were totally convinced that she was who she was on the screen. She never had to answer their real questions, because they believed the illusion. She was, of course, far smarter than that. She was so smart she could create the illusion.

Susan Sarandon

First Amendment violations of any kind are important to me. Anything to do with kids, the homeless, AIDS, HIV. Anything where people are using my tax money to do anything I disagree with. Environmental things if they directly affect me, but usually there are enough people on environment that they don't need me. Homelessness just kills me, especially in New York. I don't see how you can ignore it.

I see myself as someone who, because of my access to the media, is helpful to people who are disenfranchised, who don't have a voice. When they wanted to cut DES, [New York Mayor] Guiliani would have gotten away with that except that people went down there. And there wouldn't have been any cameras down there if Rosie Perez and I hadn't have been there. That's just the way it works. If putting my old tired persona out there gets it into the paper, that's what your job is. It's not my job to be an expert on these things. I have to educate myself and I have to know what I'm talking about.

Once you're out there everybody comes and tells you what's happening. Once you've been identified as somebody who will be out there maybe, then they call you and let you know that this stuff is happening. Then you have to choose. My family comes first, so I have to see if I can fit things in. Secondly of all, I have to make sure that by taking a chance I don't completely nullify my power in the future. I'm not going to do what Jane Fonda did unless it's really going to pay off. I understand enough about the way that it works that I'm not going to get on a tank with a gun—and I'm not going to go to Washington to an awards show and be photographed shaking hands with people that I disagree with either. I realize that I have to be very careful, when I choose and how I choose and how I'm used.

Jane Fonda

There are a few things that I did that were thoughtless and that hurt Vietnam veterans. If my apology will help heal those wounds, it's easy for me to do it. My only regret is that my apology might come off like I was apologizing for being against the war.

I didn't apologize for that, just for the things that hurt the soldiers, because I never blamed the war on the soldiers.

Robert Redford

I became interested in Native Americans first when I was about six. My mother would drive me in the summers from Los Angeles to visit my grandfather in Texas. We would drive—we couldn't afford the train or anything and she would drive this old car, which was probably one of the best kinds of education I ever could have gotten—through the Indian reservations. I was completely taken, but I don't know why.

Once I got known I was asked to start narrating films, tiny little films about Indians trying to claim their rights for something. Pretty soon the word got out and I was asked to do more and I did more. It grew until finally I began to produce some documentaries on Indian affairs. Then I began to do political work and a Navajo scholarship fund for children.

Dennis Hopper

The Actors Studio for years had been an independent nonprofit organization, but it's gotten very expensive and it's not been able to carry its own weight. So Paul Newman, for years, has been financing the Actors Studio. It's been costing him somewhere between a million and a million and a half dollars every year. He calls it his "salad money," it comes from his salad dressing and stuff, but it's a little boring to have to come up with that kind of money every year for something. I'm on the board of directors of the Studio. Finally we got together and figured out a way that this Bravo channel, by doing these TV interviews, we could actually pay for the Studio without Paul having to dish it out every year.

Jodie Foster

Most people who are lucky enough to work in the entertainment business spend 70% of their time selling products. "Please buy this washing machine."

Michael Keaton

Actors have to know that they have to sell a movie. Otherwise you wouldn't see Meryl Streep selling *The River Wild.* If you want to do this for a living, that's what you do for a living.

William Reid

(Member of The Jesus and Mary Chain)

It's got to be a business. Being a musician you probably whore yourself less than being a painter. Picasso does a painting and somebody takes it off him for money. He doesn't see the painting ever again. I always thought that was bizarre. Being a musician, people only buy copies of what you do.

Bruce Willis

So much of what I do as a public figure has to do with commerce and sales and money. I'm embarrassed by it. I'm embarrassed by this process. Here is one of the most brilliant films of the past ten years [*Pulp Fiction*] and you ask the actors to stand out in front of it and wave their arms. If I didn't have to do it I wouldn't do it. I despise it.

Thomas Jefferson advised his nephew in 1785 about the importance of how others perceive you. "Though it can never be known but to yourself, ask yourself how you would act if all the world were looking at you and act accordingly."

Michelle Pfeiffer

Doing publicity is hard for me. Even my closest friends are constantly amazed at what they don't know about me. I'm just really private. It's the most difficult part of the job for me. I go back and forth, saying I'm never going to do it again. I do feel a responsibility for helping to sell a film I'm involved in, so it's a conflict for me.

Susan Sarandon

I don't feel that I have that much to say, but it's your responsibility to come out for a film because if a film doesn't make it in the first couple of weeks they pull it. So you have to open big these days.

William Baldwin

I feel more like Joe [the prostitute character he plays in *Three of Hearts*] right now than I ever do when I see a movie that I'm in, whether I'm nude or not. Doing interviews is truly selling yourself.

Jean-Claude Van Damme

When you do a movie it's like making a baby almost. When a movie is finished, lots of movie stars stay home. They go on vacation. That's no good, because you launch a movie and they spend money on TV and

Jean-Claude Van Damme and his wife Lisa O'Connor/Shooting Star

radio and bus stops. I've got to go and promote it. If not, I'm not responsible. It's like I'm just taking the money, do my job, and disappear. I tell the same to my wife. I've got to go and promote those movies because if not, if I flop, I know it's my fault. Now if I flop and I did my promotion, I know it's not my fault. I've done the best I could.

Jason Patric

If someone makes the decision to invite celebrity into their life, they have to pay the consequences. There are certain actors who you know about and their fame has been derived from not only their work, but by being invited into their homes, the sparkly outfits that they wear, the public statements that they make. If you've gained a certain level of celebrity through your personal life, you do somewhat owe answers, but I've tried to be accepted and known for my work, so that I had no other responsibility other than to do the most honest job that I could.

Alicia Silverstone

I feel very responsible, in all of my life. I realized about a year ago that you are completely in control of every single thing that happens in your life. It's a big responsibility, what I go through.

My problem is wanting to do too much and not having the time. I get frustrated and go crazy.

> *Getting famous means less time to write. Now I'm on book tours. I'm doing interviews and giving talks. I'm being asked my opinion about things that I have no business expressing my opinion on. There's a lot of time wasted.*
>
> *—Elmore Leonard*

Jean-Claude Van Damme

They don't want you to fail, in your private life, in your marriage. They want you to be perfect, always the hero, and it's difficult because we're all human.

Natalie Cole

(Willing to discuss her battles with substance abuse?)

I don't mind. I think one of the signs of a healthy recovering addict is being able to talk about it honestly, openly, and with some positiveness to it. If you don't talk about it and you pretend like it never happened or it's not there or you're embarrassed by it or you're humiliated, then there's a good chance that you're not really recovered. You're still caught up in the active disease part. There's the active disease and then there's the recovering part. I talk about it because, I know the media is sick and tired of it, but, believe me, there are so many people out there that are helped by it. I feel that I owe it to them to give them a little bit of insight on what it used to be like and what it's like now.

James Earl Jones

I can only help through what someone else has written. I've accepted that. I cannot be an activist because I don't do it well. I don't know it. I'd rather do it through the work I do.

Andie MacDowell

It really is a lot of responsibility. You feel like you've been given a silver spoon and you want to feel like you deserve it for some reason. I can't really say that I do.

Gene Kelly

When I came to MGM, they would have scripts that would say, "Here Gene Kelly stops the show." That was it.

Jean-Claude Van Damme

You have to watch everything. You cannot even act normal in real life. You've got to be almost like a role model. So the best advice I can give to guys like me is if one day you feel bad, don't go out. Stay home.

Martin Lawrence

It took me two years [on television] to grow up. I did a line on my show the first season, I used the b-word, the bitch word, to the fellas. I was trying to show how when guys get mad and we're talking to each other, how we can refer to somebody out of their name. But that was too real for television.

I kept asking myself, "All these kids love me?" I went home and talked to my Mom and asked, "Why do all these kids love me? Why do all these babies that I don't even know love me?"

I had this little eight-year-old boy who had cancer and wanted to meet me. I was in Atlanta doing a show and I met the little boy. I gave him a hat. He was in a wheelchair—and he asked me questions. "Why do you do those jokes?" He just smiled, but a week or two later he died.

So I went home and my mom said, "Well you do have a responsibility to watch on television what you say and what you do, because now you have a whole realm of people watching you."

Marlee Matlin

A lot of deaf children look up to me because they might want to be actors. Most parents of deaf kids admire me. They ask me questions and it's nice to be a role model in that respect, but on a full-time basis it's not. There's a great deal of responsibility involved and there are a lot of people out there who resent me for that reason. But I can't live my life knowing that I have to defend every deaf person's right in life or in work.

I have my own opinions on everything, but I won't preach and I won't say this is the best for you. I'll just say this is the best for me and then you can take it or leave it. I think that's the best way to approach it. That's the safest way to approach it, because a lot of hearing impaired people are extremely opinionated, extremely political. They're very sensitive people.

Like at the Academy Awards, where I spoke the names of the nominees on international television. There were some groups of deaf people who were extremely offended. I got into bad situations with them. I wasn't doing it for them. I was doing it for me. A lot of people just didn't get the message. I'm just me and I'm just doing my job that I love to do.

Michelle Pfeiffer

When it comes down to something like deciding whether or not to adopt a baby, how the public views it is really of no interest to me. That's something that is really personal. When it comes to deciding to do a movie, first it's about how I feel about it. Second, it's about what kind of effect might this have on people. I know that movies are a very powerful influence in the images that we project on the screen. The idea of being a role model makes me really uncomfortable.

Jean-Claude Van Damme

In Sudden Death, *when I was playing* with that plastic pistol and the gasoline, I was calling the studio saying, "Guys, I think this can be dangerous to play with. Kids may do the same stuff with the fuel." They said not to worry, but I was worried about it. I was scared because lots of kids are following me. They love you and they want to do the same as you. You become an image. It can be a lot of responsibility.

Marlon Wayans

Your parents are your role models, your parents and your teachers. I'm just a person. I try to live righteous every day, but I can't take that pressure. I might guide you the wrong way. If you want to take me as a role model in terms of being successful in comedy, in that area, fine. But not on a personal level. The only people I can be a role model for are my nephews and my nieces.

Michael Jordan

There are a lot of kids who admire athletes. That's something that we certainly didn't ask for, but that's the way it's been. We all try to live a positive life and kids are going to look at it from that respect. I think it puts some undue pressure on people like Mike Tyson, myself, and other professional athletes, because no matter how you look at it, we're human. We make mistakes. The one thing that we have to illustrate to the kids is that it's part of life to make a mistake—and it's how you rebound from that mistake.

Shaquille O'Neal

There's many definitions of role model. When I was coming up, a role model was a person that you could talk to when you had a problem about the birds and the bees, about why not to do drugs, and why to stay in school. My role model was my father. Parents need to do a little better job of being there as a child's role model, instead of saying, "Be like Shaq."

I can relate to being a role model because I have two younger sisters, a younger brother, a nephew, and a niece. Some guys who don't have younger siblings can't relate. I think we as athletes just need to stay out of trouble, do the right thing, and say the right thing. But it's kind of hard to just tell some people, "You're a role model," because they can't relate. I have no problem with being a role model.

Luke Perry

As Charles Barkley so eloquently put it, "I ain't nobody's role model."

Jon Bon Jovi

I don't know if I have a responsibility to be a role model or not. I've always found it difficult to be a "role model," because I don't think I walk on water. I go home at night and I have as many problems as anyone else.

I'm growing up in front the cameras, as I've been forced to do for years, too. I don't find it easy to be a role model. I'm afraid of that. I don't want somebody to go, "Well, Jon did it." "If Jon jumped off the bridge, would you?" I don't want people to do that.

I like to do as many positive things as I can, but I've always considered rock 'n' roll to be entertainment. Period. Then you turn off your radio. It's my life, but it's your entertainment form.

Robert Wuhl

We have to, as responsible human beings and parents, delineate between somebody's profession and somebody's personal life. Because

somebody's a terrific actor doesn't mean they are a terrific human being. If somebody's a sports hero it doesn't mean they are any kind of role model whatsoever.

Robert Wuhl

Michael Jordan's got a gambling problem. We know that. But Michael Jordan, to me, was the sportsman of the year when he was the best in the world at what he does and he quits to play a game in the minor leagues—where he has to buy the team a bus—for no money, because he loves the game. To me that's the ultimate sportsman. In that instance, he is a role model. Does he gamble? Yeah. That part you don't look up to. People are not all black or white.

The U.S. Department of Health and Human Services held back a Public Service Announcement made by Red Hot Chili Peppers front man Anthony Kiedis to promote safe sex after learning of the singer's legal problems involving charges of indecent exposure and sexual battery.

Connie Selleca

I do not like being a role model. I do not like anybody holding me up as an example of perfection in any area because I am so far from perfection. I fall just as anybody else will fall. I can hope that by example I will touch some people in some good way, as God is giving me this path in life, but to actually know that someone is going to look at me as an example of whatever, as far as my being a national spokesperson for MADD [Mothers Against Drunk Driving], being a mother, being a Christian, being anything, it's not a role I'm comfortable in. But it comes with the territory. The hardest role model position I have is that of a mom. That's the most important thing for me.

Madonna

I'm flattered by people who copy me. On the other hand, my message is always to be your own person, to be an individual, so it's a little bit strange. They'll get over it, though. I like to think of it as a bad phase they're going through.

Shaquille O'Neal Bob Greene/The Kobal Collection

Ian McKellen

(On the courage he displayed by publicly "coming out" as a gay man)

I think that courage is too flattering a word. I was forty-nine when I came out. When I see kids of sixteen and seventeen telling their parents and starting their adulthood on their own terms, convincing all around them, their family and friends, that to be gay is to be as normal as to be straight, then I don't look very brave. Perhaps I'm trying to make up for lost time. There's a sense of conscience that I've got that I let myself down, at any rate, by not being honest at an earlier age.

> *At some point you begin to realize that you have a limited amount of time and an unlimited amount of opportunities.*
>
> *—George Lucas*

Laura Dern

A lot of people criticized Roseanne for going public about being abused as a child, but when a celebrity comes out and says, "This happened to me," it makes the little people say—they're not little people to us, but in their minds—"I'm just a little person in the middle of Middle America, and I was abused. If it's okay for her to talk about it maybe it's okay for me to talk about it." Magic Johnson changed the world. He saved thousands of lives.

Sigourney Weaver

As an artist, I try to do what's interesting to me, but I have a daughter and nieces. There are a lot of very interesting actresses now who are all trying to find and make interesting roles, complete people who are active and who are complicated. It's something we are all aware of.

Annie Potts

What I think is horrifying is when people are nice to somebody and then they're not very nice back. There's a special privilege that comes with that treatment. Public people get to be public people because an audience has borne them on their shoulders somehow to that position. I think that that has to be respected.

Rene Russo

At a certain point you have to draw a line and protect yourself and so, "No, no I won't do that." It takes a long time to learn that. I think about that every day. What will you let people get away with. I mean, I want to be liked. It's pitiful!

Robert Downey, Jr.

I bought into this whole, "You should give back to the system" thing. I was out there doing this Heal The Bay here and supporting this guy there or making a stand against this proposition. You know, I've got plenty of other stuff that needs looking at—and it's not going on down at the Ambassador Hotel. It's going on here in my mind, here in my family. I'm a lot less apt to go crusading for things.

Jimmy Smits

Every time I work, in a way, I do give back to the community—and I've got letters to prove that. If a kid writes to me from Chicago or East Los Angeles or South Florida, I'm giving back. That role model thing is important.

Sigourney Weaver
William Norton/Shooting Star

Sean Connery

I learned pretty quickly, you can't get more than a pint into a pint bottle. You do as much as you can do, as well as you can.

Dean Roland

(Member of Collective Soul)

The more exposure you get and the more popular you become, the more people want your time.

Robert Downey, Jr.

I don't believe you should do things because you feel like you're supposed to because you've been given some gift in life. I believe everyone creates their own reality. I don't mean to be too harsh on people who don't get successful even though they're talented. There's a bit of onus for me on that "you have so much" and the guilt trip that goes with it. "Now get out there and go feed the homeless on Thanksgiving."

It's like, "If I want to. And if I didn't have success and I wanted to, I'd do it then, too."

I find that sometimes there is that little dig that people want to get in on you. "This friend of yours has this malady and you really should be out being a spokesperson for this."

And I'm like, "Why shouldn't she? She's the one who has the disease. And get the fuck off my back, man." Everyone's telling me what I should do because of the "gift" I've been given. Hey, I went out there and worked my ass off and I got successful. I didn't get lucky. I'm good.

Rosie Perez

Sometimes I feel guilty. People go, "Do you have a lot of money?" You go, "No." You don't want to talk about what you have. I feel kind of guilty because I am so happy. It's hard to say yes, I accept all this, because so many other people need so much.

Laurence Fishburne

There's no real good reason for me to be guilty about the success that I've had. I've worked very hard.

Larry Drake

You feel a little more self-conscious about things. I found myself tipping more.

Paul Newman

The salad dressing and all that, that all started off as a joke and now they're outgrossing all my films. We're planning a hostile takeover of Paramount next week.

It's a wonderful way to use celebrity in a positive way. Our motto is: "Shameless exploitation in pursuit of common good."

Roseanne

All those people want me to do benefits for them, but good luck to ya. I've gotta sleep sometime.

Substance Abuse

The propensity for drug and alcohol abuse among celebrities is well documented and easy to understand. The pressure of stardom cries out for relief. The exuberance of success cries out for celebration. In our current cultural climate, the response to either of these emotional extremes is often the same. Throw in the youth and inexperience of so many stars and the recipe for disaster is obvious, especially in the music world where substance abuse is considered to be part of the heritage.

Dean Roland

(Member of Collective Soul)

It's all available, man. It's whether you want to take part in it or not. It's all there. Anybody who says it isn't is wrong.

Steve Walsh

(Member of rock group Kansas)

I think everybody who is creative indulges in things to an excess in one way or another. If not for anything else, just to see what it's like. When I was early on in life, it was drugs. Yeah, I'm self-indulgent.

It's really hard to take care of yourself on the road and perform every night, take care of your throat, and not be self-indulgent.

Ray Manzarek

(Member of The Doors)

Jim Morrison drank himself to death. It's one of those things that happen with stardom. You take a sensitive poet, a sensitive human being, and you put him in the middle of a maelstrom, which rock 'n' roll became....So Jim took to drink to quench the fire, to put out the fire. Instead the alcohol made the fire burn that much more insanely inside of him. Ultimately, through excessive behavior, he died in Paris on July 3rd, 1971. I wouldn't recommend his lifestyle to anyone. It killed him.

Nick Mason

(Member of Pink Floyd)

Rock 'n' roll, in comparison to motor racing, is so much more dangerous. I've known so many more people who have been really awful casualties of the music business and drugs. It's higher risk than people realize.

Dennis Hopper

Janis [Joplin] died. [Jimi] Hendrix died. These people were full of life. These were not people who were on a suicide bent. They thought they could do it and live. They thought other people OD'd. We all did.

Robert Blake

When I quit Hell Town, *I'd been working* for fifty years. I started in 1936. I was burned out on work. I was burned out on life. I was taking sleeping pills every night so I could sleep fast. I'd get up with six cups of espresso in the morning and a ton of sugar. By the afternoon I was dragging ass and I was sipping brandy to get through it. I thought about all of my friends that were gone, Dick Boone and David Janssen and Lee Marvin. All the people who said, "Robert, don't let 'em get you." They all stayed there and got got. I said, "I don't want to die. If I'm going to die it ain't going to be in front of this camera." So I left.

Dennis Hopper

I should really be dead. There's no question about it. For numbers of reasons, I should be dead. It's amazing that I wasn't just killed. I mean killed, boom. I bottomed out so badly that it's just amazing that I'm here. I was hearing friends of mine being murdered in the next room. Also I was given an anti-psychotic drug and I was one of the five percent that it gave Parkinson's disease to. So I ended up in this place having Parkinson's disease, shaking like this, and they all said, "God, look what the drugs have done to him." I couldn't make sentences. I couldn't speak. I couldn't do anything. I was in this state for over two and a half months, before my personal doctor got to see me. When I got out I was just going to go home and kill myself.

Natalie Cole

I got into some heavy cocaine abuse. It was what they call "crack" or "freebasing." That's what I was doing. It very slowly but surely destroyed

On Tuesday, April 5, 1994, Kurt Cobain locked himself in the greenhouse of his six bedroom home in a wealthy and quiet Seattle neighborhood. The lead singer of the ultra-popular, ground-breaking grunge band Nirvana placed a stool against the door. Cobain then turned over a potted plant and jabbed a pen through his suicide note into the pile of soil on the ground. He injected himself with a large dose of heroin and arranged some personal effects around him, including the plaid hunter's cap he used to disguise himself when he left the house. He laid down on the ground, placed the Remington Model 11 twenty gauge shotgun between his legs, and put the barrel in his mouth. Then he pulled the trigger.

everything that I had worked for. The signs became very visible to me. I was affected financially. I was affected physically. I lost tons and tons of weight. My voice suffered. My vocal chords suffered. I had polyps removed. That was the beginning of some serious drug abuse, over a period of three or four years, while I was still recording, some of it while I was having some very major hits. But it finally took its toll.

I believe that the Lord had a lot to do with it, because I am His child and He gave me this gift and I was abusing it. It's like a parent saying to a child, "Okay, you've had enough. Now you've got to take your punishment." So I had to pay for it. You just can't continue to abuse a gift of this nature and get away with it.

Sting

Basically as a rock star, your nearest equivalent in history is a Roman emperor. You have enough money to fill a room with cocaine and women and drink. You can debauch yourself to death. The point is if you don't, you can actually enjoy life better. I don't want to be a casualty of this business. There are too many already. Being intelligent is not a prerequisite for being a rock star. That's why there are so many casualties. The stupider you are, or the vainer you are, increases your chances of making it.

Anthony Kiedis

(Member of the Red Hot Chili Peppers)

Drugs are a very multi-dimensional thing. For someone who has a problem with drugs, obviously they'd be better off not doing them. Drugs can also be a non-detrimental part of someone's life, depending on how they use them. Not everybody needs to eliminate them from their package. Personally, my package is much better suited without the use of narcotics, because they tend to destroy whatever it is that's beautiful in my life. I'm a very self-destructive person by nature, and so it was kind of an all-or-none proposition for me. So I don't take any drugs any more of any kind.

Belinda Carlisle

I think that I probably would have had a problem if I was a secretary, or whatever, with substance abuse. I was one of those personalities. I had a good time. I don't regret any of it because I did take a lot of it with me. I know I don't have to be back there. I don't want to go back to that place in my life that was horrible after a while. It was a great thing that sort of spun out of control. I'm glad I went through it. It was an important lesson in life, no question about it.

Cheech Marin

I believe in the legalization of marijuana. I think it should be treated like alcohol, without a judgment value as to whether it's good or bad, because it's just a fact of society that that is the preferred intoxicant of a big generation. It's quasi-legal right now, depending on where you go. The decriminalization of marijuana will do a lot to bring down the crime rate in our country.

Jack McDowell

(Baseball player and recording artist)

Musicians can sit there and talk about rampant drug use and it's okay. They're creative. But if an athlete does that he'll never play again. That's a strange phenomenon to me.

Carrie Fisher

The spark for Postcards from the Edge *was the guy* that pumped my stomach after my drug overdose sent me flowers. I was sent a letter, after I did an interview in *Esquire*, by a publishing house which was forwarded to me in the rehab. "Would I like to write a book of nonfiction articles on Hollywood?" That was what *Postcards* started out being. But I found that writing nonfiction, you had to adopt a snide overview. The conceit is that I'm better than Hollywood. Well, how can I be better than Hollywood? I am really a product of it.

Richard Dreyfuss

When I was a little boy, I used to think that if you have no secrets no one can hurt you. And when I went through what I went through I figured if I tried to keep this a secret, if I tried to live as if it had not happened, then I would twist myself around and ultimately fall apart. I didn't do it because I wanted to be a role model. I did it because I wanted to keep current with myself. It's not that I don't lie and it's not that I don't have secrets. But secrets and lies are in a tough little drawer and you constantly have to open that door and go, "Oh yeah, that's my secret, oh yeah, okay!" Because you'll forget. With that big one, I don't want to have any secrets. It's just easier. It's more mobile.

Ultimately, when you talk to your kids, I want my daughter to say to me, as she has, "Are you an alcoholic, Daddy?" And I say, "Yes, I am. I got a credential. I know what I'm talking about." I don't want her to say, "I heard at school that you were an alcoholic. That's not true, is it?" I don't want to hear that.

If my SECRETS were publicized, they would hurt me. My secrets have never been publicized. Part of my life has been publicized, but those have not been secrets. When thirty-four cops take you out from under a broken car and you're busted for cocaine possession at Cedars Sinai, that's not a secret. That's like living in a glass bubble.

Dennis Hopper

We can talk about doors of perception. We can talk about drugs opening doors for us and letting us see on another level, but that door suddenly will close on you and it becomes a black abyss. You're dealing with something that was given to you free to open your doors of perception and suddenly there's a dealer standing at the other side of the tunnel who's selling it to you. Your personal life becomes a nightmare and then your work life becomes a nightmare and then you lose both. There's only one way back, to deal with the problem that you have, which most people won't deal with because the drugs and the alcohol are such a euphoric situation that you're in denial most of the time that you have a problem. It's the other people that have the problem. You don't. You can handle it. Anyway, that's my story.

Robert Downey, Jr.

It's very in, in the "recovery nineties," to talk about those drug-taking days as "the dark times." It's very moralistic, isn't it? It's very self-inflating to talk about how, "Now I have an inner life." Well who were you then? Were you just some beast walking around? You had a life. You did stuff. You made it to holidays. You were fucked up half the time and it wasn't great, but you didn't do it because you thought it was horrible and you wanted to stay horrible.

Carrie Fisher

Drug addiction is a way of saying, "This isn't it. Did you have something else in maybe a blue?"

Dennis Hopper

I was doing like a half an ounce of cocaine every three days. I was drinking half a gallon of rum a day with twenty-eight beers. I never had a problem. It was other people crawling around on the floor, blithering idiots, who had the problem. I wasn't doing that. What's wrong with these other people? I never thought I was a drug addict or an alcoholic. Well now, come on. I didn't have hangovers in the morning. I did more drugs and more alcohol. I didn't hide it. I just did more. I thought everybody in the world was doing what I was doing. Everybody I was around was doing drugs. I don't know how I ever worked during that time. When I came out of my dressing room door to go onto the set, God knows who was going to come out of that door.

I showed up for a press conference for Navy SEALS, and, I mean, who was I trying to fool? What was I thinking? You look back on that stuff and it's so embarrassing, so shameful, that you had to present yourself in that manner, in that frame of mind.

—Charlie Sheen

Charlie Sheen

New York ate me alive when I was making *Wall Street.* Everything was a phone call away and I was making a lot of phone calls. I'd see a scene where I was rested the night before and only had twenty drinks as opposed to three hundred and was able to do something good with the work. Then the scene later, when I hadn't slept for two days before shooting, the work sucks and I know it does. The whole film was a roller coaster for me of embarrassment and distress.

Al Franken

In the old days on *Saturday Night Live,* certain drugs kept certain people awake. I think there's a difference between addiction and recreational drug use. Recreational drug use can lead to addiction and is very serious —and with certain kinds of drugs is serious in and of itself. I am the last

Dennis Hopper The Kobal Collection

person to advocate drug use as a way of achieving good art. If anything it destroys a lot of people's talent.

Robert Downey, Jr.

Back in the eighties, when I was doing drugs and getting high all the time, I really felt like I was disappearing into this numb place.

Harvey Korman

I don't know how it is with the new set of people, but with the people I've known intimately there are no free lunches. There's always pain underneath it somehow. There's always abuse of some kind, whether it's alcohol or drugs or whatever. Being a star—you better really know who or what you are about because it can be a terrible, destructive trap. It happens more often than not, I think.

Doug Gray

(Member of the Marshall Tucker Band)

Just the little bit of success that we had turned me into the cocaine person that I was. Turned me into the drinking person. Some of the friends that I had were not truly friends. They were just hangers on. That happens if you're in Garth Brooks's position or if you're in the Marshall Tucker Band at that point in time. We were rock 'n' roll. I was terribly into doing everything that was supposed to be fitting into that image. We were Southern rock. We were the party kids.

Belinda Carlisle

I was doing a lot of drugs. A lot of drugs. What happened was I had to make a choice between my relationship with my husband or continuing on the path that I was on.

I quit, cold turkey, on my own. Part of the addiction was physical, but most of it was psychological. It was just a matter of going to meetings, getting a support group, and behavior modification. It took me a while to get out of that mind set of walking into a restaurant and trying to figure out who was carrying.

Rick Wills

(Member of Foreigner/Bad Company)

You learn the hard way. When you do lose control you have to come back to earth with a bit of a bump.

Charlie Sheen

Rehab was difficult. It was AA [Alcoholics Anonymous]. It was CA [Cocaine Anonymous]. It's a 12-step program. You stay there and do meetings every day—and personal therapy and group therapy. God, you get an hour for lunch and that's the only time you don't think about your problems. But I guess it has to be that disciplined, because it has to universally apply to people. Like they have a ten scale and a guy comes in at four and another guy comes in at nine. They have to have a program that supports them at both levels of problems. I was about a twelve and a half coming in.

Charlie Sheen

It was scary to return to work on *Hot Shots* after rehab—and then I realized that with the amount of energy that I had, with the amount of rediscovered concentration that I remembered having in the earlier films before I went over the edge, I felt like I was finally back in touch with myself. The drugs and the alcohol were no longer creating that numbness, that insulated cloud that I was constantly spending so much energy fighting through—and then trying to act.

Charlie Sheen
Ron Davis/Shooting Star

Treat Williams

I was living life in a very fast lane when I got off the train and started to have a life. It was wild times, John Belushi, late nights, Cafe Central in New York, and all that stuff. I just got tired. I got real tired of it and decided very luckily to get off the train, because a lot of guys got killed. The train kept going faster and faster and it killed them.

George Carlin

My wife and I had our major problem to deal with in the middle of the seventies, which was use and abuse of things. In our case it was corrugated paper, but people have different substances that they find that get them off the center track of life. We had our hassles with that and came out of it. We're very lucky.

Robin Williams

Did I have a drug problem? No. Everybody had it. That was the problem. I learned that I wanted to live. I didn't enjoy being paranoid and impotent most of the time.

Robin Williams

You can't be coked up at five o'clock in the morning going to your kid, "Hey, Daddy loves you. Want to play?"

Natalie Cole

I went to a drug treatment center once and hated it. As a result, of course, it didn't work. A week after I was out I was back into it again. In the meantime, my marriage had gone by the wayside. Everything was crumbling around me. The jobs I was getting weren't as good. The money I was getting wasn't as good. It was a pretty known fact that Natalie Cole was in trouble and promoters were a little leery of whether I was responsible enough to show up, because I had had some problems with that. I even went on national television and said I was clean and I was sober—and I wasn't. Because I had gained the trust and respect of this industry to such a degree, when I fell from grace it was a blow, not just to me, but even to the people who had believed in me. "How could she do this?"

After examining comedian John Belushi on the set of The Blues Brothers movie, his doctor was very upset. Belushi looked horrible, suffering the visible effects of drug abuse. The doctor pleaded with Belushi to clean up his act, but the comedian just listened passively. The doctor then warned the producer of the film that Belushi had to straighten out. Otherwise, he said, get as many movies out of him as possible because he doesn't have much time to live. Three years later, Belushi was dead of a massive drug overdose.

And my family was really hurt, but they did not give up on me. It was to them that I wanted to prove most of all that I could get myself together. But that still wasn't quite enough, because when I went to my first treatment center it was for them that I went, and not for myself.

Robert Blake

You say, "Well, he oughta stop drinking or it's gonna kill him." So you take the booze away from him and he blows his brains out because the booze is still his solution and it's not time to take it away from him.

Charlie Sheen

I remember a moment when I was first starting to question myself. I was in a bar with some friends, doing the usual, and I said, "Man, this doesn't work anymore." When it takes fifteen times as much of the substance or the drink to get where you got when you first did it, when it takes that much more, I think your body is saying, "Hey, we're a little saturated."

Robert Downey, Jr.

When it's kind of over and pretty obvious that it's turned into something that isn't that fun any more and isn't serving you but you're still doing it, when it's turned into that old lizard-brain addiction thing, then it's, "Oh, my God." Then you feel ashamed and you feel like an imposter and you're hiding and all that shit.

Natalie Cole

It was really because of my manager and—of all people—my lawyer and my accountant, who came to my home one evening and said, "Please, do something. We don't want your money. We just want you to get well." To have someone say that to you, someone that you'd never expect to say that, it reconfirmed to me that all lawyers and accountants are not humanoids, that they really are real people and they do care, for some reason that really struck me. So I went away to Hazelden. I went for a month. I ended up staying for six months. I went from wondering when I was going to get out of there, to not sure when I was going to get out of there, and not sure that I wanted to get out of there. I didn't know if I'd ever be able to get back to this point again.

When I think about it now I get chills. I know that there were people out there that said, "She'll never be as big as she was. She'll never get back to that place again." I'm living proof that anything is possible if you really want it. My sobriety date is November 29, 1983.

Charlie Sheen

I first used coke and booze as an insulation, a means of putting something between the public and myself, and not feeling like they had a right to know me, the real me. I would become a different person with these elements and hence deal with them on their level. I thought I was above it all. And I wasn't. I was as ground zero as the rest of 'em.

I was able, for a couple of years, to shut it down. I'd get a physical role like *Major League,* where I had to get in shape and get my pitching arm back together, and I'd turn it off for three or four months. And then I just lost the button. I lost the ability to shut it down. It just became a necessity. It was always part of the plan. "We can't do this unless we do this." And what preceded the events was always the drugs, the alcohol. Then it snowballed—and that's when the intervention happened.

Charlie Sheen

I went to my dad's birthday party, or what I thought was going to be his birthday party on August 3rd, and it was an intervention that had been planned for several months. I stepped into the worst episode of *This Is Your Life.* Of course, all they could do was try to bring it to my attention and offer this means of directing me towards a solution. And I accepted it. I knew that it was time to shut down the madness flow, to get back into myself, to reprioritize my life.

Martin Sheen

I knew he [his son, Charlie] was going to get killed. He had two bullets coming at him and I had to get in the way or knock him out of the way. I saw what happened there with Marlon [Brando] and Christian. I said, "That's not going to happen here if I can help it." And so I just tried to interfere.

We did an intervention. It was planned, calculated, rehearsed. The people we got together were family and very close friends, with an interventionalist, a very powerful man, a very compassionate guy. He orchestrated the whole thing. We went at it. We chose my fiftieth birthday because we knew we could get him on that day. We could get him isolated away from all the sycophants and bums he was hanging out with who were pulling his juices away.

I'm being very open and honest with you. I was nourished by it and I thank God for it. We all had to put our hearts on the table and everyone shared their concern, their brokenness, their love—love above all. Listen man, it was life or death. The guy was very clear about it. He said you call the people that you'd call to carry him to his grave. Call those people now. Ask them to say what they'd say if they were carrying him to his grave, because that's where he's going.

I was grateful to Marlon because I saw the love of a father and I saw what he called "the angel of misery" visiting his home. I saw that angel coming and like in the days of old went out and stood in front of the house and tried to get him to pass by. It was the thing with Marlon that did it.

Anthony Quinn

I said to my three young Italian sons, "I promise you, if you never smoke cigarettes or marijuana and you never drink, when you're eighteen I will buy you each a Ferrari." When Frankie turned eighteen and came to claim his Ferrari, I told him he was too young to drive a Ferrari and I bought him a Jeep. As each one came I got him a Chevy or a little Ford, because they still weren't old enough for a Ferrari. Still nobody's got a Ferrari, but still nobody smokes or takes dope.

Doug Gray

(Member of the Marshall Tucker Band)

We were opening a show for Waylon Jennings in Harrisburg, Pennsylvania. I could see Three Mile Island in the back, okay. I got off the stage and this black bodyguard that was with me says, "You sure are white."

I said, "Is that supposed to be some kind of a joke?"

"You just look sick."

I went back to the hotel. The next morning when I got up I couldn't touch my skin because the poison had got to me. I had these polyps, I was all infected inside. I said, "Can you give me something to let me go on to my next show on Long Island?"

They said, "Yeah, we can give you something. But you'll never wake up."

I said, "Well, I guess it's time to get fixed up then."

They cut me open, cut a few feet out of me, fixed me back. I had to wear a colostomy bag for about two months. Lost my money, most of my friends. I didn't care about anything any more.

Dennis Quaid was so accomplished at partying, he even cultivated his own alter ego, named Buck Gibson. Gibson enjoyed being a celebrity, said Quaid, adding that since he cleaned up his act, Gibson's now in Jamaica.

Dennis Quaid

At one point in my life I did have sort of a crazy lifestyle. I was drinking and doing drugs and stuff like that. I was living in the New York candy store. I had a wild time in my life, but I couldn't do that these days. Nor do I want to do it these days. I had that time in my life. I even quit smoking, because I didn't want to be smoking around my son. People can change. For the most part they don't change, but they can change.

Dennis Quaid
Ron Davis/Shooting Star

Dennis Quaid

I have some wreckage back there. It didn't take place in a vacuum.

Ethan Hawke

I really thought that if River Phoenix had friends who were interested in the same sorts of things that he was, the whole lifestyle out in L.A. isn't exactly conducive to a work ethic or anything to put your pride in. It's all devoted to Hollywood. There's so much judgment out there that you can really go crazy about people not liking you. I know that it bothered River, people talking about you and thinking you're this or thinking you're that. It can be terribly, terribly upsetting, especially if you're living in an environment where it's all that anybody thinks about.

Samantha Mathis

River [Phoenix]'s death was a life-changing experience for me. It was a little more complex than just a "price of fame" incident, but certainly that had a lot to do with it. He never felt comfortable in Hollywood. Clearly. He lived with his family in Florida and was very separate from the business. He felt very restless when he was here. The business is just a very strange thing to exist in.

River Phoenix

Life is interesting if you make it interesting. It can also be a bore, no matter what your context is.

Jean-Claude Van Damme

I know what I've got, and I cannot—sorry for the expression—fuck up, because I worked so hard for so many years. I became famous and then I became kind of lazy, the life and parties and all that stuff. Now I know what I've got and I want to make it better.

Some good people work hard for me and they're depending on me—and some other people were having fun with them. But it was like empty, deep inside, and I started to realize that.

Eddie Murphy

I've been to the Oscars once and the Grammys once to see what it was like. Not to take anything away from those shows, it's just the whole Hollywood glitz. "Hey, how are you!" I'm not a "Hooray For Hollywood"

Staggering around the crowded Viper Room music club in West Hollywood after ingesting the mix of drugs that would shortly kill him, River Phoenix spotted two celebrity photographers approaching, their cameras dangling ominously from their necks. In between seizures and vomiting spells, Phoenix looked up at them with terrified eyes. His last words before lapsing into unconsciousness were, "No paparazzi. I want anonymity."

type. Hollywood is a great town for someone who wants to try from everything at the banquet. That's what it's good for. But once you have everything and you're lucky enough not get some poison, leave the banquet.

Hugh Grant

(Asked how he handles the pressure?)

There's always alcohol. That helps, I suppose.

Jason Robards

I never drank to get falling down drunk and sing and do all that. I drank so I wouldn't have to face a lot of things.

Nick Nolte

I used to booze to get away from work. That got me in a lot of trouble. Now I just integrate it in. I go home and when I look at my son, he's there. It's like not carrying the issue of not having to shut off. I don't want to have a home where I'm one person and be another person at work.

Harvey Korman

Oh, I drank on Carol Burnett. I really found it terrifying to go out and do a show every Friday. It really terrified me. I was insecure that I wouldn't cut it from week to week. I got away with it again, one week, then another week. This went on for ten years.

Harvey Korman

I became a drunk. And I'll tell you why. Why shouldn't I? Why shouldn't you know everything?

I had been so used to being a failure and I was in my early thirties. I had been kicking around New York and everywhere trying to make it and I couldn't make it. Finally I got the shot on the Danny Kaye show and it scared me. I don't know if you have had the experience of finally finding yourself in a successful situation and having it scare the hell out of you, that you are not good enough, that they'll find you out, that it will be over soon, that you'll never been able to cut it, that you'll never be able to sustain it. I became a serious drinker. I was staggering around because I couldn't handle success. I remember when I won my second Emmy—I won FOUR—I remember that my acceptance speech was, "I want to thank my wife for helping me through the bad years and my psychiatrist and my bartender for helping me through the good years." Sometimes, somehow, the good years are not so hot. Because you can't handle the success.

Ozzy Osbourne

I was drinking like a complete fool, heavily, heavily. I was just like an animal for months. I just gave up.

> *All the great good fortune that came to me kept me sober through the years.*
>
> *—Sidney Poitier*

Jason Robards

People always said to me, "You and [Peter] O'Toole and [Richard] Burton are out there drinking all the time. Why are guys hanging around drinking? You have a lot of talent. Why are you doing that?" No one knows. Peter and I had a lot of fun, at times. I was out there with [Christopher] Plummer and [George C.] Scott. I think it's part of the profession in a strange way. After the release of doing that part on the stage every night, our day starts at eleven or midnight. We have dinner. We have a few drinks. We stay up 'til four and go to sleep. It's a whole turnaround life.

After I quit drinking Sam Peckinpah was mad at me for two years, but he finally gave up.

Peter Tork

I was very fortunate because I found myself to be an alcoholic and there is a community that is out to help and who will love you just because you're an alcoholic who wants to get better. That was the beginning of my retrieval as a human being. Otherwise I'd be a bubbling pile of protoplasm in the gutter someplace.

Liza Minnelli

[Alcoholics Anonymous] has been great. For me, anybody saying, "Look, you can fix what's wrong with you," is just the best message I've ever heard. If you have all of this over here—your health, your brain, your senses, your intuition—and that all depends on just not doing this? Fine. That's really cool. I was just so glad to find out that I had something. I just thought I was going nuts. I didn't realize that it was from having a disease.

I suddenly thought, "I really think I'm going to die here." I felt like I had blood cancer or something's wrong with me. People's denial systems are such that you don't realize what it is. But, boy, I went to find out. And that's the first step saying, "Excuse me. I don't feel good. Can I fix this?" Somebody will help you. Raise your hand, man.

Jason Robards

The time that I stopped drinking was very odd. I was doing a play called *Moon for the Misbegotten.* It's about a guy who has a choice between living and dying, really. In the play he dies. I suddenly realized that the play made the whole circle for me of all the O'Neill plays. I suddenly realized that this was the crossroads, that death lay on the other side. That was it.

Harvey Korman

Dracula: Dead and Loving It is the first picture I've done sober. Not to give you the impression that I drank while I was doing pictures, but I would certainly have a drink at five o'clock, whether I was in my trailer or not, and then I would have to face the hangover in the morning. The difference between coming to the set with a hangover and without a hangover is considerable.

Alannah Myles

Drugs won't help you. Money won't help you. Sex won't help you. You've got to go inside to find that anyway. It's a very easy thing to cast that off and say it. It's another thing to try and actually put that into practice and literally try and figure it out.

Elliott Gould

Bob Costas asked me on camera if I ever had a drug problem. I said, "No, I never had a drug problem. I had a problem with reality, but now that I accept it it's no longer a problem. Reality has to be my friend because that's the way it is. So long as I can accept the way it is, then, perhaps, I can do something more. If I don't accept the way it is there's no longer enough nature—and then there's no place to hide."

Judge Reinhold

All of the physical frontiers have been explored. We have to find a new definition for success.

Richard Dreyfuss

All of these crazes now are so familiar, with celebrities talking about their addictions, it makes you want to cry.

Martin Sheen

My wife is still a mystery to me, but she tells me the truth and nothing but the truth, all the time. I'm very lucky to have someone like that in my life, even during the bad times. You know, I'm an alcoholic. I don't drink any more and I struggle with a lot of my demons, but she's been there through all of that. I hope now that [his son] Charlie's married, I hope that he can find in Donna the same kind of companionship and trust. You have to fall in love with the truth—and that's a tough, tough companion.

Charlie Sheen

The producers of Wings of Courage *wanted me to take* a drug test. I was very insulted and I didn't do it. I'd done like thirty-one movies up until that point and a lot of lead roles and here I am showing up for a week and three scenes and they want a friggin' drug test. I was like, "Read my shoulder, pal." I've got a new tattoo. It says EMA. It stands for "Eat My Ass."

Charlie Sheen

I think I should write a letter to Marisa Tomei. I saw the movie again and I changed my opinion of her [Oscar-winning] performance. Keanu [Reeves]? No, I'm sorry. I gotta stick with what I said [in *Movieline*]. Rosie Perez? I don't think I could spend eight or ten weeks on a set with her. Her voice would drive me back to heroin.

Nowhere to Go but Down

Fame can be fleeting. Once you win the attention of the public, worrying about losing it can become obsessive. One thing is sure once you reach the pinnacle of success. There's nowhere left to go but down. Many stars reach the top already burdened with a deep sense of unworthiness. But no matter how secure you are, it's just a fact that there are always ups and downs. And the further up you are, the further down it is.

Tom Hanks

I'm very much aware of the fact that that's rarified air that I'm breathing there for a while. Even Sir Edmund Hillary eventually came down from Everest and he wasn't up there anymore. There's one side of me that believes that I've peaked, that says, "That's it, man, I'm just on the highway to infomercial hell." You feel that after a bit, because, literally, what could be more special than this?

Belinda Carlisle

It's downhill from number one. Where do you go?

John Landis

I worked with Michael Jackson when we did "Thriller." "Bad" came out and "Bad" did not match "Thriller's" sales. The press said, "Look at this. He's gone. He's over." I mean "Bad" is only the second most successful album of all time!

Whitney Houston

If I felt the pressure to duplicate "I Will Always Love You," it would make me crazy. And I don't think that we would get the best product if I was trying to outdo what I did before. I can't take that approach to records, because you will kill yourself trying to do that.

> *Success puts more pressure on you. Before I didn't have anything to lose really. People are a lot more generous in the discovery period.*
>
> *—Michelle Pfeiffer*

Quentin Tarantino

The thing you have to keep in mind—and REALLY keep it in mind—is it's a groovy time for me right now, to be sure. But it's not going to last and I know that. Right now it's [snaps his fingers twice] the thing. The thing is going to go away. I'm hot now. I'll be cold later. I'll be hot again. It's not about being hot. It's about a lifetime of making films. It's about a life. It's not about the movies I've made—both of them.

Robert Redford

I don't care about what I do being related to what I've done. It's just never been the case. It was never a question of, after *Ordinary People*, could I top it or could I repeat it. It just doesn't enter my mind, but it does enter other people's minds and then I have to deal with it.

Richard Dreyfuss

(Commenting on being the youngest man to win the Academy Award as Best Actor in 1977 for The Goodbye Girl*)*

It was a great compliment, a great gesture. It put me in great company. It also told me that I had arrived, and I don't like that feeling. I was much more comfortable on the hustle, trying to make it. I didn't like, I don't like, the psychological stance of having already proved it.

River Phoenix

(Recalling his feelings when he didn't win the Academy Award)

It would've been hell. I totally respect the Oscars and their history, but if I had had it my way I wouldn't have won, and I had it my way. I didn't win. I cheered when Kevin [Kline] won and I lost. I felt great. It was good enough to be in that company. What's the point in winning? What would follow? The expectation. The whole political future—beat it next time around or if you don't you're considered a failure. All that junk. Not that it wouldn't have been great to win it—to go down in history—but who needs it?

Nick Nolte

You work very hard at being able to approach awards with some kind of semblance of sanity. That is blown out of the water very quickly by the hype that goes along with it. You do end up discovering that one part of you all of a sudden is going with this desire to want to have this award, but I wrote little notes to myself before I went into that on perspective and what's important in life and what's not important in life, and the day after I didn't get the Oscar for *The Prince of Tides* I just looked at those notes.

The situation of those kind of things is how long do you want to carry it. How long can you afford to carry that? How long can you afford to carry not winning or winning it? Either way. How useful for you is it in life? It's not a very useful thing.

Anjelica Huston

It's an odd thing, the Academy Award, because on the one hand, yes, you want to be nominated, and following that of course you want to win, but the tension leading up to it, the decisions on what to wear and what to say start to override your life. All of a sudden it's the only thing in your life and they're the only two questions people ask you. Finally, what seems like a very incidental and faraway thing takes over and you feel like the oldest debutante in the world.

Glenn Close

(Commenting on the fact that she's received more Oscar nominations than any other non-winner)

It's getting kind of embarrassing. I feel very sorry for my family and my friends. They have to go through the entire evening and then have watch me lose again. They feel much worse than I feel. I honestly don't care if I win. I don't know what one has to do to win anymore—and if I ever cared I really don't care now.

John Landis

I was very privileged to have lunch with Alfred Hitchcock quite a bit. He was a big fan of *Animal House.* I was there with him the day he was told he was going to receive an honorary Oscar. He said, "Well John, it looks like I'm going to die."

Joanne Woodward

By the time he [her husband Paul Newman] finally got around to winning the Academy Award he wasn't there anyway. We were sitting in the living room in New York. The kids were there and we all were waiting. It went on and on and on and Paul went to sleep. Finally it came to the time and we said, "Paul, wake up, wake up." So he woke up and he won. We all said, "Darling, congratulations." "Daddy, congratulations." And then we went to bed. The thrill was gone by then. I always felt he should have won much earlier.

When I won it was exciting because I was very young. That was like a dream come true. It was unbelievable. Absolutely.

Jason Robards

The second Academy Award I won, I was in a play in New York. Instead of saying, "He's in a play in New York," to make a joke for Bob Hope they had me playing poker with [Marlon] Brando and [George C.] Scott, which I don't think is funny. So I've never gone back again.

Rob Lowe

(Recalling his dance number with Snow White at the Academy Awards)

You're going to tell me that Meryl Streep is a better actress than Jessica Lange, or Jessica Tandy? I have a hard time buying into this contest—and I'm not the first actor to say this. Give me a break already. I'd love to win an Oscar. I think it would be fabulous. But a little levity is called for here. The last time I checked we were all entertainers. We go out and we have fun. And I'm into taking chances. Part of being an entertainer is putting yourself out on the line like that and doing things that people don't expect.

Anyway, that's my Oscar statement.

Strung out on drugs and distraught over his breakup with a long-time girlfriend, pop star David Bowie hopped into his car in the middle of the night. He began circling in an underground garage, going faster and faster, hoping he would hit one of the pillars and end his life. As he hit forty, then fifty miles per hour, Bowie wondered about James Dean. But Bowie never hit a pillar and later turned the incident into a song, "I'm Always Crashing the Same Car."

Billy Crystal

(Why he stopped hosting the Academy Awards telecast)

I did it as well as I could do it. I had great moments on the show that will always be in my memory, but I really love not having the tension of thinking about it.

I watched Michael Jordan's retirement conference and I understood exactly what he was saying. "I've done this. I don't feel excited. And if I don't have fun and I don't feel excited, there's no sense in me playing." The thought of doing it was not fun. So I'm going to start playing with the Yankees.

Peter Frampton

It's much easier to make it than it is to stay there.

Elliott Gould

I'm still trying to forgive myself. I didn't know how tough things were. I didn't know how things could be in the world. I was the hottest male movie star at one time—and I didn't know anything. I didn't understand anything. I was aware that something was going on, and then it was to be or not to be and I took the chance. I didn't know I had no perspective. I didn't know I had no judgment. I still had to go for it, though, because I felt that that's not what it's about. It's not about being anybody. It's not about materialism. It's about being at one with something more than yourself, of which yourself is a part of.

I had to let it be taken away from me. I didn't want it to be taken away from me, but I couldn't allow myself to be enslaved to it. I was right, but I didn't know how to play the game.

Keenen Ivory Wayans

In retrospect, I probably would have done things differently when it came to leaving *In Living Color.* I don't have any regrets, but I do think that had I had a better understanding of what the bigger picture was, that I would have responded differently. The decisions made by Fox I took personally, and they weren't directed at me personally. It was a business decision. If I would have had that perspective then I probably would have approached it from a business standpoint.

But I took a personal offense to what was going on and creatively felt that it was being abusive, so my reaction was from the point of view of an artist and not a business person.

I've now talked it over with my brothers. I'm the Daniel Boone of the family. I'm the one who goes and gets bit by the bear and then comes back and says, "You know, it's real dangerous over this corner. Y'all look out."

Tom Hanks
Lisa O'Connor/Shooting Star

Tom Hanks

(Asked about a sequel to Forrest Gump*)*

It'll never happen. Listen to me right now. The studio would love *Forrest Gump II* to come into existence. They would love it. It would make us all a fortune and it would be half as good as the first one and it would dilute how special the movie was.

That wasn't just lightning in a bottle. It was three strikes of lightning in a bottle. We'll never be able to do it again and I don't even want to try.

Richard Gere

(Asked about a sequel to Pretty Woman*)*

It probably can't be done. Everyone saw that. It made an enormous amount of money. You think people haven't tried to do that since then. You can't do that. You can't recreate magic. It's hard enough to do it the first time.

Paul Hogan

(Asked about a third Crocodile Dundee *movie)*

I don't think so. I've had a lot of tempting offers and about seven hundred bad suggestions for reviving Crocodile Dundee. It was a complete story to me. He was a simple bushman. He started where he started and he finished back there. It's not like *Batman* or *Lethal Weapon* where you just think of a new villain and you can do another movie. No one's going to bring Crocodile Dundee out of retirement and send him to Paris to capture a planeload of terrorists, because he couldn't handle it.

Leonard Nimoy

(Asked about another Star Trek *movie with his Spock character)*

It's over. It's over. It's over. O-V-E-R. Done. The studio head doesn't even have my phone number.

Mel Brooks

I get a call a week ago from Warner Brothers. "*Blazing Saddles 2.* Come on. Let's go. We can do it." I say, "Jeez, I've covered the west. I can't think of another cliché that I haven't covered. For further adventures of this stuff maybe it should be on Saturday mornings as a cartoon."

Ted Danson

The syndicators said for *Cheers* to be picked up, the Charles brothers had to be involved and I had to be involved. So, yes, indeed, the decision to end *Cheers* was mine. I made the decision for myself. The decision was kind of a biological clock that went off. Time to go get scared. Time to do other things.

It's like losing someone in your family, eleven years of this great excuse to get together with people that you love and make each other laugh every day, is now gone.

John Cleese

The only problem with always being asked about Python is I feel a certain regret when people say, "Are you ever going to get together again?" I know perfectly well that they want me to say yes, just as we'd all love to see the Beatles together. I hate being negative about it, but what I do say is that I think we will work together in pairs and trios. But it's very hard now because we've all done a couple of decades in the business and we all have a fairly clear idea what it is that we really like. It's harder and harder for us to just sit down in a room and agree on what we should do. That is why, in my opinion, *Meaning of Life* was a mess.

Cheech Marin

Cheech and Chong broke up because of the real classical creative differences. We came to that point. Usually groups cite that because they can't stand each other anymore—and there was an element of that. But it really came down to he wanted to stay doing those three-chord dope movies and I didn't. I couldn't do them anymore. I had used all my dope jokes and I wanted to move on. I thought we could incorporate other things into the mix and he just didn't want to do that.

Richard Dreyfuss

I know definitely that I will have another down time. Maybe that's one of the things that happened to me before, that I had never thought it through enough when I was twenty-eight and twenty-nine to say to myself, "Of course I'll have a down period," so that when it started to happen I panicked. I know I'll have that.

I'm not in it to be at the peak of the mountain every day. I have a career. I do this for a living. I like my work—and one day I'll retire with a Swiss watch. Between that time and now I will have lows and highs and I don't have to be married only to the highs—or fear the lows.

Henry Winkler

No one stays that hot, but I thought I could. The Fonz [his character on *Happy Days*] was so big that I thought that I might be able to go from mountain top to mountain top and never go into a valley. I thought, "Maybe I'll be able to beat the system." Of course, you find out that there's no such thing. It just doesn't happen.

It's very important that you don't stay hot all the time, because you don't learn a lot from staying hot. You learn about yourself and you learn about living your life when you are not so hot. When you take a journey into the valley.

Rene Russo

I've been up. I've been down. I've learned in my old age to just enjoy it when you're on the top and enjoy all the different stages you go through. So I can't say that I'd be any happier winning an Academy Award than I am now. I was very successful in one career and I'm glad I was successful early because you get to realize that all stages are interesting and a challenge in different ways. They all come with their own set of horrors and joys.

William Hurt

What's more important: fame or happiness? There's a tarot card with a man who sits with his back to the viewer. And there's a river and there are four or five cups of the treasures he was given to work with in his life. One is smashed at his feet and you understand that he's weeping. The river is his tears for what he's lost, but there's also the accompanying knowledge that he will go on and use what he's got left better. Some people don't seem to have had the good fortune to survive. We have to learn from our mistakes as well as what we've got. I'm not going to say that someone who dies is unfortunate, because I don't know.

Robert Blake

I don't know what that mystery ingredient is that makes some of us make it—and some of us cross the line and never come back. I think of all the times I wanted to kill myself, I think of all the times I tried to kill other people, and I don't know why I'm here.

Olympia Dukakis

(1988 Democratic Presidential candidate Michael Dukakis's cousin)

You can't defeat that man. He doesn't go and sit in the corner very easily. His wife is getting her degree as a substance abuse counselor. They are very happy together.

But I wonder sometimes. He's so used to being at the heart of things. He's such a brilliant man that could and should be useful.

Peter Tork

I did make a pretty fair amount of money with the Monkees. Not much by today's standards, but a pretty fair amount. But I let it all go because I didn't understand value then. I didn't understand value in myself. What I've learned since then is you can't handle money well if you don't have an appropriate sense of self-value.

Steve Walsh

(Member of rock group Kansas)

When you're sitting in a big mansion and you've got all these things that money buys and you want for nothing and you think of nothing but relaxation, it becomes a "what the hell have I done to myself" kind of thing. "What am I going to do?" You've worked all these years and people say, "You're so fortunate, you're so lucky. But work is where you get the most pleasure out of life.

> ***Being famous has little to do with happiness.***
>
> ***—Barbara Walters from a headline in USA Weekend magazine.***

Yoko Ono

In the years that we [she and John Lennon] spent in New York together as a family, the five years they call "the missing years," it wasn't a missing period at all for us. It was the most fulfilling period for us, but from the other side it's "the missing years."

Tim Robbins

I really resented seeing John Lennon in *Forrest Gump.* I felt that it was self-serving for their purposes only. It had nothing to do with who he was. They used him. What scares me about that is because of a certain kind of new technology people can be used in that way. I don't like that. As an actor, I don't like seeing visual images with mouths being manipulated and words being put into people's mouths. I find that frightening, to tell you the truth.

Dennis Hopper

All these guys who became heroes during the sixties lost their position in life. They didn't finish their universities. They successfully stopped a war and started a free speech movement and fought for civil rights, but later became only curiosities at dinner parties. They had no income at all and couldn't really take menial labor jobs, or felt like they couldn't. What were they going to do, be busboys? Abby Hoffman became a drug dealer, got busted, went to prison. What a rough way to go. All these guys had leadership abilities, obviously, or they wouldn't have been the leaders that they were during that time. So there's a tragic side to all this.

Jeremy Leven

(Psychologist who directed Marlon Brando in Don Juan DeMarco*)*

He and my wife sat around talking one time. He always likes to talk about how much he hates acting. "I hate this. I hate it. It's like scrambled eggs on your face. I don't want to do it."

And my wife said, "Well Marlon, if you feel that way why do you do it?"

"Because it pays very well and I have lots of bills."

I think he uses that. That's a great way to protect yourself. If everybody believes that you're only doing it for the money, you can never fail. They can't say to you, "You gave it your best and it didn't work." But the reality is, he is so invested in acting.

Jack Lemmon

One of the best things about this business is that when you do something that doesn't work at all, it disappears quick at least. People tend to remember ones that work more readily than ones that don't work, thank God. I remember I did a picture called *Alex and the Gypsy.* I thought it was going to be the greatest thing since steam, my performance. It was not.

Comes the very first preview, I bring Walter [Matthau] in and I plunk him down beside me. Our wives are sitting over here. Ten minutes into it I know, "Oh Jesus, this is a disaster." People are getting up—and it ain't for popcorn. It isn't to go take a leak. They're going home. The lights come up at the end. There's practically nobody left. Walter's just sitting there. I go, "Okay, Walts, what do you think of the film?"

He says, "Get out of it."

Bruce Willis

I've had some of the worst things they've ever said about anybody said about me. And I'm still here. I walked through the fire and the gift that I got from walking through the fire was realizing that it doesn't affect me anymore.

Rob Lowe

The first step in getting over Atlanta [where he was videotaped having sex with a teenage girl] was admitting my mistakes and bad judgment and accepting responsibility for that. That's the first step. Just like any man would do, stand up and take responsibility for your actions.

> *Everything is funny as long as it is happening to someone else.*
>
> —*Will Rogers*

Rob Lowe

My mother, I'm sure she was embarrassed and hurt and all those things, but the one reaction that I saw was that she was furious with the forces down in Atlanta. All of it. I was like, "Mom, mom, don't get on the plane." I could see my mom swinging her purse in Fulton County Airport, "Leave my boy alone!"

I remember my dad saying something to the effect of, "Don't worry about us having a bad time because of what you've done, because there have been thousands of times when our lives have been made happier because of what you've done."

Warren Beatty

In today's way of seeing movies in two thousand theaters where you succeed or fail in a few days, there's a tremendous information machine out there that far exceeds our capacity to use it. If the people who are releasing your movie aren't your friends you should go home and take a nap. That's what I learned from *Ishtar.*

The man who ran the studio [David Puttnam], I have not met to this day. It was a very strange situation. I'm told that he never saw the movie, yet he was in charge of stirring up enthusiasm for the movie. He said a lot of negative things about me publicly. I never met him. He said a lot of negative things about Dustin [Hoffman]. I believe Dustin may have met him once. He managed to get publicity for himself by attacking people who are well-known and ironically he came in to run a company where two people he had used for this were releasing a movie. *Ishtar* became an orphan.

The picture cost far too much. Dustin and I tried to take our money on the back end. The company wouldn't permit us to do it because the money that was paid on the cable deal was 50% of the negative cost of the movie, so they wanted the negative cost to be as high as possible. We even asked if they would insist on us taking the money. We said, "If you're going to insist on us taking the money, we will, but let's keep this private and not publicize the cost of the movie." They agreed—and then they were all fired. New management came in and this guy absolutely made a crusade about the cost of the movie. There was nothing we could do. Then everybody reviewed the budget.

Sylvester Stallone

Many, many actors look for father figures. And the father figure, believe it or not, is the audience. They look for approval. That's their nurturing, their gratification. So it becomes a psychological dilemma. When you're rejected by critics or rejected by the audience, it takes on a whole different emphasis than if a football player is criticized by his coach. If you don't have a support system, you live and die by that. That's why I always believe that actors die two times. The second time is easy. The death of a career is beyond torture.

Shelley Long

I think our business beats pretty hard on us when they want us—and when they don't want us, man, they kick us right out the door. There's not much in between.

Elliott Gould

I'm still trying to overcome the brutality with which I came and went, at that period of time, in the late sixties and early seventies.

Sting

I'm pretty anxious about the whole idea of creativity just disappearing one day. Often it does. You can't guarantee that you'll be creative on any particular day. You'll find a song. Sometimes they come in a great bundle and you're very grateful, and the next day it's gone again.

Belinda Carlisle

You have all these years to come up with material for a first record—and then a year to come up with material for a second record.

David Bowie

Didn't I retire in 1990? I can't remember.

Nicolas Cage

There is a fear factor in never being able to be anonymous. Let's say I suddenly don't ever work again. I become the guy, "When's your next movie coming out?" Or "What happened to you?" That's scary stuff. You gotta put a little money aside for the Cabo San Lucas house so you can leave town.

Keith Carradine

The nature of this business is pretty cutthroat. You can have huge sums of money and praise lavished upon you one day, and withdrawn the next. If you don't have a strong grounding, if your basic character isn't well-founded, you can get lost in that. There are an awful lot of people who have allowed themselves to be victimized by the business. I don't say that people are victims of this business, because I think everybody has to take responsibility for who they are and where they go in their life. But this can be an incredibly cruel place to try and ply your trade, and if you're not prepared for that you can get in a lot of trouble.

Alan Young

After Mr. Ed *I retired,* but nobody noticed I'd left. No one puts a bookmark in when you leave. So I had to start all over again—and that's when I wrote *Mickey's Christmas Carol.*

Julianne Moore

You never know what's going to happen to you as an actor. You just pray you'll get another job. One of the horrible things that's driven me nuts since I started acting, is people who come up to you before you've even finished a job and say, "Well, what's next?" And then immediately I start to feel guilty and I start to worry. "I don't have another job." It's terrifying. It can end, man. People just disappear. They fall in these black holes and you never hear from them again.

Mary Stuart Masterson

You always think you're never going to work again. The function of this kind of life is every time you finish a job you're unemployed. You face that kind of fear. Even though people tell you not to worry about it, you worry about it.

Treat Williams

I could not get a job in the movies. I couldn't get in the offices. I couldn't get an audition. Six years ago I did about three pictures that all were really awful and I said to myself, "Look, I'm not going to do this anymore. I'm either going to take a job in a movie which I know is going to be a good movie or I'm not going to do them any more. I'll make my living in the theater or in television, but I don't want the four or five people left who like my work to keep saying, 'Why is he doing this stuff?' I'd rather do the best of television than the worst of cinema." I kept trying to get jobs in films and was having a really hard time through the agency, through a couple of agencies. That was about four or five years of that—and then *Things to Do in Denver When You're Dead* came along. Go figure.

Treat Williams

When you're in it, what you think of as a decline, you say to yourself, "What did I do wrong? Who can I apologize to?" As you look back on it you realize that careers have periods that are quiet. I realize that also during that period of quietness I grew up. I met my wife and got married. We had a son. We developed property in Vermont for ourselves that's a little farm now. I had the life I never had when I was pursuing my career. That life I have now is very strong, and is the more important part of my life. It's almost as if I had to really find myself as a person before I could allow the work to come back in and let it happen.

Bronson Pinchot

Someone's wife died and her husband said, "I get halfway to her room and keep expecting that she's going to be there." It's like that for entertainers. You do something that you like and you know it's good—

Nicolas Cage and Patricia Arquette Ron Davis/Shooting Star

and then it's just gone. Some executive pulled it. Someone made an X on a page and it's pulled. You can't do anything about it, but it's still there inside your head.

Jamie Lee Curtis

It's the only time I've ever heard of the producing entity canceling its own show. The network didn't cancel *Anything But Love.* Fox Television canceled *Anything But Love*—the day after New Year's, when the entire crew thought they had another thirteen weeks of employment after Christmas. I thought that was just abhorrent.

Nick Mason

(Member of Pink Floyd)

There are problems with being in an old, established band. It's disappointing to feel that you've become part of the establishment, rather than staying at the sharp end. You felt that you were really radical, and suddenly everyone's going, "Ugh, they're really boring, really old."

Chevy Chase

I miss having that forum, *Saturday Night Live,* I loved that forum, but if you're doing movies you can't do both.

> *Every day I have something pop into my head where I go, "You know, that would make a great sketch or a great character on Saturday Night Live." But unfortunately, that arena is closed to me now.*
>
> *—Dan Aykroyd*

Eric Idle

Sketch comedy is a young person's game. You can write lots of short pieces when you're younger, but as you get older you become more interested in writing longer pieces with character and plot. When you're younger you're so sure of your moral parameters that you can know who to attack. As you get older everything gets grayer and you become the people you're attacking.

Michael Keaton

Once people do get to a certain point, maybe they lose that edginess. A lot of comedy comes out of anger or fear. Do you need to be a little angry or frightened to be not only funny, but to be talented? Or a little neurotic or a little crazy or a little off? Some people feel they need that edge.

There's that debate, if you're totally happy can you be really artistic? So if you have a choice, I think you should say, "Fuck art," in the end.

Mel Brooks

It is tougher to be funny as you get older. You figure that comedy is kind of unseemly and adolescent. Why do you want to do it as a mature person? But there's nothing like comedy. It blows the dust off your soul. Comedy and music are the two great emotional adventures in our business.

Kirk Douglas

A couple of months ago I was playing golf. I said, "Let those old guys go ahead."

And my friend says, "Kirk, those 'old guys' are about ten years younger than you are."

I don't think of myself that way. Sure, I know that I've been in the movies for forty years, but I don't think of myself as an old guy.

You stay off the screen for three years and people say, "My dad used to watch you in the movies." Time slips away.

—Paul Hogan

Paul Hogan

I'm yesterday's news. I haven't had a hit for a couple of years. I had one movie, it got us our money back, but it wasn't a hit. They're not going to hand me a check and say, "Go make a movie." If I do a movie with a studio, experts are going to be attached to the money. Some guy who can't even make his wife smile is going to be sitting across the table from me saying, "No, no, no. Wear a purple hat. That'll be funnier."

Al Pacino

I see the mountain in front of me. We're all headed for it. It's just gotten a little closer. I'm doing more publicity. I used to work every couple of years. I went four years without making a movie. Maybe because I've become a little more comfortable with movies, making them, having made my own picture, *The Local Stigmatic,* I feel a little bit more connected with the movies than I ever did.

Virna Lisi

Hollywood is not interested in Virna Lisi now. Virna Lisi of a certain age in a certain kind of role, yes. For me now, at my age, no.

Mary Tyler Moore

Somebody will nudge her pal in the ribs and say, "Hey! Look who's here! You know who that is, don't you?"

She looks at me and goes, "No. Who?"

"Mary Tyler Moore."

"Oh."

So you're always running the risk of fame turning around and biting you in the heel.

Isabella Rossellini

(After being let go as a model by Lancôme)

If you pick up *Vogue* or *Harper's Bazaar,* you don't see a forty-year-old model. It's a perpetrated tradition. I don't like it. I don't think it's necessary. The sales at Lancôme didn't go down because of my age, and yet the tradition is so strong.

Robert Redford

I don't want the burden of having to go through my life having to adjust myself so much cosmetically that it changes who I am, because that's what I have to give. If I started altering who I am then it's all lost. There's no point. If the country is that obsessed with youth or glamorous looks, then I'll just have to live with that.

Rod Steiger

The terrible thing about age for an actor on the screen is that when you get older, and you live in a nation that worships youth and has a terrible fear of death, it becomes longer in between getting decent parts. They're writing very few pictures like *Driving Miss Daisy.* That's very bad for a person like me, who's mentally much happier when he's working and can feel some kind of need come from the world I live in. It refurbishes my respect and gives me a desire to continue.

I had a depression for almost eight years. It slowed my career all the way down. Nobody wants me to talk about it because people

Al Pacino Ron Davis/Shooting Star

misunderstand, but I insist on talking about it because I have learned that depression is a disease and often a chemical imbalance. It has nothing to do with insanity at all. Years ago, fifteen years ago, you mention depression and people think you're talking about someone who's weird, strange. I came out of that thanks to my wife, who saved my life many times.

Robert Blake

I took off six or seven years. I decided finally I was ready to go back to work after being through hell and back myself several times. I woke up to the fact that I had been seriously physically and sexually and psychologically abused when I was a kid and hiding from it all my life.

Anyway, I decided to go back to work. Ha. I went out looking for agents and they're all twelve years old, man. I signed with one of the three giant agencies. I went there one morning for the morning meeting, where they have like thirty or forty agents, and all the assistants were sitting around having coffee. Then a bell rang for the meeting to start and the assistants all sat down. They were the agents! They were all twelve years old—and the guys and the chicks look exactly alike. They've all got ponytails and earrings and baggy black suits on. They all wear makeup and they sound alike and they all act alike. I felt like some mastodon from the La Brea tar pits. They don't even know who John Garfield was and he's my hero. I lasted there about a month.

Rod Steiger

The only problem I have now, which is a problem of ego and pride, is that there are a lot of people in their mid-thirties who are in executive positions. I'll go in and have a talk with them about a movie and the young person will say, "Can you do a Southern accent?"

I say, "Well, I got the Academy Award for *In the Heat of the Night.* Did you see it?"

And they say no. You have to remind them who you are. It's a test of your ego, because you really feel like saying, "If you're supposed to be one of the heads of the studio you should know about good films. You should know who I am."

Robert Blake

Some casting lady from New York called me. She started asking me questions like, "What have you done?"

I thought she was teasing me. She was dead serious. She wanted me to send her an 8 x 10 glossy and "my tape." I said, "What tape?"

She said, "All actors have a tape with little clips of their films on it."

I said, "I'll tell you what I'll do. I'll send you $20 and you can go the nearest video store and get twenty different movies that I've done and make your own goddamn tape."

Diane Ladd

I asked her [daughter Laura Dern] not to be an actress. I said, "For God's sake, do not be an actress." This business is extremely tough on men. It burns up their manhood. It's a very hard on business on the male ego. But if you think it's hard on men, it's manure on women, and not the kind that necessarily makes the flowers grow. It's very difficult because it's a subjective business. It's not an objective business.

I have other hobbies that I do that have helped my life evolve. I have a Masters in psychology. I work with doctors. I lecture. I teach metaphysics. I'm a certified nutritional counselor. You go out on those lectures and someone comes up to you after and says, "Oh, Miss Ladd, thank you so much." There is such a feeling of respect and appreciation.

In this business you do a part. You get your reviews. You win awards. Then five minutes later you go in and you're interviewed by someone who's never done anything in the business before and knows nobody's credits. You're a piece of meat, being examined from ALL angles. But perhaps Van Gogh or some of them felt the same way about their art.

Bette Midler

My God, when you look in the magazines and everyone's so young, you say, "Well what happened to my generation?" I know how older people feel now. This magazine no longer speaks to me. They're still speaking to the same age group, it's just that you're not in that age group any more.

Vanessa Redgrave

It's not just my generation, there are another two generations older than me, of actors and actresses who want to work, who need to work, who could do wonderful work, and have not got any work at all. It's a very bad situation. There's a brilliant English actress who I know, who has already done starring roles in major theater productions and films, who just can't get work. And if you do get a job, you're not even getting paid for it.

Jack Lemmon

The older you get, there are great parts, but there are fewer of them. The waits are longer in between, believe me. When I was in my twenties, I very often would say in an interview—and really mean it—"I can't wait to get older because the parts get richer." They'd look at me like, "What kind of bullshit is that?" What they didn't tell me is they might get richer, but there are fewer of them.

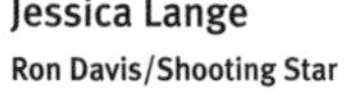

Jessica Lange
Ron Davis/Shooting Star

Paul Newman

The problem is not that you can't get a job. The problem is that the jobs that are out there aren't that interesting.

Jane Fonda

Hollywood is in a place now where it's the world of *Batman* and *Lethal Weapon.* It doesn't feel too hospitable to me now.

Gregory Peck

I knew that I wasn't going to be making three pictures a year after I was sixty years old. Why would I want to? I don't have a mad ambition to stay on top of the heap at my age. I did all that thirty years ago.

Esther Williams

The problem with being a movie star, a woman especially, is you peak too young.

It's all over too fast. Just about the time you're learning—I watched myself learn to act on the screen—it's over.

Jeanne Moreau

How can I give the best I can if I'm not allowed to age and be riper and richer inside? A woman is not just a piece of meat with a pair of ass and some tits and a beautiful face. Life has to do with experience.

I think Bette Davis said it as articulately as anybody: "Gettin' old ain't for sissies."

—Paul Newman

Daryl Hannah

Just recently I got asked to do a film where the guy was exactly the same age as me and they go, "No, she's too old."

Esther Williams

My mother [a psychologist] told me, "You have consciousness of supply. If you have consciousness of supply, nobody can take away what's yours." They can take away your money—husband number two did. They can steal your car. They can take away everything that you have, but you'll just get it all back again. Don't think I didn't think about that for twenty-two years when I was married to Fernando Lamas.

Elliott Gould

I let myself be known before I understood myself, so therefore politically and business-wise I haven't always been so sensible. So this appears to be a return, but I never really left.

Jessica Lange

I haven't met one actor, no matter what, who at the end of a project doesn't say, "I'm never going to work again. This is going to be it." In some ways, that's the nature of the beast. You always feel this is the last time anyone's going to hire you for a part.

Patrick Swayze

I don't know what's coming up next. I think I'm going to play Flipper.

Dustin Hoffman

I'm still competitive. I'm sad if I don't get asked to do parts I would like to do, like The Joker or The Penguin in *Batman.* When you first hear of it you think, "Ooh."

James Caan

Kramer vs. Kramer, which I turned down, I still consider it middle-class bourgeois horseshit. So who knew? Would I take it now if I knew the end result? You know, when I was flat broke I took a self-induced hiatus. Some people are missing for two weeks. I was missing for a decade. Even during that time, I never took a picture for money. I remember one time doing a picture for [French director Claude] Lelouch, which did three dollars over here. I think four people, including my mother, knew it was a movie. I did that for one-fourth of the money I was offered somewhere else. So the answer is no, I probably wouldn't.

Ellen DeGeneres

The hardest thing is starting out. You can compare it to walking as a baby. You don't have as far to fall. When you fall now you break a hip. You don't, but our grandparents do. When you're starting out as a baby and you fall it's no big deal. When you're starting out doing stand-up you're in front of ten people—and probably nine of those people are so drunk that they don't know who you are, and they don't care. You've got to win those people over.

I don't want to be in a position where my movie's expected to be great every time and I'm expected to be great in it.

—Leonardo DiCaprio

Then slowly you're playing to bigger and bigger crowds and it's the most frightening thing in the world, to walk on stage and have to change an entire roomful of people's opinions. They automatically think you suck, especially being a girl on stage. "You're not going to be funny—you're a girl." That's a huge thing to overcome.

Then when you get popular and people come to see you they already like you. So you've won that battle. They paid the twenty bucks or whatever to see you and it gets easier. Then you pass that point and everybody's waiting to see you fail. You can't still be good anymore because you used to be good. You're constantly fighting this roomful of people.

Kevin Bacon

I still live in Connecticut. I find myself spending a lot of time in Los Angeles and working out there. I'm just not happy when I'm there. It's like the city of fear to me. When I look back at the first time I ever went to L.A., '77 or '78, I was overcome with this kind of anxiety. I felt like I was driving in from the airport looking for the city and I couldn't find it. I saw a couple of buildings over there. Century City. A couple of buildings over there. That's downtown. Where's the damn city?

There are times when I like to go out and play the game. Go to the parties and go to the premieres. It's a good place to be when you're really the talk of the town and things are going great, but when they're not it's just so in your face. The fact that you're not doing well is everywhere you look. You can do a movie, for instance, and they'll put the billboard up on Sunset Boulevard and you'll drive by it every damn day of your life. And the movie can go in the toilet and not open and they'll leave the billboard up there for another three months. You've gotta drive by every day and it's screaming out, "Bomb. Bomb. Bomb. You're in a bomb. You're still in a bomb. You're going to be in a bomb tomorrow." It's a nightmare.

I never read *Variety* or the *Hollywood Reporter* [the entertainment industry trade papers] while I'm at home. I can't help it when I'm in L.A. It's there. I pick it up. It appears places. It's like it grows out of the ground or something. I just need to buffer myself from that still, because what it does is it makes me define myself on the wrong terms. I define myself by things like box office, or reviews, or tables in a restaurant, or guest lists. That's no way to think about yourself.

Lawrence Kasdan

The reaction to *Wyatt Earp* was bullshit. In this country, it's very rarely about the movie. It's about the event. And if it's a big expensive movie with a star [Kevin Costner] who's had a lot of hits and it's time to bring him down, it's very hard to see the movie through all that stuff.

What's it like to go through it? Terrible.

Judge Reinhold

I did this movie called *Vice Versa.* It was my first movie with my name above the title and it didn't perform. It didn't do well and my career crumbled and I realized that my whole personality was wrapped up in what I did, instead of who I was. I hadn't paid any attention at all to the inside. So I left for New Mexico, bought a small house and pulled myself together.

Treat Williams

When I was sitting on the floor of a sitcom that Shelley Long was starring in, I used to turn to Teri Garr all the time. We were on this sitcom that we knew was dying and, on the worst days, I'd say to Teri, "You know, we used to be movie stars."

Billy Crystal

I was not a happy man for a year [after his *Mr. Saturday Night* was released]. Especially in Hollywood. You walk into a restaurant after your movie didn't open and people look at you. "Huh. $4.7 first weekend." You can hear it. You can feel it. You can't express how painful it is when the phone call comes and they know pretty much Friday night how it's going to do for the weekend.

I've been thinking about moving back East.

Billy Crystal
Yoram Kahana/Shooting Star

Dennis Miller

The thing I like about show business is it's clearly delineated. They meet you at the town border on your way in and say, "Listen, this is a bloodless, mean place. You still want in?" And if you say, "Yeah," it's on you. Nobody promises you anything here.

Mel Brooks

You've got to be very careful. You've got to spoon yourself out in very small doses to the public. If they get too much of you, they jump off you.

Lawrence Kasdan

The media knows only two stories. One is people going up and the other is people coming down. This story is boring on the level when people are successful or when they're doing their work. No one talks about the work. They don't say, "This is what's in this work."

What they say is, "This person used to make $300,000 and now he makes $7,000,000."

"Now he makes $5,000,000."

"Ooops. He slipped. Now he's making $10,000,000."

Those are "good stories."

I truly love this business between action and cut, but there's a certain energy out there that wants to bring down somebody who's on their way up. We're slowly becoming a nation that's demoralized in aspects of living, one that's very sad. There's an element of "let's find something on somebody so we can bring them down." It's not about the truth. It's about seeing people squirm.

—Kim Basinger

Michael Keaton

There seems to be so much focus now on show business and success and failure. It gets all eaten up so fast, I don't know that it would be as much fun to be starting out today. When I started, making a fool of yourself was not such a big deal—and it shouldn't be.

Paul Hogan

You have to consider how short the attention span is about who's hot and who's not. I never held the system in high regard anyway, so I wasn't that disillusioned. I thought, "They're not very classy." If I go in and make two blockbusters in a row for a studio, it would make them very cheerful because I would make them a huge profit. Then if I were to make another cheap little movie and all they do is get their money back eventually, there would be no losses. If they had half a brain, they would want me to have another four or five goes, because most people have nine flops. A lot of people have five or six flops and a couple of hits. Then there are those big superstars like Arnold [Schwarzenegger] and Tom Cruise, who have blockbuster hits almost all the time. On my track record, I've made three movies for under $40 million, which is the average of nearly every budget, and they grossed $680 million, theatrically. I'd probably be entitled in a sane business for four or five goes, but then the studios change hands all the time. I used to deal with Frank Mancuso. He wasn't at Paramount any more when I went back there. I think Brandon Tartikoff was. So who are you dealing with half of the time? Hopefully nobody.

John Landis

In terms of these huge salaries, first of all, they're not new. Mary Pickford was given a million dollars a picture. It sounds like a joke, but that was when a million dollars was a million dollars. That was before Federal income tax, when a dollar was worth like sixty dollars today. There's no comparison, the fees that are paid now to Arnold Schwarzenegger and Tom Cruise and Eddie Murphy, to the silent film stars. It's not even close.

However, having said that, it's all about box office. They're separate issues to me, stardom and box office. I was quoted extensively about Eddie, saying he was like Marilyn Monroe. Eddie's a movie star. When I say a movie star, I mean like Clark Gable, like Humphrey Bogart, like Gloria Swanson, like fifty years from now Eddie's a movie star. Not like John Travolta.

Steve Guttenberg

John Travolta was the greatest box office star of our time in 1976. Then probably for about ten years Hollywood spat on him. I remember seeing a trade ad for *Look Who's Talking* and it didn't even have his name on the ad. They were trying to sell the movie. It was sitting on the shelf for two years. That's just the way this is. It's like saying the boxing game is a tough game. You gotta get beat up. That's the game.

You have to get over that hurt. Living well is the best revenge. Why do actors get paid so much money? Lots of reasons. One of them is because you get beat up so much.

Our job is to not be bitter. Once you're bitter, things start screwing up. Most actors get kicked around, so that's why you create so many Frankensteins. A lot of stars are pretty mean because they got kicked around a lot. Even when you're a success you get kicked around a lot.

Bill Pullman

How quickly the movies evaporate. All there is is the last six months. People say, "What did you do before *While You Were Sleeping?*"

Then you have the albatross around your neck. "Well, did you see *Singles?*"

"Yeah. I don't remember you in that."

David Caruso

There's a great account of when Francis Coppola was casting *Apocalypse Now.* He went down to Los Angeles to try and get a leading man for the

Martin Sheen role, a big movie star. He went to the people that he MADE movie stars in his other movies—people he fought for—and he got turned down by everyone. So he went back up to the house in Napa Valley and took all his Oscars out in the backyard and broke them all.

Jimmy Stewart

(Recalling his fears starting It's A Wonderful Life *after World War II)*

It was Lionel Barrymore who got me back in the corner and said, "Now look. There's a story going around that you're scared that you've forgotten how to act or something. Well now stop being such a dumb [pause] actor and get down here and work. Don't ever let me hear anything about you wondering if you've been away too long. You're doing fine. Acting is a very important thing that takes hard work and it demands hard work. You have shown that you are capable of hard work, so just get in there and work at it. And stop complaining."

I almost said thank you. Maybe I did. He really gave me a bawling out.

Harvey Korman

It almost works in inverse proportion. The more accolades you get, the more Emmys you get, the more everything you get, the scareder you get. Because you know it's an accident, you know it may not happen again next week, that you've been getting away with murder. That's the way it has been with me. I just recently, about a year ago, stopped drinking. I found it was the best thing I've ever done. I have a lot more clarity.

John Travolta

I don't know if I can ever get too much of it. The hot streaks I've had, there was the *Saturday Night Fever-Grease-Urban Cowboy* hot streak. Then there was the *Staying Alive* for a few minutes hot streak. Then there was the *Look Who's Talking* hot streak—and then there was the *Pulp Fiction* hot streak. None of them lasted long enough for me to know if it was too much.

The comparative is one time I rented a boat in the Caribbean. I rented it for a week and I couldn't get enough of it. So I said, "Some day I'm going to stay on that boat as long as I want." I did that and I found out that two weeks was enough. I wanted off that boat, big time. As for being in hot movies, if it's too much I'll let you know, and then I'll have to magically disappear.

Hugh Grant

It will be very humiliating when my bubble bursts and I'm back to square one. I keep asking people in Hollywood, "What happens if my next movie flops, will I be back to square one?" The people I pay say, "You'll be fine, Hugh. You've got years." And the people that I don't pay say, "You'll be back to square one."

William Reid

(Member of The Jesus and Mary Chain)

We've been through it maybe eight or ten times, to be honest. A lot of people in Britain are incredibly irritated by us, because they realize that they never built us up and they can't cut us down. If you make good records a certain amount of people will buy them. When you start making bad records that's when you're in trouble. If you're fashionable and you start making bad records, you're in deep trouble.

Mark Wahlberg

When my record came out I had such a voice, especially to young people like myself, and then once I got into the underwear thing [as a Calvin Klein model] I didn't have a voice. I was stripped of my voice and then I was introduced to a much older audience. They didn't have any idea what I was about from my music. So it was kind of a conflict, but through the trials and tribulations of careers I got my voice back. I was very fortunate.

Chubby Checker

Somewhere along the line I just lost it. I lost control of it. Everybody enjoys my dance. Everyone enjoys the success of my creations. And I just sat around.

Bob Cousy

I was supposedly the highest paid player in the NBA when I quit at $30,000. So there's been a slight escalation. Needless to say, I'm going to work until I'm seventy, which isn't too far away.

I left after thirteen years and I could've physically played another four or five. I left, frankly, because I was spaced out. I had enough of the stress and constant pressure of being in the limelight—and I was getting

Jimmy Stewart The Kobal Collection

one-tenth of what these guys are getting. It reached me after thirteen, but as we saw with Michael Jordan, it reached him quicker.

> *I always find that it is insecurity that drives us the hardest.*
>
> *—Demi Moore*

John Doe

I have no bitterness toward people making a lot of money. I feel sorry for them because then you have to follow up that hit song with a yet bigger and better hit song. And if they don't, they're a disappointment. Buying into it is crazy.

Peter Frampton

It took a long time for Michael Jackson to follow up "Thriller," and you know that he watched what happened to me.

Morgan Freeman
Nikki Vai/Shooting Star

Cybill Shepherd

I get nervous sometimes when I'm in crowds. You think, "Oh God, these people are going to ask for my autographs." But there's also the other side of the coin—what if they don't? I really went through a period in my life when people asked for my autographs and then I went through a period when people forgot who I was. I went to the grocery store in Memphis, Tennessee, and nobody noticed. Now I'm famous again. People come up to me and say, "This is terrible, a certain publication does this and this." I'm always so happy to have my name spelled right.

Morgan Freeman

You don't want to spend your life worrying that you're going to lose it. If you get to get it, then that's all there is. Fame isn't what you want. Stardom isn't what you want. That's the result. What you want is to work, isn't it?

Meeting the Queen, and Other Good Stuff

Okay, enough whining. Fame is toxic. But it is also euphoric. After detailing all the pain, how about sharing a little of the joy. After all, if stardom is such a miserable thing, how come so many people pursue it so desperately?

Sting

I think we're in danger here of crying too much as celebrities. "Isn't it terrible that we have all this fame?" The fact is we're incredibly well-paid. We all live in nice houses. People generally are very kind to us. Is it any more difficult than being a coal miner or a factory worker? I doubt it. I actually have a nice time being famous. I quite enjoy being famous. Generally I would say that for me 70% of the experience of being famous is pleasant. The other 30%? That's what I'm paid for.

Quentin Tarantino

It's been a blast. Yeah, there's been a sour note here or there, but I'm not going to whine about it because the scales, you know, definitely one's going up and the other's going down when it comes to the good and the bad of the situation.

There's no way I can list the stuff on the bad side of the scale without sounding like an ingrate and a jerk and annoy everybody.

John Cusack

I hated high school. The first movie I did I got to hang out on the set and look at Jacqueline Bisset for twelve hours a day. I just remember feeling like I had won the lottery. And I loved acting. It was thrilling to be in front of the camera in *Class.*

I'm a guy who got D's in school. My family is borrowing money from me now. There's something weird here, but I'm not complaining.

—Pauly Shore

Rosie O'Donnell

It's sort of a hard thing, but you can't really complain because you knew going in it would be like this. And you get to be a millionaire, so what can I say?

Clint Eastwood

If stars take themselves seriously it's kind of a sad thing. That obviously means they don't have enough on their minds to keep occupied.

Marlon Wayans

I've got a Range Rover, but the best thing I've done with my money is put two of my little nephews and one of my little nieces in private school. That was the best gift. That and Christmas. Everybody gets something great on Christmas. I can't reach out to every kid in the world 'cause I'd be broke, but if each man was to take care of his family like the guys in our family take care of ours, then we can get out of the situations that we're in.

Mary Elizabeth Mastrantonio

I only got Robin Hood: Prince of Thieves *because Robin Wright* got pregnant. I was in London, I had just finished a run in a play, when I got a call one day. They said, *Robin Hood.* I laughed. Maid Marian? She's supposed to be about eighteen. Where were they going to put the camera? But they couldn't have Kevin Costner robbing the cradle. So I just thought, "Hells bells, we just bought a house."

Olympia Dukakis

At the time that *Moonstruck* opened, we were sending our daughter to college on credit cards. That immediately ceased, I'm happy to report. That's number one. We paid our mortgage. So fame impacted me financially.

Esther Williams

Those speaking engagements are ridiculous, $25,000 for forty-five minutes, and I free associate without writing anything down.

Howie Long

Broadcasting football games is stealing money. I get paid to talk about hitting people. I got a horseshoe stuck somewhere.

Anthony Kiedis

(Member of the Red Hot Chili Peppers)

We're able to live in nicer houses, drive nicer cars, take our friends out to more dinners, and perhaps travel around the world more freely, but it certainly isn't what we're striving to attain. We're striving to attain honesty in our expression of music.

Uma Thurman

For a celebrity to say that they have it tougher than anyone in the real world is kind of pushing the envelope.

Melanie Griffith

Michael Douglas and I were shooting *Shining Through* and we were invited to this Shirley Bassey concert for the Prince's Trust, Prince Charles's thing. They said, "The Prince and Princess would like to meet you."

We said, "We don't know what time we're going to be finished because Twentieth is making us work as late as possible." So we said we'd get there when we could. When we got there they ushered us in. The next thing we know the door was opened and there they were! It was just Prince Charles and Princess Diana. That was it. We just hung out and talked. We talked about the kids, Diana and I. I don't know what Michael and Prince Charles talked about.

They said, "Where are you sitting?"

"We don't know. We don't really have seats."

They said, "Come and sit with us," and all of a sudden somebody's going, "All right, you're on his right, and Michael, you're on the Princess's left." They opened the doors and it's the balcony seating of this huge theater. All the people of the theater stand up—and we're there with the royalty! It was quite amazing. I felt like Cinderella.

We were watching the show and Shirley Bassey starts singing "There's No Business Like Show Business." We were kind of looking at each other going, "Yeah, no kidding."

Elle MacPherson

I met Princess Diana and Prince Charles in Australia. I wasn't expecting to meet them at all, but suddenly I was pulled aside. One of the most satisfying things that I've ever had in my career was the front page of the *Herald Tribune*, which is a very posh newspaper, printing a big double page picture of Princess Diana and myself. It was such a beautiful photograph.

Ian McKellen

I don't say receiving a knighthood was an ambition achieved, but to be nominally in the same company as people I've always admired like Sir

Laurence Olivier, Sir John Gielgud, Sir Ralph Richardson, Sir Alec Guinness, and all the rest, is very, very satisfying. You can't buy a knighthood, you know. You can't lobby for it. You can't ask for one. You just get given it. It's given by the Queen on behalf of the nation. That's the theory. I think it's a very appealing idea, that the nation should say thank you, choosing to say thank you to me. It's not for me to note that they're also saying thank you to all sorts of people that I don't like and that I really think should be struck off the register. But I knew that my gay work would be enhanced by having a knighthood available to write certain letters, to knock on certain doors, and to make a fuss. Also, I noted that I was practically the first openly gay man to be given a knighthood. Maybe that suggested that the government was a bit more alert than it had been to the fact that there are gay people around in the world.

Jodie Foster
Ron Davis/Shooting Star

Jodie Foster

Things like winning the Oscars are radical changes in your life because you realize that your instincts got you this far, so you don't have to listen to people being negative and saying, "Better be afraid of that." You don't have to listen to them because you got these Oscars by doing just the opposite, so you might as well just continue.

I keep my Oscars right next to the bathtub, so I can take a bath and look at them. What else are you going to do with them?

Al Pacino

When you get one, awards can be very positive injections into a career. An actor is sitting alone in his room, wondering when the phone is going to ring. Somebody calls and says, "Hey, you got an Oscar nomination."

"I'll close the window now. Now I won't have to jump."

Anjelica Huston

(On winning the Oscar for Prizzi's Honor*)*

There's that moment when you hear your name and there's a ringing in your ears. The stage seems very far. I remember motes of dust in this blue emptiness of the stage on which Marsha Mason and Richard Dreyfuss look very small, and finding my way up there. Such are the Awards that you're panicked about what you're wearing and what you're going to say. That overrides everything else, including the prospect of winning or losing. I remember very little about my speech, except I forgot to thank my producer and my co-star, Jack Nicholson, who was then my boyfriend, then leaving the stage to return to the audience, which is generally not done. Normally you go behind to the press room. I remember seeing my dad [director John Huston] and saying, "Dad," and his not looking at me. Tears were gushing down his cheeks and I'm thinking, "That's strange." And then my making my way to my seat where Jack was crying—and feeling extremely by myself and astonished.

Martin Lawrence

I've been called a buffoon. I've been called a clown. I've been called a lot of things. So when I got the NAACP Image Award it was beautiful.

It's nice to get all the awards. But if I never won an Oscar or an Emmy or all that, it's nice to be recognized by your peers, but I realize one thing. I make a lot of people laugh. I make people smile. If it's only for a moment, I take their mind off the violence or whatever.

Henry Winkler

I've lived a life that could not be duplicated if I was reincarnated eleven times, because of The Fonz [his character on *Happy Days*]. I'm one of the very few men in the 20th century who has been able to photograph the Hopi Indians. I have a jacket in the Smithsonian Institute. I have earned an incredible living. I have traveled all over the world. I have been invited into about 85% of the population's homes for dinner. I've been able to direct. I have a really good time and a really good life.

William Shatner

The celebrity accrued to me from *Star Trek* has given me the opportunities to do so many things and realize so many ambitions. I'm three jumps past lucky. I'm one of the luckiest people alive.

Sophia Loren

I have received so much from life. Sometimes I was dreaming a lot and I really had from life much more than I was dreaming about. Even now, I don't know if I am deserving of all that is still happening to me. I'm not a kid anymore. It's wonderful.

Ozzy Osbourne

They always thought I was a clown and a fool, but I've proved everyone wrong. It was the biggest prank I've ever pulled off in my life. I've proven every one of them wrong. They all thought I was nuts and I was crazy, but out of my craziness I've given a lot of people happiness. There's no harm in that.

Tina Louise

It's taken some getting used to, but now that I really realize how much people love *Gilligan's Island.* Love is really powerful. It makes them happy. It's taken so many turns and forms. There was this woman who came up to me in a restaurant who said that her husband had died of cancer and how much joy I brought into his life. He loved me so much. I can't argue with that.

Michael Crawford

When fame finally did come to me, in the way that it did with *Phantom,* first in London and then in New York and then in Los Angeles, it's something to be savored, so beautifully. You can't say it's just like a great wine. It's what you've worked for, it seems like for hundreds of years. I've been in the profession now about forty years, because when I was a child I started, and if I'd had anything any earlier I wouldn't have felt as rich as I feel now. It's not a financial thing, because in the theater you don't earn as you earn in movies. You have sufficient when you become successful, but it's far greater reward than that. People do seem to have respect for what you do.

Christian [Slater], John [Travolta] and I threw a party for the crew of <u>*Broken Arrow*</u> *up in Montana. We rented out this place and we had a karaoke machine and a disco room. We were all out there dancing. They put on "Saturday Night Fever" and John did a little dancing, nothing too showy, but we were like, "Oh my God, this is really cool." Then they put on the last song of* <u>*Grease*</u>*, "You're the One That I Want." I turned around and he was singing it to me. We started doing it, I just went with it, and the next thing I knew we were acting out the entire end of the movie. We were dancing and he picked me up and he twirled me around. The crew just stopped. They were watching us and cheering. It was unbelievable. It was a childhood dream come true. I saw* <u>*Grease*</u> *twenty-three times when I was a girl. It was pretty huge.*

—Samantha Mathis

John Ratzenberger

Going someplace you've never been, someone recognizes you, and instantly you can find out where the best restaurants are, places to go, places to avoid, because you've been part of their family for eleven years. People are very warm, instantly, usually.

James Garner

I've been famous for almost forty years now. Early on the fame was a little difficult. You'd go places and it was kind of like rock 'n' roll, crowds of people at airports and things like that. I was happy to get out of that.

Now, I'm like an old sweater around the house. I fit well and everybody knows me. They're very friendly and pleasant. I like that. There's not all this furor about it. Everybody treats me like I'm part of the family.

Dennis Miller

It is a fun thing. You come into rooms, people want to hear what you say. It's kind of neat. If you try to make it completely nothing then you've missed the point. It should be fun and you should be able enjoy it once in a while and pride yourself on it.

Jerry Mathers

The fans of Leave It to Beaver *consider everybody* in the show like a friend. My wife and I will be walking down the street and people will just say, "Hi Beave." It's not like they stop and scream and just go crazy. When I go to almost any airport, while I'm getting my bags, somebody will come up to me and ask, "Aren't you Jerry Mathers?" or "Aren't you the Beaver?" I ask them if they're from this city and if they say yes I ask them where the best restaurants are. So it's really like having friends all over the country, or like people you went to high school with and you haven't seen in a few years and then you run into them at some place. It's a very, very nice relationship.

Jean-Claude Van Damme

Every time I go to an airport, people stop me and ask me for an autograph for themselves, for their son, for their daughter. When this happens, I feel popular. When they come up to me, I feel good.

George Burns

I walk out on the stage, everybody stands up. Let me tell you something. I do about a hour on the stage. If you asked me to get up and stand for an hour I couldn't do it, but the audience gives you that love, that vitality.

Marisa Tomei

I live in New York and even though people recognize me it's kind of low key. People just shout out, "Hey!," across the street. It makes it like a little bit of a smaller town in a way. I actually like that.

Alfre Woodard

You feel like your neighborhood is a big place because somebody will always say, "I see you. I'm pulling for you."

Geraldine Chaplin

I always felt that everybody was rooting for me, because everybody loved Daddy [Charlie Chaplin] so much.

Howie Long

When we played exhibition football games in Japan and in London, it really blows your mind when you get off a plane and people are walking around with a "75" jersey on.

Esther Williams

That love you get is in perpetuity. It's because they've lived with you so long. They know all about you and they've got thousands of scrapbooks. They know about your kids.

Bo Derek

You can make yourself miserable about it and say you have no privacy, or you can arrange your privacy in your home, which anyone can do, and look at it as a very lovely way to go through life. I have like this bubble and when people enter it and see who I am I see the best side of them. Wherever I go in the world everyone is so wonderful and lovely to me. I hear horror stories about other people's experiences, but I really do see the best side of people.

Mike Nichols

It seems to me I have the best of it, which is I can get a table, but nobody cares whether I'm there or not. That's what I've wanted all my life. My marriage [to TV newswoman Diane Sawyer] changed things a little bit, but neither one of us, apart or together, are people who like to be out in public a lot for other reasons. By and large that stuff is about how much you think about it. I don't think it's profitable to think about it, so I don't, and then it's not a problem.

Mel Gibson

I always get a table at a restaurant, even when it's booked. That's the upside. And believe me now, I didn't used to take advantage of that because I thought it was unfair, but I used to get pissed off about the bad stuff. Now I don't get pissed off about the bad stuff, but I milk it for everything it's worth because you have to have some balance in your life. If there are free seats to the baseball game, you bet I'm there.

Linda Fiorentino

I played sports all my life. To be able to have the opportunity to present an ESPY Award—I know that's not important to other people—to me it is. If the price I have to pay is the ups and downs of my film career, it's worth it, just to have the opportunity to be in the same room with maybe Clyde Drexler.

I met Kareem Abdul-Jabbar and Wilt Chamberlain on the same night at a party over Christmas. I was like a little kid. To me, they are the stars. Movie stars do nothing for me. If I had been born a man I probably would've been a professional basketball player instead of an actor.

Jason Alexander

I miss the anonymity at times, but most of celebrity comes with enormous perks that, while I don't feel they're necessarily merited, I'm very happy that they're there. Just for example, I went to Disneyland with my kid yesterday. There are forty thousand people there. It's three hours per line. We had a VIP guide and we zipped through the park. We went in separate entrances. That doesn't suck. For doing what I want to be doing anyway and being paid very well for it, celebrity is fine.

Jack McDowell

(Baseball player and recording artist)

The things that are cool about celebrity, like me being able to go to a club to see a show and the people there know me so they'll bring me in and give me good seats, it almost has to happen if the celebrity is there. If I go into a show and I'm out on the floor, I can't watch the show because people are all over you. So the good things that come with it are almost a necessity that has to come with it because the celebrity is there. So the negatives definitely outweigh the positives because the positive isn't a positive above and beyond normalcy. The positive is a positive 99% of the time because it has to be.

Arnold Schwarzenegger

The great thing about films is you can do certain things even when you're married. When you get to my age and you're a married man, this is probably as close as you ever get to a woman in a legitimate way. Kissing her and making out, for the art of the movie, and no one can complain about it.

Keenen Ivory Wayans

It's Hollywood. It's dreamland. You get to cast the most beautiful women in the world and you write that they want you. You live your fantasy. For six weeks I was the man and it was great.

Martin Lawrence

My girl fucked me over and I talked about it on stage and it helped me, where I would have wanted to chase her down and wait outside her room, "C'mon out!" It helped me to go on stage and say, "Yo, I was hurt and man, she got me good." It helped me to see. Through my standup I realized that no matter how hard it gets, if it don't work out with one lady there are many others out there.

Woody Harrelson

I'm very balanced. I'm an exhibitionist, but I'm also a voyeur.

Jonathan Taylor Thomas

I deal with adults on a regular basis. A lot of kids aren't in that position. I'm with my mom a lot, which I think is a great benefit. She's there helping me and so we talk a lot. That helps. Often today parents are at work or doing something else. They don't get to talk to their kids. They don't really know what's going on and it's very tough for them to relate. Kids don't get any real adult perspective and understanding until they actually have to bridge the gap and enter an adult world. Often times they have no experience with adults or living in an adult world, so they're completely lost.

Lukas Haas

I was in Japan doing promo for *Witness* and I had dinner with Harrison Ford and Jimmy Stewart and my mother, in a sushi bar. We were all drinking warm sake and there was this terrible looking piece of sushi. Jimmy and Harrison were rooting for my mom to eat it, so she ate it, and for the rest of the night she was throwing up. That was pretty cool.

Jeanne Moreau

To be famous is a reward. Good God! You want to be an actress? You want to be on stage? You want to please people. You're successful? That means you have fame. If you have fame you have more parts. And the more it goes the better it is. Why should I resent fame?

Bruce Willis

Whatever power you think is assigned to being famous really comes down to just being able to decide which films I want to do and not having to work in someone else's film just to get the job. I can say yes or no primarily on what interests me.

Alan Alda

When I hear myself talk about this I get a little nervous, because I envy myself. The ability to do what interests me is a fortunate thing in my life. I do a science program on public television that I just love, catching sharks and rattlesnakes and climbing to the top of Mount Vesuvius. I really have a great time. And we do some good with that show.

I do movies that interest me—and I don't have to worry, "Can I pay the rent?" That's a terrifically lucky position to be in.

Ellen DeGeneres

I love doing the sitcom and working in front of a live audience every week. I love doing films now. I can't wait to do my next one. I'm really, really fortunate that I'm not just stuck in a medium. I can do film or television. I wrote the book. I hosted the Grammys. I'm able to do so many different things right now. It's really flattering and it's really fun.

Ed O'Neill

It's one of the ways you keep score. Being famous means I've accomplished something.

Steve Martin

You go from—I don't want to say a nobody—but a nobody in show business to a somebody. It doesn't happen to many people, so it's kind of thrilling. But more important than that is your work came to fruition. Suddenly it's, "Uh, I wasn't wrong. What I was doing meant something. It was understandable and had a point and had a logic."

Mary Elizabeth Mastrantonio

I like to act. It's like two musicians standing up and jamming. You know the basic structure of it, but you don't exactly know where it's going to go and where they dynamics are going to be. That to me is sweet. Sometimes doing Shakespeare, it just takes you. It's fabulous, all that it says and all the questions that it poses. I love to take a bit of human behavior and throw it up at people and say, "Just watch it."

If it's a devil's bargain then I made a hell of a good deal. It's given me a degree of artistic freedom in the conduct of my business, great comfort for my family certainly, and security for my future. And I haven't had to kill anybody.

—Harrison Ford

Michael Jackson

Dancing is really showing your emotions through bodily movement. I think it's a wonderful thing to get out on the floor and just feel free, do what you want and just let it come out. When I dance I feel free. It's escapism, getting away from everything and just moving your body, letting all the tension and pain out.

Harrison Ford Ron Davis/Shooting Star

John Hall

I played a show with Orleans opening for the Wailers in Boston and I was a serious Bob Marley fan. I sat in the front row listening to their whole set. After the show Marley came backstage to me and said, "How do you play guitar so fast, man?"

I said, "I don't know. How do you play so slow?"

He said, "The spliff, man," reefed in clouds of ganja smoke. But it was a legitimate contact between the two of us that I had no reason to expect. I'm proud that I just had those few sentences with the man.

Samuel L. Jackson

My mother gets to go to movie theaters free now in Chattanooga, she can take her friends to the movies free. She's very large now. The whole time during the Academy Awards thing I would call her and she would say, "I can't talk to you now. I'm doing an interview."

Robert Townsend

The best thing about celebrity is everybody's excited to see you. People are really happy, like "HEY, ROBERT TOWNSEND! HEY, ROB!" If a plumber got treated this way I would be a plumber. "COME ON IN! FLUSH MY TOILET, MAN!"

Robert Conrad

Last night, coming from Northern California where I live to Hollywood to do business, I stopped off at a Denny's. I was recognized and it was a hoot. Wendy came over and said, "It's my birthday and you're my idol!" After she left I thought, I've been doing this thirty-five years and I've entertained this woman. What a nice feeling for me.

Michael Richards

I've been in this business for sixteen years. *Seinfeld* is my third television show. I've made a handful of pilots. I've done just about every show that was on television in the last twelve years. Maybe if this had all happened to me earlier I wouldn't have been able to handle it, but now I'm grateful when they come up to me and say, "We love the TV show you're in." I've been in television shows where they didn't come up and say a word to me on the street. So I'm like, "You like the show? Good! You really like it?

Do you want an autograph? I'll give you an autograph. Pictures? Give me your address."

Tony Curtis

A lot of people who are put into the spotlight cannot handle fame. Fame is a little too much for them. It's too personal. The magnification is intense. Some people fit in it like a glove. It fits me like my jacket fits. It's well-tailored. I like it. I like being famous. Fame likes me. I like people and people like me. I don't find anything abrasive about it or clumsy about it. People have this deep affection for me because they've grown up with me, and I've grown up with them, even though I don't know them. I find it a privilege and an honor to be Tony Curtis. I mean it.

Richard Gere

You have to stop seeing it as an assault on you and see it as an opportunity to do some positive things. That's a major click of technique, of changing your mind. I've had the opportunity to have a lot of practice at transforming those emotions.

Patrick Swayze

Movie stars are the royalty and the role models, whether you deserve it or not. When you start taking that seriously you start going, "Wait a minute. This could be a cool thing. It doesn't have to destroy me. I can do good things with this." And so it gives you a purpose when you key into that place. You can affect people in a good way and maybe change their mind set or position through something you do that has some artistic fulfillment. It's kind of a neat thing.

That's the reason I like doing press. If I can communicate that one thing that I got to learn as a kid to kids around the world, then I get a chance to do something worthwhile in this world.

Harry Belafonte

Ever since I was a kid, there was never any question in my mind that my life, no matter what I did, would forever be in concert with battling injustice. I grew up with it. I saw it take its toll on my family, etc. So when I became this American thing, and ultimately this world thing that had celebritydom tied to it, I saw it as an excellent opportunity to say things and do things that will help me on this quest to change the way people are doing business and see if we can't do it a bit better.

John Ratzenberger

Cheers *padded my checkbook enough* that instead of being thrown out of parties because I was so obnoxious with my environmental views I could do something. An opportunity presented itself and I hired engineers and we got to work devising a different packaging to take the place of expanded polystyrene, which is the scourge of all Christmases when it goes all over the living room.

Mary Tyler Moore

How often I have been on the verge of saying, "Well, what am I here for?" We all do. It's the big "What's it all about, Alfie?" question. I have mine answered to a degree. I know if I do nothing else I have made a big difference in people's lives.

I feel I'm one of the luckiest people alive. I've had the ability to validate my having been on this Earth, having done something that made a few people happier or richer or less lonely. I've made myself very happy.

Roseanne

Fame saved my life. It allowed me to turn my life around. It allowed me to do the work I need to do and to meet people who I have inspired and who in turn inspire me back.

[Meeting the Queen, and Other Good Stuff]

In 1944, some Americans came to my house when I was just six. They were G.I.s. My mother and father invited them over for tea and things like that. They were getting ready for D-Day. Their names were Cooney and Durr. They brought me some colored marbles and chewing gum. I'll never forget. I remember the Saturday morning they left. I was riding on this little tricycle in the garden and this guy said, "That's a heckuva machine you've got there."

I remember standing on the gateway watching them with my mother and father—I can't say this without choking up—and we never saw them again. They were both killed in the Battle of the Bulge.

About two years later, I was on the bus with my mother and we ran into this American sergeant who was having difficulty with his change, with the British money. It was rainy and he looked lost and my mother said, "Would you like to come back to our place? My husband will give you a lift where you're going." And he said, "Oh, I'd love that."

My father comes in and there's an American soldier sitting in the house. I remember I was fascinated watching this guy. He came from New York. His name was Sam Arrat. They became friends, he and my father. My father asked him whatever happened to that outfit that Cooney and Durr were in. He said, "Oh, they were all killed." A few months later we got a letter from Cooney's wife thanking us for the friendship and confirming that her husband and his friend Durr were dead, bedded into the fields of France.

And I always wondered if I'd ever see Sam Arrat again. He used to send us food parcels and Look magazines and I became obsessed with America. Totally obsessed with America. I always wanted to come here.

I did this CBS television thing two years ago, 60 Minutes. I was down in South Wales, my birthplace. My mother came down for the trip and they asked her to say a few words. My mother said, "Oh, no, no." But they put her on camera and she couldn't shut up. She just kept talking.

Fade out. Six months later Sam Arrat is sitting down in his house in Florida. He turns on the television set. "There's Muriel Hopkins! My God, that's the woman who looked after me, she and her husband. And that's Tony Hopkins!" He didn't know the connection until then. He contacted CBS—and he's coming out to California next week to see her after fifty years.

Index

Celebrity Index